Tricksters and Trancers

TRICKSTERS and TRANCERS

BUSHMAN RELIGION AND SOCIETY

Mathias Guenther

Indiana University Press Bloomington & Indianapolis

This book is a publication of
Indiana University Press
601 North Morton Street
Bloomington, Indiana 47404-3797 USA

www.indiana.edu/~iupress

Telephone orders 800-842-6796
Fax orders 812-855-7931
Orders by e-mail iuporder@indiana.edu

The paper used in this publication meets the minimum requirements of American National Standard for Information Sciences—Permanence of Paper for Printed Library Materials, ANSI Z39.48-1984.

Manufactured in the United States of America

Library of Congress Cataloging-in-Publication Data

Guenther, Mathias Georg.
Tricksters and trancers : bushman religion and society / Mathias Guenther.
p. cm.
Includes bibliographical references and index.
ISBN 0-253-33640-6 (cl. : alk. paper). — ISBN 0-253-21344-4 (pa. : alk. paper)
1. San (African people)—Africa, Southern—Religion. 2. Africa, Southern—Religion.
BL2480.S24G84 1999
299'.681—dc21 99-35078

1 2 3 4 5 04 03 02 01 00 99

Contents

MAPS

Preface

The domain of culture dealt with in this book is in any culture as complex and variable as it is opaque and elusive; indeed, the more a researcher immerses himself in the study of one particular religion, the more perplexing its abstruse features appear to become, confounding the analytical or hermeneutical effort undertaken. This is the case especially with respect to the culture featured in this book. Notwithstanding its basic homogeneity, with respect especially to phenotype and socio-economic organization, Bushman religion—for reasons that are explored in this book as they constitute its key problematic—seems to be an inexhaustible font of ideas, beliefs, stories and symbols, and ritual practices and expressive performances. Many appear and reappear in countless versions and variants, especially once one takes one's examination beyond just one band or related bands and scans the religious and expressive culture of the various Bushman "tribes" or linguistic groupings of a region or of all southern Africa. On the Bushmen's cosmological and symbolic landscape, we find the three permanent waterholes to be myth, art, and ritual.

Even though it is as long as most and longer than some, this book thus does not do justice to the richness of the field it covers. I have throughout made reference to other works—which in Bushman studies are quite abundant and for the most part quite accessible—to which the reader might refer to supplement the exposition and to complement the analysis of Bushman religious and expressive culture here presented. Especially useful as reference works are the two "big books" in Khoisan studies on the Bushmen (and their herding neighbors and cousins, the Khoekhoe), Isaac Schapera's *The Khoisan Peoples of South Africa* (1933), a compendium of early ethnographic and ethnohistorical information, and Alan Barnard's recent *Hunters and Herders of Southern Africa* (1992), an update, in some ways, of Schapera's classic.

While the ethnographic literature on the Bushmen is not generally concerned much with the cultural domain covered in this book, it is nevertheless relevant to it. One of *Tricksters and Trancers'* insights is that foraging is a mindset, an ethos or ideology that informs religion. Foraging is the socio-economic process also underlying most of these other studies, which deal with cultural-ecological parameters. More recently, some writers have argued that in Bushman society people also forage socially, for relatives and exchange partners, and a theme of this book is that they forage also for ideas. Because of this common thread, foraging, all the rich literature on Bushman economic, social, and political organization becomes germane to the present study. Two chapters recognize this point and reign in much of the literature on infrastructural and structural parameters of Bushman social organization, thereby sketching out the social context of Bushman religion. It is through this context that, as anthropologists, we may understand whatever there is of structure, as well as of meaning, within Bushman religion.

Five of the chapters of the book were presented, either fully or in part, as conference papers; they have been reworked extensively for this book. One section of chapter 1, on the ethnohistory of the Ghanzi District, was presented in August of 1994 at the *International Conference on People, Politics and Power: Representing the Bushman Peoples of Southern Africa* at the University of the Witwatersrand and Johannesburg Art Gallery in Johannesburg, South Africa. Parts of chapter 4 were included in a paper entitled "Jesus Christ as Trickster in the Religion of Contemporary Bushmen," which I presented at a conference on "The Ludic—Forces of Generation and Fracture" at the International Science Forum at the University of Heidelberg, 25–31 October 1993. A version of chapter 5 was presented as "Story Telling in the Foraging Context: The Case of the Moon and the Hare," at the *Seventh International Conference on Hunting and Gathering Societies* (CHAGS 7), Russian Academy of Sciences, Institute of Ethnology and Anthropology, Moscow, 18–22 August, 1993. Chapter 6, too, was a conference paper, titled "Myth and Social Reality: The Case of the Kalahari Bushmen—and Women," and presented at the *Interdisciplinary Conference on Myth and Knowledge* held at Memorial University of Newfoundland, Sir Wilfred Grenfell College, Cornerbrook, Newfoundland, May 1991. Finally, chapter 9 had its origin in a conference paper I gave many years back, as "The Failure of the Bushman Mission," at the *American Academy of Religion Annual Conference,* Dallas, November 1980.

Having presented so much of the contents of this book at conferences has increased the exchange of my ideas with colleagues and friends. I have benefited enormously from that exchange, over the past years and decades, and extend my thanks to the following individuals: Alan Barnard, Megan Biesele, Kuno Budack, Pieter and Maude Brown, Alec Campbell, Peter Carstens, Thomas Dowson, Irenäus Eibl-Eibesfeldt, Hans-Joachim Heinz, Robert Hitchcock, Dirk and Pollie Jerling, Rocky Jacobsen, Susan Kent, John and Jill Kinahan, Richard Lee, Braam and Willemien LeRoux, David Lewis-Williams, Lorna Marshall, Raymond Martin, Alan Morris, E. W. Müller, Mark Münzel, Shawn O'Hagan, Nigel Penn, the late Andries Rampa, Helmut and Marianne Reuning, Sigrid Schmidt, the late Marjorie Shostak, George Silberbauer, Pippa Skotnes, John Steffler, Renée Sylvain, Joachim and Hiltrud Walter, and Polly Wiessner.

My greatest intellectual debt goes, of course, to the many Bushmen and women who, over the past three decades, were generous enough to talk to me about their beliefs, to discuss ideas with me, and to tell me stories and myths, and who allowed me to be present at trance dance performances. Here, I would single out !Khuma//ka and his late wife N!aba, who were our next-door neighbors when my wife and I stayed at Dekar village from 1968 to 1970, and who became, and have remained, friends.

I acknowledge a debt of gratitude to the Office of the President of Botswana for permission to conduct fieldwork among the Bushmen (or Basarwa) people of the country. Thanks also are extended to Wilfrid Laurier University for granting me a sabbatical leave to write this book. I also received from the same university funding for some of the field and archival research that has gone into this project, and for some of its publication costs; this, too, I acknowledge with thanks.

Tricksters and Trancers

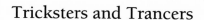

Introduction: The Challenge of Bushman Religion

> *I told him [a colonial officer] about the scientists who had begged to come with me, some because they wanted to measure Bushman heads and behinds, others to measure his sexual organs, others to study his family relationships, and one to analyze his spit; but when I asked them if they were not interested in the Bushman's mind and spirit, they replied: "That is not our department of science." We seemed to have destroyed the Bushman without ever bothering to find out what sort of person he really was.*
>
> —VAN DER POST 1961: 116

I have shared some of the same discontent with the work of "the scientists" on the Bushmen as expressed by the late Laurens van der Post, in one of his Bushman books. And I agree with Alan Barnard (1989)—who cites the passage in a critical, anthropological evaluation of these books (works of ethnofiction[1])—that, for all their hyperbole, Sir Laurens's grumblings do contain "a grain of truth" (Barnard 1989: 108). What was written then, and has been written since then, by well over a hundred anthropologists, has generally not concerned itself much with the religious, expressive, and symbolic domain of Bushman culture, or, using van der Post's formulation, with "the Bushman's mind and spirit." While an astonishing volume of anthropological research and writings has been produced on the Bushmen, creating an ethnographic record richer than that existing for most other African peoples, that record, for all of its wealth, has gaps.

My frustration is with these gaps, not with the actual studies that have been written, which are of the highest scholarly caliber and which I hold in high esteem. They are meticulous studies of virtually all of the cultural ecological parameters of Bushman society, some of them—such as Richard Lee's—path-breaking, paradigmatic contributions not only to the field of Bushman studies but also to the study of hunter-gatherers generally. However, they are works that mostly continued along the materialist trajectory Bushman research had followed before, a predominant concern of which, at the time van der Post wrote the cited passage, had been the physical traits of the Bushmen. From the 1960s through the 1980s research interests dealt with such issues as ecological adaptation, demography, spatial organization, modes of production, division of labor, gender and property relations, and the like, as well as kinship and political organization, and socio-cultural change.[2] The latest issue to be debated, the relative degree of isolation and autonomy of hunter-gatherers vis-à-vis state neighbors, is an issue to which belief and ritual have no relevance.

Thus, despite all of this copious research, with the exception of some recent studies to be mentioned below, the symbolic gap has remained in our studies of the Bushmen, which have yielded ever more information and understanding of the infrastructural and structural working of their society, leaving the area of belief and myth largely unexplored. The overall impression created by this work is that these hunter-gatherers are a particularly prosaic people, with adaptive, pragmatic ways, living in a natural and social landscape with which they interact rationally and which is altogether free of the sorts of elements of enchantment—animal spirit keepers, bear- or tiger-walking shamans, songlines, ancestor spirits, reincarnation beliefs, and the like—one comes across in the symbolic and religious domain of other such peoples.

Any contention that there is a gap here in Bushman studies might be greeted with surprise or even disbelief by those conversant with the ethnological literature on the Bushmen, especially the earlier writings. What about the extensive writings of Wilhelm and Dorothea Bleek and Lucy Lloyd, from the later nineteenth and early twentieth century, on Bushman folklore (of the now extinct Cap /Xam)? What about the prolific ethnographic accounts of Bushman religion that were gathered by early, oftentimes clerical writers (such as Dornan, Lebzelter, Vedder, Estermann, and Gusinde), mostly about religion and, in the context of a lively academic debate, about "primal monotheism"? And the educated and interested settlers or farmers who had much firsthand knowledge of the Bushmen, and wrote popular, at times insightful, and much-cited books on the culture and religion, prime among them the grandiloquent Laurens van der Post (1958, 1965, 1975), but also E. W. Thomas (1950), Erik Holm (1965), Fritz Metzger (1952, with P. Ettighoffer), or Ilse Schatz (1993)? With the exception of the last category, which I will touch on in passing, I will address and assess most of these writings in the chapters that follow. It will become clear from that review that most of these early works are in one way or other methodologically flawed, as well as greatly dated with respect to the problematic posed.

While this old work has thus not done much to close the symbolic gap in the understanding we have of Bushman culture, more recent studies have. They have been on such areas of Bushman religion and expressive culture as rock art, by David Lewis-Williams (1981) and Thomas Dowson (Lewis-Williams and Dowson 1989; Dowson and Lewis-Williams 1994)[3]; on the trance curing dance, by Richard Katz (1982), Megan Biesele, and Verna St. Denis (Katz, Biesele, and St. Denis 1997[4]); and on folklore, by Roger Hewitt (1986), Sigrid Schmidt (1980, 1989), Megan Biesele (1993), and myself (1989). Moreover, Lorna Marshall's book on !Kung religion (in press) is anxiously awaited by Bushman researchers, who might expect it to expand on her masterful article on the same topic in the journal *Africa* a generation ago (Marshall 1962). In writing this book on the same cultural system, I have greatly profited from these recent works, as will be evident to the reader who will note frequent references to the facts and ideas they present. My book is as much a complement to my colleagues' work, as it is a compliment.

As I address these works in the course of the ensuing chapters, the distinctiveness of the present study will become apparent. In contrast to the ecological, psychological, structuralist, or folkloristic analytical focus taken by one or another of these studies, my framework is essentially sociological (or functionalist). On the social-anthropological assumption that people's ideas and feelings are ultimately grounded in society, I consider the articulation of Bushman beliefs, myths, and rituals with social structure and organization, social institutions, processes, and values. While society is treated as the ground and being of Bushman mental and spiritual processes, these express themselves more explicitly in specific cultural forms, pertaining, loosely and heuristically speaking, to the cultural domain of religion, things such as beliefs, myths, stories, rock paintings, dances, music, curing or initiation rites. Because of the explicitly symbolic, and mental, mystic, and spiritual garb of these elements of culture, which concern themselves with existential and supernatural issues, some of them portentous or ultimate, I will focus on these cultural forms most extensively; as the embodiment of the "Bushman's mind and spirit"—although not quite as envisaged by Sir Laurens, whose bent was Jungian—these matters constitute the substantive component of this book.

The Challenge of Bushman Religion

Other than lack of theoretical interest or its uneasy fit into a materialist theoretical framework, there is another conceptual reason for the neglect of the religious dimension of Bushman culture. It is tied to the theoretical wariness with which so many anthropologists are inclined to approach the field of religion in general. Religion deals with matters "imaginative and emotional" and contains so many "intrinsic difficulties" and "uncertain elements of knowledge" as to make religion "to some extent unintelligible." This, as I will note again, was Morgan's well-known view on the matter, showing how far back into the history of the discipline the theoretical unease about religion reaches. As we will also see, Morgan's pronouncements on religion generally were not far off the mark, as regards the specific case at hand. The hallmark traits of Bushman religion are fluidity, flexibility, and variability, each manifested to a striking degree. Thus, the knowledge one can gain of so ambiguous a field is indeed uncertain.

Uncertainty starts at the level of description, as there is so much variation that one hardly knows where to start and stop. When the task becomes the analysis of this domain of culture, the challenge is akin to nailing a custard to the wall or ladling water with a sieve. The conceptual fastening or holding devices at one's disposal in the anthropological study of religion are unsuited for so variable, contradictory, and protean a cultural mass—or mess—as Bushman religion. Because of its pervasive ambiguity, Bushman religion presents a special challenge to anthropologists of religion. So many of them subscribe, explicitly or implicitly, to theoretical notions about religion that are quite inapplicable to the specific case before us. One is the theoretical notion that religion is the core institution of society, its moral charter, its social glue and grease that holds together and integrates all other institutions. The other holds religion, specifically myths, to be the repository of a culture's basic structures of logic and thought. As the following chapters will show (especially the conclusion), the paradigms based on these two notions, functionalism and structuralism, have severe limitations in the context of an analysis of Bushman religion.

The trickster and the trance dancer are the two central, key figures of Bushman religion (and the pivotal characters of this study) who dramatically bear out its basic (anti)structural constitution. We will see the trickster figure as the embodiment of the ambiguity that pervades Bushman mythology and cosmology, much the same as the trance dancer embodies this state with respect to ritual. Both are ontologically ambiguous, confounding such basic categories as natural–supernatural, humanity–divinity, human–animal; in addition to these the trickster confounds every other conceivable category. Both figures are also ontologically fluid, ever ready to change who, what, and where they are, through transformation and, in the trancer's case, transcendence by altered states of consciousness. Both figures are equivalents of each other, the trickster active primarily in the sphere of myth and lore, the trancer in ritual, and thereby embedded in real-life society. Yet, the two figures frequently enter one another's domain, such as at the trance dance, at its climactic moment, when the trancer "dies" and his spirit takes over and proceeds with the curing task on a mystical plane. At this moment of the trance dance the trancer's spirit may encounter the trickster-god, who is attracted to the curing dance. The trancer and trickster are alike in other ways as well; both are curers who may employ identical methods, and in one of his numerous personas the trickster is "the magician." Both may use flight, and the wives of the latter may attempt to seduce the trance dancer.[5]

Somewhat surprisingly, perhaps, I bring one other key figure into this study of Bushman religion, the forager. Why would (s)he share center stage with the trickster and trance dancer, given her/his secular, odd-(wo)man-out status vis-à-vis the other two figures? The reason is that I hold foraging to be an integral dynamic of Bushman religion, reflected by such terms or concepts as "foraging for ideas," "foraging ethos," and "foraging ideology." These terms have been used in recent studies of Bushman society and culture, and will be examined and applied to Bushman religion, in an effort to explain its fluid state. The point to be argued, simply, is that the fluidity of Bushman religion is an ideological counterpart to the fluidity of Bushman society; the former provides the foragers with a set of cosmological and symbolic notions and a basic mental outlook that is congruent with foraging. It is a view that fosters a top-down analytical approach to foraging and contrasts with the bottom-up approach of previous cultural-ecological studies. The latter explains fluidity in terms of ecological adaptation, the former, in terms of social structure, ethos, and belief.

In the context of Bushman religion, the issue of super-infrastructural articulation raises a host of questions in the minds both of students of Khoisan people (and foragers generally), and of anthropologists of religion. These questions derive primarily from the manner in which religion, so devoid, in the Bushman case, of many of the functions or properties conventionally ascribed to it by anthropologists, works its way within their society and culture. Another line of questions has to do with the nature of Bushman society, to which religion is so loosely linked. Like religion, this cultural system, is profoundly different in the ethnographic case at hand from other societies, requiring one to rethink the nature of society and of the articulation between society and religion.

What is the religion of a society that is fluid, loose, and labile like; a society, that is, which is lacking in a structural "center," in stability and corporateness (and, for that reason, may not even be a "society," but something altogether different, as suggested by some theorists)? Does, can, religion, in such a loose society, act as the integrating force that conventional functionalist wisdom—i.e., Durkheim—holds it to do, in the context of another foraging society (and in society generally)? If religion is itself fluid and ambiguous, how can it fulfill such a function? Indeed, in the context of anthropological theory of religion and its above-mentioned a priori premises, *can* any religion be infused with ambiguity to the extent that I suggest, on the basis of my reading of what strikes me as an exceptionally complex and ambiguous religion? Given the discipline's classic axiomatic assumption that religion is a culture's ultimate repository of order and meaning, must serious doubt not be cast on such a reading? Should I not attribute such a fanciful notion to errors of observation (as have some students of Khoisan religion)? And if, in fact, there are no such errors or misreadings, what can a researcher who is epistemologically steeped in reason, structures, and order do or say about such a religion? Given that religion in the majority of human societies holds, as its primary function, the endorsement of power, what happens to religion if the society within which it functions is free of hierarchy and power structures? Similarly, if one of the prime functions of ritual is the resolution of conflict, what is the role and content of ritual in a society that is able to resolve its conflict by means of "secular" mechanisms?

Another line of questions, less sociological and more ecological: How far would a "vegetable school" approach to religion (for instance, of the venerable Frazer) take the analyst in a society that has no agriculture, no need for cyclical, calendrical harvest rituals, fertility rites, rain magic and the like, because of its relatively abundant supply of food drawn from nature's storehouse? Is religion, in such a society, linked to ecological or productive processes?

The attempt to answer this barrage of questions constitutes the theoretical program of this book. One or another of the questions, sometimes several, run through each of the chapters, especially the conclusion, wherein the key questions, about ambiguity and how to handle this troubling state analytically and methodologically, are dealt with explicitly.

In addition to addressing these theoretical questions, a study of Bushman religion contributes to the anthropology of religion and comparative religion in substantive ways, relating to specific features of Khoisan supernaturalism. To begin with, there are the rather too well known misapprehensions about Bushman religion, deriving from the racist stereotype Westerners held about the people, who were deemed incarnations of natural, feral man, in Hobbesian rather than Rousseauian guise (Guenther 1980). In an effort to separate fact from fiction, I will examine these at times fanciful notions: about "prelapsarian" conceptions of God, on the one hand, and moon and mantis—and even devil—worship on the other, about "rain dances" and transplanted cults of Isis and Osiris.

The Bushman religious figures of greatest interest to the student of comparative religion are the trance dancer and the trickster. The latter is relatively little known in the large and growing field of trickster studies[6] and I take delight in introducing this complex, unusual, and highly interesting character to the world's rogues' gallery of such figures. What makes him different is his dual persona, on the one hand, as protagonist—of whimsical or outrageous tales—and, on the other, as god. In the latter persona he appears in myths and in ritual, as a figure of numinous power and portent. While tricksters in other parts of the world may also hold religious or sacred significance (Hynes 1993: 39–42)—for example the Greek Hermes (Doty 1993) and the West African Legba (Eshu) (Pelto 1993) are both "messenger gods" who were subject to ritual attention—nowhere does the figure's status as divinity appear to be defined as clearly as in Khoisan religion. The case at hand compounds what is already a daunting problem, to define and conceptualize a figure of confounding "plurality, plurivocality and ambiguity" (Hynes and Doty 1993: 9), for which as many as sixteen defining traits have been delineated. This exercise is all the more difficult, and considered impossible by some (Beidelman 1993), if the attempt is made to delineate this figure as a universal, cross-culturally comparable religious type (Doty and Hynes 1993: 22–28; Beidelman 1993). The Bushman case will no doubt add further grist to the mills of comparative religionists preoccupied with typological questions.

The second major category, the trance dancer, whom I (following Lewis-Williams) refer to as shaman, is a figure rarely encountered in African religious studies, wherein spirit possession, divination, witchcraft, and sorcery constitute the predominant forms of preternatural operation and machination (Guenther 1997b). As the Bushman trickster forces definitional reconsiderations, so does the trance dancer–shaman, who does not fit into the classic, Siberian-derived category of shaman (because he does not experience spirit possession). Yet, with altered states of consciousness, as well as outer-body travel as his principal modus operandi, and curing and hunting as his main spheres of ritual activity, the Bushman trance dancer falls in line, more or less, with shamanic figures in other parts of the world. The case adds further fuel to those students of religion—for instance Jane Atkinson (1992)—who, in a postmodernist spirit of relativism, advocate a deconstruction of "shamanism" ("writ-large") as a universal category, to be replaced by the pluralized term "shamanisms," which encompasses "historically situated and culturally mediated practice[s]" (ibid.: 308).

There are two other, very basic categories which are questioned conceptually by this study. One is "society," the cultural domain to which Bushman religion is linked (to be examined in chapters 1 and 2). As already noted (and to be discussed in the conclusion), the sorts of "social formations" people like the Bushmen live in and by, "band societies," are not considered by some hunter-gatherer researchers to be exemplars of "Society." With respect to the second broad category, religion, there have been writers—mostly, as will be seen in chapter 9, nineteenth-century missionaries laboring among the Bushmen—who would call into question the most fundamental category of this study. The contention has been, simply, that the Bushmen have no religion, because of a basic state of cultural and spiritual benightedness. As the theoretical questions raised above suggest, Bushman religion does, indeed, present a conceptual challenge, even to contemporary anthropologists free of the racism that clouded these earlier writers on the subject.

Bushman Religion: A Brief Summary

While it is difficult to summarize so divergent and variable a field as Bushman religion—as well as misleading, since the opposite impression, of clarity and coherence, is conveyed through such a summation—it is nevertheless of heuristic value to provide a skeleton outline. It provides a framework for the rich and dense information to be presented in some of the chapters that follow, or a large-scale road map through the multi-featured landscape of Bushman myth, belief, and ritual.

In the area of belief—as against ritual, the second, and among the Bushmen less elaborated, area of religion—the most prominent figure is the trickster, whom we have already met. His principal abode is the world during its first phase of being, at primal time, when beings and states were inchoate and dreamlike, as well as fluid and flawed and ever-ready to change their forms or being. Akin to the Australian Dreamtime, the "First Order"—and its inhabitants, the "Early People"—are a key element of Bushman mythology and cosmology. The First Order's landmark features are described in chapter 3, along with its many and varied inhabitants, who frequently blend human with animalian traits. Therianthropes are also featured in rock art, and transformation into an animal, or a close sympathy bond to it, is a feature of ritual and of hunting. It is an expression of another key cosmological element, human kindredness with animals. Women especially are symbolically linked to animals, especially game antelopes, and held to be spiritually attuned to the hunters' prey. At certain ritual occasions, women merge with the eland or springbok, so that the hunter's wife, or the girl at menarche, become "meat" (rendering sex and marriage as cognates to hunting). While the First Order of Existence is a time primarily of chaos, it is also the setting for creation—as the features of nature and of culture are created or decreed—as well as for existence (in particular death, which is the subject of a key myth which I explore in chapter 5). The agent of creation is frequently the trickster, as well as the more nebulous god figure, who is another significant (although not, perhaps, indigenous) feature of Bushman belief. As will be seen in chapter 6, another creative agent is womankind, whose representatives are well-profiled beings of primal time, more prominent, astute, and effective than males. Women's primal, mythical prominence and their symbolic and spiritual link to animals are the ideological underpinnings of the position of equality females hold within Bushman society.

A slight gender bias is evident also in the two principal ritual patterns, the trance dance and initiation rites. The former favors the man, as in most (though by no means all) instances the trance dancer is male. With its symbolic and mystical link to hunting, which is evident in the dancer's affinity with an animal and the ritual routine of animal transformation, as well as the trance dance's close link to rock art, wherein it is a frequently depicted motif, this shamanic ritual is symbolically set to a male key. Women, however, are an integral ritual and symbolic element as well (as we will see in chapter 8, which will examine this ritual in some detail). In addition to transcendence and transformation, another dynamic of the trance dance I will consider is its function as a mechanism for cultural revitalization. Initiation (the subject of chapter 7) is especially elaborate with respect to women, whose importance to, and complementarity with, men is a well-defined symbolic theme in the conceptualization and performance of the rite. Its male counterpart, especially in one of its two forms—the "bush school," as against the "First Buck" ceremony—is less prominent and less elaborate in its symbolic and ritual content, nor is it, as in the female case, pressed upon the individual by his culture; his submission to the rite is optional. Both men and women, in the context of the liminal transition phase of the rite, experience a close spiritual affinity with—yet again—animals.

In addition to these principal features, Bushmen groups in various regions and at different times have acquired elements of belief and ritual from neighboring Khoekhoe or from non-Khoisan groups, enriching their religious traditions, and rendering them all the more complex. Such "foraged" elements include certain trickster figures (including Jesus Christ!), certain myths and tales, possibly the concept of a creator god, the concept of ancestors and their worship, totemistic ideas and practices, male circumcision, sorcery and witchcraft beliefs and practices, certain concepts of disease and means of treatment, and divination practices. One source for new religious ideas is Christianity, most directly the missionaries; their effect on the Bushmen is examined in chapter 9.

Notes on Methodology and Orthography

Some of the information presented in this study is drawn from sources that are short-term or impressionistic, if not altogether fictional, such as the popular writers like Laurens van der Post and Erik Holm, or Namibian white farmers like Fritz Metzger and Ilse Schatz, who, for all their familiarity with the language and customs of their farm Bushman laborers, present information that is derived without following the protocol of ethnographic data gathering. The same must be said of the early ethnographic field-workers (such as Lebzelter, Vedder, Gusinde, and Fourie, one of whose gaffes I describe in the conclusion), who often spent only a few days among the people they visited, some of them farm workers called by the white *baas* to the porch, where the visiting researcher was entertained by his farmer host, to chat with the visitor about "Bushman customs." However, as already noted, I only sparingly draw from this early ethnographic record. Most of the information I use is more or less factual, based on the long-term observations of trained ethnographers. The extent to which these factual accounts are also reliable and truthful depends on the quality of a particular researcher's work. I could, at this juncture, get caught up in self-defeating, postmodern quandaries about the relativism and self-delusionary nature of ethnographic truth claims and feel challenged to demonstrate the hermeneutical validity of the facts I report and rely on in this study. However, such is not the intent of this book; while I critically evaluate the methodological competence of some of my more dubious sources, I permit myself to assume that the evidence I have at my disposal is basically reliable and provides a suitable empirical basis for what I offer as an account of Bushman religion.

The primary ethnographic information on which this study of Bushman religion is based is derived from the Nharo of the Ghanzi District of Botswana, the site of my fieldwork since 1968; as well as other Ghanzi Bushman groups with whom I had dealings, such as the G/wi and //Gana, who are related to the Nharo, the !Kõ (or !Xõ) and the !Kung-speaking ≠Au//eisi (or ≠Kao//'ae, also known as Auen or MaKaukau). In addition, I have drawn extensively on the ethnographic descriptions of other Bushman groups (map 1), in order to convey the scope and variation of the religion of a tribal group which, while

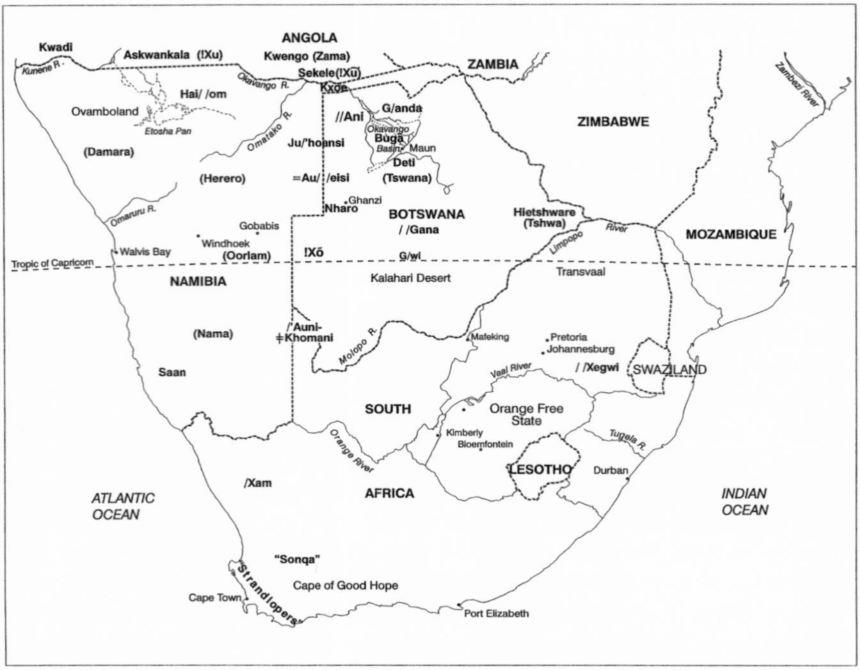

Map 1. Bushman Linguistic Groupings in Southern Africa. (Names in parentheses indicate non-Bushmen tribes.)

small in numbers and uniform in some of its basic social structures, is nevertheless an astonishingly heterogeneous culture. This study of Bushman religion is thus one of regional comparison; however, unlike another recent comparative study, of Bushman culture and society in general (Barnard 1992a), which emphasized structural uniformities, my examination of Bushman religion and society emphasizes divergences (see also Guenther 1986c, 1995a).

Regarding the as yet unresolved matter of what to call the people featured in this book, which Kalahari students have debated for the past three decades, the term I am using is "Bushman," despite its onetime racist, and continued sexist, connotation. For reasons outlined in detail elsewhere (Guenther 1986d), I prefer the term to "San" (or the official designation used in Botswana, "Basarwa"), pejoratives used and perceived as such by many people in Namibia and Botswana. Moreover, at present "Bushman" seems to be the preferred term also of the people themselves, as I learned again most recently in Ghanzi, when polling various farm Bushmen on the matter. However, there is still little agreement on the question and as many writers use the one term as use the other. The issue has recently become revived in post-apartheid South Africa, primarily by Coloured intellectuals or political spokesmen (such as Henry Bredekamp from the University of the Western Cape, who sees himself as "something of a Khoisan"), in the context of constructing an identity that is properly—and profitably—aligned with new official approaches and policies to ethnic plurality (Bredekamp 1994; Hitchcock 1996: 84–85; Bank 1998).

Finally, the inevitable note on orthography that accompanies any book on the click-speaking Khoisan. It will be short, in view of the fact that there is as yet no official orthography of the Bushman language I draw from most, Nharo. The orthography produced by Alan Barnard (1985) in his useful dictionary is in the process of being superseded by Hessel Visser (n.d., 1994) who is currently conducting an ambitious linguistic research project among the Ghanzi Nharo. However, in view of his employment of consonants to represent the various clicks, a practice not in keeping with anthropological usage, I do not follow this otherwise excellent orthography. A succinct summary of !Kung orthography, based on the linguistic research of the late Patrick Dickens, appears in Megan Biesele's recent book (1993: xiv–xvii), as well as in Dickens's Ju/'hoan dictionary, published posthumously (Dickens 1994). The other vernacular terms and names cited in the book come from a large variety of phonemically (and grammatically) different and distinct Khoisan languages. This diversity of languages precludes putting together an orthographic key common to all of them.

In this explanatory note I will thus deal with only the one most distinctive linguistic feature, the clicks. The four that are best defined, as well as universally found and uniformly pronounced across Khoisan language groups, are:

1) dental (/), produced by placing the tip of the tongue against the back of the upper incisors, creating a sound similar to our "tsk, tsk" (used, for example, when chiding a child);

2) lateral (//), produced by placing the sides of the tongue against the sides of the upper rows of teeth, creating a sound similar to what we might make when urging a horse on to greater speed;

3) alveolar (≠), produced with the tongue against the bony projection on the roof of the mouth (alveolus);

4) cerebral or alveo-palatal (!), produced by placing the front of the tongue behind the alveolus, creating a cork-popping sound.

1

Bushman Society

> *As a general rule, families live one beside the other in great independence, and little by little develop a grouping of small societies . . . which have no definite constitution, so long as internal conflicts or an external danger, such as war, does not lead one or several men to disengage themselves from the mass and become leaders. Their influence, which rests peculiarly on their personal titles, only extends and has sway within marked limits set forth by the confidence and patience of the others. Every adult remains in the eyes of such a chief in a state of complete independence. That is why such people, without any other internal organization, are held together only by external circumstances and through the habit of common life.*
>
> —WAITZ 1858: 359

This description of the social organization of simple, egalitarian societies was written over a century ago and, a generation later, appeared in Durkheim's *The Division of Labour in Society* (1964: 177–78 [1893]). I open my description of the social organization of one such society—the Bushmen—with this quotation, in part because it already captures, in so early a conceptualization, a number of key attributes of "band societies," and in part because it serves to set the sociological, rather than ecological, tone of the account of Bushman society here presented. Moreover, the formulation hints at another neglected dimension in recent study of hunter-gatherers: their "external circumstances," that is, the contact of such a "grouping of small societies" with outside societies, in the course of history.

The society of Waitz's *Naturvölker* is autonomous and atomistic, small in size, fluid in composition, loose in "internal organization." It is without a "definite constitution" and lacks well-defined leadership, is egalitarian in ethos and consists of members who are independent. All this changes when the society's "external circumstances" change, for instance, as I will show below, through encroachment and aggression, at which point the society can become more centralized and organized. In surveying the society and societies of the Bushmen, on the basis of recent ethnographic and ethnohistorical information, we can flesh out, situate historically, and refine the surmises of this nineteenth-century armchair anthropologist about hypothetical, iconic "natural societies."

The key features of Bushman society, its organization, and its institutions and ethos, are flexibility, adaptability and diversity, fluidity and amorphousness, ambivalence and ambiguity (Guenther 1996d, 1986c; Barnard 1993: 36–37). One notes these features both when looking at one specific Bushman society—that is, the band or bands of one particular "tribe"—and, especially, when looking at Bushman societies and tribes comparatively, across southern Africa. Such a regional-comparative perspective yields a dazzling spectrum of social and cultural diversity (Biesele, Guenther, et al. 1989; Barnard 1992a; Guenther 1986c, 1995a, 1996a, 1996b). On the one end, one finds loose, nomadic, family-based and -sized foragers, and on the other sedentary, palisaded, multi-band aggregations, politically organized, with chiefs, tribute, and stock; moreover, some groups are relatively isolated, while others have lived, in some cases for centuries, in economic and political association with agro-pastoral neighboring groups, either as traders or as serfs (Solway and Lee 1990; Wilmsen 1989; Wilmsen and Denbow 1990; also see Barnard 1992b). The explanation for all this diversity is, on the one hand, the inherent flexibility of Bushman social organization and structure and, on the other, Waitz's "external circumstances," ecological and socio-political ones, such as prolonged droughts and aggressive settlers, respectively. In the course of a history of contact that was turbulent and prolonged at certain times and for certain groups, these outside conditions, to which a Bushman band or tribe was constantly forced to adapt, have stretched the resilience of Bushman society to its limit, manifesting thereby virtually all of the organizational possibilities Bushman society is capable of manifesting.

I will begin my investigation of the flexibility of Bushman society by describing one case—the Nharo—with whom I am familiar as a result of my own ethnographic and ethnohistorical research. The account will be diachronic, covering almost two centuries, in the course of which Nharo social organization has taken on a range of different economic, social, and political configurations. After sketching the historical developments of the Ghanzi District in the nineteenth century, and the socio-political patterns of the Nharo during that period, I will deal with the recent and contemporary situation. Here I will turn from the Nharo case to other Bushman groups, in an effort to present a synchronic analysis of the social parameters of flexibility. Its ethnographic base is derived from Bushman linguistic groupings from all over southern Africa. This analysis will be followed, in the subsequent chapter, with a consideration of ideological and psychological parameters of the same structural trait, in an examination of Bushman ethos and the individual.

Nharo Society, 1790s to 1890s

As I have shown in a number of papers on the ethnohistory of the Ghanzi region (1992a: 96–99, 1993/94, 1996b, 1997a), during the course of the previous century the size and scale of Nharo society—as of the ≠Au//gei with whom the Nharo were either at war or to whom they were linked as subjects or allies—seems to have undergone a drastic shift. While some of the groups probably lived as small-scale, egalitarian foraging bands throughout the century, written and oral historical sources suggest that others, those living along the water- and game-rich Ghanzi veld stretching from Rietfontein to Kuki, were large, politically organized and centralized societies, whose "captains"—also referred to, by Passarge, as "paramount chiefs"—led troops of up to a hundred armed men (Passarge 1907: 114–16; Baines 1864: 136, 151). Passarge (ibid.: 119) suggests that this complexity may have been an element of the hunting economy of the Ghanzi Bushmen, a "hunting people par excellence" whose "social and economic relations, all laws and rights, the entire political organization" were based on hunting (ibid.: 119). Given the species, volume, and style of hunting, this conjectural, cultural-ecological appraisal of the nineteenth-century Ghanzi Bushmen has a ring of plausibility. The Ghanzi veld was extremely rich in such big-game species as elephant, giraffe, and eland, as well as huge herds of springbok and wildebeest, and all of the other antelope species. This was prior to the arrival of white, black (BaTawana), and yellow (Nama) big-game hunters, who exterminated some species and decimated the rest, and, following them, Boer settlers for whom the Ghanzi veld and its pans and wells provided cattle grazing land, which was parceled out to them as freehold land. The old Bushman hunting practices in use prior to the arrival of the commercial hunters and herders consisted of driving herds of animals down through rows of fences, into deep pits that were dug by the score in the river bed. They were as high-yield as they were labor-intensive, and they may have formed the base for more complex labor regimens and property relations, and more regulated and restricted access to land and resources, than can be seen among contemporary Ghanzi Bushmen, and other Kalahari Bushmen.

In his 1907 book about the Bushmen of the Ghanzi and adjoining Kaukau veld—the first ethnographic monograph on the Bushmen[1]—the geographer Siegfried Passarge provides a vivid account of what was no doubt the largest and most complex of Bushman state-like societies that might have existed in the Ghanzi region throughout the previous century or centuries. Basing his description on information obtained from "my good, old //Koschep," Passarge's Nharo interpreter, the geographer refers to the society of the Bushmen of the Ghanzi veld as a "well-organized state form," and likens it to the "feudal system prevailing amongst the Bantu" (Passarge ibid.: 116). Corresponding roughly to the farming block of today's Ghanzi District, it was ruled over by an autocratic war-chieftain—the "mighty ≠Dukuri (Passarge ibid.: 115; Guenther 1993/94: 34–36)—whose name is remembered by some of the contemporary farm

Bushmen in the Ghanzi and Gobabis districts to this day. He exercised his power and control with the assistance of a body guard of "warriors" who surrounded him at all times, ruling over his Bushman subjects as "paramount chief" and "supreme judge," and as collector of annual tribute (consisting of furs, ivory, and ostrich eggshell bead necklaces) from family groups in his realm (Passarge ibid.: 115). His subjects were both from his own ≠Au//ei tribe, and from the //Aikwe whom he subjugated, thereby adding territory, fighting power, and tribute to his strength. The //Aikwe came to be known as the "Narro" (Nharo) at that time, according to Passarge's informant, meaning "people who are not worth anything"[2] (Passarge ibid.: 115). Another gloss of the appellation of the ≠Au//eisi at Rietfontein for the //Aikwe, "Naru," is "subordinates" or "slaves" and is reported by Lebzelter (1934: 68) to reflect the relationship of the latter people toward the former. So powerful was ≠Dukuri (and other, lesser Bushmen chiefs like him), that the BaTawana to the east are said by //Koschep never to have dared enter their land, while the Hottentots to the west only ventured into the Ghanzi veld on brief raiding skirmishes (ibid.: 115).

While doubtless exaggerated,[3] Passarge's account of the Ghanzi Bushmen as a politically well organized, proud, and independent people, with the capacity to maintain their autonomy and territorial integrity is nevertheless borne out to some extent by other early writers, especially those traveling through the region in the first half of the century, for instance, Joseph McCabe, Charles Andersson, James Chapman, and Tomas Baines (Guenther 1993/94, 1997a). These explorer-hunter-traders are given to comments on the tallness of stature, "manly independence," fearlessness, and boldness of these "Lords of the Desert Land," and they contrast the Bushmen met in the Ghanzi region with those encountered further to the south, west, or east, who were described as more timid and submissive. They also report on the local black people's wariness of the Bushmen—the BaTawana regarded them as the "*Swart*-serpents of the desert," "whom they could neither pursue nor dared engage" (Baines 1864: 175)—and they write nervous log entries about the well-armed Bushmen who pay altogether too frequent visits to their caravan of ox wagons, occasionally "upwards of 100" strong (Chapman 1971, 1:8; also see Guenther 1997a).

Oral traditions of the Ghanzi Bushmen also tell of Bushman chiefs and black raiders, and acts of resistance carried out by a valiant Bushman chief or a clever Bushman child, by means of poison arrows or through cunning. Some of these stories suggest that apart from political mobilization, massing, and centralization, the Ghanzi Bushmen employed the other tactic available to them for dealing with the colonizing, dominating herders that encroached on their lands: the tactic, consistent with their loose, flexible, and nomadic lifeways, of hit-and-run, lightning attacks or ambushes, by fleet-footed hunter-warriors and archers—who loosened poisonous arrows on their enemies, in salvos or one or two at a time, at unexpected moments—with superior knowledge of the terrain and of tracking and stalking. It appears that these "low-profile tactics" (Bender and Morris 1988: 7; also see Myers 1988: 264–65 and Rao 1993: 510

for examples from hunter-gatherers in other regions of the world) were used alongside the other strategy of resistance: strength-in-numbers aggregation and political consolidation (Passarge 1907: 117). Certain of the oral narratives, set in the late nineteenth century when the BaTawana had placed much of the Ghanzi region under their control, indicate that stealth and cunning, rather than massed confrontation, were the tactics then employed. I have provided the texts of the narratives I collected elsewhere (Guenther 1989: 152–55); they are dramatic, spun-out tales of valor too lengthy to be put down here.

Family memorates constitute another source of historical information. An example is the story of the Nharo chief[4] Tsabu, which I collected from /Xamku Moses, an old Nharo man, who was born around 1907 and raised in eastern Ghanzi, near Kuki. When his mother was a young girl, her brother Tsabu had the following hostile encounter with black raiders:

> This happened before there were any Europeans in Ghanzi, except for some, very few. In those days there was an old Nharo man; his name was Tsabu. He was the chief of the Nharo. He had two sisters at ≠Xoi tsa farm, an older one and a young one. [The latter was the narrator's mother.] When he stayed at that place, visiting his two sisters, the Tswana came from Ngamiland. They had heard that he was at ≠Xoi tsa and they came to kill him, along with other people, and to take their people to Ngamiland. And they came, especially to kill him. When they came Tsabu defeated them and he killed them and the rest of the Tswana men ran away, back to Ngamiland. More Tswana came, and they came and they killed him. What happened was that after the first battle had ended Tsabu had spoken with his people to tell them to get away but the people refused. So he told them that he, too, would stay; "I won't move, I'll just stay at this farm." This is why the Tswana found him there, when they came back the second time. When they came they made a kraal and put it around them and put all the children inside. They caught the chief and two men and tied them to a tree. They spent a day asking him questions and then tried to take him to Ngamiland to make him a servant. He refused. They talked to him till five o'clock and then shot him dead, and also as those other two men. And the people ran away. Tsabu's two sisters were there; the oldest and a younger one. And those two girls scattered. And there was then no longer any chief. . . . (Field Notes, Dekar, 29 Oct. 1969)

Such raids became more and more frequent in the second half of the nineteenth century, as well as more and more difficult to repel, as, thanks to the extremely lucrative ivory and feather trade, the perpetrators were now armed with guns and mounted on horseback. The raiders were primarily the BaTawana from Ngamiland and the Nama-speaking Oorlam (Orlam) Afrikaners (or "Oorlam Hottentots") from Gobabis, both of which had become mini-states in the previous century, with ever more determined expansionist and hegemonic intentions on the Ghanzi veld and its faunal and human inhabitants (Vedder 1934: 522–25; Lau 1987: 67–68; Nettleton 1934; Sillery 1952: 144–47). The game was needed to satisfy the insatiable demand for ivory (Wilmsen

1989: 105–23; Gordon 1992: 33–40). The BaTawana also co-opted the services of their Bushman serfs as hunters, utilizing their superior tracking and hunting skills; moreover, they collected tribute from them in the form of ivory, ostrich feathers, and other game products (Chapman 1971, 1:185; Schinz 1891: 381; Passarge 1907: 122; Stow 1905: 143–44). Other services they exacted from their Bushman serfs were to act as spies and messengers, providing information on strangers approaching or traveling through Tawana or Oorlam territory, as well as to mislead white travelers and hunter-traders, whenever they voyaged on trails the BaTawana considered risks to their political or economic security (Andersson 1856: 384; Baines 1864: 196–97, 231–32; Chapman 1971, 1:185; Passarge 1905: 84, 1907: 121–24; Wilmsen 1989: 119–21).

The number of white hunter-traders rose steeply throughout the latter half of the nineteenth century, after some cautious venturings, at the middle of the century, into what one early traveler (Andersson 1856: 374) had referred to as a "howling wilderness . . . with every inch on the ground ahead . . . unknown to Europeans" when he first approached it at its western edge at Rietfontein, with his companion Sir Francis Galton (Andersson 1856: 374). The two men did not then dare enter this stretch of African terra incognita, Andersson doing so only some four years later, on a return journey that took him to the Tawana at lake N'gami. He was probably the first white trader to travel the west-east route, Walvisbaai-Gobabis-Rietfontein-Nagami, while others (Moyle, McCabe) had traveled the Ghanzi-Lake N'gami stretch entering from a southern route, through the Kalahari, or the "Great Southern Zahara" (Campbell 1822: 116), following routes BaThlaping, BaRolong, BaNgwaketse, and Griqua cattle raiders or traders had taken to Lake N'gami some years or decades before (Campbell 1822: 114–19; McCabe 1855; Guenther 1997a). In subsequent years others followed in rapid succession, so that the "howling wilderness" fast became one of the most widely traveled trade routes in southern Africa (Lee and Guenther 1993: 192–95), enabling the Swiss botanist-explorer Hans Schinz, in 1884, to find his way by simply following the well-marked ox wagon trails leading through the land (Schinz 1891: 385).

By the end of the century travelers and traders became colonists and herders. These took over the Ghanzi region from the BaTawana, who claimed it as their land, and, of course, from the indigenous Bushmen who, while recognized as the rightful owners of the land, were nevertheless not considered, let alone included in any treaty negotiations, when the British colonial agents engineered their expropriation (Silberbauer 1965: 116; Tlou 1975; Childers 1976: 6–8; Russell and Russell 1979: 13–14; Maylam 1980: 146–48, 196–97; Guenther 1986a: 40–45; also see Guenther 1997a). In 1898, after five years of negotiation with the BaTawana chief Sekgoma, and one false start (in 1895, forcing the Ghanzi settlers to retreat and return to the Cape), the Boer settlers arrived for good. Each was allocated a farm of approximately four thousand hectares, with the Bushmen either continuing to forage on the land between the farms, or providing labor on the ranches. As the number of farms increased, the farming block expanded, and the veld corridors disappeared, foraging became less and less an option. Farm labor became the subsistence base for the majority of the Ghanzi Bushmen who lived within or around the farming block (Guenther 1976, 1986a: chap. 5, 1996b).

We thus have two societal and personality types among the hunter-gatherer Bushmen of nineteenth-century Ghanzi: on the one hand, a politically organized, mobilized, and centralized mini-state of individuals of warlike mien and independent bearing, with a robust big-game-hunting and gathering economy; on the other, loose, egalitarian, politically unorganized, and passive bands of "harmless people," pursuing a foraging subsistence pattern and mode of production. The former type was found in and around the Ghanzi region during the first half of the previous century, the latter in the second. The latter is attested to by later writers, such as Hans Schinz (1891: 388–99), Siegfried Passarge (1907: 16–75), Hans Kaufmann (1910), Dorothea Bleek (1928), and Viktor Lebzelter (1934: 65–79), who all provided early ethnographic accounts on the Nharo and ≠Au//ei Bushmen of the Ghanzi region. They describe a people and social and economic way of life that is like that of most other contemporary Kalahari Bushmen (Guenther 1997a), except that it has somewhat more institutionalized headmanship than other groups, as well as (in the ≠Au//ei case) a somewhat warlike tradition that is reported to have revolved around territorial raids and feuding (Kaufmann ibid.: 138; Lebzelter ibid.: 66, 72–73). To this day the "Makauakau," as the ≠Au//eisi are locally known, have the reputation of ferociousness among the people of the Ghanzi district (Bleek 1928: 41–43; Guenther 1986a: 7). The "Makaukau" hold the same reputation in the Gobabis region, where the attack on the District Magistrate and his party, resulting in the former's fatal wounding with a poison arrow, is still talked about by the elder farmers (Budack 1980; Gordon 1992: 92–100). During a recent visit to a number of Gobabis District farms and farm ≠Au//eisi, the story was told to me in a number of versions, some of them embellished as a tabloid melodrama.[5] The perception of the "Makaukau" as a once-bellicose people is held also by some contemporary ≠Au//ei farm Bushmen, as well as their Nharo neighbors, both in Gobabis and Ghanzi Districts. For instance, I was told by two old ≠Au//eisi on a Gobabis farm how, when they were small boys, men would practice their warrior skills in play raids. Such war games evidently involved shooting blunt, wooden arrows at one another.

For the Ghanzi Bushman the nineteenth century thus ended quite differently from how it had begun, with a reversal in their political structure and fortune. Having once been described rhapsodically as "Lords of the Desert Land" (Baines 1864: 144), whose rich game resources sustained a strong, well-organized, and politically and culturally autonomous hunting economy, they had become squatters on their own land. The encroaching settlers that had encapsulated them with an ever-tightening noose, at first with guns and on horseback and then through arrogant treaties that excluded the Bushman as negotiating partners, had now moved onto their land fully and irreversibly.

Hunting and gathering territories were carved up into freehold ranching spreads, game was displaced by cattle, and a free-ranging foraging economy was supplanted by sedentary farm labor and dependency on a patron-*baas* (Guenther 1976a, 1986a). Moreover, the gross overhunting, not only of elephants but also of game antelopes and other species, had seriously depleted the supply of game, contributing to the drastic depopulation of Ghanzi Bushmen in the last two decades of the previous century (Passarge 1907: 10, 58, 75, 119; Wilmsen 1989: 123–29). Outbreaks of malaria and smallpox—the latter "a thing hitherto hardly known to the people of this country" (Chapman 1868, 2: 298)—in the second half of the century contributed further to the population decline (Chapman 1971, 1:183; Kaufmann 1910: 136; Bleek 1928: 40).

All of this—encroachment, encapsulation, enserfment, labor exploitation —was a repeat of the same story that had played itself out among Bushman groups in other parts of southern Africa, as well as among the hunting and gathering peoples of Africa generally (Woodburn 1988). And so was the reaction: like Bushman groups in the other regions, the Ghanzi Bushmen offered determined resistance. Contrary to the image portrayed of contemporary Bushmen as a "harmless people" or as "flower children of the Kalahari" (Guenther 1981), they responded with resolve and efficiency to the acts of aggression and expropriation brought against them. They did so by the same basic process that was followed by beleaguered Bushmen in the colonial Cape or in northern and western South West Africa. Developing a bellicose and "territorial" ethos, which not infrequently struck fear and terror into the hearts of encroaching settler groups, they organized themselves politically, activating the structural capacity of Bushman social organization for large, multi-band aggregation (Guenther 1986b, 1995a). They rallied around a leader, who sometimes was an outsider of mixed blood, conversant in the cultural and political ways of the colonists. Thus, in early colonial South West Africa, around Grootfontein, Karakubis, and the northeastern stretches of Gobabis District, white settlers had to contend with a number of short-lived, large, and predatory Bushman groups, up to 350 strong, that consolidated around bellicose Bushman or Nama "Captains." Such Bushman groupings led brigand lives and constituted an ongoing threat to German settlers (Seiner 1911: 140, 1913: 39–40; Lebzelter 1934: 60–61; Wilhelm 1955: 154; see also Schott 1955: 145; Gordon 1992: 77–88; Guenther 1993/94: 36–37). As suggested by one early writer (Wilhelm 1955: 155), the !Kung around Karakuwisa and in the Kaukauveld of South West Africa, like the ≠Au//eisi and Nharo to the southeast, had a tighter, more centralized political structure until the early nineteenth century. Like the Ghanzi ≠Dukuri, their war chieftains led their followers into brutal raids against enemy bands (ibid.: 156–58) and their control over their lands was so firm that "the neighbouring Hottentots and Bantu tribes seldom dared enter Bushman territories" (ibid: 155). A century before, and on a larger scale, the same process of political consolidation under a war chieftain (Marks 1972; Szalay 1983: 170–79, 212–13, 255–57) and fierce, and for a time effective

(Marks 1972: 74–75; Szalay 1983: 171), resistance and attacks had taken place among the Bushmen of the Cape, against white, as well as black, settlers.

As seen in this brief discussion, and more fully elsewhere (Guenther 1997a adduces further ethnohistorical evidence), the Ghanzi Bushmen were not unlike their compatriots in other regions of southern Africa, offering a like process of resistance to encroachment, subjection, and domination, and undergoing a like social-structural process of politicization. Living in a more remote and obscure region than the rest, and one that until recently lay outside the colonizing orbit of white settlers and black state societies, the Ghanzi people and their story of resistance did not enter the written historical record, except as a footnote. Yet, as I have briefly shown here, and more fully elsewhere (Guenther 1997a), the Ghanzi hunter-gatherer Bushmen were part of that history, as active, at times even proactive, agents, aware of the new realities and how to control and exploit them.

Nharo Society, 1890s to 1990s

Turning now to the social organization of the Ghanzi Bushmen of the twentieth century, we note two main socio-economic and political patterns, farm labor and government settlements. The first began in 1898, after the establishment of the ranchers within the Ghanzi district. As described in detail elsewhere (Guenther 1976a, 1977a, 1979b, 1986a, 1986b, 1996b; also see Silberbauer 1965: 114–26; Childers 1976; Russell and Russell 1979; Barnard 1980c: 138–39; Osaki 1990), until the 1970s farm labor was for the most part paternalistic and exploitive. It created for the farm Bushmen a life of dependency, oppression, and deprivation, the latter consisting of malnutrition, hunger, and a rising incidence of disease, including a high infant mortality rate. Laborers worked for pittance wages and rations and lived in village compounds attached to the farmer's residence. The farm villages consisted of several families or bands, living in close proximity, not only leading sedentary lives, but also adhering to a Western work regimen marked by regularity and punctuality. Such a lifestyle was foreign to many Bushmen, as were many other elements of the new life situation, such as cash, schooling, political regulations, and direct or indirect contact with Christianity, through the ministrations of the Dutch Reformed Church mission at Dekar. A consequential economic change is the diminished subsistence role of hunting and gathering, the latter eroding the productive role of women and with it their personal mobility and independence as they and their children are tied to their male kin and providers. Thus, the farm Bushmen were required to make numerous changes and adjustments that are necessitated by a transition from nomadic hunting and gathering to sedentary wage labor. In addition to engaging in wage labor, a number have become petty, penny-capitalist entrepreneurs, killing vermin, collecting bones on farmers' lands, or building fences, all on contract to farmers; selling home-made brew or, for a fee, hauling wood or roof grass by donkey cart for fellow villagers; or making handicraft items to sell to marketing outlets or the occasional tourist passing through Ghanzi village (Guenther 1986a: 156–61). Another problem, that became progressively serious throughout the second half of the century, was the erosion of farm jobs for farm Bushmen due to the preference for black workers on the part of some farmers. As more and more Kgalagadi, Tswana, and Herero came to settle in the district, unemployment and poverty became additional problems for the farm Bushmen.

Whereas the farm villages offered the Bushmen living and working there a life of close supervision and restrictions imposed by a paternalistic *baas,* the second main socio-economic pattern for farm laborers, the cattle post hamlets, offered more freedom. Like black herders, the white ranchers divided their herds up into "camps," each at a windmill-driven (now diesel-powered) water reservoir. One or several Bushmen are placed in charge of these remote herds and in some cases the closeness of the veld allows them to snare or hunt game animals, and lets their wives gather wild plants. However, the laborers' main activities revolve around the employer's herd, as well as the Bushman's own few head of either small stock or cattle. These may constitute part of the laborer's remuneration. The women, who are not employed and thus not tied to any job, have more freedom of movement than the men, not only to go gathering but also to go off for visits to other villages or hamlets. The farm Bushmen generally regard life at the cattle posts to be less stressful than at the farm villages.

There are eight government settlements in the District. They were established throughout the late 1970s and 1980s, in order to provide for the farm Bushmen, whose employment prospects and living conditions were becoming increasingly precarious, a place to live, grazing and water rights, and the opportunity to develop herding and plant cultivation (Guenther 1986a: 304–14, 316–17; Heinz 1978a; Heinz and Lee 1978; Wily 1973, 1982; LeRoux 1995b). The government also set up boreholes with diesel pumps, paddocks, schools, and stores in most of the settlements, as well as agricultural training programs, leather tanning and working shops, and bee-keeping schemes. All of these programs are designed to foster economic initiative and self-reliance among the people. The settlements consist of four to five hundred people and some have officially recognized headmen, who act as spokesmen for the community and the group. A prolonged drought, in the 1980s, required the government to provide famine relief to the settlement residents. This initiative held back the development of economic self-sufficiency of these communities.

One other economic and socio-political development of the Ghanzi farm Bushmen that should be mentioned is Kuru Development Trust, an NGO operating at Dekar that grew out of the Gereformeerde Kerk mission at the same location in 1986. Its aim, like that of the government settlements, is the economic self-sufficiency and self-reliance, and the political self-direction, of the Ghanzi Bushmen. The former objective is pursued through a variety of farming and income-generating schemes, as well as educational and cultural projects, the latter by involving the hundred or so Bushmen attached to the settlement at Kuru directly in decision making (Kuru Development Trust 1991/92; Morupisi 1992). Just under half of the members of the Kuru Development Board of Trustees (of fifteen) are Bushmen. Over a dozen projects are run at Kuru; they include cattle ranching, a market vegetable garden, a cochineal harvesting operation, a preschool program, a tannery and leather workshop, a craft marketing scheme, and a Bushman art project (Turkinson 1992).

This survey of Nharo social organization over the past two centuries has revealed the many diverse forms this society is capable of assuming: big-game hunting or small-scale foraging; tributary dependency relationship to regional state societies, or military independence and resistance, as quasi-state societies; sedentary life with wage labor and marginal herding and cultivating, as well as petty entrepreneurship at farm villages or cattle posts, or as economically self-sufficient and politically self-directing larger village communities (albeit, the latter as yet in its rudimentary phase).[6]

These diverse social formations are all variations on the theme of the foraging band. It remains as the underlying social blueprint of the societal patterns of today's Ghanzi Bushmen, notwithstanding their sedentary lifestyle, wage labor, and other subsistence and economic patterns, such as hunting on horseback, hunting with spear and dogs (Osaki 1984; Ikeya 1994), dry farming (Ikeya 1996b), road construction (Ikeya 1996a), and goat keeping (Sugawara 1991; Ikeya 1993). As Nurit Bird-David (1992a) has convincingly argued, inherent in these "other," non-hunting-and-gathering economic activities by Bushman and other hunter-gatherers, are the same elements as are found in traditional foraging, such as flexibility, variety, and opportunism. Such was my conclusion in a monograph on the Nharo farm Bushmen of the late 1960s and early 1970s, whose social and cultural changes I described. In assessing their effects on Bushman band society after three to four generations of farm life I concluded that, on balance, they had "not been that far-reaching, indeed, neither singly nor in combination have they brought about anything like a transformation of Nharo society or culture . . . the band, the fundamental structure of Nharo society, is still basically intact. That this should be so, after nearly a century of quite intensive contact, is rather remarkable" (Guenther 1986a: 289, 292). Much the same conclusion was reached by George Silberbauer and Adam Kuper, in their study of the contemporary serf relationship of Bushmen with Kgalagadi villagers in western Ghanzi: "It is true that there has been a modification in the hunting-gathering way of life, and that serf Bushman villages are more stable than 'wild' Bushman encampments, which are frequently shifted, but *Bushman band organization and kinship structure seem to have remained intact*" (Silberbauer and Kuper 1966: 179, my emphasis).

A like conclusion was also reached by one researcher about contemporary Bushmen in the Kalahari generally (Barnard 1988: 12). After listing the extensive changes the people have undergone on the economic and technological front, and noting less pervasive change in the domains of social organization and religion, as well as retention of their own language, Barnard writes:

> Specific forms of band organization are changing, due to dependence on material goods from the shops and the easy access to water afforded by boreholes put down by the Botswana government, district councils and local ranchers; but the ideal of the band society is in many parts of the Kalahari very much intact. (Barnard 1988: 12)

The reason the integrity of traditional band society has been maintained is its flexibility. The various manifestations of this hallmark trait and its structural parameters will be my preoccupation for the rest of this chapter. Shifting from a diachronic account of the on-the-ground society, I will now consider Bushman society synchronically. This approach is well suited for identifying the structural and institutional makeup of what Barnard refers to as the "ideal of the band society."

Bushman Social Organization

For all of its organizational simplicity, Bushman society, and band society in general, is, in fact, structurally differentiated. Ideally, the structure is three tiered, consisting of the family, or, using Barnard's term (1992a: 226), the domestic group; the band; and the band cluster.[7] While these three tiers make up an inclusive system, this system—as everything else in Bushman society—is not tightly integrated. Like the segments of an earthworm—Durkheim's somewhat stretched analogy for the workings of "mechanical solidarity"—each is potentially autonomous and, depending on "external circumstances," may actually become so, for varying lengths of time. In any of its three forms Bushman society is, in fact, capable of social reproduction. This structural feature renders Bushman society flexible and resilient, capable of assuming and sustaining whatever is the situationally adaptive structural form. It also provides an explanation for the diversity of forms we noted in Nharo society over the past couple of centuries, a diversity found within Bushman societies over all of southern Africa.

For most of the time families are a part of co-residential, co-nomadic bands or camps, the former referring to all potential members of this multi-family group in an abstract sense, the latter to the members of the actual group at any one time. According to Lorna Marshall (1965: 258) the individual family is a domestic group of great emotional cohesiveness. Ideally, it occupies one hut and tends one hearth, and consumes a woman's gathered plants and a man's small game.

Among some Bushman groups, such as the G/wi and //Gana, there may be yet another social unit, sandwiched between the family and band (Silberbauer 1981: 166–67; Barnard 1992a: 102). It consists of two or more families, who cluster their huts in close proximity to one another and engage in extensive interaction, intervisiting, and gossip. Silberbauer refers to these units as "cliques." He emphasizes the transient and unstable nature of these multi-family sub-band units; in fact, in periods of aggregation, they may also be supra-band with respect to their segmentary position, as they may be made up of members from more than one band. They reconstitute themselves anew after each move the band makes to a new campsite. It is only during periods of extreme drought that cliques may become more permanent, moving about as tiny bands, or "family clusters" (Barnard 1992: 102), until the drought is over (Silberbauer 1981: 167).

Bands, in turn, are parts of a larger social unit in some tribes, such as the !Xõ (Heinz 1966: 93–110), the Nharo (Guenther 1986a: 173–74; Barnard 1992a: 138–39) and the G/wi (Silberbauer 1965: 76, 1972: 302–304, 1981: 178–90). The "band cluster," "band nexus," or "band alliance" may be formally absent from the social structure of other groups, for instance, the !Kung (Marshall 1965: 246), although in times of severe drought and prolonged drought periods members from various groups may come together (Lee 1993: 33; see also Barnard 1992a: 229), forming aggregations that are much more spontaneous and unpatterned in their social, political, and cultural integration than groups such as the Nharo or !Xõ. The strength of ties among the constituent units of a "cluster" thus varies from tribe to tribe, as well as within different ecological or historical contexts. The loosest are the G/wi "alliances": sporadic, ad hoc aggregations, through loose, open, and unnamed networks that are based on frequency of intervisiting and exchange (Silberbauer 1981: 178–81). Next on the solidarity scale are semantically recognized or named "nexuses" that are related through kin, friendship and age-group ties and territorially defined (Heinz 1966: 91–93; see also Barnard 1992a: 64–67). The most tightly and durably knit are the politically integrated and centralized quasi chiefdoms, such as were found, for instance, in nineteenth-century Ghanzi, as a reaction to Nama and Tswana encroachment.

However, like the normal aggregation phase, set in motion through ecological, rather than political, adversity, these more complex forms of aggregation rarely proved to be permanent. Once the external threat facing the Bushman people in a certain region had subsided, the political leaders and institutions that had given a relatively high degree of stability and complexity to aggregation subsided with it. This did not happen in situations (such as in southern Angola) where Bantu-speaking peoples had established themselves permanently, either because they remained a permanent threat, or because, through acculturation or incorporation, the Bushmen had acquired statelike forms of political organization. However, a more common form of permanent accommodation to strong state-organized neighbors was to enter, through force or as a matter of course, into a dependency relationship with them.

As I have shown more fully elsewhere (Guenther 1986a: 291–94, 1986c, 1996d: 79–81), each of the three structural sections—family, band, band cluster—is capable of assuming its own existence, for varying lengths of time. The family group is usually the unit that moves back and forth from band to band, either to visit or because of social tension, when a conflict in the band has reached an impasse. Also, in seasons either of resource abundance (!Kung, Nharo) or shortage (G/wi, Saan), it is the family that traditionally lives and moves about together. In the acculturated setting of the farm Bushmen, this social unit gets defined through the economic and social guidelines that underlie the European wage economy and society, as set by the white employer vis-à-vis his Bushman farm laborer. Remuneration paid them, especially the allocation of rations, is set by the farmer's standard of what constitutes a proper number of dependants for his employees.

The camp/band is together for most of the time, especially during certain seasons when a group of this size seems to be optimally efficient for the exploitation of available resources (Lee and DeVore 1968: 245–48). For the Zhu/'hoan !Kung, for instance, this is the rainy season (R. B. Lee 1976), whereas for the G/wi, living in a more arid environment, the rainy season is the time of year in which people aggregate, around water pans and resource nexuses. They are forced to disperse during the dry season, when no surface water at all may be available and people are reduced to satisfying their thirst from the moisture in tubers or the rumen of killed antelopes (Silberbauer 1981: 104–106, 218–19, 242–44; see also Barnard 1992a: 223–36). It is the social unit that "owns" a certain territory, is "led" by a headman, and is made up of a core of consanguinal kin (siblings and their parents). In situations wherein a Bushman population are serfs to Bantu-speaking or Nama neighbors, the social unit to stand in a dependency relationship to a specific overlord is often a band (although it could also be a family) (Passarge 1907: 121; Silberbauer 1965: 127; Silberbauer and Kuper 1966; Lee 1979: 407; Guenther 1986a: 178–81).

During the aggregation phase of the year the multi-band group assembles, more or less regularly. Here, ideally, the Bushmen are very much like many other hunter-gatherers, such as the Eskimo—the classic case, thanks to Mauss's (1905) paradigmatic analysis. Aggregation is as dense morally as it is physically, interaction revolving around such vitally and socially important matters as courtship, marriage brokering, visiting, exchange, ritual, storytelling, and—among non-Kalahari Bushmen—painting. (Lee 1979: 364–66; Guenther 1984: 30–34). As seen above, in the account of the Nharo of nineteenth-century Ghanzi, and elsewhere, in the colonial Cape and South West Africa, such multi-band aggregations sometimes became politically organized and centralized, forming bands of mounted "banditti," up to one thousand strong (Szalay 1983: 179).

Thus, depending on the season, or on other ecological or social circumstances, one or another of the units of Bushman society would become situationally activated. While normally and ideally oscillating, in tune with the seasons, between large aggregation and small dispersal units, either could remain the operational unit of social organization for a long time—potentially indefinitely—as were the loose, and probably endogamous, family groups of Saan in the Namib (Trenk 1910; Vedder 1934: 25), or the militaristic colonial Bushman multi-band tribes. As a result of these short- or long-term structural oscillations, Bushman social organization is kept flexible, over the course of time.

Apart from these external, situational forces which sporadically realign and flex social structure, Bushman society is also inherently flexible and dynamic. A basic reason is the mobile economic and social life, the "nomadic style" (Lee and DeVore 1968: 11–12), which causes people to move hither and yon or to and fro—as they exploit unevenly distributed plant resources and largely migratory game, or follow the seasonal round—between aggregation and dispersal locales. The social reasons for spatial mobility are the pull of visiting kin or trading partners and the push of social tension within the camp (Lee 1979: 364–68). Such movements, by individuals or family groupings, from band to band and over adjoining territories, is possible because of the openness of social groups. Their respective territories can usually be entered for the asking, and their resources utilized. Reciprocal access to resources, rather than territorial exclusiveness, is the basic ethos regulating inter-band relations (R. B. Lee 1976; Guenther 1981; Barnard 1992a: 229–36). It is a rule that makes ecological sense, given the unevenness and unpredictability in the distribution of resources over space and time, and the consequent need for a flexible territorial "policy" (R. B. Lee 1976: 91, 1978: 108, 1979: 361). The fact that kin and trade partners are spread far and wide makes cross-territorial movements and inter-band visits that much easier. Thus, there is much coming and going in a Bushman camp, not only during the dispersal phase, but also in the more stable aggregation period; from week to week the number and composition of the members of a group will vary (Bleek 1928: 4; Lee 1979: 354–60; Guenther 1986a: 185). Indeed,

> the constant circulation of population makes it appear at first that there is no stable basis of residential life and that the !Kung are a mobile people who can live anywhere and with anyone, but in no place for very long. (Lee 1978: 107)

The same flexibility and fluidity that pervade the structure and composition of Bushman society mark its institutions and values, to which a certain looseness and indeterminacy attaches, contributing to the "organizational lability" of Bushman society, as Silberbauer (1981: 185) put it, writing about the G/wi.

With respect to economic institutions, we see a striking range of diversity, from "immediate-return-style" gathering hunting, through "Plains-style" big game hunting and mesolithic fishing, to herding and cultivating. As I have argued elsewhere (1996d), such diversity, in the economy as well as the other cultural systems, bespeaks institutional flexibility. This is also the condition of the two subsistence patterns followed by the Bushmen and -women. What one notes is the relaxed, laid-back, loosely scheduled pace of both gathering and hunting, women working two to three days per week, men a bit more, on an uneven, ad hoc work schedule (Lee 1978: 105, 1979: 261–90). The "stop-and-go" rhythm of hunting has both ecological and social reasons, having to do with the unpredictability of game and the social expectation that the good hunter will hold back for a while and let other hunters bring in the meat (Lee 1993: 54–59). Women and men gather and hunt either alone or in small groups; hunting tends to be an individual activity more frequently than it is a collective one (Lee 1979: 118, 1978: 104). This applies especially to snare hunting, an activity that is always done by a single person—young or old (Hewitt 1986: 30; Guenther 1986a: 152, 211; Lee 1993: 52), male or female (Kent 1993a: 489–90). Hunting and gathering are both opportunistic, open-ended activities in which luck, as well as dreams and divination, all play a significant part (Lee 1978: 104).

Neither subsistence role is gender-specific except in a general sense; the "fuzzy boundary" between man the hunter and woman the gatherer (Kent 1993b: 9) renders ambiguous in practice what ideally is clear-cut. As noted, snare hunting is done by women among the Kutse Bushmen, while "mobile" hunting, most commonly a male task, may also occasionally be performed by women (Lee 1979: 235; Shostak 1981: 93, 244; Heinz and Lee 1978: 120). In addition to plants, women will also gather such things as insects, birds, lizards, locusts, and tortoises (Hewitt 1986: 34; Lee 1979: 235). Among the "River Bushmen" of the Okavango region, women do most of the fishing (Gusinde 1966: 172). This inclusion of animals within the female category of "getherable" further obscures the category of man the hunter. Conversely, the role of gathering is by no means exclusive to women. Men, whenever they are out on a hunting excursion, will also gather plants (as well as firewood) for their own use, and bring back supplies thereof, in the event that they fail at hunting (Lee 1979: 123; Barnard 1980a: 116; Guenther 1983: 13; Kent 1993a: 490). The /Xam Bush*men* of the Cape also were the ones to gather honey and ants' chrysalids (Hewitt 1986: 35); among the G/wi, on the other hand, termite gathering is done by everyone, including the children (Silberbauer 1981: 216–17). Men, like women, keep a look out not only for animal tracks and sightings, but also for locales where food plants are to be found.

The division of labor regarding other work chores is, again, not clear-cut. Tool making tends to fall into the province of men rather than women; however, housing (among the !Kung) is made primarily by women (Lee 1979: 276), while clothes, once made by men—for instance, among the Nharo (Bleek 1928: 9)—is now made by both (Barnard 1980a: 116). Housework is the responsibility primarily of women; however, men will share in the work whenever necessary, without any stigma being attached to such activities; for example, when their wives are ill or away (Guenther 1986a: 205; Kent 1993a: 490). Among the !Kung, between 20 percent to 40 percent of household work is done by men (Lee 1979: 177–80, 452). This tends to exclude childcare, a sphere of responsibility considered to belong to women (Lee 1979: 452). Yet, among the G/wi "the importance of the mother's role is at least equal to that of the father in the rearing and socializing of the children, and the strength of the emotional bonds between mother and child is no less than that between father and child"

(Silberbauer 1981: 158); indeed, in the case of a divorce, it is the father who assumes custody of the children (ibid.: 157). In a recent survey of the preschool program operated by Kuru Development Trust in a number of farm Bushman communities, Willemien Le Roux reports how fathers are taking an active role in the rearing of their small children, especially with regard to their attendance at and involvement with the school (Le Roux 1995b: 35–36).

As we will see below, political or ritual leadership positions, such as headman or trance dancer, are usually, though not necessarily, held by men (Lee 1979: 344; Katz 1982: 161).

The !Kung exchange pattern of *hxaro,* described by Polly Wiessner (1982: 68) as "partnerships that are not economic contracts with set terms but . . . bonds of mutual help," is viewed by the same author as a risk-reducing strategy for coping with occasional food shortages. As such, hxaro "is geared to unpredictability" (ibid.: 67) and a person who has given to his hxaro partner aims to store his debt until he needs to receive. Consistent with the looseness and openness of this system of reciprocity is the individualist, egocentric fashion with which hxaro partnerships are established—by each person, in the course of a wide-ranging, mobile life—bringing her in contact not only with her own partners, but also with their partners' partners. While most frequent and intense among consanguinal relatives, hxaro partnership networks radiate beyond the confines of a person's own family, band, and neighboring bands, each camp being a node on a hxaro path which extends over hundreds of kilometers (ibid.: 70; Wiessner 1986; Lee 1993: 105). The Nharo have a closely similar exchange system (called *//aĩ-ku*); partnerships extend over the entire farm block and beyond, linking farm Bushmen and -women through individual, extra-kin networks and acting as a buffer against unemployment and poverty (Guenther 1986a: 162–63; Barnard 1992a: 141–42).

Flexibility and looseness, as well as a degree of ambiguity and moral ambivalence, apply to the two key social institutions, kinship and marriage. Child rearing, usually growing from the latter, is also relaxed and informal, as well as indulgent. When small, the child receives affection from all members of the band and, when older, is required to do little work (Blurton-Jones, Hawkes, and Draper 1994; LeRoux 1995b: 40–42). While these remarks apply to today's Kalahari Bushmen, it seems that among the /Xam of the Cape, who hunted a relatively large amount of big game, with labor-intensive techniques (Hewitt 1986: 32–33), children were required to participate in subsistence work from an early age, the boys in hunting (for instance, in game drives) the girls in gathering. (Hewitt 1986: 30). The socialization training of the small child is a group effort in which neither parent is especially prominent (Draper 1976; Konner 1976; Silberbauer 1981: 163). The parent-child relationship contains a degree of emotional ambivalence as it is, on the one hand, one of indulgent affection—especially when the child is young (a */wa,* in Nharo)—and, on the other, one of avoidance-respect, when the child is big (a *//go,* in Nharo) (Guenther 1986a: 211). The comment of one of Silberbauer's adult informants about his parents reflects this ambivalence: "I love them and I fear [respect] them as I do no others and will always obey them because they made me" (Silberbauer 1981: 165).

According to Alan Barnard (1992a: 243), Bushman kinship is "based primarily on notions of social interaction and presumed common descent, rather than on an ideology which requires everyone to be treated as kin." Thus, among the G/wi, kinship is characterized by "a virtual absence of lineage structures or other corporate kin groups beyond the nuclear family"; moreover, because of the system's loose and somewhat arbitrary nature, it is marked by a "ready facilitation of fission and fusion within and between groups of kin" (Silberbauer 1981: 142). Kinship is a broad social field; one of the common, pan-Bushman elements is its broadly classificatory, "universalistic" scope (Barnard 1978, 1992a: 243–45, 265–66). This means that virtually everyone within one's social network is classified as kin, at least at the "ideological," if not always on-the-ground, level (Barnard 1992a: 266).

Kinship is also beset with ambiguity and contradiction, brought on especially by another of its widespread characteristics, the distinction between joking partners and avoidance partners (Marshall 1976a: 204–208; Silberbauer 1981: 143–49; Guenther 1986a: 196–98; Barnard 1992a: 280; Lee 1993: 69–71). While not without a certain logic as a device for sorting out one's relationships to the various kin recognized by the system of universalistic kin, these two principles "are often completely at odds" (Lee 1993: 74; also see Silberbauer 1981: 147). The key problem is that this dual system may clash with other kinship principles, such as the namesake relationship and the principle of the joking relationship between members of alternating generations (Lee 1993: 69–74), as well as, in the G/wi case, the principle of "congruency," whereby ego assumes a joking partner's joking and avoidance partners (Silberbauer 1981: 147). For instance, while the relationship toward one's namesake entails joking, this becomes awkward if the joking partner belongs to one's proximal generation, toward whom the general rule of avoidance applies. Such an incongruent joking-namesake "father" creates problems with respect to the latter's relatives, to whom, by the principle of congruency, ego now stands in the same relationship as does his namesake. This may be the opposite of the relationship ego would normally have toward them. For instance, while his namesake's father would normally be his joking partner by virtue of the principle of alternating generations, vis-à-vis ego's elder namesake partner, this man (the namesake's father) now becomes his avoidance partner, having been lowered from the alternate to the proximate generation.

Such impasses are frequent in Bushman kin relationships—the Ju/'hoansi call such conundrums *sa ge a//keni* ("they are in the middle")—and much energy is spent by a person to devise ingenious stratagems to work out such impasses in a way that serves his or her interests (Lee 1993: 74; see also Silberbauer 1981: 147). In its employment of interest-motivated designs and stratagems, working out one's kin relationships and its contradictions may, indeed, become a process of "'foraging' for relatives" (Barnard 1993: 33).

As already noted, another ambiguity inherent within the joking-avoidance principle is created by the relative-age principle, according to which deference is extended to the person older than oneself (Lee 1993: 74–76). The latter principle prescribes an emotional and moral deportment toward joking partners in one's grandparents' generation that differs from that exhibited toward those in one's own (such as brother, cross-cousin, spouse, sister-in-law). The former is restrained, and, especially from the elder's perspective, indulgent and affectionate; the latter free, ribald, and gibing. However, as there is "a gradation of decreasing reserve in joking relationships" (Silberbauer 1981: 143–44), the emotional tenor of these two types of joking is not clear-cut. During my stay with the Ghanzi Bushmen I found improper behavior toward one's joking or avoidance partners to be a constant issue of tension in interpersonal relations. Devising little schemes that would avoid such tension, as well as serve one's own ends, is what keeps the Bushman kinship system flexible; such actions lead to "ad hoc distortions of formal structure" (Silberbauer 1981: 147) within that system, as within Bushman social organization in general.

The institution of marriage and post-marital residence rules seem to be as variable as they are flexible among the Bushman groups of southern Africa. Regarding rules of residence, the most common preference seem to be uxorilocal, with bride service performed by the suitor or husband for several years (Marshall 1976a: 169; Guenther 1986a: 202; Barnard 1992a: 112; Lee 1993: 81). However, other groups have other residential preferences, such as virilocal among the Bugakhoe (Barnard 1992a: 127) or ambilocal among the /Xam (Hewitt 1986: 29). Following an initial, preferred residence arrangement, a !Kung couple usually has a choice and residence enters its neolocal phase, with a large number of options, given the personal mobility of people and the wide range of kin (Marshall 1976a: 170–71). "Much discussion surrounds the making of this decision" (Lee 1979: 242).

In Bushman society there generally are no strictly exogamous groups; nor are there any strictly endogamous ones (Marshall 1976a: 252; also see Hewitt 1986: 29). The band tends toward exogamy; however, given the fluidity of membership, permissible marriage partners are very likely in a camp at any one time. Marriage prohibitions are not clearly defined; instead, there are degrees of approval of marriage: preference, permission, toleration (Marshall ibid.: 261). The nuclear family incest proscription is followed; since first cousins, ideally, are joking partners, they (among the !Kung) are considered ideal as sex partners. However, due to another complication—the likelihood of cross-cousins being putative siblings because more than one of them bears a grandparent's name (Barnard 1992a: 52; Wilmsen 1989: 178)—marriage between cross-cousins is less likely, though, once again, not impossible. Indeed, it would seem that the !Kung can marry just about anyone—"any people you know" (Wilmsen ibid.: 178)—including those you don't, "that is persons of other races, persons of other Bushman language groups, or other !Kung outside the Nyae Nyae region" (Marshall 1976a: 262). A case in point is the German–South African anthropologist Heinz, who married the !Xõ woman Namkwa (Heinz and Lee

1978). More standard cases of inter-ethnic marriages are the not infrequent instances of Bantu-speaking men taking Bushwomen as wives or concubines (Silberbauer 1965: 127; Guenther 1986a: 203–204). This scenario, marrying strangers, "brings in a touch of the anomalous," however, as such persons "fall outside the joking system" (Marshall ibid.). It is yet another kin-incongruity—a spouse who is a non-joking partner—still, while not without its problems (Lee 1993: 131), its disconcerting effects on the people seem to be slight. The reason, simply put, is that the "society tolerates the anomaly" (Marshall 1976a: 262).

While monogamy is the most common form of marriage, polygynous and even polyandrous marriage can also occur. The reason is typically ad hoc, perhaps because of the closeness of two sisters or two friends, who did not want the marriage of either to separate them. Silberbauer describes one such case, a polyandrous arrangement:

> A woman had left her husband for his widowed best friend. The two men "fought" and the second husband went away with the woman. However, a triangle has three sides; and the two men missed each other, and the wife missed her ex-husband, who, in turn, had refused to take a second wife because he missed his first wife so much. The absconding couple returned after two years and the original husband moved in with them. The band had discussed the solution to this problem at great length before the return of the couple. Although the polyandrous solution was unprecedented, it was accepted by everybody. (Silberbauer 1981: 155)

Marriages can be readily dissolved by either spouse (Barnard 1992a: 112, 146), particularly the woman (Marshall 1976a: 286; Lee 1993: 83), and divorce is especially easy for a childless couple (Marshall 1976a: 286; Silberbauer 1981: 156; Guenther 1986a: 203). Little formality accompanies divorce (Silberbauer 1981: 156), as well as little acrimony, and "ex-husband and wife may continue to joke and may even live in adjacent huts with their new spouses" (Lee 1993: 83). Like marriage, divorce is a matter of mutual consent in a society free of the institution of the bride price so widespread in other African societies. Furthermore, in a society without descent groups the matter of custody of children is a non-issue, the more so in view of a "familistic" social structure that allows children to be reared by caregivers other than the mother or father (Lee 1979: 452, 1993: 83–84; Silberbauer 1981: 157–58).

Another reason divorce is easy for young couples among some groups (such as the G/wi and Nharo) is that early marriages may be quite informal. Again, one finds variation on this social practice; for instance, marriages may be formal and involve extensive ceremonies among some of the Eastern and Northern Khoe Bushmen, such as the Bugakhoe, G/andakhoe and //Anikhoe (Barnard 1992a: 127). Writing about the Nharo, Barnard (1992a: 145) states that "marriage is a gradual process, and there is no absolute distinction between the boyfriend/girlfriend relationship and the husband/wife relationship." While early marriages are usually arranged between the prospective spouses' parents, the Nharo expect these to be provisional and tenuous, preceded by a "trial" phase, which the Nharo call */robe* ("to borrow"). The couple can test their congeniality toward one another and their in-laws, as well as decide whether or not the marriage would bear children (Guenther 1986a: 201–202). The breakup of such trial marriages is considered regrettable, but is accepted philosophically, as an inevitability, in view of incompatible personalities (Silberbauer 1981: 154).

First marriages are also frequently arranged by the principals' parents, especially those of the bride, who may be a young, prepubescent girl at the time. She may express strong opposition to the designs of her elders, and defy these through fierce outbreaks of temper and a refusal to leave her family's hut or place and move in with her husband. She may refuse to sleep with him for weeks or months and attempt, repeatedly, to run away from him (Lee 1993: 82–84). While this display of temper and stubbornness may, to some extent, be explained in terms of cultural expectations—a remnant, perhaps, of some sort of marriage-by-capture practice—it also exemplifies the strong-willed nature of Bushwomen, as well as the occasional pitting of the individual against the group.

Turning now to politics, we find that the institutions and processes of leadership, decision making, and conflict management are all loose. They have the same flavor of ad hoc indeterminacy, ambiguity, and ambivalence as the other social institutions. This looseness of Bushman politics, coupled with the equally loose and ambivalent attachment of the individual to the community (as to be shown below), have led one Khoisan scholar to think about them in terms of "anarchy," à la Kropotkin (Barnard 1993). The same term is applied by another student of egalitarian societies to the political "system" of such peoples, because of their "having leadership but no government or true legal sanctions" (Barclay 1993: 241).

Once again, it is necessary to qualify: not all Bushman groups of southern Africa, at all times in the history of the region, displayed such loose and "anarchical" traits. As noted earlier, there were Bushman societies (such as the Ghanzi ≠Au//ei and Nharo) with complex political organization and centralized leadership. At the other end of the spectrum of variation in this Bushman institution are politically amorphous and acephalous groups, for instance the G/wi, among whom "every adult member of the band has rights equal to those of all other members" (Silberbauer 1965: 73). In between are groups such as the !Xõ and the Nharo, the former with a more institutionalized leadership role than the latter (Guenther 1986a: 192–94; Barnard 1992a: 139). In the !Kõ case this included the organization of hunts, the delegation of gathering trips, and the performance of "ceremonial duties" (Heinz 1966: 55).

Except for the most politically organized and centralized, the exercise of leadership by a headman, rather than being generalized, is usually limited to situations that require it: for example, reaching a group decision or organizing a hunt or a group move. As put by Andrew Smith over a century and a half ago, when visiting the Bushmen around Kuruman in the northeastern Cape, leadership is exercised "when the union of strength and an agent to direct its application may appear to be especially required" (Smith 1975: 179). "At all other times," Smith continues,

> these functionaries sink to the level of the other inhabitants and find themselves possessed of no other means of protection than those which their own physical power can afford, when the duty for which they have been selected is no longer required.

Despite this diversity, most Bushman groups had some sort of leadership, more or less weakly established. Once again, the !Kung serve as the representative case: headmen, Lorna Marshall reports (1976a: 194), who "are as thin as the rest," hold little authority, nor any regalia of office of special honors. In Bushman politics, leadership is "situational, temporary and non-binding," so much so, Susan Kent (1993c: 243) suggests, that the headmen's definition as leaders may, in fact, be nothing more than a matter of ethnographic labeling. Alternatively, where it is found, the headman concept may have been created by political fiat, either through the national government (as among contemporary Nharo at some of the settlements) or by Bantu-speaking neighbor groups, such as the Tswana in Ngamiland, who wanted to incorporate the Ju/'hoansi into their hierarchical system (Lee 1982: 50–51).

In the absence of a practice of defining leaders, individuals possessing a certain degree of firmness of personality, as well as expertise in one field or another, will take the required decision and people will generally follow him (or her). This expertise may be in hunting, in locating plants, or in saying things in difficult decision-making situations that have the right ring to them and that cut through an impasse. Such expertise as a person may hold in one field of activity does not, however, become generalized or "'overflow' into habitual success," for it "may be seen as not at all relevant to another field, and even in matters closely related, leadership shifts unpredictably among acknowledged experts with the occasional inclusion of a 'dark horse'" (Silberbauer 1981: 170, writing about the G/wi, among whom leadership is especially loose).

As Richard Lee (1993: 94–96) found out, headmen are a most elusive political species in Zhu/'hoan society. After searching in vain for "the headman" of each of a number of *n!ore*'s (band territories), Lee finally located an alleged headman, who reacted to the allegation with "surprise, shock, disbelief and laughter." The now classic one-liner set the questioner straight on the matter of Zhu headmanship: "Of course we have headmen! In fact, we are all headmen. Each of us is headman over himself!" (Lee 1993: 95).

There are ecological and social reasons for the weakness of leadership in Bushman society. Undifferentiated access to resources and a general absence of "territoriality" obviate the need for internal coordination and coordinated protection of resources (Gulbrandsen 1991: 92). The smallness in numbers and scale, as well as the absence of property and a "fierce" egalitarian ethos reduce the structural need for leadership. As in other egalitarian societies around the world (Boehm 1993), social mechanisms of "reverse dominance" are in place in Bushman society that limit the authority of those who hold, or aspire to, power. Of the five mechanisms for keeping persons with power aspirations in check—public opinion, criticism, ridicule, disobedience, extreme sanctions—it is the third at which the Bushmen (and hunter-gatherers in general) excel. Laughing at authority figures, or at individuals with authoritarian, arrogant, or boastful airs, is one of the most effective mechanisms for smothering dominance within a small group and for preventing the entrenchment of authority within social relationships (Clastres 1977: 121).

It is thus not surprising that the frame of mind of persons who hold positions of power or privilege is also one of ambivalence. This is so all the more whenever anyone is seen to strive for such a position, displaying thereby a demeanor of arrogance and self-importance. As we will see more fully in the discussions of values in the next chapter, not only are such persons ridiculed, but they are also expected to ridicule themselves, thereby taking the wind out of the sails of their ambition. As noted by Boehm (1993: 233), the frequently employed anthropological designation for leaders in societies such as the Bushmen's, primus inter pares, is inherently contradictory. The term reflects the deep-seated ambivalence of such leaders. On the one hand, they are expected to be generous, unassuming, unaggressive, modest, and soft-spoken; on the other, their actions must at times also be strong and decisive. It is not surprising that a person generally does not seek out the position of headman or that the position has not become institutionalized within society. It holds no rewards; such privileges as an authority position may potentially hold—"honour, love, obedience, troops of friends"—are surrounded by stated or unstated proscriptions and evoke invidious sentiments from others. And, to boot, "all you get is the blame if things go wrong" (Marshall 1976a: 195).

Decision making, like leadership, is unstructured and ad hoc. It is done through "talking," either between two persons, or within small groups of the group as a whole, in discussions involving the entire camp. Talking is engaged in with much zeal and zest, lustily and argumentatively, as a cherished pastime and as something of an art form (especially in its manifestation as storytelling). The importance of *n//a,* ("talking" in Nharo), is reflected among the Ju/'hoansi in two terms of collective self-designation: "owners of argument" and "people who talk too much"—"we have to talk this way," an old Ju/'hoan woman told Harriet Rosenberg (1990: 24); "it's our custom." Such talk may be lengthy and heated as it is the unspoken goal of the group to reach a decision based on consensus, wherein all people affected by the decision have had access to all the information and the opportunity each to contribute to its formation (Silberbauer 1982: 31). As shown by Silberbauer (1982), Marshall (1976b) and Lee (1979: 372–76, 1993: 97–98), talking follows a variety of techniques and forms, depending on the issue at hand, and on the degree of disagreement and agitation. They may be subtle and discreet, consisting of spoken or sung monologues, or of dialogues—in earshot of the party at whom they are aimed, forcing him or her into such response-ploys as the "forced eavesdrop" or "auditory withdrawal" (Silberbauer 1982: 26–27; Marshall 1976a: 288–93). Among the !Kung these are to some extent semantically distinguished, ranging from heated, but good-natured, joke-peppered conversation or discussion (*hore hore* or *oba oba,* translated by Lee [1979: 372] as "yakity-yak"), to a stylized, staccato "talk " (*n≠wa*) that may suddenly flare up when tension and disagreement rise. The talk my culminate in a "shout," a verbal explosion for which the !Kung have no name (Marshall 1976a: 291). At this point insults are traded, which, in their sexual form (*za*), may turn anger into rage and fighting as they are considered the worst forms of verbal abuse in the !Kung lexicon of swear-words (Lee 1979: 373). The latter is morally ambiguous, since it is, on the one hand, a favorite mode of banter between joking partners and, on the other, a grave affront that almost always leads to a fight (Lee 1979: 372–73).

The ambiguous and ambivalent blend of tension and laughter that pervades Bushman decision making also underlies conflict management (Marshall 1976a: 287–93; Silberbauer 1982; Lee 1982: 372–76, 1993: 69–99; Luig 1990). Among some Canadian subarctic hunter-gatherers, "risibility," a laughing personal deportment, is a calculated form of behavior employed by individuals to protect themselves from being the target of sorcery attacks by others (Hallowell 1967; Guenther 1992a: 103). The laughter so frequently heard by the field-worker in the Kalahari, constituting the auditory backdrop to Bushman interpersonal relations, similarly cannot be taken as an indication merely of nobly savage jollity and harmlessness. Such was the mistaken impression of the Rousseauian-minded Hauptmann Müller during his brief stay among the Ju/'hoansi on a patrol through the Kaukauveld. He describes the interaction, one merry evening, of the small band that had attached itself to his camel troop of *Schutztruppler*:

> Here such merriment prevailed as to border on madness. The laughter was so refreshing to one's heart that one could not help but laugh along.[8] (Müller 1912: 540, my translation)

There is more than meets the eye and ear to the mirthful, thigh-slapping banter, the "joke-peppered conversations," one might witness among the Bushmen. The social and emotional subtext of such outbreaks of fun is often to hide or dispel tension: for example, people cracking jokes around a person who has just been bitten by a poisonous snake and is in pain and mortal danger (Shostak 1981: 266). Such incidents of ambivalent mirth are comparable, to a degree, to Eskimo song duels, which, despite their ludic performance elements, are intense and serious contests. "Simply because these arguments happen to be funny," Richard Lee (1993: 97) notes, "doesn't mean that they lack seriousness. In fact, they proceed along the knife edge between laughter and danger" (Lee 1993: 97). A person may laugh to dissipate conflict or anxiety, because he feels it rising within either himself or the group (Marshall 1976a: 292). "A joke may burst the bubble of tension," reducing "the entire camp, including the disputants, to helpless laughter" (Lee ibid.: 99). "One is astonished," Richard Lee states elsewhere,

> to see two men chatting amicably together who only a few minutes before had been shouting abuse at each other. To a certain extent verbal battles appear to be a game played principally for the fun of laughing about it afterwards. (Lee 1978: 111)

I came across this ambivalent blend of conflict and anger with laughter and playfulness among the Nharo, in what some of my informants referred to as the "war game." It is different from the game with the same name Dorothea Bleek (1928: 21) described fifty years earlier, which involved two rows of young men squatting opposite each other, striking their chests—Yanomamo fashion—and the ground before them, hissing and groaning, and, through facial grimaces, expressing contempt for the opponent group. The more recent version of the game is apparently[9] a good deal more agitated and uses verbal abuse, rather than grimacing, to express contempt for the adversary. It also appears that the performance is not initiated as a game but grows out of a rancorous verbal quarrel between two individuals. As they hurl insults at each other, which become more and more excessive (reaching the !Kungs' *za*-level of abuse and potential for physical fighting), people from the camp begin to gather around the two antagonists in growing numbers. They respond to the quarrelers' string of insults with cheering and laughing; this results, at first, in an intensification of anger to rage, as well as in confusion in the two combatants. This reaction is caused by the inappropriateness of the group's response—mirth—to the quarrelers' feelings—anger. But the more the latter intensify their anger, expressing it with ever more outrageous invectives, the greater the sense of hilarity among the bystanders. Their mirth eventually infects the two antagonists, so much so that they laugh as well, despite themselves, so much so that they might even rush toward each other, bent over and eyes streaming with laughter, to slap each other on the shoulder.

Thus, in this case of the ambiguous blend of anger with laughter, mirth came to hold the upper hand and the danger of anger was dissipated. Again, one is reminded of the Inuit song duelists who may become "so engrossed in the mere artistry of singing to forget the cause of the grudge" (Hoebel 1954: 93). I observed a small but telling version of this transformation of tension into harmony, by means of a ludic performance that suggests this ambivalent approach to conflict may have deep cultural roots. A woman was cutting some food with a sharp knife. Her small toddler suddenly grabbed the knife, wanting to play with it, a "no-no" for a small child in Bushman culture, as anywhere else. Nevertheless, she relented after a couple of seconds, letting the child hold the knife for as long. She then snatched it away, resulting in the child's startled and frustrated crying, whereupon she immediately gave the knife back to him again, for another few seconds, then snatched it away again. Again the child roared, received it back, and again had it taken. After half a dozen times, the child reacted with laughter to the game the mother was playing with him. His anger had vanished and, a few minutes later, he tired of the game.

The trance curing dance can also be regarded as a more or less overt device for ludic conflict resolution. According to the psychologist Richard Katz, who studied the !Kung trance dance in the field (Katz 1982), its "synergistic" performance has a Durkheimian, morally integrating effect that can soothe tempers and tension (ibid.: 35, 54–55). A dance may be performed after a big kill—the division of which could cause friction—after a contentious session discussing marriage gift exchanges, and sometimes at the end of a fight (Lee 1979: 272, 377; Katz 1982: 54; also see Hall 1988: 144–45). Megan Biesele reports how, in the event that

> there is bad feeling between two men, others will contrive to put them next to each other in the dance: participation in the form of brotherhood paves the way for brotherhood to re-establish itself. (Biesele 1993: 78)

Among the /Xam it appears that the sanctioning effects of the dance were more explicit, as criticism of a certain individual was expressed directly (Hewitt 1986: 39).

Moral exhortation, sometimes about specific social tensions, may be part of the chants Zhu/'hoan dancers utter, thereby airing and alleviating conflict and grievance (Biesele 1993: 78). Megan Biesele cites excerpts of such chants from unpublished field notes by Richard Lee; they range from such general exhortations as "How is it that you are full adults yet you refuse to give each other an agreement? . . . You people here who are arguing and glaring. . . . You are battling it out [over an argument about cattle] and you are killing each other," to more specific instances, such as "His blanket, help him put it over his shoulders; can't you see he is trembling? Help him cover himself." As Biesele remarks, such exhortations implicitly posit the connection between a person's sickness and the tension in the social relationships among the people around him: "He lies there dying; while you sit above him wrangling and fighting, and arguing and glaring, arguing and glaring and glaring, arguing and glaring . . ." (Biesele ibid.). That social conflict and individual sickness are interconnected is the underlying assumption in the theory of sickness and well-being of many African people. Witchcraft beliefs are based on it, not only among villagers of central and southern Africa, but also among some of the more sedentary Bushman peoples (Guenther 1992a).

The key question, sociologically, that these ludic conflict resolution mechanisms raise is this: Having been transformed into a ludic performance, is the issue of conflict forgotten? Is it resolved for good? I think some issues may be; in the case of others, however, where the disagreement is deep and resentment has run high, such measures that attempt to "jolly" a person out of his anger work only temporarily or not at all. Katz observed that, for all their effectiveness at tension soothing through a trance dance at which two families quarrel over gift exchanges for an upcoming marriage, "the conflict is not resolved to the total satisfaction of either family" (Katz 1982: 55). Disputes puzzled Richard Lee (1978: 111) "for their apparent lack of clear-cut outcomes." For the same reason, they are unlikely to be resolved through such side-stepping actions, and conflicts may continue to escalate and assume ever more determined and aggressive expressions. These may include vicious physical fighting (Kent 1989a: 706–707; Lee 1979: 371–72, 1993: 97–99), leading to homicide and executions, feuding and "blood vengeance" (Lee 1979: 382–400; Bleek 1928: 35–36; Wilhelm 1955: 156). Having reached such levels of intensity—which happens relatively rarely—conflicts are no longer capable of resolution by so informal, gentle, and discreet a set of mechanisms as "talking," teasing, and laughter.

There is one other mechanism available to Bushmen in a conflict situation, one widely and not infrequently resorted to and, perhaps, more effective than all the others: withdrawal. In an impasse, one of the parties in a conflict simply gets up and leaves (Lee 1979: 372, 1978: 111). He might join another band, or make a separate camp, and a few months later, he might rejoin the band, when all is "forgotten and forgiven." More or less: again, one should not over-idealize the efficaciousness of this method of handling a conflict issue. The fact that the issue of contention had culminated in the "walking off" mode of reaction toward anger suggests that it had been a fairly drawn out, contentious, and acrimonious one to begin with—perhaps a case of adultery or repeated laziness and stinginess. Being a serious and salient moral breach it may not yet be forgotten; moreover, it may not yet be resolved, given that it may be an ingrained and habitual shortcoming on the part of one of the antagonists.

The vigilance of members of a group over the sociableness and the tensions within interpersonal relations of other band members is an ongoing preoccupation of people (Silberbauer 1982: 30). In Bushman moral culture, the values which mediate this process of vigilance over one another's actions are themselves beset with contradiction—between communalism and sociableness, and individualism and self-interest (Marshall 1976a: 287–88; Lee 1982: 53–56; Barnard 1993). It creates ambiguity within ethos, and an individual who is loosely and ambivalently attached to his or her community. And working out these contradictions, in ways similar to the stratagems and games people employ in the social and political sphere, are everyday issues of concern to members of a Bushman camp and "central themes" of their culture (Lee 1982: 54). The following chapter will explore the ambiguities and ambivalences of Bushman ethos and of the individual.

2

Values and Individuals

"When I kill anything, it is usual for our fellows, especially my Bushmen, to exclaim: 'How small!' The wounded one that escapes is pronounced wonderfully fat."

—CHAPMAN 1863 [1971, VOL. 2: 79]

"Hey /Gau," I burst out, "that ox is loaded with fat. What's this about the ox being too thin to bother eating? Are you out of your mind?"

"Fat?" /Gau shot back, "You call this fat? This wreck is thin, sick, dead!" And he broke out laughing. So did everyone else. They rolled on the ground, paralyzed with laughter. Everybody laughed except me; I was thinking.

—LEE 1969 [1993: 186]

Eland fat is a very highly valued gift. An eland provides so much fat that people can afford to be a little luxurious. They rub it on themselves and on their implements, and they eat it. ≠Toma said that when he had eland fat to give, he took shrewd notice of certain objects he might like to have and gave their owners especially generous gifts of fat.

—MARSHALL 1976B: 366

The fact that a century separates the two opening vignettes—both instances of Bushmen "insulting the meat" that has been provided for them by an uppity hunter—suggests that such leveling ploys, directed against the group member who is perceived to aspire to wealth and status, are deeply rooted in Bushman normative culture. The confusion of the aspirant, one an explorer, the other an ethnographer—whose gifts of venison and beef were given in a spirit of generosity, and received by people who needed and coveted them, yet also belittled and virtually rejected them—points to one of many ambiguities of the system of values and to the ambivalence of the individuals who submit to them. These values and individuals are the topic of this chapter.

Contrary to the perspective of classic social anthropology, which looks askance at social analysis that focuses on the individual and on "psychology," the individual and his or her relationship to the social and moral collectivity is key to any understanding of a simple, small-scale tribal society such as the Bushmen. As I will show, Durkheim's assertion that in such societies "the individual does not exist," since in societies bound together by "mechanical solidarity" "individual conscience is hardly at all distinguishable from collective conscience" (Durkheim 1964: 194), is off the mark. In so small, undifferentiated, and familistic a society as a Bushman camp or band, the individual looms large. Here individual agency is a force that directly impacts social process, more so than in other, more complex societies. The person is not swallowed up as (s)he is in a large society that is based on either corporate descent or corporate industry. Instead of being a small cog in the wheels and gears of a Leviathanesque mega-society, (s)he is a big frog in a very small pond. That pond, to put the point less metaphorically, is an "intentional community," made up of "people who make up their minds" (Boehm 1993: 239), and who "forward their interests" (Smith 1975: 179).

A "transactional" perspective was recently brought to an analysis of Bushman social organization by Ornulf Gulbrandsen (1991, in a Festschrift for Frederik Barth), focused specifically on egalitarianism and sharing, and the values on which these social practices are based. In tune with that paradigm, the analysis is focused squarely on the individual, and how he or she negotiates the culture's values strategically, in order to gain something of value (Barth 1966).[1] Such a focus also attunes the student to the frequent and chronic noncorrespondence between ideal and practice in Bushman social action. With reference to the social and moral issues of egalitarianism and sharing, Gulbrandsen suggests that the analyst needs to "deconstruct" the same, by differentiating conservative, fixed, and absolute components from flexible, situational, and opportunistic ones. While static, unequivocal, and absolute as an ideology, in certain situations, and for pragmatic considerations, individuals may act contrary to that ideology—for instance, by accepting an overlord, storing wealth, or taking collective action beyond the family level. They do so after a process of transacting the values of their culture, when faced with the contingencies of certain ecological or social circumstances. The individual, vis-à-vis the values of his culture—which, qua *homo manipulator*, he engages and negotiates to work out a situationally appropriate course of action—is thus another key dimension of flexibility and ambiguity in Bushman society.

While such a process of individuals negotiating the strictures of their normative culture for pragmatic or self-seeking reasons is universal in human society, it is especially prominent in a society such as that of the Bushmen (or of hunter-gatherers generally). The key characteristics of Bushman social organization described in the previous chapter—looseness, fluidity, and diversity of composition and organizational and institutional makeup, as well as smallness in numbers—all necessarily lead to the delineation of the individual as an exceptionally sharply profiled actor and agent. Ecological adaptation, too, through maximization or "optimal foraging," fosters an opportunistic, open-ended, strategizing approach by the hunter or gatherer to the resource base and its risks and vagaries (Kelly 1995). As to be noted later on, outsiders also represent a "resource" which hunter-gatherer Bushman may approach in an opportunistic frame of mind, taking from them material and ideological goods and gods, while vis-à-vis neighboring bands, egocentric networks of trade partnerships crisscross wide stretches of the geographic and social landscape of the Kalahari. And in the context of their own band society, people in a sense "forage" for relatives. As I will argue in chapter 5, all these instances of cultural resource exploitation constitute, in combination, a "foraging ethos" that pervades all of the sub-systems of Bushman culture.

In the following discussion I will describe the values of Bushman culture, and submit them to the sort of "deconstructionist" analysis suggested by Gulbrandsen. This examination will reveal another important dimension of ambiguity in Bushman social organization. It also reveals reasons why individuals are loosely connected to their groups and why individual agency and autonomy are so well defined in this hunter-gatherer society (as well as in others).

Values

While one might be readily inclined to accept, as a commonplace, the pronouncement that a society's values contain ambiguity and contradiction, when this assertion is applied to the Bushmen, one's first inclination might well be to challenge its applicability. Since the Bushmen have been idealized or eulogized, in arch-Rousseauian terms, as "harmless people" and "flower children of the Kalahari" (Guenther 1980; Konner and Shostak 1986; Barnard 1989; Wilmsen 1989: 33–38; Jeffreys 1978) throughout the latter half of this century, the contention that such a people's ethos should be anything other than harmonious and homogeneous is likely to meet with scorn and disbelief. In anthropology, such a claim would also fly in the face of the axiomatic, functionalist, and, again, Durkheimian notion that small-scale primitive *Gemeinschaften* or "folk societies"—of whom the Bushmen are a textbook case—have a strong and integral collective conscience and consciousness, and moral consensus and cohesiveness.[2]

At the risk of sounding arbitrary, I hold the two key values of the normative system of Bushman culture to be equality and sharing. They reinforce and complement one another, and people acknowledge them as important and distinctive dictates of their own culture and way of life; they are an explicit element of the enculturation regimen adults bring to bear on children. They are a vital force of integration of what is a fragile society, in lieu of descent or age groups that provide structure and stability to more complex societies (Kent 1993a: 480). As seen in the preceding chapter, such social processes as exchange and gift giving, decision making, and leadership express, in behavior and action, the values of equality and sharing. Each is surrounded by reinforcing and complementary companion values, humility and even-temperedness for the first, generosity for the other. And running through all of them, as a basic, implicit key of Bushman (and hunter-gatherer) normative culture, is reciprocity. Jointly they all formulate a strong ethos of sociability or communalism.

While well defined as a cultural ideal, however, this value package is beset with ambiguities. In part these stem from the universal discrepancy between ideal and practice, in part because of the presence in Bushman normative culture of competing and contradictory values. The prime source of the ambiguities in Bushman values is individualism, running as a strong countercurrent to the ethos of communalism. That countercurrent, too, is underwritten by its own values: self-reliance, individual autonomy (Gardner 1991), independence. These also impinge on people's actions, albeit less explicitly than the opposite ideals. Let us review these values and examine their inherent contradictions, and how these affect a person's interaction with others.

Egalitarianism—"staunchly," or even "fiercely" asserted by the !Kung and other Bushman groups (Lee 1979: 24; Kent 1993a: 480)—is held by some writers to be the central pillar of Bushman ethos (Lee 1982: 53–56; Cashdan 1980; Woodburn 1982; also see Luig 1990; Gulbrandsen 1991; Barnard 1993; Kent 1993a; Gardner 1991: 547–48; and Clastres 1977). It is easy to see why egalitarianism could be regarded as the linchpin of the value system: all the other values that make up Bushman moral culture, both the communalist and individualistic ones, could be deemed variations of the egalitarian theme; moreover, it is a theme that pervades social organization and action at every turn (Woodburn 1982: 434; Kent 1993a: 480). Arguably, it is the Rome of Bushman ethos, to which all of the other moral roads lead.

Egalitarianism is maintained through a number of "leveling" mechanisms that curb the desires and ambitions of the individual. The latter may lead him or her to express or demonstrate a certain special skill, accomplishment, or ambition—for instance, hunting or leadership. Yet, anyone acting in such accordance with that inclination would immediately and almost automatically be brought face-to-face with the moral value of "humility" (Lee 1969, 1982: 54, 1993: 54–56, 83–88; Cashdan 1980: 116).[3] People who brag and act arrogantly and self-importantly are pounced on, and subjected to teasing and ridicule, until they are back in line. Fresh arrivals to the Kalahari, ethnographers or explorers who have not yet appreciated this quite un-Western bit of

Bushman etiquette, can be taken aback at what they deem a display of ungraciousness, or outright ingratitude, toward their well-intentioned exercise of largesse. This happened to Richard Lee, as a rookie field ethnographer, in the famous story of the Christmas ox (1969; see also 1993: 83–88), and a century earlier, as noted in the first chapter epigraph, we find James Chapman grousing about the same issue in his field journal.

As a salient figure in the economy and culture of the Bushmen, the successful hunter is an exceptionally ready target for the sanction of ridicule and humiliation. He avoids these through of a series of stereotyped, self-deprecating gestures and acts, after a successful hunt. The first (among the Ju/'hoansi) is that he is careful about semantics when he announces his success. Instead of saying "I have killed an animal," his neutral announcement is "the animal has died," a phrase that minimizes the hunter's own importance (Biesele 1993: 91). The routine of self-deprecation and modesty is especially elaborate (Lee 1979: 244–46) when the carcass is butchered and the meat distributed—the latter a socially charged undertaking, as it is one of the principal exchange events at which debts are discharged or incurred and people's "social capital" may be enhanced or diminished (Lee 1979: 244–46). By "insulting the meat" (Lee 1993: 54–56; see Bleek, "Customs and Beliefs" [1932: 240] for the same custom among the /Xam) in such a fashion the skilled hunter demonstrates to the group that his success has not gone to his head, that he has "leveled"—or "humiliated"—himself, maintaining through his display of humility the ethos of equality.

Yet, as Susan Kent (1993a: 480) argues, such displays of humility build up only the "facade of egalitarianism," as hunting skills are not possessed equally by all hunters. And in view of the highly positive evaluation of the hunt, coupled with the individualism and personal autonomy of the hunter, one might wonder if the successful hunter's heart is always quite as fully engaged in such self-deprecatory routines as it appears, all the more so since other members of the band recognize differential degrees of success and skill at hunting and extend social approbation to the hunter who is good at his task. Among the Kutse a certain hunter's lack of such skills may be a topic of conversation, calling up explanations and justifications, such as poor eyesight (Kent 1993a: 493).

This scenario—a person denying a skill that varies among individuals and that is generally appreciated, in the interest of the "facade" of equality—is a template for value contradiction that appears in other areas of Bushman ethos. One is in politics. While not an office sought after by many Bushmen, for reasons indicated in the previous chapter, headmanship, and such power and influence as go with it, is an attractive career move to some individuals. This is the case especially in some contemporary Bushman communities, such as government settlements and farm villages, in which "politics"—decision making, factionalism, conflict, along with government or NGO-sponsored community development or political "conscientization" schemes—have intensified, providing a challenge and an arena for anyone politically motivated. However, just as a person, in his public deportment, will deny his accomplishments as a hunter, so will he be circumspect about his political ambitions. Like many a Western prospective candidate for public office, he is coy about expressing his plans publicly. We recognize such a person in /Kukrib "Hartebeest," a Nharo-≠Au//gei man Dorothea Bleek met at Sandfontein in 1920, the son of a once-mighty chief, whose private thoughts about his own political importance—expressed to Bleek in "Dutch" (Afrikaans)—were very much at odds with his public utterances on the subject:

> Whenever . . . /Kukurib, called Hartebeest by white men, is speaking Dutch, which the others do not understand, he asserts that he is now chief, but when speaking Bushman he never ventures to claim this, but chimes with the rest, that there are no chiefs nowadays. (Bleek 1928: 36)

/Kukurib's "chiming equality" when in the presence of his band members may be seen as a political version of "insulting the meat."

If he fails to follow the prescribed humility demeanor, the leveling mechanisms he is subjected to consist of ridicule, criticism, or non-compliance. They drive home the fact that, while he may be, or presume to be, "first," he is so very much "among equals." Their irreverent, irrepressible actions toward "their leader" result in a scenario of "reverse dominance" (Boehm 1993) that may quite curb or frustrate a leader, who may end up being manipulated by the others, especially those that might be deemed weak and inferior (for instance women, among the sub-arctic Chippewayans [Sharp 1994]). Instead of being a figure who is "respected, admired and feared," as leaders often are (or like to be), and whose "serious labour and responsibility" is duly acknowledged (Clastres 1977: 121), he is lampooned and his authority usurped, in the service of safeguarding the maxim of equality. As shown by Pierre Clastres, egalitarian societies may also embed this power-controlling mechanism of their value culture in their myths; South American Indians' myths ridicule the shaman and his cognate, the Jaguar, normally figures of power. (It is such tales that make the study of South American Indian mythology a "gay science" to Clastres, who chides his compatriot Lévi-Strauss for too serious and deadpan an approach to the subject.)

Buttressing the value of "humility" and non-arrogance is that of even-temperedness (Marshall 1976a: 288; Lee 1982: 56). Its more or less explicit intent is to hold in check hostility and quarrelsomeness (*mingku* in Nharo), which hold the danger of violence, a danger the !Kung dread (Marshall 1976a: 288). Despite the battery of variably benign, face-saving conflict resolution mechanisms described in the previous chapter, that are designed to smother conflict before it can erupt, and despite the highly effective "withdrawal option," Bushman social life is not without social tension. As borne out by ethnographic information and statistics that astonished those students of the

Bushmen who had regarded them as a "harmless people," violent conflict is not infrequent in Bushman social life, including its manifestation in homicide. Among farm Bushmen violence may also express itself in a mystical idiom, in the form of alleged witchcraft and sorcery, of which contemporary, village-based Bushmen will on occasion accuse each other (Guenther 1992a; Vorster 1994, 1995). The concrete reason physical violence may be lethal is the Bushman hunting tool kit, the "deadly poisoned arrows which are always at hand" (Marshall 1976a: 288), as well as the spear and throwing club. These weapons can be used against another person, in a state either of uncontrollable rage (Lee 1979: 397), or premeditatedly, by means of an ambush or raid, which may trigger feuding and blood revenge. While this pattern of violence is rare among today's Kalahari Bushmen (Lee 1979: 398), "incessant warfare among the hostile bands and tribes" was reported among the !Kung and the ≠Au//ei of the past (Seiner 1913; Wilhelm 1955: 154, 158; Kaufmann 1910: 138, 154–56), as well as Bushman tribes in other parts of southern Africa.

Sharing is the other principal value and virtue in Bushman ethos (Marshall 1976a: 295–303; Lee 1979: 117–19, 1982: 54–55; Wiessner 1982, 1986; Guenther 1986a:162–66; Gulbrandsen 1991: 90–91). It is perhaps the most explicit value of Bushman ethos to which children are socialized from an early age (Guenther 1986a: 166) and the !Kung call adults who fall short of its expectations "bags without openings" (Lewis-Williams and Biesele 1978: 130) and subject them to especially pointed ridicule and other sanctions.

As a result of these socialization and sanctioning mechanisms sharing is done as a matter of course, as an integral and implicit element of interpersonal interaction. Indeed, having things shared with another becomes a matter of "entitlement," especially as regards older people (Rosenberg 1990; Lee 1993: 175–76), so that sharing may express itself as "demand sharing." As such, it is preceded, among the Nharo, with the verbal request "*mate*," rather than "*aute*." Both phrases mean "give me," but they differ subtly in meaning (as well as intonation); the first says "give me" in a matter-of-fact "demand" sense, the second in a culturally uncharacteristic, pleading, "please-style." Because of the erosion of the egalitarian and sharing ethos on the Ghanzi farms, one is apt nowadays to hear the latter phrase more frequently than the former.

Sharing is underwritten by two other key values of the Bushman normative kit, reciprocity and generosity. The chief item to be shared is food, especially meat, the more cherished and less common food item (Kent 1989b, 1993a: 491–95). In this context we might mention another expression food sharing may take, commensality (Gulbrandsen 1991: 191). It is expressed in the !Kung adage that "only lions eat alone" (Marshall 1976a: 295) and applies especially to a meal of freshly butchered and distributed meat (as illustrated effectively at the end of John Marshall's classic film *The Hunters*, where all of the camp members are seen idyllically sitting around their families' respective cooking pots, ready to partake of a joined meal). Yet it appears that such joined family meals are not the regular pattern; people evidently prefer to eat "on the run," continuously and individually, when and as they wish, rather than at regular meal times (Lee 1979: 199; Marshall 1976a: 302).

These three companion values to sharing reflect the fact that the latter is first and foremost a "social" rather than an "economic" activity, concerned more with the "fostering of social networks" (Kent 1993a: 479) than with risk management or such practical considerations as difficulties of storage or of transportation (Speth 1990). Yet, sharing is not done just with the heart; the head also is engaged (and the stomach, as regards the coveted and much-exchanged item, meat). Practical considerations of the sort just mentioned are also entertained, as well as economic and social calculations of costs, benefits, and social capital. As put simply by the !Kung researchers Henry Harpending and Pat Draper:

> The !Kung that we know share meat because it would rot if they didn't and, by sharing, they obtain meat in return the next week. They are less enthusiastic about sharing nuts, which don't rot. (Harpending and Draper 1990: 127)

While profoundly social and sociable, sharing is thus also pragmatic and subject to value considerations that may be at odds with those of communalism, deriving, instead, from those of individualism, the crosscurrent within Bushman normative culture.

It is that crosscurrent that may lead people toward an approach to sharing in which generosity takes a back seat to calculation, self-interest, or greed. A case in point is the !Kung man ≠Toma, whose "shrewd" determination of whom to give some of his surplus eland fat appeared at the beginning of the chapter. It is an instance of giving and sharing done with the ulterior motive of self-gain, rather than as an act of propriety or generosity. Giving with such a mind-set leads a person toward deviating, in spirit and letter, from the sharing ideal. Resentment may be harbored toward such a person; he or she may be accused of "far-heartedness" or "stinginess" for refusing to give in the proper fashion, or to give back. Such breaches in the proper ways of sharing may create different forms of disaffection in people, who may have repeatedly been refused gifts, who may be thwarted recipients of gifts, or who may be donors who always give but never receive counter-gifts (Marshall 1976b: 363–70).

By custom, none of this is ever "supposed" to happen, because of the maxim of reciprocity that underlies gift giving. Yet, it does happen and not infrequently (as I found in my own field work) vexes people. "Stinginess" is an accusation one hears especially frequently among the farm Bushmen of Ghanzi or the cattle post Bushmen in the Dobe area: people, that is, who have become partially acculturated to a different—agropastoral or capitalist—ethos (Guenther 1977a, 1986a: 164–65; Lee 1979: 412–14, 1993: 150, 153, 156; Schott

1955; Woodburn 1982: 447), which is geared toward "saving" rather than "sharing" (Lee 1979: 412–13). Individuals who find themselves on the horns of the dilemma of these two moral principles either design stratagems for reconciling them, or, in opting for "greed" rather than "generosity" (Gulbrandsen 1991: 104), devise subterfuges for escaping the vigilance and censure of the group.

Among the Ghanzi farm Bushmen these may consist of physically separating oneself from other villagers (by setting up one's hut out of eyesight and earshot of neighbors), or being sly and clandestine about receiving a coveted item from an outsider. An example is the Bushman field assistant Tsaxa, who asked the visiting anthropologist to give him things—including his wages—surreptitiously, either after dark or inside his hut (Guenther 1986a: 164). Another instance of the value conflict in which contemporary farm Bushmen find themselves occurred at a recent field trip to Dekar (in 1995). I went on a *khutsu*-gathering outing, with half a dozen women, offering the services of my truck. The availability of the vehicle allowed us to gather as much as possible of this delectable *veldkos* item (a type of truffle) and over the course of six hours we loaded close to two hundred kilograms on the truck. When we arrived back at the village at dusk, the women asked me to take each of them to her respective hut, so no one would see them carrying a full sack of truffles, and, seeing so rich a load, ask them to share.

By manipulating sharing and giving, so that they are no longer acts of matter-of-course propriety and casual, open-ended reciprocity but acts of stark self-interest, the !Kung man ≠Toma and the farm Nharo man Tsaxa demonstrate the fragility of the Bushman pattern of sharing and giving. Its inherent and expected element of generosity toward all and sundry, particularly those especially entitled (such as the old), is readily flouted, not only among labor-rendering and cash-earning farm Bushmen acculturated away from sharing to saving, but even among traditional Bushmen, such as the !Kung described by Lorna Marshall. Hoarding things—secretively and jealously, like the Nharo farm Bushman just mentioned—"guarding them 'like a hyena'" (Lee 1982: 53), is one of the most frequent and salient moral breaches, and causes for quarrelling, brow-beating, and recrimination (Lee 1982: 53–54, Marshall 1976a: 244)—including accusations of witchcraft—within sedentary Bushman communities (Guenther 1992a).

The issues of contention surrounding generosity can become especially acute during meat-sharing episodes, occasions at which great tact and social finesse have to be exercised by the person in charge of the division. It presents the opportunity both for discharging previous obligations and assuming new ones, and, in the process, demonstrating one's "big-heartedness," and for eliciting invidiousness, resentments, and the common charge of "far-heartedness" (Marshall 1976a: 295–303). The fact that a spirited dance may follow on the heels of a meat-sharing episode may have as much to do with the sense of well-being that accompanies a good food-feast as with the desire to appease overt or covert ressentiments the event may have evoked in the hearts of some of the recipients.

We see, then, a constant tug-of-war within Bushman interpersonal and exchange relations, between sharing, generosity, and reciprocity, on the one hand, and hoarding, stinginess, and self-interest on the other.

Of the former three values, reciprocity is perhaps the most basic—pervading, as an implicit moral assumption, the exchange not only of food but of gifts generally; it is the most basic of Bushman economic processes in general (Wiessner 1982; Lee 1979: 460; Marshall 1976a: 299; Guenther 1986a: 161–62; Silberbauer 1981: 252–55; Barnard 1993; Woodburn 1982: 44–42). Cooperation and mutual help are extensions of this principle beyond economic interaction into the wider moral sphere. Mutuality is found in gender relations and kinship patterns, forming the basis of the joking and avoidance relationships, as well as the !Kung pattern of name relations and the G/wi principle of "congruency" that were discussed earlier. It applies also to relations with neighboring bands, all of whom grant reciprocal access to one another's resources.

Reciprocity is inherent also in the very way the people speak to each other, attesting to the pervasiveness of this principle within Bushman social existence.[4] In its give-and-take structure all conversation is reciprocal; however, among the Bushmen this element has become conventionalized, as a stereotyped speech pattern that marks people's everyday conversation. Lorna Marshall provides a perceptive account of the "contrapuntal" flow of the conversation among the !Kung:

> While a person speaks the listeners are in vibrant response, repeating the phrases and interposing a contrapuntal "eh." "Yesterday," "eh" "at Doboragu," "eh," "I saw old /Gaishay." "You saw Old /Gaishay," "eh, eh." "He said that he had seen the great python under the bank." "EH!" "the python!" "He wants us," "eh,eh,eh," "to help him catch it." The "ehs" overlap and coincide with the phrases, and the people so often all talk at once that one wonders how anyone knows what the speaker has said. (Marshall 1976a: 290)

Thus while reciprocity (as well as egalitarianism) is at play in the constant exchange of one another's phrases and exclamations, each individual is also intent in putting forward his or her own message. Each holds forth and several conversations run simultaneously (providing the ethnographer with an abundance of information, as he "channel-flips" back and forth between diverse discourses).

All of the values here reviewed—equality, reciprocity, cooperation, mutual help, generosity, commensality, non-arrogance, even-temperedness—are facets of one encompassing ethos which is the moral template for Bushman society: sociability. It is an ethos to which people cling, because the society in which they live is so loose, fluid, labile, amorphous, and because social relationship is so fragile, "involving a serious danger of being left more or less in a social vacuum" (Gulbrandsen 1991: 104). "Seeking solitude is an absolutely foreign concept" to the !Xõ (Heinz 1966: 54). "They must belong," says Lorna Marshall of the !Kung,

> separation and loneliness are unendurable to them. I believe their wanting to belong and be near is actually visible in the way families cluster together in an encampment and in the way they sit huddled together, often touching someone, shoulder against shoulder, ankle across ankle. Security and comfort lie in their belonging to their group, free from the threat of rejection and hostility. (Marshall 1976a: 287–88)

Yet, again we note ambiguity and ambivalence: notwithstanding so intense, palpable, and "thigmotactic" (Heinz 1966: 54) an expression of sociability, Marshall notes in the same discussion that "self-interest" and "jealous watchfulness" are also ever present. Indeed, she notes, "altruism, kindness, sympathy, or genuine generosity were not qualities I observed often in their behaviour" (Marshall 1976b: 350).[5]

And, contrary to Durkheim's view of the "collective conscience" absorbing and obliterating the individual's identity (Durkheim 1964: 150–52) in societies with "mechanical solidarity," he or she is, in fact, well-delineated, assertive, and in pursuit of his and her own agenda, all this in a society and ethos that are loose and ambiguous, and grant the individual much independence and freedom of mobility. Let us turn now to the individual to see how he and she work out the contradiction of Bushman ethos, between altruism and communalism, on the one hand, and self-interest and individualism, on the other.

The Individual

As noted in the previous chapter, it is individuals, alone or in small family units, who move hither and yon in this nomadic society, changing its composition by the day through their constant comings and goings. Because of the lack of a "front stage/back stage demarcation" (Gulbrandsen 1991: 90) in social life, and the lack of privacy, the actions of the individual are subject to ongoing surveillance by the rest of the group. His "critical shortcomings and sensitive emotions" are exposed, and ridicule is dumped on him, whenever he is perceived to display "tacitly esteemed abilities like hunting skills, expressed confirmation of oratory capacity, or the exercise of social domination" (ibid.: 90).

That individuals will bristle at such unceasing group censure is evident when one looks at the life careers of the two !Kung women N/isa (Shostak 1981) and N!ai (J. Marshall 1982; Volkman 1982), as well as the !Kõ woman Namkwa (Heinz and Lee 1978). All three of these Bushwomen are revealed to be complex and colorful personalities and, each in her own way, quite nonconformist. In the case of Namkwa, the latter trait was manifested by her agreement to be married to the anthropologist Hans-Joachim Heinz, and, almost equally unusual, becoming a "business woman" who managed her own shop at the !Xõ village of Bere. As girls and middle-aged women, these three frequently rebelled at the moral directives and pressures brought to bear on them by their families, friends, and neighbors. Their many moves, away from the group—in Namkwa's case, as far away as New York—and back again, and their breakups and reconciliations with lovers and other significant others, fill their lives with storm and passion. Throughout, these three real-life women from the Bushman ethnographic literature are seen to be a good deal less demure, repressed, and long-suffering than many of their literary counterparts in Western fictional literature, say Nora Helmer, Hedda Gabler, or Emma Bovary (the latter, coincidentally, like N!ai, sexually unsatisfied by and estranged from a dull doctor-husband!). The attempts of the European trio of women to break free from the conventions of the patriarchal mores that shackled them proved futile, and this futility constitutes the tragedy of each of these three fictional life stories. While the life of any of the three Kalahari women is not free of tragic moments, tragedy is not the summation of these lives. Instead, each is a real-life drama, about the growth and affirmation of individualism, self-fulfillment, and autonomy.

Together these qualities—which one would also find in the life stories of Bush*men* (Guenther 1996c)—constitute what Peter Gardner has dubbed the "individual autonomy syndrome," which he found, to varying degrees, among hunter-gatherers worldwide. The egalitarian values and practices of Bushman society, including gender equality (Barnard 1980a; Guenther 1983; Lee 1982; Kent 1993a: 486–91) and the lack of coercion and power institutions, make up one part of the explanation. Another is the loose and fluid organizational structure of the society, which, as shown by Woodburn (1982) in a comparative article primarily on African foragers, has three implications for the individual:

> 1) Individuals have a *choice* of whom they associate with in residence, in the food quest, in trade and exchange, and in ritual contexts;
> 2) People are *not dependent on specific other people* for access to basic requirements;
> 3) Relationships between people . . . stress sharing and mutuality but *do not involve long-term binding commitments and dependencies. . . .* (Woodburn 1982: 434, my emphases)

Indeed, among the Hadza the individual's personal autonomy can be so extreme as to enable an adult person, of either sex, to live alone as a hermit for long periods of time (ibid.: 483). While among the Bushmen the sense and the need to belong would never be so weak as to drive a person to seek out his or her hermitage in some remote stretch of Kalahari desert land, Woodburn's general statements about the pervasiveness and fixedness of individualism within the social relations of egalitarian foragers apply to the Bushmen as well.

The reason an ethos of individualism and personal autonomy is fixed within the individual is that self-reliance and assertiveness are inculcated in a person from early childhood. A child-rearing regimen is in effect which, while not without elements of conformity (Silberbauer 1981: 177), places little emphasis on strict obedience. Instead, child-rearing practices are generally quite indulgent (Marshall 1976a: 315–18; Konner 1976: 238–43; Heinz and Lee 1978: 221–30; Guenther 1986a: 211; Le Roux 1995b: 11–12, 41–42), "easygoing and unselfconscious" (Draper 1976: 205). When scolded, a child might be allowed to "scowl back"; the "parents saw this as a way in which the child could vent emotions, while simultaneously grasping the nature of the offence," reports Willemien Le Roux in her survey of the preschool program for the Bushman children of the Ghanzi District (ibid.: 12). This sort of reaction to chastisement[6] also seems in tune with the assertive individualism inherent in Bushman culture and personality.

The parents interviewed by Le Roux and her assistants discouraged the beating of children (a key reason they withdraw their children from school, where corporal punishment is a form of discipline), preferring, instead, to "talk to our children. We talk to them a lot, and everybody talks" (as noted by Xgaiga, during an interview on the subject of child rearing). Habe added that "if you beat a child too much, they become stubborn, and you cannot win that child over again," and /Oe//'ae pointed out that

> it is better to give the child a reward if he has done something right, than to beat him/her when doing something wrong. You can always bribe a child to do something, if he knows he will get something afterwards. (Ibid.: 41)

Attuned to the child-indulgent ways of their culture, children might explicitly negotiate their way out of a beating, as pointed out by //Uga:

> Sometimes I have tried to beat my child, then she tells me not to do it. She also tells me when I tell her to do something: "I will only co-operate if you do not beat me." (Ibid.: 42)

These comments reveal the strength of conviction of Bushman parents that child rearing should be a process that does not bully a child. Being so young, it does "not know everything," as pointed out by the Nharo elder !Khuma//ka. It is a notion held by other Bushman groups as well, such as the !Kõ, who, from birth to about age six, are not regarded as having any sense, or as being fully human. Their "sense" develops only after that age, in two stages, pre- and post-puberty (Heinz and Lee 1978: 222–23).

Completing the above comment, !Khuma//ka states, "if you are too forceful on children, you can make that child very weak. It is important to let the child feel strong." One element of the "strength" ceded to the growing child is a solid dose of assertiveness and resourcefulness, evident in the child's negotiating stance toward the parents' authority. Individualism is allowed free rein in the child so that a wide range of personalities is created across the different families and bands (Shostak 1976: 276).

The latter process is aided also by the informality of the child socialization process. Children learn their culture's ways through observing their parents, in the course of their everyday interactions (Tanaka 1980: 101), and through a social setting in which children and adults freely intermingle, and that has no "adults only" area (Draper 1976: 202). "No subject was censored, and the child could listen to all kinds of vulgar talk, gossip and quarrel," notes Willemien LeRoux (1995b: 11), again among the Ghanzi farm Bushmen. Another source of cultural knowledge was stories told around the fires at night by adults to one another, to which children would listen, "free to make their own interpretations" (ibid.: 12).

Looking at children's, especially girls', play and games (Marshall 1976a: 322), we note a lack of competition. The reason is that this behavior takes place within multi-age peer groups, a circumstance that would discourage competition and encourage cooperation—especially among older children aiding younger ones—because of the wide variation of mental and motor skills among the players (Draper 1976: 202–203; Heinz and Lee 1978: 225; Silberbauer 1981: 177). The lack of competition in games may act as a psychological mechanism in the development of personal autonomy, as the standard of evaluating one's performance in the game would be placed within oneself, since one would not be inclined to measure up one's performance against any competing other player.

Turning from child's play to work, we note that children are not enjoined by adults to do many chores (Draper 1976: 209–13; Blurton-Jones, Hawkes, and Draper 1994), especially boys, who, throughout their pre- and postadolescent years, roam the villages and farms in play and amorous adventures (Guenther 1986a: 211). The element of responsibility, for a work task such as looking after cattle or fields (as among agropastoralists), is thus a minor component of socialization. According to Barry, Child, and Bacon (1959), and Whiting (1968), the lack of that moral element fosters assertiveness in the child. Being free of responsibilities, (s)he is not placed into a position of submissiveness and obedience to an adult. Spontaneity and self-indulgence, too, these comparative psychologists suggest, are inculcated through such a relaxed regimen that boys, when they do go out to hunt, do so "for their own pleasure rather than carrying out a task assigned by their elders" (Whiting 1968: 337). The independent initiative of the boy when he is hunting "on a whim" is consistent with the opportunism of the adult forager, whose "food quest begins each day anew" (Gardner 1991: 543).

Apart from the social mechanism of socialization that fosters individualism, such a personality orientation is affected also by the cultural process of individuation.[7] This process was first brought up by Durkheim (1964: 174–99), in a discussion that argued for its absence within societies such as the Bushmen, due to a strong collective conscience and homogeneous religion, and for its appearance, instead, in complex societies with "organic solidarity."[8] However, as mentioned earlier, subsequent fieldwork among the former type of society has shown a different picture. Instead, as noted by Stanley Diamond (1963: 103; also see Diamond 1974: 160–75 and Service 1979: 75), in a discussion of the same issue,

> the fulfilment—delineation of the human person within a social, natural and supernatural (self-transcendent) setting—is a fundamental trait of simple societies and differentiates these from complex ones.

Akin to Marx's utopian unalienated worker, who expresses his true nature—his individuality and humanity—in his work, thereby "doubly affirming himself and his fellow man" (Haralambos 1980: 229; also see Hobsbawm 1965), a member of a simple society is able to fulfil himself and herself, through control not only of the processes of production and the material resources of his culture but also of its social and symbolic ones (Diamond 1963: 91). This makes possible the achievement of maximal self-fulfillment, "the full and manifold participation of individuals in nature and society" (Diamond ibid.: 110). These cultural resources are accessible to all, in part because of the egalitarian bent of society, in part because of the relative simplicity and unspecialized nature of material and mental culture. Among the Bushmen, there are no Woody Allen types who are overcome with an anxiety attack because they cannot fix the toaster on the breakfast table (or, more intimidating yet, their home computer)!

Diamond also notes that, because of the lack of status differentiation and craft specialization, individuals in such societies do not play any roles as they interact with others. Instead of social role playing, persons are "natural" in how they present themselves to others. He chides Goffman for his over-hasty claim of universality for his concept of role playing and masking of self, which confuses the "construction of a person" with the "development of self" (Diamond ibid.: 104).[9]

Another way whereby the person is defined as an individual in foraging societies is through the basic economic processes and social relationship patterns that operate in his/her society. Opportunistic and strategizing foraging, on the one hand, and sharing (especially the demand kind), generalized reciprocity, and assertive egalitarianism, on the other, are all intrinsically egocentric, as well as (in the case of the latter three), dyadic and reflexive. They acknowledge the individual every time he or she engages in economic subsistence tasks and in social action.[10]

Diamond and Service draw a distinction between the individualism that plays itself out in tribal society and the "ideological—or aggressive—individualism" of Western society. The latter, because of its rationalized, mechanized, and secularized civilization, brings about the mechanical separation of persons from each other, resulting in the individual's "pathological loneliness" (Diamond ibid.: 104–105). Restated more recently by the political scientist Charles Taylor (who, in turn, is restating Tocqueville), Western democratic equality "draws the individual towards himself, '*et menace de le renfermer enfin tout entier dans la solitude de son propre coeur*'" (Taylor 1992: 4). Commenting on the passage, Taylor (ibid.) continues:

> In other words, the dark side of individualism is a centring on the self, which both flattens and narrows our lives, makes them poorer in meaning, and less concerned with others or society.

Taylor casts his gloomy essay on "the malaise of modernity" around three "worries" about contemporary Western culture and society: individualism, disenchantment with the world, and loss of freedom. The first is also the foremost on Taylor's worry list, because of its pervasiveness, and the fact that it is embedded in an all-embracing "culture of narcissism" which creates "an outlook that makes self-fulfilment the major value in life and that seems to recognize few external moral demands or serious commitments to others" (1992: 55). Noting the same feature—"narcissism" and a "regrettable self-absorption" in Western society—Diamond starkly contrasts the Western individualists with their tribal counterparts. Instead of self-conscious and alienated persons, Diamond regards the latter to be "natural varieties of persons" (Diamond 1972: 104), who, for all their individuation, are organically tied to the community which is the ground and being of their individuality.

In summing up his position on "primitive individuation," Diamond lists three traits:

> 1) The full and manifold participation of individuals in nature and society;
> 2) the intensely personal socialization process through which individual qualities are delineated; and
> 3) the expression of society in the person and the person in society. (Diamond 1974: 172)

All this comes close to capturing the nature of individualism in Bushman society also. However, in its romanticist-modernist tone—Diamond's formulation is presented in a book embarked on a "search of the primitive" and a "critique of civilization"—in some way it is also off the mark, especially in its lack of recognition of similarity with "civilization," and of inherent contradiction or ambiguity (the "malaise—perhaps—of modernity" in anthropology). The Bushman individualist is a person who in a number of ways would be quite recognizable to a Westerner. A Bush(wo)man is very much autonomous as a person, well defined socially, self-fulfilled, uncommitted to others, moving about in pursuit—as often as not—of her self-interest, and doing "his own thing." However, (s)he is never all of these things unwaveringly; as noted above, the social and moral chemistry of Bushman society and ethos, as well as the pragmatics of survival in a risky environment, also foster an acknowledgment of others, indeed, a dependence on them and a strong sense of belonging.

Whereas the Bushman individualist, like his Western counterpart, can be "aggressive" about his or her individualism, by asserting the opposite values which were reviewed in this chapter, he or she may be said to be aggressive also about asserting communalism. This is the key contradiction in Bushman society and culture; its resolution lies in a third key value, yet again asserted aggressively: egalitarianism. Because it is linked to both individualism and communalism, providing each with its moral underpinnings, egalitarianism is capable of mediating these two opposites of Bushman moral culture. Herein lies the difference between the individualism of the West and of the South (i.e., the Kalahari): in the West we find what Simmel (1971: 251–93; see Béteille 1986) called "individualism of inequality," whereas among the Bushman it is a case of "individualism of equality." In the West equality is a cherished ideal that lies superimposed over, and at odds with, a hierarchical social structure. It is applied aggressively or apologetically as an a priori ideological construct, to a social reality (as in India; see Dumont 1972 and Béteille 1986), that does not bear it out. Putting the idea differently, *homo aequalis* is "conceived as an autonomous agent prior to his entry into social relations" (Ingold 1986: 130).

Among the Bushmen, for the individual to enter social relations is to act in a manner which is egalitarian at every turn. It is not a self-conscious ideological premise of social interaction that is stubbornly asserted but violated in social practice (Béteille 1986: 133), but is instead an a posteriori consequence or by-product of social relations (albeit one that interrelating people monitor). Individualism and egalitarianism are manifested, not negated, through the communalist values of sharing and reciprocity; to follow the dictates of one set of values is to be true to those of the other. Exchange, too, is an expression of these two communalist values, in part because of its generalized nature, in part because much of what is exchanged is not things but ideas. A person gives up the former—a knife or a flashlight—when he exchanges it with another, but retains the latter—a song or a trance curing routine—in his or her head after the exchange. Both giver and receiver continue to have the exchanged idea; by default, the exchange becomes an instance also of sharing.

Bushman ethos operationalizes, as a matter of course, Kant's "categorical imperative"—"act in such a way that the maxims of your will may at the same time act as principle for the law of all"—and the Scripture's "golden rule." Thus it illustrates Dorothy Lee's insights about the "self and other" in certain societies which, while "differentiated . . . are not exclusive . . . [since] self-interest and other interests are not clearly distinguished—so that what [they do] for [their] own good is necessarily also good for [their group]" (Lee 1976: 12).

The Individual and Society

Loose and labile, beset with contradiction and ambiguity, Bushman society is in need of constant vigilance by its members so that its key values of communalism—egalitarianism, cooperation, mutual aid, sharing, reciprocity, generosity, sociability—are maintained, while, at the same time, the individual's personal autonomy and fulfillment are safeguarded. For the individual this is not just a matter, simply and blindly, of one for all and all for one, as the Frenchmen D'Artagnan and Durkheim would have it. Instead of standing one with the group, in the fashion either of a musketeer-soldier-swordsman or aboriginal-forager-hordesman, the individual is loosely attached to the corps or horde, footloose and fancy-free, with an "inability to sit quietly in a room" (to cite yet another Frenchman, Pascal, gloomily musing on man's urge to wander, which he deemed the root cause of humankind's troubles).

Yet, men and women are also closely tied to one another and to their fluid cliques, or camps and bands, or band clusters. And for all that looseness, these mini- or quasi-societies[11] are, in fact, inclusive groups, which "are constituted by relations of incorporation rather than exclusion, by virtue of which others are 'drawn in' and not 'parcelled out'" (Ingold 1990: 130). Bands are societies that persist, as they have over the centuries and millennia, despite their lability. Indeed, one might even say because of it, as the condition of structural lability does not bring with it a state of structural liability, as demonstrated in this and in the preceding chapter. Fluidity means flexibility, which means resilience, which means adaptability. Analogous to the multiple subspecies and species of finch on a multi-niched island environment, Bushman bands are found in many diverse forms all over southern Africa, adapted and forever adapting to diverse and forever-changing ecological and social circumstances (Guenther 1996d).

The structural and moral ambiguities and contradictions require of individuals that they ponder and negotiate the institutions and values of their society, to chart each her or his own course of action, in the context of contingencies specific to each individual. In so doing, individuals also engage each other—through "talking" and sharing—manifesting, thereby, sociability and belonging. And they do so in the context of an ethos—egalitarianism and reciprocity—which acknowledges both the individual and society.

In looking at Bushman ritual and belief, we will once again find intrinsic and pervasive ambiguity, as well as diversity and openness, along with a touch of the antic and the ludic. All that is consistent with the social and psychological constitution of society and the individual, wherein ambiguity and diversity, openness of society and lack of orthodoxy of values, and well-defined and assertive—as well as jocular and risible—individuals are hallmark features.

As will be seen in the following chapters, their religion and expressive culture is satisfying to the Bushmen because of the correspondence between two ambiguous cultural domains, society and religion. It is because of this basic epistemological quality, I sense, that religion ultimately seems real to these people, rather than—in Durkheim's or Malinowski's or Lévi-Strauss's vision of things—because of some inherent moral, symbolic, and collective integrity, rendered clear—conceptually and emotionally—through myth and ritual, and through the workings of the mind. Instead, religion rings true for the Bushmen because of its texts and subtexts of ambiguity. What these are, and how they play themselves out in the belief "system" and ritual practice of the Bushmen, is the subject for the remaining chapters.

3

Bushman Religious Belief and Cosmology

> *The growth of religious ideas is environed with such intrinsic difficulties that it may never receive a perfectly satisfactory exposition. Religion deals so largely with the imaginative and emotional nature, and consequently with such uncertain elements of knowledge, that all primitive religions are grotesque and to some extent unintelligible.*
>
> —MORGAN 1877: 5

> *One fundamental feature about Nharo belief, and one shared with the belief patterns of Bushmen in general, is its multifarious, inchoate and amorphous quality. There is wide variation in the accounts provided by different Nharo individuals when they describe the appearance and qualities of a supernatural agent. Nharo supernaturalism seems to be a confusing tangle of ideas and beliefs, marked by contradiction, inconsistencies, vagueness and lack of culture-wide standardization.*
>
> —GUENTHER 1986A: 216

While excessive in its language, Morgan's frustrated, despairing comment about religion in general—its "grotesque" and "unintelligible" aspect and the uncertainty of the knowledge one can obtain of it—rings true with respect to the case before us. As suggested by the second epigraph, Bushman religion contains much "uncertainty of knowledge." This quality is intrinsic, manifested in vagueness and fluidity, and is also present in the people's and, most particularly, the outside researcher's mind as he or she struggles to make sense of it. Bushman religion is not so much grotesque as it is ambiguous; other adjectives that might describe it are diverse, heterogeneous, surreal, and contradictory.

These remarks apply especially to the area of belief, the topic of this chapter. This is the larger component of Bushman religion, overshadowing the other component, ritual. By comparison to other African societies, where ritual and ceremonialism are prominent, the ritual life of the Bushmen is somewhat sparse (although, as we will see, such ritual as is practiced can be intense and absorbing for its practitioners). The challenge of Bushman religion, which I described in the introduction, lies to a certain degree in this property; being more "thought out" than "danced out," the greater part of Bushman religion is not open to the gaze of the anthropologist. Because religion resides primarily in the believer's mind, rather than in the arena of the social, where the ritual component is enacted, the student of religion is deprived of that part of religion that, by virtue of its being in the open, is thus more amenable to anthropological scrutiny. Also contributing to the visibility of ritual is the fact that this component of religion is frequently clearly articulated with other "open" social institutions and processes, as well as economic and political ones (Guenther 1979a: 119–26).

I will undertake, in this chapter, to put together a summary account of Bushman belief and cosmology, as much as this is possible, given the striking ambiguity and wide diversity of this cultural field. That done, I will attempt to explain the diverse and ambiguous nature of Bushman religion, both from a synchronic, social-structural perspective, and from a diachronic, historical one.

The Diversity and Ambiguity of Bushman Religion

Contrasting Bushman religion with the more streamlined religious system of the "Hottentots,"[1] Theophilius Hahn noted in 1870 how variation abounds, "not merely from one tribe to the next, but also from individual to individual" (Hahn 1870: 84; see also Lebzelter 1934: 56 for a virtually identical formulation of the same point). So diverse and formless seemed Bushman religion to Hahn that he referred to it as *wildwuchender Aberglaube* ("superstition grown wildly rank"). To his contemporary Gustav Fritsch, the grossly heterogenous, shapeless state of Bushman religion suggested that these people had no religious notions and practices whatsoever, having received various and sundry religious scatterings from neighboring groups (Fritsch 1872: 427, cited in Schmidt 1933: 548). As we will see in a later chapter, missionaries laboring among the Bushmen at the time held similar views, doubting the existence, within the culture and soul of their charges, of any notion whatsoever of God, especially a God so rarefied and spiritually demanding as is worshipped by Christians.

Subsequent generations of students working in the Kalahari continued to be astounded by the same quality of Bushman religion; for instance, Dorothea Bleek, who referred to the religion of the Nharo as a "wonderful muddle of religious beliefs" (1928: 25), especially those about the divinity Hise and the god-spirit of the dead-ghost-dream figure of //Gãũwa. The same assessment—a *Wirrwarr* ("mess")—was applied by Bleek's contemporary Paul Schebesta (1923: 116) to Khoisan religious belief in general. The early ethnographer Viktor Lebzelter, whose field work among a variety of Bushman groups throughout South West Africa focused especially on their religious domain, opined that it was an exercise of futility to search for any coherence within Bushman religion as this trait was altogether absent from their cultural system. He explained its absence in terms of the highly individualistic nature of Bushman thought, specifically notions of causality (Lebzelter 1934: 56). His contemporary Isaac Schapera referred to Bushman beliefs about their supernatural beings as holding "a good deal of variation in details among the different Bushman tribes" (1930: 177), especially those about //Gãũwa, which are "vague, inconsistent and ambiguous." His lengthy summary of the literature of the time on Bushman religion (1930: 160–201) reveals a dazzling range of variation (see also Schmidt 1933: 537–695, especially pp. 584–90 and 602–11). In his recent "update" of Schapera's comparative work on the Khoisan herders and hunters, Alan Barnard includes a recent regional-comparative survey of Bushman religions (Barnard 1992a: 251–64, also 1988). Its focus is on the considerable "fluidity of religious belief and discourse" (while it also mentions an underlying structure, an analytical paradox to which I will return later).

Gusinde referred to the system of religious practices and beliefs (especially about divinity) of the various !Kung groups he visited on his Namibia-Botswana tour of 1950 and 1953 as a *verknäulter Komplex* ("a complex tied up in knots") (1966: 79), made up of elements gathered and garnered by the Bushmen from all directions. He tried to trace these directions, "culture-historically" (with little success, as I will discuss later). Visiting the same group at about the same time, Lorna Marshall comments on the same diversity and profusion, as well as inconsistency, of beliefs, especially about divinity, whose many (eight) "names, terms, titles or descriptive phrases" she (like Gusinde) attempted—with admitted futility—to sort out in terms of borrowings from different sources at different times (Marshall 1962: 223–29; also see Biesele 1993: 180–81). Richard Lee's account of !Kung theology is more streamlined. He distinguishes between only two divinities—a "big-big god" and a "little god"; however, he notes that "there are many puzzling aspects of the High God/Low God dichotomy" (1993: 113), that include divergent and contradictory views on the divinities' moral qualities (ibid.: 113–14). !Kung myth and oral tradition are similarly seen to be diverse, complex, and fluid (Biesele 1976: 304, 1978: 162, 1993: 180–81).

The same can be said of the myth and lore of other Bushman groups, such as the Nharo and /Xam, on the basis of a comparative study of their oral traditions (Guenther 1979a: 106–11, 1986a: 216–18, 1989: 30–36, 1996d: 72–74), as of Khoisan folklore in general (Schmidt 1989). In both cases versions abound, and, as will be seen more fully later, the degree of textual and textural variation is high (Bleek 1875; Lloyd 1889; Bleek and Lloyd 1911; Guenther 1989). As for /Xam Bushman religious beliefs and concepts of divinity, Lewis-Williams (1981: 124) points to the "shifting and elusive nature of Bushman thought" and the futility of expressing Bushman belief "in single English words without serious distortion."

Turning to the southern neighbors of the Nharo—the G/wi and the !Kõ—we note, in the former case, beliefs about supernatural beings and "the (to us) natural phenomena of sun, moon and rain," that strike the ethnographer writing about them as "casual, confused and very difficult to obtain and put into any sort of order" (Silberbauer 1965: 102; also see 1972: 319). The belief systems, as a whole, of the G/wi (and the !Kung, to whom comparisons are made) "vary significantly" (Silberbauer 1996: 52). Holding the !Kõ to be a people with an intellectual bent that is basically prosaic and pragmatic, Heinz (1975a: 19, 22, 23) presents their religious beliefs (especially about god) as lacking uniformity, showing "more differences than resemblances," and beset with uncertainty, confusion, and discrepancy.

Diversity, ambiguity, confusion, contradiction, incoherence, vagueness, heterogeneity, fluidity, ineffability—such are the qualities that commentators on Bushman religion have variously attributed to the beliefs over the past century. They run through all of the elements that make up the realm of Bushman belief, cosmology, and myth.

Divinity

Bushman belief shares with the religions of the rest of Africa a belief in a creator god. The beliefs about god's nature, however, vary widely, so much so that virtually every conceivable facet—"from atheism to monotheism" (Schebesta 1923: 116)—one might think of attributing to, or taking away from, a divinity can be found in the Khoisan area.

The most common pattern seems to be a dual divinity, such as postulated by the !Kõ and G/wi, who name their two deities *Gu/e* and */Oa* (Heinz 1975a: 19–23), and *N!odima* and *G//awama* (Silberbauer 1965: 95–97), respectively. Similar to the latter are the names and concepts employed by the Nharo, a people geographically and culturally close to the G/wi. They name their two gods *N!eri* (*N!adi*) or *Hise,* a creator god associated with the sky, and *//Gauwa,* the veld-associated trickster-god who, in the fashion of a demiurge-figure, is sometimes seen to rival god (Bleek 1928: 25–26; Guenther 1986a: 218–25; Barnard 1992a: 113–14, 254–55). The latter personage has many attributes and multiple personas, and different Bushman groups may perceive him in one or the other of his many preternatural guises. Thus, Alan Barnard, who also worked among the Nharo, talks not about any single divinity, //Gãũwa, but about the *//gãũne,* the evil spirits (Barnard 1992a: 254). In terms of this researcher's understanding of Nharo theology, there is only one divinity. However, he recognizes that among other Khoisan groups, this supernatural being may be recognized as a god, usually, though not necessarily (Lebzelter 1934: 57) an evil one (Barnard ibid.: 259).

The next chapter will reveal the complex relationship of the two divinities to one another, which may be one of opposition or apposition, of antagonism and rivalry or cooperation, of equality or servitude. In fact, according to some of the beliefs held by Bushman individuals or groups, the two god-figures may be merged, either having one and the same name, or holding different names while sharing the same identity. Some of these may be unutterable, divine names; others, "earthly names" that may not only be uttered, but even derided.

In line with the Bushman god's somewhat "schizoid" identity is his ambiguous moral constitution. It results in an attitude of ambivalence in people toward their divinity, to whom they attribute a nature ranging from numinous to frivolous. What this moral ambivalence about divinity ultimately derives from is the lack of any clear association of their one or two gods with the moral values of good and evil. It is true that the lesser god frequently shows a destructive, malevolent, and adversarial side. In his guise as //Gãũwa, which is widespread in Khoisan belief (Schapera 1930: 396–99), he appears almost always as either "the evil god, the evil aspect of the good god, the evil spirits, or the spirits of the dead" (Barnard 1992a: 259). As such, the missionaries have pounced on this figure of Khoisan supernaturalism, in their search for an indigenous concept and name for the Devil, and as the Devil or Satan this figure appears in their early writings, as well as in the religious views of many Christianized Khoisan individuals or groups (Schapera 1930: 387–88; Lebzelter 1934: 10, 57; Gusinde 1966: 7). As we will see in the next chapter, this is an egregious distortion of a complex figure, however. He can also be beneficent, either in a fashion that is deliberately magnanimous, or more capricious and spontaneous.

The lesser god's magnanimous side is especially in evidence whenever he is perceived as merged with the creator god, whom people generally esteem as a good and providential divinity. Yet, that this god is not wholly good is also suggested by this merger of the great god with the lesser god, deemed a "cheating" and a "bluffing" god by the !Kung (Marshall 1962: 247). To the !Kung, //Gauwa is one of the six divine names and guises of god. While doing both good and evil deeds, god in his guise as the lesser god //Gauwa is primarily concerned with "death-giving" and "evil-doing." Another element of ambiguity is that the god //Gauwa may in fact not be a god at all, as among the Angola !Kung, but "a man who lives in the forest and has his house in a cave in the ground" (Lebzelter 1934: 6).

Turning to the Kxoe of northeastern Namibia, we meet a god, *Kxyani* by name (or *Yice*, his old name), who is described by Köhler (1978/79: 20–23) as basically good but also capable of assuming an evil, destructive guise, bringing, in this "emanation," epidemic diseases to humankind. The Kxoe god's moral ambiguity is mirrored by his gender: he is bisexual. The male Kxyani is perceived as a "Master of the Animals" and of the hunt figure; the female one, as a "Mistress of the Bush and the Water" and of gathering. By contrast, the G/wi, who also attribute a godlike role to god's wife, see her as primarily the protectress of the animals. Most commonly, however, the gender of the Bushman god is male; and he may live singly, or with a wife or wives, and with children (for instance, see Marshall 1962: 225–26). The divine household may be run just by the couple, or with a staff of servants. To my knowledge, with the exception of the wives of each of the Kxoe and the G/wi gods who hold divine status, none of these godly wives holds the status of divinity. They may play a minor mystical role in certain rituals, such as initiation, among the Nharo and Kxoe (see chapter 7), or in trancing, among the Hei//om (see chapter 8); however, nowhere on the supernatural landscape of this hunter-gatherer society is there anything like a goddess.

Generally, ideas about the creator god tend to be clouded in vagueness, probably because this divinity, unlike his trickster-adversary, is fairly remote from the affairs of people. He may be prayed to in situations of adversity, especially drought, as the sky, clouds, and rain are the key elements of his celestial domain. For instance, in the language of the Nharo, the words for sky and clouds, respectively, are *N!eri k'i* ("God's face") and *N!eri /oo* ("God's hair"). The association of divinity with rain was especially marked in the /Xam belief about *!Khwa* (whose name means "rain"), a threatening, rather than benevolent force, who could kill people with lightning and punish girls for transgressions during menarche by transforming them and their people into frogs and other water animals (Hewitt 1986: 40, 65–89). We will meet this enigmatic divinity again, in chapter 7.

The G/wi see god as being somewhat closer to the affairs of the living, as do most other Bushman groups (Silberbauer 1965: 51–52). The divine couple *N!adima* and *N!adisa* live in the region above the visible sky, which the G/wi hold to be a stretch of veld rich in water and game. Omnipresent, eternal, and omniscient, they direct the lives of humans—their children—by appearing to them in dreams. The animals, too, are the offspring of the couple, specifically N!adisa, whom, as noted, the G/wi hold to be mother to all of the mammals of the Central Kalahari. Being the animals' parents, the two deities are also vegetarians. As we will learn in the following chapter, among other Bushman groups, such as the /Xam (Hewitt 1986: 40; Lewis-Williams 1981: 56–57; Guenther 1990a: 244), the Hai//om (Wagner-Robertz 1976: 540, 546), and the !Kung (Shostak 1983: 300; Biesele 1993: 94), the divine role of "spirit keeper of the animals" was assumed by the trickster-god.

One other portrayal of god, which was likely derived from or through European missionaries, is his persona as Lord. It is in terms of this conceptualization of the divinity that Gordon explains one of the descriptions Lorna Marshall received from a !Kung informant: a white man, mounted on horseback and wearing a gun (Gordon 1992: 217). Such iconography displayed the regalia of power of the new white overlords. Over a century before, Livingstone received a like account of god from a Ngamiland Bushman, except that the lordly figure embodying god then was black, namely chief Sekoni (Sekgoma) of the Tawana, then overlord of the Bushmen of the region (Gordon ibid.: 266)

In sum, god in Bushman religion is a being that is both ambiguous and diffuse. He is comprised of varying and opposite ontological and moral traits, and different linguistic groups, bands, and individuals may hold diverse and contradictory conceptualizations or beliefs about this divine being, and extend feelings of ambivalence toward him (and, on the rare occasion, her).

Mantis and Moon "Worship"?

Another enigmatic figure in Bushman supernaturalism is the mantis, a large green insect related to the grasshopper. While in the beliefs and tales of the /Xam, Mantis was a trickster protagonist (Bleek 1923), and his name, /Kaggen, was also the name of the /Xam god (Barnard 1992a: 84–85), which gave the insect a numinous aura (Schapera 1930: 180–81; also see Gusinde 1966: 71–72; Schmidt 1973; Lewis-Williams 1981: 119–20; Hewitt 1986: 40–42; Barnard 1992a: 84–85). Among other groups, such as the Okavango !Kung, this insect was evidently just that, a "useless thing . . . which we throw out of the hut if it enters it" (Gusinde 1966: 71). The Nharo with whom I discussed this animal—as well as the chameleon, toward which similar feelings are extended —were more divided on the question of its preternatural quality. Some regarded it as just a *xoxo*, a "bug," toward which one reacts with indifference, while others held both animals to be uncanny creatures, to which oracular powers were attributed and which were vaguely associated either with rain (chameleon) or with //Gãũwa (for whom the mantis, as well as other insects, may spy on hunters as they plan their stalk of an antelope). However, any suggestion that people might pray to the insect was considered ludicrous, and dismissed by them as categorically as by any Westerner. The Nharo praying to the mantis is no more likely than the mantis praying to God!

Whether or not the moon and the sun, or even the stars, were godlike supernatural beings has been a matter of controversy in Bushman religious studies. Earlier writers attributed Wilhelm Bleek's Müllerian portrayal of the key elements of /Xam religion—"worshipping sun, moon and stars" (Bleek and Lloyd 1911: 435; also see pp. 56–59)—to other Bushman groups also, holding this "sidereal" package of beliefs to have been the pattern of Bushman religion in general, either at present or in the past (Bleek 1927; Schapera 1930: 435; Lebzelter 1934: 6; Potgieter 1955: 29; Köhler 1978/79: 16–19). Later students showed that what was considered to be moon worship was a misinterpretation of fact. For example, while a number of Bushmen do engage in ritual during moonlit nights, this was likely a matter more of practical convenience than of spiritual conviction. "Yes, we like to dance on moonlit nights," I was told by Nharo trance dancers, "because that way we can see what we are doing. We are less prone to bump into each other." A similarly prosaic and profane explanation was given to Gusinde by some of the southern !Kung to whom the moon is no more numinous than the headlights on Gusinde's truck. Both were appreciated by his informant for the same reason: they light up the road at night (Gusinde 1966: 39). In an elegant exegetical account of Nharo beliefs about the moon—as well as the sun, to which it is symbolically and mystically linked—Barnard (1992a: 153; 254–55) suggests that both stellar bodies are children of the god N!adiba; the element common to all three is the sky. Once again, this assigns to the moon the quality of light. So does the Kxoe notion that the keenness of vision of the hunter is enhanced by the light of the moon (Köhler 1978/79: 17).

Yet, in so far as in Nharo the sky is semantically, as well as mystically linked to god, there is, perhaps, also a divine element to the moon, at least in the minds of some individuals. Indeed, on the basis of her fieldwork among the Nharo, Dorothea Bleek felt justified in asserting that "the moon is still worshipped" (Bleek 1928: 26). Yet, they were also "very shy to admit it" (a reticence, one wonders, based on perhaps not knowing anything about it, yet being nevertheless pressed on the matter by the ethnographer). We find a similar discrepancy about this belief among the !Kung, again revealed by ethnographic information provided by Dorothea Bleek, who was, it would seem, beholden to her father's Müllerian views (a point to which I will return again later). Unlike the !Kung to whom Gusinde talked in Namibia and Botswana, Bleek's informants in Angola evidently extended ritual attitudes toward the moon (Bleek 1927: 119–20; Lebzelter 1934: 6; Estermann 1976: 12–13). It appears that to some Bushmen the moon represents, in its crescent form as the new moon, life and well-being, as among the /Xam, whose menarcheal rites were timed by the new moon. Alternatively, we find that the Nharo associate the waning moon with death: its crescent is seen as a boat carrying dead souls to god. Indeed, as we will see in chapter 5, because of its waxing and waning, the moon appears as a symbol of life (and death) and regeneration throughout Khoisan belief and myth.

In sum, we once again find a considerable diversity and divergence of views on this enigmatic stellar body which to some Bushmen was numinous, to others merely luminous.

In the context of an unwavering argument for Bushman monotheism, Gusinde (1966: 69–74) suggests that the notions of mantis and moon worship were all Western fabrications, designed either to titillate the European reader's sense of exoticism about the primitive Bushmen,[2] or to devise a dehumanizing stereotype with which to further the oppression and expropriation of the Bushmen by European colonists[3] (Gusinde 1966: 69–74; see also Guenther 1980: 129). Gusinde documents his case against the "Hottentot God" and its defaming perpetrators, early European settlers, by drawing from early South West African missionary reports (by such writers as Burkhardt, Lemue, Bisseur, and Rolland). These sources reveal not only that moon- and mantis-worship were European fabrications, but that, in addition, they were deliberately inculcated within the minds of their Bushman and Hottentot servants. That the latter greeted these quaint notions with skepticism and resentment is evident from the comments of one of them:

> The . . . [Boers] . . . told us, the God, the creator of heaven and earth, was not our god; they [showed] us a kind of fly, which the [Boers] call Hottentot-god, and they said: "Look and behold your god!!" Whenever they spent some time praying on Sundays, and we wanted to listen a bit at the window, they chased us off right away; their religion, they said, was not for us. Thus it was that we remained in a state of complete uncertainty. . . . We were also told that after death all was over with us, and since we suffered so much among the [Boers] of this land, we came to long for death, in order to be redeemed from all suffering. (Gusinde 1966: 73, my translation)[4]

Cosmogony: Primal Time

Bushman cosmology posits two orders of existence, a primal one and the present order, which succeeded the First Order and, according to some accounts, reversed it (Guenther 1989: 31–33, 86–114, 1990a: 241–45; see also Biesele 1993: 21–22, 95, 116–38; Schmidt 1995: 158–62). Because the Second Order is both a continuation and an inversion of the First Order, the mythological past and primal time pervade the historical present and contemporary reality. This confounding of past and present, and myth and reality confers on the present order an abiding aura of ambiguity.

It was in the First Order, however, that ambiguity reigned supreme. Beings and states were in flux and boundaries were fluid; moreover, flaws attached to everything, rendering things of the First Order incomplete and inchoate. The primal humans and animal-humans behaved "without customs," violating in particular the norms and mores pertaining to eating, sharing, marriage, proper kin relations, and menarcheal proscriptions. As will be seen in the next chapter, in many of these moral transgressions the trickster had a hand; as the First Order's most prominent citizen, he roamed its landscape in many guises, well suited, by his ambiguous nature, to its unformed makeup.

Another transgressor, in /Xam folklore, was the "first maiden," whose violation of menarcheal taboos was especially dangerous, as it was likely to incur the wrath, in /Xam mythology, of the ineffable and ambiguous rain-, thunder-, and lightening-divinity !Khwa, an impersonal force that sometimes manifested itself in mist or a whirlwind, and that was associated with certain animals, especially reptiles. !Khwa took these forms when setting out to punish the violator, or he embodied himself as a "rain bull" to abduct her on his back (à la Zeus and Europa). Even more typically, his punishment was to transform the maiden and all of her family members into frogs. This reversal of "cultural" (albeit precariously so, in the case of the Early Race) humans into "natural" animals was accompanied, and underscored, by another transformation: the change of the items of material culture of the Early Race back into their original natural forms—bows and digging sticks into shrubs and trees, leather cloaks into antelopes, jackal-tail swats into tails attached to jackals (Hewitt 1986: 75–88; Guenther 1989: 105–11). Thus, just as the social and moral condition of the Early Race was not firmly fixed, so also was their ontological state fluid and precarious. The latter condition of ambiguity applied especially to the many therianthropic beings who inhabited the First Order, along with humans proper and the trickster figures. These (m)animalian beings combined within themselves predominantly animalian traits with human ones. They are the most beguilingly enigmatic creatures in the Khoisan mythscape (Guenther 1988). They all had animal names, and each displayed certain anatomical and behavioral traits of the animal whose name and personality he or she bore. Thus Mantis was, at times, a "little green thing" that, in dangerous situations, might suddenly spread apart its wings and take to the air. Aardvark (the "Anteater") burrowed in the ground and ate ants, and the Ticks lived in sheep's fleeces. Mason Wasp had an absurdly slender waist that so embarrassed him that he concealed it from his wife's view under a leather cloak. Lion had a roar which he had obtained through bullying Field Mouse. As is the case sometimes with dwarves and giants, whose sonority of voice is incommensurate with their body size, it was the mouse who originally had the "big voice," as against Lion's thin squeak. The latter told him that so big a voice ought not to reside in so little a creature and commanded him to give his voice over to Lion. Regarding Lion—a central character in Bushman mythology—it should be noted that the mythological persona of this animal is somewhat ambiguous. On the one hand, because of his bullying, greed, and man-eating habits, he inspires fear; indeed, along with ogres—and, in tales set on farms, the Boer *baas*—he is probably the most fearsome being of the First Order. However, he is as frequently depicted as a bungling and laughable fool, who is easily duped and who is "everywhere the vanquished party" (Bleek 1928: 304; Guenther 1989: 128–30).

Each of these were-creatures is also human, in speech and gait, and in physical and social deportment. These Early People are therianthropic tribes of hunter-gatherers who live in bands, intervisit, intermarry, adopt one another's children, and quarrel over bad manners, stinginess, laziness, boisterousness, adultery, and in-law tensions. The latter interpersonal problem was especially likely to arise because marriages of the Early People crossed "species lines" with wild abandon. Thus, the Blue Crane's husband was a small unidentified songbird, and another such bird was married to a beetle. Animalian Early People also married humans; for example the aforementioned Wasp had a human wife, as did the Agama Lizard. (The latter's wife eventually left her lizard-husband because he persisted in procuring tainted meat—his own flesh—whenever he hunted. I will return to this strange and symbolically rich tale again later.)

A glance at the genealogical composition of !Kaggen-Mantis's band will demonstrate the wide range of indiscriminate affinal ties that linked the members of the Early People. The example also reflects the random array of animal species inhabiting the social landscape of the "First Race."

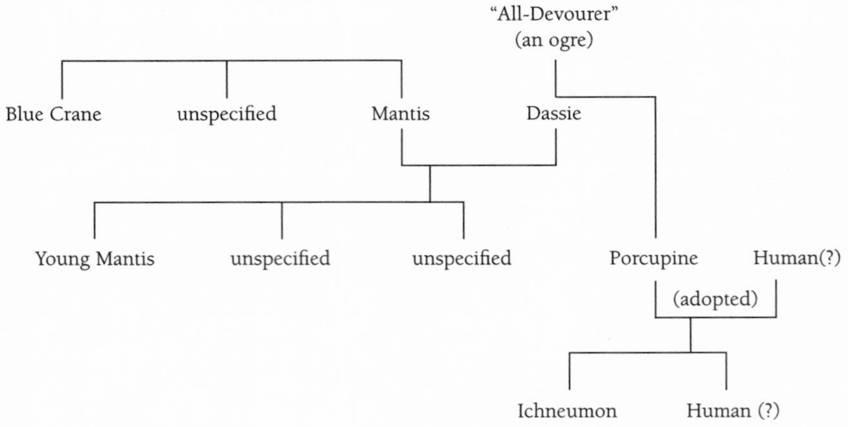

Another category of ontologically ambiguous thing-being, from the primal skyscape, was stellar bodies. Like animals, they were personified in Bushman mythology, especially among the /Xam, to the great beguilement of Bleek, as they provided an exemplary case for Müller's theory of myth, to which the linguist was drawn (Hewitt 1986: 59). As noted above, Nharo belief holds sun and moon to be husband and wife, whereas in /Xam mythology, the two bodies were seen as two men standing in an antagonistic relationship to one another. The sun had been thrown into the sky by the Early People (Bleek and Lloyd 1911: 44–65; Guenther 1989: 75–80). His antagonist, the moon, was a dangerous old man in the myths, feared by /Xam hunters and children (Guenther 1996c). As will be seen in chapter 5, one child in particular had cause to dread him, the Hare-maiden, whom he punished sorely after she had distorted the message about eternal life Moon had exhorted her to take to mankind. Some stars were also personified—although, again, not by all Bushmen (Heinz 1975a: 25)—and falling stars, the !Kung believe, turn into "ant lions" (that is, ant-eating insects which trap their prey in cone-shaped tunnels that are common in the sandy soil of the Kalahari).

Through a series of creative acts the inchoate and imperfect state of the First Order of existence became altered, and the Early People became more discrete and distinct one from the other, as well as less flawed. The result was the establishment of the Second Order of existence, which replaced—though not entirely—the First Order.

The establishment of a new order is a central theme of Bushman mythology; Sigrid Schmidt (1995: 152) refers to this pivotal moment of Khoisan cosmology as "die grosse Wende" ("the great turning-around"). Predictably, we once again find much variation in the accounts given by different Bushman groups of this portentous cosmogonic event. Among the Nharo, and, it seems, also the /Xam, it was, simply, an act of reversal—the transformation of First-Order animals (and therianthropes) into humans and of humans into animals (Guenther 1989: 32, 41–42; Schmidt ibid.: 159). There are tales, for example, of quagga, gemsbok, and ostrich of the First Order becoming humans in today's order, as well as of the reverse process, which, in one version of a widespread tale, features the hare—a boy changed into a hare by the angered moon (Maack n.d.: 34–35). Thus, the humans today were the animals of primal time and the present-time animals, the primal-time humans. To most other groups "the great turning-around" was less straightforward, however (Schmidt ibid.: 158–62). In the view of the /Xam, the human element of the therianthropes was reduced or eliminated and their animalian elements were brought to the forefront. Thus, what took place here was not a reversal so much as a transformation. That is, a man-animal creature merely developed to its fullest extent its animal component, while its humanoid component shriveled away and either vanished altogether from the makeup of the being or remained as a vestigial element. The latter explains why a "human" smell attaches to the modern quagga, or why a small section of the hare's body still contains human flesh, which the hunter has to discard when butchering the carcass (Bleek and Lloyd 1911: 60–61; Guenther 1988: 193). The creation of the new animals was accompanied with the admonition that each marry its own kind. The creative agent to bring this change about might have been the trickster (see next chapter) or one of the early animals, such as the "Anteater" woman among the /Xam (Guenther 1989: 83–85) or the Kori Bustard man among the !Kung (Biesele 1993: 110–38). It is unclear from the transformation tales just what was the fate of the early humans; it appears that ontologically they remained the same throughout, while cleaning up their act on the moral front.

There is one other way whereby the fluidity of the animal–human boundary was in evidence among the early humans: the readiness with which a woman could become "meat," that is, a game animal to be killed, butchered, and eaten by men, including at times the husband, along with his family. This is the grisly outcome of a number of tales, after the husband has been prodded by his badgering family members into realizing that his wife "is meat," that he "has married meat." While this may be merely a mythological account of marital (and in-law) strife—a chronic problem of "customs" besetting the Early People—it likely holds a deeper meaning than that. As shown eloquently by Biesele (1993: 139–70; also see Guenther 1989: 33, 92–95; McCall 1970; see Graburn 1976: 49 for a parallel case from the Inuit[5]), what is shown by these "animal wife" stories is the symbolic complementarity of hunting and sex or marriage, and the metaphorical link of women to game and to the hunt.[6] In her study, sententiously entitled *Women Like Meat,* Biesele shows this link to be the key to understanding a number (though not all) of the major myths of the Ju/'hoansi, as well as of their curing and initiation rites, gender relations, and productive and symbolic labor.

Bushman myth also presents a male version of this motif: man the hunter as meat, providing his flesh for his wife or wives, in lieu of the expected game which he has been unsuccessful at procuring (Guenther 1989: 101–104). In some tales he shares his ill-gotten meat with his wives, in others the story may take a different twist, becoming a cautionary tale about food greed: the hunter, having become "a veritable quagga to his own flesh" (Guenther 1989: 101), eats himself. This figure, the unsuccessful hunter who offers his own flesh as meat, thereby perpetrating an act of cannibalism on himself or on the unsuspecting womenfolk of his family, not infrequently is the trickster. In tune with his lewd and antic ways, what he presents to the women may be his testicles, anus, entrails, or buttocks (Schmidt 1989, 2:127–34, 1995: 89–91, 213–15; Biesele 1993: 171–73).

Cosmology: The Human–Animal Nexus

To a certain extent, the ambiguity of the First Order, with its ontological fluidity, its trickster protagonists, were-beings, and meat-women, still persists in the present world. In part this may be due to the fact that this new order is, in Bushman belief, vaguely overseen, or perhaps overlooked, by a god who is diffuse and remote, and toward whom people feel ambivalent. In part it may also be because the tales of the First Order are—or were until recently—told with great frequency, in a culture that is highly oral, creating intra- and inter-group variety in storytelling performances (a point to which I will return again in a later section). This immersion in *hua* ("old stories") also keeps people aware of the First Order and the Early Race, and attuned to its strange and dreamlike ways. The two elements of Bushman cosmology that convey ambiguity more directly and compellingly than any others are the people's attitudes and conceptualizations about animals and the processes of transformation and transcendence central to Bushman ritual and art. The two elements of ambiguity can also merge, when the transformation and transcendence are human-to-animal—of the dancer at a curing rite or initiation site, or of the initiand. At that point, the humans of the present order can experience a return to the conditions of existence that prevailed at primal time, suspending not only ontological states, but also chronological ones. Ambiguity becomes a palpable state, as ordinary reality is suspended through trance, human becomes animal, and present and linear time converge on the mythic past.

Here I will explore the ambiguity inherent in the Bushmen's notions and sentiments about animals; chapters 7 and 8, respectively, will deal with the ritual manifestations of transformation and transcendence.

What renders ambiguous and ambivalent the relationship of Bushman hunters—as of hunters generally (Shepard 1973, Kent 1989b:11–18)—toward animals, especially those he hunts, is that it is a relationship both of encounter and exploitation, sympathy and distance, intersubjectivity and object-otherness. The game animal encountered on a hunt is, in short, both a significant other, and, simply, an other (Guenther 1988).

These sentiments are conveyed hauntingly in Elizabeth Marshall-Thomas's (1990) remarkable essay about lions, written from the triple perspective of herself, as an ethnographer, of the !Kung Bushmen, and of the lions themselves. On the basis of her extensive observations of the latter two parties, she is convinced that what has developed between the Bushmen and the lions, over centuries or millennia of living in close proximity to the same waterholes and hunting the same antelope species, is a relationship of mutual respect. In fact, what the two fellow predators have set up is a sort of contractual relationship, along with a truce, that allows each party to go about its predatory ways without interference from the other. The truce is sustained through an exchange of respectful, at times forceful exhortations, elicited whenever one species gets too close to the other, usually accidentally. The !Kung, Marshall-Thomas states, communicated with the lions on many occasions, "with spoken and gestured commands that were designed for other human beings and then applied to lions" (89). In turn, "these were correctly understood by them," so Marshall-Thomas is convinced. The one problem was that the people were not able to understand "Lionese," resulting in a number of impasses and, to Marshall-Thomas especially, tense situations. Not being "understood," the lions intensified their vocalizations, roaring in frustration, sometimes for hours, until the Bushmen's stern exhortations for them to go away had their effect. Marshall-Thomas sees evidence for a sympathy bond between the lions and humans in the interest the lions appear to have in humans, whom they watch frequently and intently. She notes her own experience of being "studied" by a lioness that she was watching, both of them acting in a casual manner.

> In time I yawned. To my amazement, without taking her eyes off me she also yawned. Was it a coincidence, her enormous red gape? Was it empathy? Fascinated I deliberately yawned again. She yawned again! I yawned again and again. But I had done it too quickly. She simply watched me through half-shut eyes. I waited two to three minutes and then yawned once more. She yawned right away.

The author sees her theory of empathy and encounter between human and lion borne out by the fact that, with the exception of a small crippled girl, not one of the approximately fifteen hundred deaths people could recall over the previous one hundred years was caused by a lion. She notes that this is not the case regarding other predators, such as leopards and hyenas, who have caused human deaths. Toward them no relationship of respect is extended, nor any truce.

As I have suggested elsewhere (Guenther 1988; also see Biesele 1993: 88–92, 95), the reason for humans' consummate interest in animals is the basic ontological ambiguity of the animal, a being both very much like humans, and unlike them. The Bushman hunters are closely aware of both these traits, as animals are culturally elaborated (and their flesh culinarily appreciated) and they become creatures that inordinately fascinate people. Tracking, stalking, killing, and butchering has yielded a vast amount of knowledge and understanding of animals; anatomically Bushmen know animals inside out, they can read their tracks with uncanny accuracy (Lee 1979: 212–13), and they know an astonishing number of things about the behavior of a wide range of animal species (Blurton-Jones and Konner 1976; Heinz 1971, 1976/77, 1978a: 151–59, 1978/79; Heinz and Martini 1980; Lee 1979: 226–35; Silberbauer 1981: 63–77; Guenther 1988; Tanaka 1996), including insects (Nonaka 1996; Heinz 1981/82). In addition to the regular names these species hold, the !Kung also have a secret name each for the species hunted, which is used in certain situations by the hunters. One such situation is tracking a wounded animal, which requires circumspection lest the animal gain strength from the hunter's speech about it (Lee 1979: 206; Biesele 1993: 90).

The Bushmens' knowledge about animals is in excess of what is necessary for survival; for instance, Heinz 1978a: 152–53; also see Heinz and Martini 1980), in an examination of the ornithological knowledge of the !Xõ, is struck by how many of the birds on the !Xõ's checklist are devoid of economic importance. They have names for sixty-five of the seventy-seven birds seen during Heinz's investigation and know the rest by their songs. Heinz notes that they are able to distinguish by song species very similar in appearance, and that they are skilled at reproducing the song of each bird. The interest in small, obscure songbirds is also reflected in Bushman folklore, which, as seen in chapter 6, features these animals with relative frequency. That the people's interest in animals goes beyond their economic value is also revealed from the fact that a hunter in shooting range of an antelope—the most interesting of all species to Bushmen—might get so absorbed in his encounter with the animal that he may forget all about shooting it, until it is out of range, breaking what seems like a spell of enchantment (Blurton-Jones and Konner 1976: 334).

This supererogatory element pervading the Bushmen's interest in animals suggests that, beyond knowledge and exploitation of animals, the cognitive and interactive modes are understanding and encounter. Animals, to the hunter—as well as to the trance dancer, storyteller, and artist—may become "Significant Others," with whom and through whom a person may gain heightened understanding of himself or herself, as a "strange being," rather than the familiar social self. A Bushman hunter, in the presence of an antelope, may experience sentiments similar to what D. H. Lawrence experienced when encountering "A Doe in the Morning":

> I looked at her,
> And felt her watching;
> I became a strange being.[7]

That such may be an element of the Bushmen's cognitive processes about game animals is suggested by the bond of sympathy that a hunter feels toward his quarry, especially when stalking the animal after wounding it with a poison arrow (Lewis-Williams and Biesele 1978; Biesele 1993: 90–91). It is acute also at the outset of a hunt, manifesting itself in "sensations" in those parts or spots on the hunter's body that correspond to the quarry's salient anatomical traits; for instance, the springbok's horns, black facial stripes, and back hair. These create "tappings" on the hunter's head and face, and down his spine, as he contemplates his prey animal (Bleek and Lloyd 1911: 331–35; Hewitt 1986: 124–25; Guenther 1988: 192, 198–99). These mystical tappings, which the /Xam called the "Bushmen's letters" (and contrasted them with those found in European books), allowed the hunter to project himself into the animal and look at himself qua hunter, approaching his prey. He could "read" the animal, its actions and reactions, through this act of projection and empathy. The /Xam called the premonitions, and the practices of respect and sympathy that accompanied then, *!nanna-sse* (Bleek and Lloyd 1911: 271–83; Hewitt 1986: 124–29). It could be seen as another instance of the woman- (or hunter-) as-game-meat projection noted above, which heightens the human's sense of appreciation of the animal as a kindred being, at either the mythological or experiential level.

That kinship is evident in a number of ways. Humans and animals share the same anatomical plan; it is in evidence every time an animal is skinned and butchered, laying bare the subcutaneous anatomical homology between the hunter and the carcass. The understanding and encounter of animals has revealed them to the Bushmen as beings with sentience, morals, a social organization, and language, and as consisting of different tribes (or species) (Barnard 1980b; Silberbauer 1981: 63–77; Guenther 1983, 1988: 197; Kent 1989b: 12).

Some animals, such as the game species and baboons, possess the same mystical weather and curing powers (known in the !Kung language as *n!ow* and *n/um*) held by humans. These may affect humans, adversely or positively, thereby bringing animals within humans' deepest preternatural and ritual spheres. Such traits are attributed to actual veld animals, of the present order. Such symbolic acts of anthropomorphization link the wild animals of today more closely to the mythic human-animals of the first order; thus, echoes from the mythological past resound through the world of animals of the present. "The dividing line," Dorothea Bleek noted in a series of articles on /Xam notions of animals (1931–1932), "between mankind and the animal world is never very deep with the little hunters."

Yet, there are also differences. Animals do not have, for instance, the incest taboo, or any kin categories (Barnard 1980b). They are also different in their external, supercutaneous aspects, sporting horns and tails, trunks and tusks, stripes and spots, claws and wings. Notwithstanding a profoundly and extensively perceived similarity between man and beast, the latter are also very much other than human; they are also deeply strange and alien.

As already noted, this ambiguity may be what lies at the heart of the Bushmen's (and humankind's) fascination with animals (Guenther 1988). It has the potential also of creating feelings of ambivalence in people when they set out to hunt, kill, and eat animals, as such actions are metaphorical acts of cannibalism. As a wife or a hunter can be meat and game metaphorically, so game animals can be (and were once) human. When the Nharo eat game animals, whom they call *k"o /wani* ("little meat children"), this act is akin to the Inuit eating "souls," rather than seals (Briggs 1982: 115, citing Birket-Smith 1959: 166). The Inuit see this as a situation fraught with mystical danger, yet, all the while, they hunt animals with pleasure, enjoying especially the element of the kill. The Bushmen, too, enjoy hunting and seem unconcerned and not the least squeamish about killing the wounded and exhausted animal. Eating the flesh of most species likewise evokes nothing of the apprehensiveness it does among the Inuit. The eating of some species may be surrounded with circumspection and moral ambivalence, however, especially if the animal eaten (such as the elephant, among the !Kung) is *kaoqkoaq* (a "thing to be feared") and *tci dore* (a "bad, strange thing") (Biesele 1993: 150). Such animals people either will not eat at all, or they will do so warily.

The problem is that such animals are "too much like humans." This is the reason many Ju/'hoansi give to explain their refusal to hunt elephant, an animal believed to be "a person," possessing intelligence like a human, utilizing its trunk like a person uses his hands, and uttering human-sounding shrieks (Lee 1979: 234). Biesele's informants add to the list of human traits possessed by the elephant. The female has two breasts like a human, which stick out in the young animal, and hang down in the old; the males have penises like humans; elephant's skin is like that of a human, and at death the animal smells like a person (Biesele 1993: 149–50). Moreover, the elephant has both "people's flesh and bush-animal's flesh"; in short, "you don't eat it because it's like a person" (ibid.: 150).

The /Xam extended the same ambivalence toward such animal species as the baboon, the quagga, and the hare. Baboons have wives like humans; they have speech, as well as songs; and they understand the human language and call the Bushmen by their names. They have diseases like humans and medicines which also cure humans—a belief shared by the Nharo (Guenther 1986a: 237)—and, on their deaths, they make the same "cloud" as a dying human (see below for a discussion of *n!ow*). "Its actions are still like a man's, although it is a baboon" (Bleek 1931: 174). Killing this animal was dangerous to the hunter, as the "baboon's death would live in his bow" (ibid.: 174), and it was killed not for its flesh but to obtain its potent medicine called *sso/a* (ibid.: 168). Also, when a hunter shoots at it with an arrow, it will take the arrows and shoot them back at the hunter, as "it would also like to kill the man, because he seems to be trying to kill it" (ibid.: 174). The Nharo told me that they would never kill a baboon; to obtain the animal's medicines a curer would just follow the animal until it led him to the place where it grows. The baboon's belly resembles the quagga's and both animals "smell of people" (ibid.: 176). When butchering a hare, the /Xam evidently cut out and discarded a portion of its flesh, as it was not hare, but "human flesh" (Bleek and Lloyd 1911: 61). So treated, with the "human flesh" excised and its human essence exorcized, the /Xam would then eat the hare. They also ate quagga meat, especially the liver—raw, the same way the Jackal-Man of /Xam myth kills and eats his Quagga-Wife, especially relishing her liver (Hewitt 1986: 112–13). And while in /Xam mythology "little significance is given to these instances of apparent cannibalism," in terms of their moral impact on people, who told and listened to such stories, they were treated, according to Hewitt (ibid.: 113), "as curious and sometimes brutal absurdities."

Inasmuch as most animals were members of the Early Race in the First Order and Significant Others in the second one, moral ambivalence surrounds eating the flesh of all animals, rather than just the "special" ones deemed particularly close to humans. While greatly cherished, at the gustatory, gastrointestinal level, meat eating may thus be troubling at the moral, cultural–symbolic level. The many food taboos, most of them concerning meat, that are imposed on persons in symbolically marginal situations—children, old people, menstruating women, especially at menarche (Tanaka 1976: 112; Hewitt 1986: 279–86)—are, perhaps, recognition of the ambiguity of the animal they are applied to. The fact that humans and animals standing in the taboo relationship share the same liminal ontological state symbolically asserts their kindred nature.

Moral ambivalence about killing and eating animals reverberates also through the /Xam tale of the "Chaser of Food," a man of the Early Race who went around the veld beating and kicking game animals so that they would be afraid of humans and run away from hunters (Guenther 1989: 161–62). It echoes also through the above-mentioned Kxoe idea that the divine couple, the master and mistress of the animals and the bush, were vegetarians.

The way the Bushmen of today deal with the bloody business of killing, butchering, cooking, and eating animals is to focus on the "other-than" side of their being. Notwithstanding the aforementioned bond of sympathy, this is the foremost perspective hunters bring to bear on their quarry, thereby precluding any cosmologically and symbolically generated qualms about committing the abomination of cannibalism. In the context of a hunt, or the discussion preceding and following it—or "seminars" with the hunters about their animal knowledge that are arranged in the Kalahari by anthropologists (Blurton-Jones and Konner 1976)—their comments about animals may be detached and analytical. The two seminar leaders were struck by the prosaic, factual bent such discussions tended to hold, evident in the hunters' descriptive and inductive observations about animals, their distinction of observed facts from hearsay, and their avoidance of inference, as well as of magico-religious elements (Blurton-Jones and Konner 1976: 333, 344; also see Guenther 1986a: 251–52).

It should be noted that the hunters, when assuming the "other-than" attitude toward animals, are never so detached as to derive from this attitude the moral green light to hunt in the fashion of white safari hunters. Bushmen hunt for food, not for sport; even though an element of excitement accompanies the hunt, they "show respect to the game" (Bleek and Lloyd 1911: 271). I have heard Ghanzi Bushmen comment disdainfully about the wastefulness and senselessness of trophy hunting (see also Marshall 1976a: 136; Lee 1979: 207). The Bushman hunter's and meat eater's suspension of the "anthropomorphizing" perspective on animals could be seen, perhaps, as a "distancing device," designed to obfuscate, for the individual, the morally troubling repercussions of his own actions. Serpell (1986: 150–70) has distinguished between four such devices, in the context of the human–animal nexus in cultures worldwide: detachment, concealment, misrepresentation, and shifting the blame. In the context of Bushman culture, the device employed would seem to be a combination of the first three.

As meat and metaphor, animals fill the collective Bushman stomach and mind. They are eaten and talked about with relish and are as prominent in Bushman religious and expressive culture as they are, or once were, in the Kalahari landscape (Guenther 1988, 1989: 31, 86–87; Tanaka 1996: 21–26). In art, animals, especially the game antelopes, make up almost all of the images represented in the rock engravings, and about half of those in the paintings. The big species, such as the eland, gemsbok, and giraffe, were painted elaborately and in multiple colors, as against the smaller bucks, rendered in monochrome red. Animals continue to captivate the imagination of contemporary artists, such as the ones at the Kuru Development Trust in Ghanzi. In a sample of their work (received in 1991 in a preliminary analysis)—fifty-nine paintings and engravings—animals are the subject matter in thirty-three paintings. The species are predominantly antelopes (especially eland and gemsbok), as well as birds (predominantly raptors) and insects, caterpillars, and snakes (Guenther 1995a).

Storytellers dwell on those sections of a narrative that feature these animals. An example is the /Xam youth /A!kunta, who, in his lengthy rendition of the story of the Moon and the Hare (see chapter 5), lists all of the creatures the moon exhorts, as he contrasts his own immortality with the mortality of "things that walk the earth": antelopes, birds, carnivores, humans. Like the roll call of the animals entering Noah's Ark, the "flesh-things" are listed by species, twenty altogether. The selected passage leaves out those species for which Lloyd could not provide a translation—some with beguiling onomatopoeic names, such as the *//'koä*, the *!kon!kouru*, the *!koen/ku* and the *kwakwara*.

I die, I live; living, I come again;
I become a new moon.
Man dies; man, indeed, dies; dying he leaves his wife.
When I die, I return, living.
The gemsbok. The gemsbok dies, the gemsbok dies, altogether.
The hartebeest. The hartebeest dies, the hartebeest dies, altogether.
The she-ostrich. It dies, it indeed dies.
The kudu. The kudu indeed dies, and dying, it goes away.
The springbok. The springbok dies and, dying, it goes away forever.
Myself, I die; living again, I come back.
The korhaan [bustard]. The korhaan dies; the korhaan, dying, goes away.
The cat does [die]; it dies. The cat goes away, dying.
The jackal. The jackal dies; dying, the jackal goes away.
The lynx goes away, dying.
The hyena. The hyena dies, it goes away, dying, dying.
The eland. The eland dies and, dying, it leaves.
Myself, I die. Living again, I come back.
People see me; people say: "Look, the Moon does indeed lie here; it is grown, it is a Full Moon."
Things which are flesh must indeed die. . . .
(Guenther 1996c)

The !Kung, likewise, delight in enumerating the animals, in a "highly stylized, almost rhapsodic fashion." Here they differ dramatically from the hunters' relatively restrained and matter-of-fact style of discourse about animals they assumed during the animal "seminars" mentioned above. Biesele's account of how animals feature in Ju/'hoan storytelling (as well as everyday conversation), by a folklorist interested as much in the verbal surface of Bushman folklore as the meaning, fleshes out the /Xam storyteller's text and points to textural elements that suggest that animals were important not only for cosmological reasons but also for aesthetic ones:

> They count graphically and visually, putting successive fingers up to their lips as each animal's name is called. There is a certain way of stressing the syllables that appears in no other context. "*N!hoansi . . . /aosi . . . n!angsi . . . ≠oahsi,*" and so on. The list becomes a singsong. Almost, the eyes glaze over. The first syllable goes down in tone. The second, the pluralisation, goes up high and then comes down again, trailing off from near-singing into silence. People love to do it, and they count off the animals at every opportunity. (Biesele 1993: 61)

Another favorite and frequently told genre of animal tale is the telling of the hunt—one either recent or distant—sometimes after the event, while sitting around the cooking pots (as shown at the end of John Marshall's classic film *The Hunters*). Like animal details in folktales, such narratives portray the hunt "step-by-step, in microscopic and baroque detail" (Lee 1979: 205).

Animals are important elements of Bushman ritual. Trance curing dances (as well as recreational dances) are frequently named after an animal, usually a game antelope, which the person who first composed the song may have seen in a dream or vision and which he holds to be a source of healing potency into which the dancer will tap during his trance experience (Bleek 1931: 168–70; Lewis-Williams 1981: 83–100; Katz 1981: 39, 51; Brearley 1988; Guenther 1990a: 239–40; Biesele 1993: 93–94; Tanaka 1996: 22–23). Some of the dance steps may simulate the movement of the animal that is the mystical "sponsor" of the dance. As we will see in chapter 8, another moment at which animals become a prominent element of the trance dance is when the dancer undergoes transformation into a game antelope or a lion.

As we will see presently, the mystical curing power that is lodged inside the body of the trance dancer and the trance antelope (as well as in some plants [Köhler 1978/79: 35–36, 40–41]) can also be a killing power among some Bushmen, for instance the Kxoe. They hold the healing–killing potency *tcõ* to be so potent in game animals that a hunter has to undergo a purification rite after killing an antelope, to purge its dangerous effect on him (Köhler 1978/79: 43). Thus, in addition to being sources of medicine, animals can also cause disease, such as the springbok who can send disease arrows to the /Xam (Bleek and Lloyd 1911: 277), or the Spirit Keeper of the Animals, who will punish the Hei//om with disease if they abuse a game animal (Wagner-Robertz 1976: 539–40).

Some animals—for instance, the eland (among the /Xam)—were god's favorite animal and the being whereby he would impersonate himself (Lewis-Williams 1981: 117–26). At initiation rituals, as cogently argued by Lewis-Williams (1981: 41–74), the eland assumed, for the /Xam, the status of an *animal de passage*. As we will see in chapter 7, at menarche the eland provides the exterior form and symbolic substance for the widespread dance performed by elder men and women.

Animals, in fact, are frequent subjects for recreational dances, as well as games and spontaneous play, wherein certain species are impersonated and caricaturized (Marshall 1962: 314; Brearley 1988). The ludic approach toward animals that dwells on the whimsical traits of one or another species seems also to be evident in some paintings, which appear to be caricatures of the animal (Guenther 1984: 25–28).

Along the same ludic lines, there is the quite frequent use of an animal's name as a person's nickname (Guenther 1986a: 210–11). These serve to enhance individuality by reflecting a person's physical traits or behavioral idiosyncracies, or by referring to some singular event in the person's life. Examples from the Ghanzi farm Bushmen—among whom European terms (Wireless, Sixpence, Spitfire, Reliable) have begun to compete with animals as source material for nicknames—are *N/au* ("Duiker," in recognition of the bearer's skill at snaring this small antelope species), *N!abe* ("Giraffe," reflecting the bearer's long neck), *Tsara* ("Bird," a fairly common girl's name, reflecting a petite stature), and *G/aro* ("Ostrich," reflecting the person's gait). In addition to these rather common faunal nicknames are more specific ones, such as *Gwe k"i* ("Cow Face"), *//Auxa* ("Bull Hump"), */Xu //xama* ("Pig Hartebeest," reflecting the person's deep and hoarse voice), and *!Owe k"am tsara* ("Leopard's Saliva," in recognition of the bearer of this name having once been mauled by a leopard). Assigning this kind of nickname is a practice which simultaneously recognizes an animal's diagnostic traits and fosters an identification of a human with an animal. Blending an idiosyncratic anatomical or behavioral trait of a person with that of an animal renders both the person and the species the more salient.

There is another, mimicry-based mode of communicating about animals: hand signals. A large lexicon of such signals exists among some Bushman groups, used by hunters to identify different species of animal, communicate their sex and age, and signify some of the actions of stealthy, stalking hunters (Marshall 1976a: 136, 314; Silberbauer 1981: 209–11). Hand signals represent a further cognitive and expressive technique for symbolically and aesthetically processing animals.

Among the !Kung (Marshall 1957; Barnard 1992a: 58–59; Biesele 1993: 87–88), as well as, probably, the /Xam (Hewitt 1986: 138) and the Nharo (Guenther 1986: 234–35), one finds another concept of sympathy, linking humans not to animals but to the weather, specifically the wind and rain. The !Kung call it *n!ow* (*n!ao*) and the Nharo, who may have acquired the concept from their !Kung neighbors, refer to it as *//ga* (their word for the gusty winds that accompany a thunder storm). Among the /Xam, too, it was associated with wind, as well as clouds (Bleek and Lloyd 1911: 397–401). In a fashion akin to the pathetic fallacy in a Shakespearean tragedy, the presence of a rain storm or cold spell near or at a person's birth will form his or her particular *n!ow,* or mystical bond to the portentous meteorological event that accompanied the person's entry into the world. He remains in tune with his *n!ow* throughout his life and, upon his death, it will be unleashed one final time, sweeping through the land, blowing the thatch off people's huts and scattering their possessions. According to /Xam belief, not only does a person's wind blow, but the hair of his head turns into clouds (Bleek and Lloyd 1911: 397–99). Throughout their lives, certain individuals are held to be able to manipulate their *n!ow* through simple acts of sympathetic magic; for example, a person with rain *n!ow* may burn some of his hair or urinate in the fire, to cause the sky to form rain clouds and release water onto the hot land. Animals, too, may have *n!ow* and upon a game animal's death at the hands of a !Kung hunter its *n!ow* may interact with that of the hunter, causing the requisite weather condition. As noted above, baboons, according to the /Xam, "make clouds" when they die, just like humans.

Being the Significant Others they are in Bushman cosmology—beings who are close to humans physically and mystically despite their otherness, beings talked about frequently, literally or metaphorically, prosaically or poetically, in everyday parlance or oral literature, beings represented through art, ritual, dance, and mimicry—it is perhaps not surprising that some humans should have the ability to assume animals' identities. The eland dance referred to above may be so intense and self-absorbing a ceremony that one wonders if the performer may not, at certain moments, actually feel as though he or she has transcended his or her species boundary and assumed the identity of the animal that lends its name and symbolic substance to the dance (and stands as the favorite Bushman game species, identified—symbolically and, in a number of Bushman languages, also semantically—with rain, the Bushman's favorite natural phenomenon).

Ambiguity of Bushman Religion: Social and Cultural Factors

How can we account for the ambiguous quality of Bushman religion, especially religious belief? In searching for an answer to this key question, I will turn to Bushman social organization and ethos. As seen in the previous chapter, the nonreligious domains of Bushman society are themselves shot through with ambiguity and fluidity. Thus, when these traits appear within cosmology, belief, and ritual, there are no extra-religious social-structural forces at work to counteract the anti-structural quality of the religious sphere. Inasmuch as religion is everywhere grounded in experience, in the case of the Bushmen the social matrix that provides the ground is itself fluid. The fluidity of social organization and the ambiguity of religion are structurally consistent and mutually reinforcing.

There are several interrelated structural elements of Bushman society and culture that have a bearing on the condition of ambiguity and fluidity of the society's belief system. Social-structural factors are such things as fragmentation of society, absence of specialization, low degree of political organization, lack of formal socialization, and high degree of individualism and individuation. In addition to these "social" factors are such "cultural" ones as the nonexistence of "religion" and "cosmology" as emic categories of thought, the absence of writing, and the influence of acculturation. I will discuss these factors in turn.

A third set of factors, to be considered in the conclusion, are not structural but methodological. The issue here is whether the confusion and diversity of Bushman religion may be a function of a diverse, at times contradictory, number of theoretical and interpretive paradigms being brought to bear on Bushman religion, sometimes by researchers with scant ethnographic data and even scanter linguistic facility.

Social-Structural Factors

The fluid composition of Bushman social groups and the frequent movements of group members, as well as the relative isolation of bands or band clusters from one another, likely contribute to the fragmentation of belief patterns. These conditions would lead to the development of regional religious "dialects," as well as to personal idiosyncrasies in the package of beliefs of individuals. Individuals and groups may range widely, taking people to different regions and even different linguistic groupings, as well as to non-Bushman groups, adding yet different elements to a person's or group's religious brew. A striking illustration of the latter is provided by the Ju/'hoan man //Gaugo, who picked up a mine compound dance during his employment as a mine laborer in Johannesburg. Back home at /Xai /Xai, //Gaugo formed his own version of the dance which he called the "Trees Dance," blending old with new traits, such as the dancer's pair of assistants, which he named "Bossboy" and "Foremana." The dance became a hit in the Dobe–Nyae Nyae region in the late 1960s (Lee 1993: 121). Thus, due to the openness and fluidity of groups and the unsettled nature of group members, beliefs are prevented from coalescing, remaining instead fluid and unstructured.

The strong individualism of Bushman ethos further contributes to the development of interpersonal variation. Each individual picks up his or her own version of beliefs, early as well as later in life, in his own way and at her own pace. Children listen to the stories people tell, in a learning context that is informal, while adults who have had the experience of trance draw from this altered state of consciousness their own religious and cosmological—at times dreamlike and surreal—visions and notions. In fact, among the Nharo it may be a certain dream or a number of dreams that provide individuals with their version of beliefs concerning such things as the names and nature of divinity (especially the trickster-god) and the physiological or mystical nature of the soul and its fate after death (Guenther 1986a: 241–45). The beliefs related to the last point may range from the soul's dissolution into nothingness, through its manifestation in different types of ghosts, to an elaborate afterlife (the features of which were described earlier). Highly varied as well are explanations of disease and the physiological and mystical ways for treating one or another disease (Guenther 1986a: 240–47).

When individuals bring their own views and visions into conversation and into their narratives when stories are told, they generally receive rapt attention from an audience that enjoys hearing a good tale and appreciates the embellishments and twists an individual storyteller may apply to the story. Megan Biesele was impressed by how much the !Kung appreciate individualism in storytelling, as well as in general conversation, and by their propensity to grant "great latitude for individual artistry" (Biesele 1993: 66). Indeed, the substance of an individual's narrative may so intrigue listeners that they adapt it into their own stories, duly altering it to fit their idiosyncratic versions (Guenther 1996c). In this fashion variation is created on an ongoing basis, in dialectic and dialogic interplay among creative and expressive individuals, who employ the elements of their expressive culture—conversation, storytelling, dancing, singing, painting—as modes of individuation. I return to this matter in chapter 5, in which

I explain the astonishing range of variations of one tale largely with reference to the factor of individualism.

In addition to altering the specific images, motifs, or tales of local belief patterns through idiosyncratic twists, an individual may also radically change entire expressive genres: for example, styles of painting or beadwork, which show regional variation (Rudner and Rudner 1978; Wiessner 1984), or forms of song and dance.

The importance of the individual in the development of an item of expressive culture within the group and region can be illustrated with the example of the giraffe curing dance of the !Kung, as reported by Megan Biesele (1993: 67–69). Thanks to her long-standing research among the Ju/'hoansi, Biesele was able to trace the inception of their most popular song, the Giraffe song, to an old woman named Beh. She was able to interview and film Beh, just before the old woman's death. Biesele learned from her that decades back, probably in the early 1950s, the song had come to Beh in a vision—of a herd of thundering giraffes whose rolling hoof beats mingled with the thunder of a sudden rain. The composition quickly replaced the song currently enjoying popularity, after Beh's husband /Ti!kay had recognized his wife's production as a medicine song. As such he developed it (Lee 1993: 117), so that he was the actual inventor of the curing dance, from a song first created by his wife. It spread rapidly eastward, to Botswana, and by the late 1960s, when I was in Ghanzi, it was the top hit of curing songs and dances of the district (Guenther 1986a: 255). Throughout the 1970s and 1980s the giraffe dance appears to have continued its spread southward and is reported by Jiro Tanaka (1996: 27) to have reached the G//ana and G/wi at Xade by 1989, and to have become the predominant "hunting dance" among all of the Kalahari Bushman groups.

In Ghanzi, where trance dancing is more elaborate than among the Ju/'hoansi, a variety of songs and dances other than the giraffe dance were performed in the 1960s and 1970s (Guenther 1986a: 254). These originated in the same way, with individual dancers, and the impact of a curer's dance on the repertoire of other curers would differ, depending on its popularity, its reputed efficacy, and the incumbent renown of its originator. I also noticed highly individualized dance routines among the dancers (Guenther 1986a: 256–57). As for the singing by the women, as noted by Dorothea Bleek among the Nharo at Sandfontein (1928: 22), "the time is perfect but no two in a chorus seem to hit the same note." Yet, "the general burden of the tune is kept up," as all of the singers "go up together, and all go down together, each hitting any note they please." No singer, Bleek points out, ever seemed to hit the same note twice. The performance style of the women's trance dance song expresses in crystallized form the nature of Bushman expressive culture, the balance between individual freedom of expression and collective constraints thereon that derives from the group context provided by the performance setting.

As an individual brings his or her personal, at times quite idiosyncratic, stamp to bear on a certain item of belief, ritual, or art, before a receptive audience which responds well to innovative twists, the religious and expressive repertoire of the group becomes altered, enhancing the diversity of this field of culture. At the same time, as a result of positive audience feedback, the individuality of the performer is reinforced. Encouraged to be all the more creative in the delivery of his or her performance, the storyteller or dancer becomes thereby all the more individuated, as a result of the group's appreciative acceptance of his or her expressive uniqueness. Creativity leads to innovation, enhancing the range of diversity of the culture's symbolic and expressive elements.

The process of defining and reinforcing an individual's identity and self-awareness is especially evident with respect to the trance dance, which is an exceptionally potent individuating force, by virtue of its element of altered states. In being "melted away into the other-world"—as Jiro Tanaka described the experience, which he himself went through (1996: 27)—trance enables the dancer to go "beyond his ordinary self by becoming more himself, or by becoming more than himself" (Katz 1976: 287). Katz notes how one dancer, after not having danced for a number of weeks, explained his desire to do so again soon by saying: "I can really become myself again." (ibid.). Katz takes this comment to mean that "he wanted to experience again what he felt was his more essential self." The experience of trance takes a person beyond his ordinary, worldly, and social reality, presumably dissolving his social self—as mediated and defined by the others he engages in social interaction—and defining his "essential self." The process of individuation has its wellspring within that second, inner, "I"-focused self, defining and confirming an individual's unique identity and capacity.

Another source of change and diversity in the trance dance is its lack—among non-acculturated Bushmen—of specialization or professionalization. Instead of being an esoteric rite that can be performed only by a select few, it is generally open and accessible to a large number of adult men and women, who are able, with varying degrees of adeptness, to perform the dance, and to achieve trance and cure. Thus, the aforementioned low degree of status differentiation on the political front is found equally at the ritual front; just as almost anyone can be a headman, so one out of two men and one in three women can be trance dancers. As a diffuse ritual practice shared by a wide range of people, its belief elements have become widely divergent.

The low degree of ritual specialization is possibly another factor explaining the fluidity and diversity of Bushman belief. The absence of ritual specialists deprives Bushman culture of its "religious formulators" (Radin 1957): custodians, as it were, of belief, myth, and lore. In such a capacity they would render systematic and intelligible the culture's complex beliefs, as well as transmit those "packaged" beliefs to other individuals and across generations. There is an element of teaching and learning to the trance dance, in that a person is usually trained to become a healer, by either a relative who has *n/um,* or an unrelated dancer (Guenther 1986a: 263; Lee 1993: 117). However, each of these teachers is himself an individualist with his own idiosyncratic program, who teaches an apprentice who will soon leave him, setting forth to do his own ritual thing.

The lack of political organization and the concurrent absence of any institutionalization of power, also means that religion in Bushman society is freed from one of its most essential and universal roles in society: the legitimization of power. Wherever power is wielded in human society, religion is co-opted in order to "celestialize" that power, through more or less subtle, covert or overt, means. In societies where there are no power institutions such as chiefs, kings, elites, classes, or governments, or where these are rudimentary, religion loses what is frequently its key raison d'être. Ritual can turn away from the affairs of state, toward altered states, and perform trance and healing rites instead of rites of installation or rebellion, both of the latter again directed at the powers that be and each serving its own hegemonic end. Myth, too, is able to remain within its proper, mythic time, where order is inchoate and power absent, rather than be called upon to spin out charter myths that legitimate temporal order and power. In short, religion can be disengaged from social and political reality, hover above it in a state of suspended animation, allowing its form and content to be surreal, amorphous, and fluid (Guenther 1979a).

Another reality-related function that baroque functionalism attributes to religion plays a reduced role in the Bushman case, namely its function as a coping mechanism in the face of misfortune. The Bushmen undeniably do experience their own share of "the real tragedies of human life and the conflict between human plans and realities" (Malinowski 1948: 71)—which to Malinowski is what has brought about religion and sustains it in human life and society. Yet, the fact that the resources of the Kalahari environment are modestly abundant, that the people's state of health is relatively sound, and that they are resourceful and effective in dealing with conflict (which they smother through laughter rather than confrontation) all conspire to undermine the function of religion as an antidote to existential and social adversity.

Cognitive-Cultural Factors

Another reason for the ambiguity of religion may be, simply, that it is not defined in Bushman culture as a separate domain, with a distinctive "perspective" (Geertz 1966: 24–40) and singular concerns, states, and beings. The Bushmen are not unique in this respect; as I have argued elsewhere (Guenther 1979a: 125–26), anthropologists have long recognized the fact that "religion," as a distinct cultural and experiential category, may be a Judaeo-Christian construct projected, willy-nilly, onto non-Western societies, distorting understanding of their cultures and religions (Saliba 1976/77: 181–82). In such societies religion may be undefined as an institutional complex or a separate cultural reality, and instead may be diffused through the other cultural subsystems and the people's experiential reality. Yet, this diffuse quality of Bushman religion, from the perspective of the rationalist and dualist idiom of Western belief systems, is likely to go unnoticed, along with the other cardinal religious traits: ambiguity, fluidity, and variability. I will return to this point again in the next chapter, on the trickster, a figure that has suffered considerable distortion as a result of projection and conflation with a Christian model, namely Jesus Christ, or his adversary, Satan.

Another cultural factor that may partially account for the ambiguity of Bushman religion has to do with the cognitive style whereby Bushmen transmit information. This is oral; unlike the written style, which is fixed, orality, by its very nature, creates variation. This, according to Jack Goody (1992: 15), is because of the innovation each performer brings to the performance (of storytelling), shaping the traditional text, which he remembers only selectively, to his present interests. Consequently, the storyteller, not remembering a narrative element correctly, will substitute one that is functionally equivalent. This mechanism of variation is so inherent a part of oral transmission that the folklorist Sigrid Schmidt calls it a "law of oral narration" (1995: 167). Goody also rejects, for lack of "justification in practice or theory," the structuralist-rationalist notion that each performance is a "deviation from a disembodied ideal or that hidden continuity lies at the level of deep structure" (ibid.: 17). Instead, what is produced from performance to performance is wanton variation, unstrictured by structure. I will return to this dynamic of change and variation of Bushman myth and lore in chapter 5.

Megan Biesele has examined the nature of orality—by nature "protean, changing, and often puzzlingly contradictory"—in Ju/'hoan expressive and mental culture[8] (1993: 51–67). Their oral tradition—like that of oral cultures generally—consists of variants "as uncountable as the grains of sand" (ibid.: 65). Among other things, she notes how oral texts evince a greater propensity for being metaphorical and oblique, confounding any straightforward attempts at interpretation (Biesele 1993: 52). The interpretation problem is all the more difficult with respect to the Ju/'hoansi, given that people's strong metaphorical bent (ibid.: 23–27). "Metaphor permeates Ju/'hoan expressive life," writes Biesele (ibid.: 23), "which in a few words can be characterized as highly oblique, indirect, and allusive." Another significant observation she makes is that people in cultures based on orality may consider communicated messages as being "the same," despite differences in verbal content. Outsiders such as anthropologists or folklorists coming from a culture with writing might perceive only the differences, and gain the impression that people's ideas and beliefs are much more varied in their meaning than is the case from the native perspective. This tendency Biesele attributes in part to the outsider's culture of writing, which directs the Westerner to concentrate not on the message as such but on "words *per se*," "a phenomenon of alphabetic literacy which has long distorted our understanding of communication in oral societies" (ibid.: 67). Orality constitutes a sort of "meta-language" for the members of the oral culture to which the visitor from the written culture is not attuned.

Another element of the cognitive style of Bushman mental culture that may affect their thoughts, comments, and actions about religion is their alleged prosaic bent, which has received comment from a number of writers, such as Lebzelter (1934: 24), who attributes the lack of imagination and fantasy of the !Kung to the well-honed empirical bent of these *scharfe Naturbeobachter* ("keen observers of nature") (see also Bleek 1928: 41; Heinz 1978; Blurton-Jones and Konner 1976: 344). It is in evidence even in the trance dance, for all its mystical aspects. Its pragmatic side, to Heinz (1975a: 28), lies in the !Xõ's realization that the cure the dance provides is none too efficacious for persons who are seriously ill. Such patients are not treated by dancers. As an example, Heinz points to the smallpox epidemics, victims of which were evidently not treated by !Xõ trance dancers. A prosaic mind-set seems to underlie Lee's observation that "Ju do not spend their time in philosophical discourse in the abstract" (Lee 1993: 114). Similarly, the G/wi tend not to "ponder the nature of N!odimo" or hypothesize about his attributes (Silberbauer 1965: 95). Instead, people get on with the "concrete matters of life and death, health and illness in their daily lives" (Lee 1993: 114). Being thus not given to reflection about their religious beliefs, the people are less likely to notice, think through, and iron out its inherent ambiguities and contradictions. In this respect the Bushmen are similar to other tribal cultures, the classic example being the Azande (Evans-Pritchard 1937: 127–28, 318–19).

On the basis of my own fieldwork among the Nharo, I am suspicious of this characterization of the Bushmen. While I, too, found some individuals that could be deemed "prosaic," there were others with a reflective bent, as well as an interest in "philosophical" questions, who at times engaged me in extensive conversation about such issues as the nature and difference between body and soul, life after death, the ontological and moral makeup of //Gãũwa, moral and political issues pertaining to the apartheid system of the Boers, and many other topics. Like so much else that is reported about Bushman mental culture, such a characterization is subjective and impressionistic, and, as I will argue more fully in the conclusion, possibly a projection of the observer's own mind-set.

"Foraging for Ideas": The Factor of Acculturation

The Bushmen have adopted, and adapted to, a wide range of religious traits from neighboring Bushman and non-Bushman groups, as a result of their mobility and openness as a society and people, and their flexible and nondogmatic ethos and religious ideology. "Religious tolerance" is extended toward individual members adopting new religious patterns and experiences (Biesele 1993: 47), as well as toward outside religious practices and beliefs. As Alan Barnard points out, a characteristic trait of Bushman myth and belief is "that ideas can pass from one group to another, from one system to another," traveling "across linguistic, cultural and environmental boundaries" (Barnard 1992a: 261). And, in being moved across Bushmanland by mobile foragers, the ideas, beliefs, and stories are locally adapted and newly interpreted and recreated, so that they fit the "current emotional needs and imaginations of the people who are now living" (Marshall 1962: 233; also see Gusinde 1966: 55 and Jolly 1996: 278–79).

Just as they opportunistically forage for plants and game—picking up and bringing home whatever comes their way, at times while venturing through neighboring band territories, as well as the cattle camps, villages, and towns of black and white settler groups—people forage for ideas (Guenther 1996d: 73–74). Each individual, family, or camp adds new features that come their way to the store of religious beliefs and practices each holds individually or collectively, compounding diversity and complexity, as well as contradiction. Even in the beliefs of isolated groups, such as the !Kõ (Heinz 1975a: 32–34), one can come across Bantu as well as Christian trace elements, reflecting the people's mobility and receptivity to outside ideas. There may be just one individual in a remote band who starts telling a strange story he picked up on a distant journey from which he has just returned, perhaps from a person who himself hailed from a distant place, such as the itinerant preacher who provided one of Barnard's storytellers with the tale of the Tower of Babel (1992a: 261). Such a scenario is analogous to the case of the leather-clad !Xõ individual Phillip Tobias (pers. comm.) came across in the 1950s in a remote region of the Kalahari in whose mouth he found a tooth filling. He had received it from a mobile dentist years earlier, when he was visiting kin in the Ghanzi farming block.

It is probably impossible to sort out which Bushman group obtained what trait from which group at what time, as some earlier writers attempted to do in the 1930s when such "culture-historical" studies were in vogue (Schmidt 1933: 539–695; Hirschberg 1933; Schapera 1930: 177–95, 195–99). Later anthropologists dealt with other, more "synchronic" issues; however, some continued the effort to make sense of Bushman religion by differentiating between genuine and derived traits, by tracing out the possible inter-tribal Bushman and non-Bushman connections, especially with respect to the myriad names and attributes of god and the gods (Marshall 1962: 223–25, 233; Gusinde 1966: 39–77). Such an undertaking is extremely difficult, in part because there is very little information on the migration and movements of bands and linguistic groups within a region; in part, because the "Common Bushman" core of beliefs that constitutes the benchmark for differentiating indigenous from derived items is too varied and fluid to serve as a standard for evaluation. Summing up his own "which-is-what" exercise, Gusinde declared !Kung religion to be a "vielfältiges Durcheinander von Ideen und Gebräuchen, aus mehrfachen Richtungen hier und dort zusammengetragen" ("a multiplex mix-up of ideas and practices, gathered together here and there, from several directions") (ibid.: 10).

As regards Khoekhoe, as well as Bergdama (Wagner-Robertz 1976: 533–56), influences on the religion of the Bushmen, the tendency today is to treat the two groups not as discrete socio-economic and cultural entities but as one people and culture. Its Khoi and San elements have become variously blended, in different regions of southern Africa, as a result of a long and varied history of contact between and migration of the two constituent, nomadic peoples (Barnard 1992a, chap. 2). Even Schapera, who subscribed to a "two peoples" view, found "striking resemblances" in the religion of the two groups (Schapera 1930: 395–99). Writing about Khoisan folklore sixty years later, Biesele (1993: 34–37) notes that the two traditions are "practically indistinguishable."

In the same vein, I have distinguished a "Khoisan Religious Tradition" (Guenther 1989: 33; also see Barnard 1988, 1992a: 251–63) from other religious traditions of Africa, especially with respect to its low development of ritual and ceremonialism—which are elaborate components of the neighboring Bantu religions, manifested in such ritual patterns as ancestor worship, agricultural rites, installation ceremonies, divination, magic, witchcraft, and sorcery (for example, see Schapera 1953: 58–66). The core elements of the Khoisan tradition, which are abstracted from a multifaceted, fluid, and highly variable complex of beliefs, are a dual notion of divinity; a trickster figure who is both protagonist and god; vaguely defined spirits of the dead; a cosmogonic notion of an early order of existence and race of people, and its transformation into the present order; a closeness to animals, who are significant economically, mystically, and symbolically; ritual trance, both as a curing technique that draws on a mystical force or potency and as a means for transformation and transcendence; and male and female initiation rites (Guenther 1989: 33–36, Barnard 1992a: 252).

Most of the Bushman groups have Bantu-speaking neighbors and in many instances the social and economic contact—at times, contract—between the two groups has been of long standing, going back one or two centuries (as in eastern Botswana, northern Namibia). This interaction and exchange has brought not only material goods to the Bushmen, but also beliefs and ideas, as well as ritual practices. Thus, some of the Kxoe and !Kung Bushman groups of northeastern Namibia, east of the Okavango, who have had extensive contact with Mbukushu and Tawana peoples, have a rich complex of magic and notions of witchcraft, as well as a belief in ancestral spirits and a variety of ritual patterns. The latter include such elements as prayer, libation of food and tobacco, propitiatory "first fruit" rites, and the use of large drums in the curing dance (Lebzelter 1934: 48; Gusinde 1966: 30–32, 33, 42; Köhler 1978/79: 25–26, 28–37), as well as bodily mutilation consisting of the chipping of the upper two central incisors, either for aesthetic or ritual reasons, the latter to allow the person's spirit to escape at his death (Huruwitz 1956: 22). Contact between the southeastern Bushmen, east and west of the Drakensberg, with Nguni and Sotho peoples has left its mark on the rock art and ritual practices of the former people (Jolly 1996). The practices of the latter people include the removal of part of the little finger (Lebzelter 1934: 103) and circumcision, a practice (likely derived from Bantu speakers) also reported among some of the Northern and Eastern Khoe (Dornan 1925: 158–60; Almeida 1965: 32–36; also see Barnard 1992a: 131–32).

The Nharo of Ghanzi, as well as the Khoe and !Kung of Schmidtsdrift, have incorporated Bantu-derived witchcraft and sorcery beliefs into their culture (Guenther 1992a; Vorster 1994, 1995), and practice some forms of divination (Guenther 1986a: 251–52; see also Eibl-Eibesfeldt 1973: 247). The latter ritual pattern is not employed to any large extent, however, and is not as integral a component of decision making in puzzling or uncanny situations as it is among the neighboring Tswana. As Dorothea Bleek observed of Nharo divination two generations earlier, it is "very babyish" in its practice; people go on throwing the divining pieces "until they get a favourable answer" (Bleek 1928: 28). Talking about Bushmen in general, Bleek notes that the frequency in the use of divination coincides with the degree of Bantu influence to which a certain Bushman tribe has been exposed (Bleek 1929: 29; see also Schapera 1930: 201). Yet, the divination practices observed among the relatively unacculturated G/wi and !Kõ seem to be quite different from any Bantu pattern. They incorporate a mystical element from the trance dance, consisting of pressing the oracular bones to the armpits and moistening them with sweat or saliva (Eibl-Eibesfeldt 1973: 247). This may suggest either that divination is an indigenous Bushman trait or that, like witchcraft patterns, it has been creatively integrated within the indigenous religious complex.

Another religious concept found among some of the eastern and northern "Khoe Bushmen" is totemism (Dornan 1917: 53; Barnard 1992a: 125–26). It would seem to be very much a non-Bushman ritual pattern, as the elements of segmentary kinship and social organization to which totemism is structurally linked are absent from Bushman society. For this reason Dornan describes it as rudimentary and suggests that it is of Bantu, specifically Tswana, origin (also see Schapera 1930: 85). However, unlike the Tswana pattern (Schapera 1953: 35), totemism among the northeastern Bushmen defines exogamous units (called "clans" by Dornan) through such animal species (or animal parts) as eland, impala, zebra, hare, hippopotamus, elephant, crocodile, lion, ostrich, monkey, dog, cow, and "heart (or testicle) of goat" (Cashdan 1986: 147, 170). As with the Tswana pattern (Schapera 1953: 35), members of a totemic group observe an ideology of refraining from eating the flesh of their totem animal (Cashdan ibid.: 170). The discrepancies between the Bushman and Bantu patterns of totemism suggest to Barnard (1992a: 126) that the former may have an earlier origin, prior to Bantu contact.

Other elements of belief that show outside influence are names for divinities, myth, and lore. As shown by Schapera (1930: 190–92), a number of names for god reveal Christian influence, reaching Bushman groups via the Khoekhoe or the Tswana, whose Christian-derived names for god—Elob and Modimo, respectively—found their way into Bushman theology. While the folklore traditions of the Bantu-speaking peoples of southern Africa differ from those of the Bushmen in a number of significant ways—for example, by being less surrealist, more moralizing, and more closely linked to power holders[9]—it nevertheless has left its mark on Bushman oral traditions (Biesele 1993: 32). Biesele (ibid.) suggest that the story motif of the hunter entering the other world through a hole might be Bantu in origin. The hare and the rare spider trickster figures in the tales of some Bushman storytellers are very likely Bantu characters (Guenther 1989: 139–43; Tanaka 1996: 27; also see Roberts 1989: 22–30), as are the "All-Devourer" ogre figure of the /Xam (Schmidt 1973: 120) and the chameleon messenger figure (Schmidt ibid.: 116) in some of the Khoisan-wide origin of death myths (see chapter 5). The trickster person of Jackal, and his sidekick and dupe, Hyena—so prominent in the stories of the Ghanzi farm Bushmen (Guenther 1989: 132–34)—are found also among the Herero and Ovambo in Namibia (Arnold 1987: 44–49, 81–96), as well as among other Bantu-speaking groups in that country (Knappert 1981: 166). The story of the tar baby trapping the stock or vegetable thief (Guenther 1989: 135; Schmidt 1989, 2:200–201) is found also in Bantu folklore (Seiler-Dietrich 1980: 237–39; Knappert 1981: 167), as well as among African Americans, from their earliest slave days (Roberts 1989: 41–42). However, this may not necessarily make it a Bantu item; as shown by Schmidt (1989, 2:200–201), the tale is found also in the story repertoire of Nama and Dama storytellers, and their children may read the story in an Afrikaans school anthology, in which the central element of the tale appears as *teerpop*.

Another extra-Bushman source of belief and myth is the religion and folklore of the Europeans. It is mediated directly through missionaries, Boer farmers who hold devotional services with their Bushmen on Sundays, or schoolbooks; and indirectly through other converted Bushmen or Bantu. Thus, the exposure of Bushmen to Christian notions is usually sporadic and often second- or thirdhand. Their sources on this or that idea might have been another Bushman, a Boer farmer, or a Christian Tswana or Herero. The Christian names or notions I found in the mouths of farm Bushmen with whom I talked about religion were the following: Adam and Eve; Mary and Joseph; a "good place" and a "bad place" to which people will go after death, depending on their actions throughout their lives; the notions of sin, soul, and miracle (especially the resurrection of Lazarus); the Tower of Babel (Guenther 1989: 45–46, 50, 71; Barnard 1992a: 262). There is general awareness of the sacraments of baptism and communion, as well as of Christ's Last Supper. These latter two Christian features, along with Christ's miraculous feeding of the multitudes, presumably strike a cultural chord with the Bushmen because of the element of commensality and food sharing which is one of the pillars of Bushman ethos. Baptism is likened to the Bushmen's own initiation rites (*/ri kaxu*). "Kissmes" (Christmas), too, is well known. The Ghanzi Bushmen's familiarity with this Christian festival precedes the arrival of the mission church (in the mid-1960s), as the local Boer and English farmers, who arrived in Ghanzi from the Cape in the late 1890s, have always included their Bushman farm laborers and their families in the celebration. This involved the giving of presents, including the slaughtering of the "Christmas Ox," as well as holding an outdoor devotional service on Christmas day for the Bushmen, in their village. The latter was conducted every Sunday by the more pious farmers (Guenther 1979b: 97; Russell and Russell 1979: 95).

As I have shown more fully elsewhere (Guenther 1997c), I found a wide range of variation in the Christian beliefs and ideas farm Bushmen talked about. They spanned all three of Firth's (1964: 261) levels of personal understanding and variation of belief, from the "core" ("firmly held and in essentials usually simple to state"), through "ancillaries" ("personal variation of a fluctuating kind"), to "periphery" ("vague, involving either difficulty of formulation or lack of clarity and conviction"). The first would apply to catechists and recent converts, as well as residents at the mission station and active church members; the remaining farm Bushmen would fall into the other two categories in equal numbers. For them Jesus Christ is frequently a "person of great difficulty." In order for them to make sense of this figure, as well as of other elements of the new religion, these new ideas are filtered through the mesh of their traditional belief system. Indeed, in that process of redefinition these borrowed beliefs may lose their quality of newness. Personal understanding of such items moves up from the periphery, to the ancillary or even core position; so much so, in fact, that some informants would comment on them with the greatest authority and confidence, claiming, in some instances, that what they were telling they heard from their parents and grandparents, that it stemmed from the "old, old, old people." Thus, "great difficulty" gives way to clarity as Jessu Kriste takes the place of Jesus Christ, the complexities and uncertainties pruned away from the latter figure.

As shown in a number of revealing texts collected by Sigrid Schmidt among the Nama and Dama of Namibia (1970, 1977, 1985, 1991; see also Biesele 1993: 35–37), the influence of European tales on Khoekhoe folklore has been pervasive. Stories featuring such standard figures as Cinderella, Tom Thumb, Hänsel and Gretel, Red Riding Hood, Snow White, and Howleglass (Eulenspiegel) have become so integral a part of the narratives of the contemporary descendants of the Khoekhoe that storyteller and audience may be quite unaware that what they tell and hear is anything other than "stories of the old people." However, one should note that it is not always clear whether the similarities in plot and character are due to historical diffusion or spurious coincidence. For instance, while a number of the Jackal-trickster tales were likely modeled on the European Reynard the Fox (Bleek 1864; Schmidt 1980: 224–25), other jackal tales in the Khoisan corpus seem to bear little resemblance to the European Reynard, being, in some instances, devoid even of the trickster element (Guenther 1989: 147).

European elements have also found their way into the oral repertoire of Bushman storytellers. This has come about either indirectly, through the connection of Bushman folklore with that of the related Khoekhoe, or directly, via stories from local European settlers (Guenther 1989: 45–46, 50, 71; Barnard 1992a: 261). Again, they are usually presented as *hua* ("old stories"), having been foraged from the outside and molded to Bushman textual and textural standards.

The most recent evidence of amalgamation, within the expressive culture of contemporary Bushmen, of old and own with new and derived is provided by the work of contemporary Bushman artists at Dekar and Schmidtsdrift, in Botswana and South Africa, respectively (Guenther 1995a, 1998). The paintings and prints depict a shreds-and-patches collage of foraged motifs. They range from "traditional" ones such as veld animals—painted in either "natural," whimsical, or even "traditional rock art" styles—as well as veld plants and trees and gathering women and hunting men, to "modern" ones such as trucks, minibuses, helicopters, hunting or army rifles, soldiers, army tents, raid scenes, crosses and angles, houses, kitchen utensils, chairs, cups, pails, bottles, radios, jeans, boots, buttons, numbers and letters, identity cards, fishes, and one dinosaur! The latter the artist had seen on the back cover of a telephone book, in a phone booth in Durban, on an exhibition trip to that city. Such motifs are frequently combined or juxtaposed, creating whimsical or disjunctive compositions: two fighting Boers and bemusedly onlooking veld birds, a helicopter surrounded by antelopes, elephants and antelopes standing or bounding through the backyard of a European city home, a dancer in rigid trance pose around whom swirl a slew of buttons. The artists all obtained their idiosyncratic set of motifs in the course of their own lifetimes—from people met, places visited, things seen, stories heard—creating a rich body of art, highly varied and disparate, at times strangely fractured and seemingly discordant. The hybrid, de-centered, montage- or collage-like collective oeuvre of the modern Bushman artists strikes the onlooker as decidedly postmodern. As I have argued elsewhere (1995a), the art can be seen as a counter-hegemonic discourse on such "modernity" as affects the contemporary Bushmen living on White- or Black-owned ranches, or in government settlements and army tent cities (as at Schmidtsdrift), whereby select traditional elements of culture and of the new economic, social, and political reality are expressed or embraced and newly configured, all in an effort to make sense of that new reality and to find a place and space within it.

The acculturative process whereby a Bushman derives select religious and narrative elements from the store of beliefs and tales of neighboring bands and non-Bushman settler groups both stems from and contributes toward a loose, flexible, and tolerant ethos and belief system. Paralleling the openness with which outside individuals and groups are allowed to utilize a band's own food resources, outsiders are also given leave to forage the group's mental resources. In both processes the spirit of sharing and reciprocity prevails, especially in the exchange of ideas between fellow Bushman bands and tribes. With respect to the non-Bushman groups from whom Bushmen draw material, the borrowing process may be more unilateral; however, as shown by Schmidt and Biesele in the cited works, Blacks and Whites have both also adopted Khoisan elements into their respective bodies of folklore. In the course of this receptive and reciprocal interaction, individuals and their ideas—and the cultural field of belief and myth from which they derive—become yet wider, more open and multifaceted, adding further elements of complexity and ambiguity.

While beliefs and ideas interact in creative, syncretistic fashion in any acculturative situation, the openness, the fluidity and flexibility of the Bushmen (as of foragers elsewhere) renders their "penchant for acculturation" (*Akkulturationsbereitschaft*) (Köhler 1978/79: 13) a basic socio-cultural tendency. Indeed, according to Gusinde (1966: 55), it is nothing less than a "tendency in tune with their nature" (*natureigene Neigung*).

All the more appropriate, then, to extend the central dynamic of Bushman social organization, foraging, to the realm of ideas. They, too, are a resource which people hunt and gather within the mental *n!ores* of their neighbors, on the basis of reciprocity. I will return to this point—a leitmotif of this book—in later chapters.

Socio-Cultural Change and Religion

While the process of acculturation contributes toward the fragmentation of Bushman belief—into a shreds-and-patches amalgam of names, notions, and practices that are added to what is an ambiguous belief complex to begin with—there is another diachronic process with opposite effects on Bushman religion. These are to simplify and streamline religion, as well as to define it as a more discrete cultural domain, rather than a diffuse ideological element of social practice. They are a part of the process of socio-cultural change that has affected the farm Bushmen. Its main ingredients are marginal herding and cultivation, wage labor, sedentism, dependency, and social and political marginalization (Guenther 1976b, 1977a, 1986a). These are the ingredients of the life situation not only of the Ghanzi farm Bushmen, but also of farm Bushmen in other parts of southern Africa, as far back as the Cape frontier of over a century ago (Guenther 1986b, 1996b).

The two main effects of these socio-economic and political changes on farm Bushman religion is a reduction of the range of interpersonal variation of belief and an increase in the degree of ritual specialization, as the trance dancer becomes more professionalized and his knowledge acquires an aura of the esoteric and exclusive. I have suggested elsewhere (Guenther 1979a: 11–2, 114) that these developments can be related to an increase in the level of social and political stress experienced by the farm Bushmen. The effects on farm Bushman religion of oppression, despondency, frustration, deprivation, disease, lowered life expectancy, and raised child mortality is to render this socio-cultural system adaptive, so that it becomes the cultural and psychological coping mechanism that Malinowski saw in religion. In the desolate life situation of the farm Bushmen, religion eschews its disengagement from social and existential reality; instead, it turns toward that reality. It is reflected, endorsed, and explained by belief much more directly than ever before.

An example illustrating this process of bringing religion to bear on the problems of existence is provided by the farm Bushmen's ideas and practices concerning disease. These have become more "rational" than they were before, more consistent and pragmatic, such that there is now an actual explanatory *system* for disease, which has become so prominent an existential threat. As I have shown elsewhere (Guenther 1986a: 240–41, 272–74, 1992a: 89–90), it is a tripartite system, reflecting the three major racial and ethnic groupings of the pluralist society of Ghanzi, attributing to each its respective category of disease and seeking from each the necessary and requisite expertise for treatment. Thus, diseases believed to have been mystically caused by //Gãũwa and other "Bushman" spirit agencies are treated by the trance dancer. Suspected or confirmed cases of sorcery and witchcraft are held to be a "black" disease and taken for treatment to a Bantu diviner. "Organic" diseases, particularly tuberculosis, which the Nharo call */ho ≠gei* ("European disease"), are taken to the clinic nurse or hospital doctor.

The farm Nharos' creator god and trickster-god, N!eri and //Gãũwa, become more personalized and better defined; in the accounts of a number of the religiously acculturated Bushmen the two divinities follow the model of the Christian God and Devil. Creation myths explain, simply or elaborately, such features of the modern situation as the ethnic composition of the society; the relative prestige, power, and wealth of the ethnic groups; how cattle were obtained by non-Bushman groups, to the exclusion of the Bushmen; the operation of banks, hospitals, and schools; and how to subvert the power of an exploitative *baas* over his Bushman laborers (Guenther 1989, passim).

Now that I have documented ambiguity within Bushman religion and explained the same with respect to Bushman social organization, the task that remains is to deal with the theoretical implications this case holds for the anthropology of religion. As noted at the beginning, all of what I have presented in this chapter poses a considerable theoretical challenge to students of the latter field. This challenge will be magnified by the chapters that follow, each of which will trace the anti-structural tentacles of Bushman mental culture through one or another domain of Bushman myth and ritual. After having presented the full scope and depth of ambiguity within Bushman religion, I thus defer my treatment of this remaining task to the conclusion.

4

The Bushman Trickster

He . . . seems to me to be just a sort of dream Bushman. . . .

—BLEEK 1923: VI

"You tawny rogue! Have you not played at beating long enough?

Have you no more loving game than this?"

—BLEEK 1864: 10

"I /ke /kaggen. !kui kua ka-g /ne te:kwa. . . . I /ke-ten !khwaiten !khwaiten. !kui ha i: /ka" ("Our name is /Kaggen. What man is our equal! . . . Our name is Penis! The man has done it!").

—BLEEK AND LLOYD 1911: 31; HEWITT 1986: 238

"//Gãũwa likes the women."

—GUENTHER 1989: 117

"Today indeed have I seen a beautiful girl at the hut yonder, fit only for you, O Haiseb to marry."

And Haiseb, hearing this, preened himself and went forth. . . .

—THOMAS 1950: 54

[The hunter] knows that it is not a louse, but it is the Mantis who is trying to cheat him, for the Mantis wants him to think it is a louse and to catch it and kill it, thinking it to be a louse. When the Mantis behaves like this, he wants the eland to get up as the man kills the louse, and he knows that the louse is vermin. So he thinks the man will kill the louse, its blood will be on

his hands with which he grasped the arrow when he shot the eland, the blood will enter the arrow and cool the poison. . . . [H]e is biting our eyes, with which he makes us look about. He bites all parts of us, for he wants us to take hold of that part, he knows that if we do so then the eland will live.

—BLEEK, "CUSTOMS AND BELIEFS" (1932: 236)

. . . They [the Nama] believe in Heitjeebib [Heitsi-Eibib], or Heitjekobib, whom they consider to have the power to grant or withhold them success and prosperity. But whether Heitjeebib is a deity, a goblin, or merely a deified ancestor, I shall not presume to say.

—ANDERSSON 1856: 327

"He [Haiseb] was our Jesus; he was exactly like God (the Christian God), he only had another name."

—SCHMIDT 1993: 11

[The !Kung] tell the tales of ≠Gao!na's doings without restraint, say his name aloud, howl and roll on the ground with laughter at his humiliations, whereas, when they speak of the great one of the east, they whisper and avoid his name. Yet they think that somehow in the rightness of things theses two beings must be the same, or so they are said to be.

—MARSHALL 1962: 228

//Gauwa must help us that we kill an animal.
//Gauwa, help us. We are dying of hunger.
//Gauwa does not give us help.
He is cheating. He is bluffing.
//Gauwa will bring something for us to kill next day.
After he himself hunts and has eaten meat,
When he is full and feeling well.

—MARSHALL 1962: 247

The trickster is the central denizen of the First Order of existence who is perfectly at home in this inchoate world and in tune with its spirit of disorder and flux. As suggested by the numerous epigraphs that open this chapter, the personas of this complex being are multiple, ranging from lewd prankster to divine creator; goblin to god; human to jackal; incarnation within the lowest of animals, the louse, to Spirit Keeper of the highest, the eland. Yet, they are only some of the many and varied, contradictory and confounding traits possessed by this embodiment of ambiguity.

The Bushman—or, more generally, Khoisan[1]—trickster is as ubiquitous as he is multifarious, having been noted and described by travelers, ethnographers, and scholars of Khoisan religion and folklore for well over a century. These wide-ranging accounts display a great deal of variation and contain much contradiction, further attesting to the ambiguity of this enigmatic and slippery mythological personage. Reports about the Khoisan trickster go as far back as the mid-1800s: for example, Andersson's account (1856: 327), cited in the epigraph (he is himself citing earlier reports), or Wilhelm Bleek's 1864 collection of Jackal trickster tales, most of which he had received from missionaries laboring in Namaqualand. About seventy years later, in a comparative summary of the writings on the Bushman protagonist received to date, Isaac Schapera noted that these were "not crystallized into clear-cut conceptions, but . . . vague and inconsistent and ambiguous" (1930: 396).

More recent accounts of this multiplex supernatural figure confirm the early assessment; for instance, Lorna Marshall finds the !Kung's "thinking vague and inconsistent" on a number of points relating to the !Kung trickster-god ≠Gao!na (Marshall 1962: 235) and Lewis-Williams sees the "kaleidoscopic" /Xam trickster /Kaggen to be "a concept [which], like so much of San thought, [is] . . . shifting and elusive" (Lewis-Williams 1981: 124). Talking about Bushman folklore generally, Biesele (1993: 17) points to the "extremely variegated" nature of the trickster figure, each mythological tradition depicting its trickster in terms very different from the others (Guenther 1989: 115–51). What Sigrid Schmidt says about the Nama/Damara trickster Haiseb (or Heiseb)—"the more you learn about this figure the more puzzling he will become" (1993: 9)—can be said generally of this character of Khoisan religion, myth, and lore. The dazzling kind and range of variation displayed by the Khoisan trickster is evident from Sigrid Schmidt's exhaustive inventory of Khoisan folklore, within which the trickster variety constitutes the largest body of tales, occupying close to half of Schmidt's "catalogue" (Schmidt 1989: 71–221; also see Schmidt 1995).

The Trickster's Many Faces

While found everywhere within Khoisan belief and oral tradition, the trickster, like the people whose mythology he represents, is known by no single name common to all Bushman groups. He is /Kaggen to the Cape /Xam, Pate and Pisamboro (or //Gawama) to the Nharo and G/wi of Botswana, Piisi/koagu to the //Gana of the Central Kalahari Game Reserve, Kaoxa (or ≠Gao!na, !Gara, Hice, or Hoe) to the Zhu/'hoansi of Botswana and Namibia, Jackal and Haiseb (or Iseb or Heitsi-Eibib, his earlier, somewhat archaic name and persona) to the Hei//om, Nama, and Damara.

In addition to the more prominent trickster figures here named, there are numerous other, more obscure tricksters and trickster-like characters in the mythological collections of the various Bushman groups. Some of them are cultural "foragings" of Bushman groups from Bantu- or Dutch-speaking neighbors (Guenther 1989: 139; Schmidt 1991, 1995: 223; Biesele 1993: 32). Some Nharo storytellers will loosely apply the name //Gãũwa to their trickster protagonist, as a general or generic label, thereby merging the trickster protagonist with a divinity bearing the same name. //Gãũwa is a "lesser god" also among the !Kung (as well as among other Bushman and Khoekhoe groups), and in the plural form, the //gauwasi are either the spirits of the dead or the children born to gods (Marshall 1962: 238). However, as we will presently discover, everywhere in Khoisan myth and belief the figure's dual personae—god and protagonist—blend into each other, creating a trickster figure of profound ontological ambiguity and moral ambivalence.

The trickster's guise may be human or humanoid, or it may be animalian or therianthropic. The human guise may be normal or grotesque and misshapen, such as the !Kung figure !O!ôtsi/dasi (known to the Nharo and /Xam, respectively, as N!are tsam ≠xi /kam and !Goe/weiten), who has an eyeless face because his two eyes are between his toes, or, depending on the mythological tradition within which one encounters this widespread figure, on his inner ankles, toenails, or the back of his feet (Schmidt 1986b: 179). Matching wits with "Eyes-on-his-Feet" in a number of stories (Guenther 1989: 117–20), we encounter the Nharo trickster Pate, a short manikin, resembling a cock-grouse in size and bearing, especially in his frequent courtings of a lusted-after girl. His thin body is ruffled and covered all over with spidery fibers. Numerous big toes stick out from all over his cocoon-like cover, as though to compensate for his having only one, eight-toed, crippled, and misshapen leg (Guenther 1989: 118). His brother, among the Nharo, is Pisamboro (or Pisiboro), a vulgarian who delights in farting and "flashing" nubile girls (Guenther 1989: 122). His body was of such huge size that, when in pain of death, he gouged out the dry riverbeds of the central Kalahari with his thrashing limbs, as well as formed rivers and rain clouds from his putrefying flesh and his hair (Marshall 1962: 236–37; Silberbauer 1965: 96; Guenther 1989: 123; Schmidt 1989, 2:125–26).

Two human or humanoid trickster figures that Sigrid Schmidt discovered in Khoisan oral literature and attributes to the folklore of the early Dutch settlers were the figure of Till Eulenspiegel (or Howleglass, as he is known in English) and the Devil.[2] Instead of duping town burgers, magistrates, or priests (Guenther 1993/94: 28–29) the favorite mark of the southern African *Uilspieël* is the Boer *baas* (Schmidt 1991).

There are a number of tricksters whose names and attributes are animalian—and at the same time also human, as the Bushmen will insist, enigmatically, whenever they refer to animalian "*People* of the Early Race." The best known is the Mantis-man /Kaggen (Cagn) of the /Xam, who will sometimes spread out stiff wings to fly, escaping from one or another of his nasty pranks that have gone awry and landed him in physical danger (Bleek 1923). The magician-trickster Woodpecker of the Hei//om and !Kung of northern Namibia is seen squaring off against the regular trickster, and either outwits his adversary, or is outwitted by him (Schmidt 1989, 2:139–41, citing texts by Heikkinen 1985 23–31 and Metzger and Ettighoffer 1952: 54–60). Hare and Cock are animal tricksters of farm and veld; the Bushmen have likely borrowed both of them from Bantu-speaking and European neighbors (Bleek 1864: 23; Guenther 1989: 139–43, 136; Schmidt 1989, 2:191–93; Tanaka 1996: 24–25). Among the //Gana, the trickster Piisi/koagu may assume the identity of a wide range of animals, from the familiar hare, through the tortoise, to the korhaan and the small songbird konkon/koagu (Tanaka ibid.: 25).

The Khoekhoe-derived Jackal of the Nharo and Hei//om roams the pioneer ranches of Namibia and Ghanzi. The favorite target of this "tawny rogue" is his trek Boer *baas*, whose work he shuns, whose workers—especially Hyena (or Porcupine), Jackal's co-worker and boon companion, as well as favorite patsy —he gets in trouble, and whose nubile daughter and matronly wife he seduces (Thomas 1950: 40–41; Guenther 1989: 124–43; Schmidt 1980: 62–95, 1989, 2:157–221). Jackal stories are especially prominent within the narrative traditions of the Khoekhoe, wherein he may either be an embodiment of Haiseb, or an adversary to that trickster figure, creating particularly humorous trickster tales, as two such figures are seen squaring off against one another (Schmidt 1995: 48–51, 215–21). Sigrid Schmidt (1986: 224–25) suggests that the figure may have been borrowed from the early Dutch Cape settlers who brought tales about Reynard the Fox to Africa. Indeed, so similar are the Khoisan jackal tales to those about his European, vulpine cousin that Wilhelm Bleek entitled his collection of Nama jackal stories *Reynard the Fox in Africa* (Bleek 1864). However, as I noted elsewhere (Guenther 1989: 124, 147), there are also Bushman jackal characters—Jackal Men (as among the /Xam) and Jackal Women (the !Kung) who may or may not have trickster traits (Guenther 1989: 147; Biesele 1993: 27–30, 122–37). If the former is the case, they may possess trickster traits not displayed by the Reynard prototype, such as the performance of providential actions that bring salvation or boon to humankind (Guenther 1989: 147–51; Schmidt 1995: 97–99, 217–18).

Each of these trickster figures is capable of transforming his shape or guise, from human to animal and back, or from one animal species to another. In addition to his ontological makeup, his social state, too, may vary. He may be a solitary figure and the one and only trickster on the mythological landscape, or he may live with a wife or wives, child or children, and extended family. In some narratives these family members are featured as ancillary trickster figures as well, while in others they take the place of the main trickster (possibly a son succeeding his father, after killing him in a fit of oedipal rage and lust). Apart from such secondary trickster figures, there may be others in that category who are not kin to the main trickster. Narratives that feature two tricksters as adversaries trying to get the better of each other—such as Pate vs. "Eyes-on-his-Feet," Haiseb vs. Woodpecker, Jackal vs. Cock, or Hare vs. Spider—have great entertainment value (Bleek 1864: 23; Schmidt 1989, 2:139–41; Guenther 1989: 117–19; Tanaka 1996: 25).

Even more varied than the features of the trickster protagonists of the stories are the personal notions individuals may have of the trickster-divinity. Some of these, sometimes surreal and Boschian, portraits may be based on some extraordinary encounter a person, especially a trance dancer, may have had with the figure, usually in a dream or trance state. These visions or encounters, which may have been experienced recently or a long time before, are salient, long-remembered moments in a person's life. While all are numinous to the beholder, they vary in the degree of mystical otherworldliness that attaches to the divinity, ranging from highly or bizarrely remote to ordinary, //Gãũwa being "just a man" (albeit a "wild man" living out in the veld).

I obtained some of the following descriptions of //Gãũwa from informants in Ghanzi, all of whom had experienced some such vision or encounter: three feet tall, black, burnt body, naked, one leg burned and shriveled, genitalia burnt away, wielding a red-hot knife; an ordinary Bushman person mounted on a horse; a red-haired ordinary person; a white man, tall, with chalk-white face and dark beard, wearing a wide-brimmed hat, whose features appear to the person beholding him at one time exceedingly handsome, at the next monstrously ugly; a black negro person, as tall as a windmill, thin, wearing a leather loincloth and riding on a huge dog. One especially haunting, Bergmanesque vision was described to me by the blind husband of a Nharo trance dancer (who sings for his wife when she performs her curing ritual): fifteen mounted //gãũwani were descending from the sky the day he saw them, causing darkness that lasted throughout their stay of several days. The G/wi-//Gana artist-shaman //Goa (Qwaa) from D'Kar village in Ghanzi has produced several pictures of //Gãũwa, the most striking of which depicts him as a spindly manikin with insect fingers, huge, round, baleful eyes, and a bloated head, the latter expressing his agitated and dangerous frame of mind, according to the artist, as //Gãũwa's head, like the hood of a cobra, will swell when he is angry (Guenther 1998). Turning to the !Kung, we come across a variety of different personal descriptions of ≠Gao!na: "the tallest of the Bushmen": aggressive in his bearing (like a Herero or white man); either yellow- or white-skinned; hairy-faced and -chested; wearing European clothes, bearing a gun and mounted on horseback (Marshall 1962: 236). It should be noted that we also encountered the latter figure in the previous chapter, as one of the embodiments of god, rather than as the trickster (-god). Such contradictions abound in Bushman belief, especially those about god, who, as we saw before, may incorporate the trickster or //Gãũwa persona within his being.

The trickster-god has a special affinity for large game antelopes—"/Kaggen is a hartebeest thing" (Lewis-Williams 1981: 56)—and his appearance may reflect this affinity. There are widespread stories that depict him fondly raising one or several baby antelopes (or, in a farm-based variant, lambs), which he feeds with honey water and other magical, strength-inducing medicines, and which he mourns and weeps over when his people kill it (Bleek 1923: 1–9; Schmidt 1995: 97–99, 191–94, 217–18). He may temporarily assume the guise of one of his antelope children, or antelope traits may be a regular part of his appearance. With regard to the latter, we find the account of the Hai//om shaman /Garugu //Kumob, which depicts //Gaunab as a Cernunnos-like figure, who wears the horns of all large game antelopes on his head (Wagner-Robertz 1976: 539).

The Embodiment of Ambiguity

The multiple and varied elements in the names, appearances, and identities of the trickster reveal this figure's central—and universal—trait: ambiguity. It is exemplified in myriad ways, such that virtually every conceivable ontological, moral, social, or physical attribute of this quixotic figure is somehow betwixt and between, topsy-turvy, neither here nor there. He confounds categories and opposites and is the embodiment of self-contradiction, requiring the storyteller narrating his exploits to resort to the oppositional rhetorical device of *einerseits* ("on the one hand") and *anderseits* ("on the other hand"), as perceptively noted by Sigrid Schmidt among her Nama and Dama narrators (1980: 244). The device may be employed more than once in a tale, given that the trickster's character may change several times in the course of one tale (Schmidt 1993: 9).

//Gãũwa may be corporeal, or he may be "just like the wind" or the sunshine "which is all over." He may be a single or multiple being. He may be human, animal, or divine, or he may blend these three ontological traits in every possible combination. Whatever his guise, it is never stable as he is wont to change himself into another being, such as a game animal, a bird, or an insect. He may even become a plant, a rock, a whirlwind, or a cooking pot—the last a ploy with which to obtain, before anyone else, the fattest and choicest pieces of meat (Lloyd 1889: 7; Marshall 1962: 239; Silberbauer 1965: 96; Guenther 1989: 58, 143; Schmidt 1989, 2:116).

The Bushman protagonist, like his trickster colleagues all over the world, on the one hand, is a creator of beings and things, as well as of rules and categories, and on the other, transforms, distorts, and inverts what he has created or decreed. As creator, as well as culture hero, he may bring into the world beings, things, and conditions of importance to nature and humankind, as well as structure and order. Thanks to his creative acts or antics there is now fire and cooking, the rivers and water holes of the Kalahari, the vocal sounds and body patterns of some animals, healing medicine and trance arrows, rain magic, and the knowledge of procreation (as well as of death) (Guenther 1989: 116–17; Schmidt 1995: 149–62, 210–11). However, the trickster's creations may also be caricatures of what the creator god has made; such is the case of the Nharo //Gãũwa, whose versions of God's horse and cow were the donkey and the goat, while his version of God's baboon was the Bushman (a poignant reflection of the collective inferiority of the farm Bushmen) (Guenther 1989: 50).

The trickster's role as inverter-transformer in creation is most explicit in those creative acts whereby he reverses aspects of the "First Order" and the "early Race of People" into the new, present order. An example is the Nama Haiseb, who cursed the people of the early times and condemned them to become those animals of the present time whose names they bore before (Schmidt 1993: 11, 1995: 149–52). Another is /Kaggen, who, in the tale of his visit and quarrel with the Ticks, arranged things so that they would henceforth no longer be people who have fires and who cook their food, but ticks, moving about in cold darkness rather than through a night warmed and illuminated by fire. Moreover, they will be "biting things' bodies [and] they will have to drink things' blood and no longer eat cooked meat" (Bleek 1923: 32). /Kaggen extended his reversal of the status quo of the First Order to other beings: fire and cooking (in pots) will henceforth be only for "real people," the ichneumon shall live in the hills, the dassie in a mountain den, and the porcupine in a hole. He reverses even himself, proclaiming that he shall become a "little green thing" with wings (Bleek 1923: 33). In the myth of the "Branding of the Animals," the key Ju/'hoan tale about the creation of the new order (Biesele 1993: 115–23), the central fire is "Kaoxa's magical fire," according to Megan Biesele (1993: 122), and the agent supervising the branding, the Kori Bustard, is Kaoxa's servant. In !Kung cosmogony the trickster-god is thus seen to be the directing divine force behind the reversal of the previous state of being. Other, more isolated and anecdotal examples of the trickster as cosmic inverter are the Nharo "Eyes-on-his-Feet," who changed the ostrich into a wild veld animal and gave it its new voice (Guenther 1989: 59), and ≠Gao!na, who changed the early person /Kai /Kini into a bird of the new order called ≠ore (Marshall 1962: 233).

In tune with the fluidity of the First Order, wherein violation of menarcheal proscriptions could bring about the reversal of humans into animals and cultural objects (such as leather cloaks or digging sticks) back into their natural state (antelopes and bushes) (Hewitt 1986: 133–37; Guenther 1989: 87), the trickster /Kaggen was able to animate his quiver, leather cloak, cap, walking stick, and bowstring, so that these objects might come to his aid when one of his pranks went awry (Bleek 1923: 17, 19, 31; Guenther 1989: 144). Being no longer things but /Kaggen's "children," at his bidding they came running or flying to his aid and /Kaggen engaged them in conversation.

The theme of the trickster's things, or the material objects of his inchoate world, breaking out of their inanimate and cultural state to become independent beings or animals is recapitulated in the trickster's body parts. Instead of being integral members of his anatomy they may be severed, or sever themselves, in order to perform unpredictable and unseemly things. One such member—not surprisingly, given the figure's Rabelaisian constitution—is his penis: perhaps his most prominent body part, so much so that, as seen in of the epigraphs, one of the trickster's names may be derived from it (Hewitt 1986: 238). Having detached itself from his body, the organ falls into the hands of a young woman who unwittingly roasts it and then beats it to soften it. As one might predict, the member jumps out of her hands and between her legs, where it buries itself in her body. That done, the trickster (Haiseb) appears beside the woman as a man, sneering and triumphant. (Schmidt 1989, 2:116). In another tale, the !Khung trickster Haiseb dismembers his cumbersomely long penis—which he carries, folded several times, around his belt—creating from it several species of snake (Heikkinen 1985: 87–88, cited in Schmidt 1989, 2:118). Other parts to sever themselves, jump into the women's cooking pot, and back to their owner to reattach themselves, are the buttocks and anus (Schmidt 1989, 2:128). Apart from these lascivious members, other body parts may also be dismembered: for example, when the trickster, having transformed himself into a dead game antelope, allows himself to be cut up.

As seen below with respect to /Kaggen, each of these body parts—head, neck, spine, thigh, ribs, shoulder blade—will run ahead of the other and jump on top of each other, re-articulating the trickster's body. However, things may not go all that smoothly; for instance, until all the parts have found their proper place and rhythm, the shoulder blade may jog alongside the legs or shoes for a while ("he was stepping along with his shoes, while he jogged with his shoulder blade" [Bleek and Lloyd 1911: 11]). One might note that tricksters in other parts of the world have the same problems with their body parts; the Winnebago's Wakdjungkaga, for example, carries his excessively long penis in a box. His member has a mind of his own—which, like its master's, is dirty—and his lascivious antics get its owner in trouble. Wakdjungkaga's anus, too, can be severed and engage in antic tricks. Another set of unintegrated body parts are the Winnebago trickster's left and right hands, which fight and work at cross purposes (Radin 1972: 17–20, 38–40; see also Koepping 1985: 207 and Apte 1985: 215).

The tales that feature Trickster within the present order, usually as a farmhand on a European farm, also dwell on the theme of the inversion and flouting of rules, in this case those set by the oppressive and irascible Boer *baas*, a modern cognate of the Lion of tales set in the First Order (Guenther 1989: 115, 125–34; also see Schmidt 1995: 210–11). The most common theme of stories about Jackal-*jong* ("boy") feature him shirking work and keeping others from work, thereby sabotaging the farmer's enterprise, stealing the *baas*'s property, and sleeping with his womenfolk. His parting words to the *baas* might be a jeering: "Thanks a lot, Baas! And don't forget: Jackal's the name!" (Schmidt 1980: 85). As flouter and saboteur of the new rules brought into the land by the oppressive colonists who have taken this land from the Bushmen and decimated its game animals and plants, the trickster-as-wayward-farmhand becomes a symbol of resistance. The tales about him may take on the flavor of oral protest literature (Guenther 1989: 128–35, 1996c). This theme has its most poignant and explicit expression in one Nama tale wherein Jackal, having killed the farmer's herd-boy, murders the farmer and his wife and takes the orphaned children as his servants (Schmidt 1989, 2:186). In another he induces the Lion-*baas* to kill his own children (Schmidt 1995: 213). Such especially violent tales recapitulate, in reverse (as is the trickster's wont), the historical plight of Khoisan peoples in many parts of southern Africa.[3]

Another contemporary setting is the veld, where people may believe him to be found, as always, either as a quixotic, multiform divinity, to be drawn to humans at ritual occasions, or as some type of "bush spirit" or "wild man" who lives in a cave, helps people who have lost their way in the veld, and is given to dancing when it rains, his singing resounding through the land (Schmidt 1995: 206). While it differs widely in detail, the above notion of //Gāũwa as some sort of wild spirit-man, "alone and palely loitering" out in the veld, is held also among some of the Ghanzi farm Bushmen.

These contemporary tales set on farm and veld point to another realm which the Bushman trickster confounds, namely time. He can be as much a creature of the mythological past—*eine fern zurückliegende Zeit* ("a far-distant time") (Schmidt 1986a: 242)—as of the recent, historical present. While the former, dreamtime-like, fluid, and inchoate First Order is his proper home, he appears also within the Second Order, within the veld of old and the farms of new.

In addition to confounding the temporal categories of past and present, he also mixes up the spatial dimensions of above and below. His abode is equally the ground and the earth and the world as it is the sky and heaven and the netherworld, where spirits of the dead and of shamans come to him. He moves along both spatial axes, walking or whirling (as a "dust devil") laterally across the ground and flying vertically up into the sky.

Dream and reality are also realms muddled by the trickster, "a sort of dream Bushman" (Bleek 1923: vi). In the often lengthy tales about the Mantis trickster we find him shifting reality sets: the narrative starts out in a dream setting, as a dream, then switches into reality, where it is set within the same scenario as before and continues the same plot. The transition between the real and surreal realms is seamless, and the /Xam storyteller, presumably attuned to this element of ambiguity in the protagonist, appears to give no indication where in the narrative the dream left off and reality set in. As a consequence, the plot of such narratives can become dense and incoherent to a reader accustomed to more linear and unequivocal perceptions of reality (Hewitt 1986: 243; Guenther 1989: 144).

Life and death is another set of antithetical states which the Bushman trickster confounds. He is, on the one hand, a living being; on the other, he is identified with the spirits of the dead, the *//gauwani* (or *//gangwasi*) or the *//awa,* as they are known among the !Kung (Marshall 1962: 226, 241–44; Lee 1993: 113–14) and the Kxoe (Köhler 1978/79: 34). To Köhler they, too, are "trickster beings," and, like the trickster to whom the spirits of the dead are linked, can appear in a variety of forms to trance dancers: like real people whom you can touch, or ephemeral and smoke-like, or one-legged, standing in midair (Lee 1993: 113). The existential polarities of life and death are mingled also in the trickster's role as custodian of both "healing medicines" and "killing medicines" (Köhler 1978/79: 34; Schmidt 1989, 2:80; Biesele 1993: 105), and by his ability—upon having been beaten, maimed, burned, crushed by rocks, eviscerated, swallowed up, or killed—to revitalize himself and to reassemble his severed body parts (Bleek and Lloyd 1911: 3–17; Bleek 1923: 23, 31; Guenther

1989: 120–23; Schmidt 1989, 2:115–18, 127–38). While very much alive in the tales and myths, and in his mystical role as divinity, the Khoekhoe trickster-god Haiseb was also perceived as dead, in a palpably concrete fashion. His graves—"Haiseb-graves"—dot the Namibian landscape, in the form of stone cairns. Underscoring the finality of Haiseb's death, these grow in height and mass through time because each passing person will add a stone to the grave, along, perhaps, with a prayer for rain, cattle, and well-being, and possibly a libation of water, food, or tobacco (Schmidt 1995: 201–205).

An example of the trickster's regenerative power, which also graphically illustrates certain other of his traits, is provided by /Kaggen. Having transformed himself into a hartebeest and feigning death, he lets himself be cut up with stone knives by two nubile sisters. Then he revitalizes himself from dead antelope, lying inert and cut-up, to man, upright and running, lustily chasing the frightened girls. He re-articulates himself, body part after body part, from the head down, and once again, "he became a man while he was putting himself together again" (Bleek and Lloyd 1911: 11):

> The flesh of the Mantis sprang together, it quickly joined itself to the lower part of the Mantis's back. The head of the Mantis quickly joined itself upon the top of the neck of Mantis. The neck of the Mantis quickly joined itself upon the upper part of the Mantis's spine. The upper part of Mantis's spine joined itself to Mantis's back. The thigh of the Mantis sprang forward—like a frog—it joined itself to the Mantis's back. The other thigh ran forward, racing it joined itself to the other side of Mantis's back. The chest of the Mantis ran forward, it joined itself to the front side of the upper part of Mantis's spine. The shoulder blade of the Mantis ran forward, it joined itself on to the ribs of the Mantis. The other shoulder blade of the Mantis ran forward, while it felt that the ribs of the Mantis had joined themselves on, when they raced. (Bleek and Lloyd 1911: 9–11)

As regards his gender, the Bushman trickster is usually male, although in some ritual contexts he may be she. However, even in the figure's male guise, which he may exemplify most convincingly through excessive phallic exploits, the figure's maleness is equivocal. Thus, the /Xam Mantis-man /Kaggen—whose "name is Penis"—is, for all this boasting, referred to by his adopted daughter Porcupine as "mild," "cowardly," and "a runaway." The figure strikes Hewitt (1986: 152–53) as mildly effeminate, an assessment of character borne out by /Kaggen's use of a woman's tool (the weighted digging stick) and the fact that he is left-handed (Bleek and Lloyd 1911: 11), in a symbolic culture that —as most others across the world—assigns male and female values to right- and left-handedness, respectively (Hewitt 1986: 153, 163). There are some Khoekhoe narratives wherein the trickster becomes a female person: for instance, Haiseb, when he transforms himself into either a beautiful maiden or a repulsive crone (Schmidt 1989, 2:117, 119). In a !Kung tale ≠Gao!na took the guise of his own sister in order to be able to accompany the women on a gathering outing. The reason for this charade was his carnal desire for his pretty daughter-in-law who had refused his advances. The ruse was successful, enabling him to consummate his lust (Marshall 1962: 32). His gender may be obscured also when, in a prank that has backfired on him, he manages to either neuter himself or mutilate his genitals.

With respect to his social status, he may either be a solitary wanderer of the veld (as //Gãũwa of the Nharo) or live with people, to whose camp or village he returns every night and after each adventure (as did Kaoxa and //Kaggen of the !Kung and /Xam). Wherever he lived in a group with other men he was wont to be "set apart notably by his marked anti-social behaviour" (Hewitt 1986: 122). For this he might be scolded or derided by his wives or children, and his people might even rejoice at the news that he has died (Schmidt 1995: 195–96). Moreover, as a member of a group, he may or may not be its headman (Schmidt 1986: 242), and in marriage he may be the patriarchal family head or a husband henpecked by his wife or wives (Guenther 1983: 21), and usually outsmarted by them (Schmidt 1993: 9). In some accounts he is a "wild" veld hunter (Biesele 1993: 103–15), in others a "tame" farm laborer, working for a trek Boer *baas* on a frontier ranch (Guenther 1989: 115, 128–35).

He may be an old man, as was /Kaggen; however, he "does not act like a grown-up person" and he has "never grown up" (Hewitt 1986: 15). Indeed, his actions may be so foolish as to result in his being hectored by his grandson Ichneumon. All the tales that show /Kaggen displaying exceptional stupidity end with moral exhortations from the trickster's grandson, who becomes the moral conscience of his grandfather as he, even though old, does not know what is right and smart. Such tales confound the opposition of old and young and flout the identification of old age with wisdom. Instead, the tales convey the adage of old age being a second childhood and exemplify the morale that "there is no fool like an old fool." Another infantile trait of tricksters is that they may be unable to speak properly. They may lisp or may be unable to master any or some of the clicks, the last phonetic sounds a child masters as he learns the language (Schmidt 1986a: 224, 1993: 9, 1995: 197–98). This makes their speech akin to "baby talk," comparable, perhaps, to the consonant distortions of Tweety Bird or Elmer Fudd of Western cartoon fakelore. This amusing textural element of storytellers in the dialog parts of the narrative gets laughs from the audience (Schmidt 1986a: 224, 1995: 197–98). Sigrid Schmidt has effectively conveyed this ethnopoetic feature, in her recent renditions of some of the Haiseb narratives (Schmidt 1995: 31–36).

The trickster's "ethnic" status, too, is ambiguous. To some he is "a Bushman," to others a black man or a white man. The latter two views seem to be especially prevalent; perhaps the identification of the trickster-god with the white and black settlers is a reflection of the divinity's destructive side. The Nharo refer to these two settler groups as "terrible"—an assessment borne out by the frequently violent history of contact between the indigenous "red" people and the black and white colonists—and in Nharo faunal taxonomy the settler people are included in the category of *n/ie /wa* (predators, literally "claw children")

(Guenther 1986a: 236–37). Yet, the attitude toward the settlers, especially the Whites, is not without ambivalence. By means of the firearm and hypodermic needle—two material objects that, along with the motor car, signify this settler group (Guenther 1986a: 89–90, 241)—they have always provided potent medicine and abundant meat for the Bushmen. Yet, at the same time, they have also brought to the Bushmen new and terrible diseases (such as tuberculosis, which the Nharo call */ho ≠gei,* "European disease"), along with depletion of game, hunger, deprivation, and oppression. There are certain parallels between the European colonists and the veld god that make his (among the Ghanzi farm Bushmen) frequent casting as a white man seem an appropriate symbolic twist: both may provide game and medicine to people, or they may as readily and wantonly deprive them of these vital substances.

In his moral disposition, the Bushman trickster, like tricksters everywhere in the world, is both vindictive and beneficent, selfish and altruistic, destructive and creative, weak and powerful, cowardly and courageous, quaking and tough, foolish and clever, childish and mature, cunning and readily duped. He may be pathetic in two opposed senses: eliciting disgust by the grossness of his shortcomings, or eliciting true pathos and pity by weeping for a creature he loved and lost, such as his son, or his tenderly reared baby antelope or lamb, both of whom die at the hands of neighbors or of his own family (Schmidt 1995: 191–94). The two overriding moral shortcomings, and the motivational elements topping the trickster's "hierarchy of needs," are gluttony and lechery (Guenther 1989: 56, 122–25; Biesele 1993: 171–79). This pair of bodily drives shares the top spot on the needs hierarchy because—in the context of Bushman moral culture that regards hunting, meat, fat, and honey as metaphors for sex—lust and gluttony become linked together as symbolic cognates (Guenther 1989: 60–63; Biesele 1993: 79–80; Schmidt 1995: 191). Sex, quite simply, is food; indeed, in the words of the !Kung woman N/isa, "hunger for sex can cause people to die" (Shostak 1981: 265).

In his appetites for these two types of food, the trickster is equally voracious. He gorges himself on meat, eating alone and without sharing, and can become so swept away with his food greed that he will start to eat his own flesh, his howls of pain overridden by his greed for food (Guenther 1989: 101). In addition to liking meat, the trickster, the Nharo say, is a man who "likes the women," and, in Nama and Damara folklore, he may have as many as twenty wives (Schmidt 1986a: 22, 1995: 90–92). But marriage does not satisfy his lust and he is forever on the lookout for amorous conquests. These are directed toward women of all ages, from maidens to matrons. The former may include his own daughter-in-law, the latter his own mother. She may become the object of his lust even when he is a baby, as in the case of Haiseb, who raped his mother shortly after his birth (Schmidt 1980: 39–40; Guenther 1983: 22). In a !Kung tale (Biesele 1993: 178–79) the boy-child to rape his mother was actually not Kaoxa but his son, who first killed his father in a fit of oedipal jealousy. His bungling attempt to have sex with his mother reveals him to be a trickster junior following in his father's footsteps: in an act of foolish futility, he tries to enlarge his boy-sized penis by placing it into a mass of crawling insects whose stings are to make it swell to man-size. As is so often the case, the rewards of his outrageous excesses are failure and pain.

In satisfying his voracious and lascivious appetites, Trickster becomes the vulgarian par excellence, exemplifying both of these moral shortcomings to gross excess. He flouts the norms and mores that regulate eating and sex, such as commensality, sharing, and avoidance kin regulations. His excesses lead him to such abominations as incest and cannibalism: for instance, when he seduces his nieces, rapes his mother, or butchers his wife—"meat"—and roasts and eats her.

Once again, we see the trickster in his role as profligate flouter and inverter of rules; however, we must again qualify even this salient and highly embellished trait of our protagonist. Aggressive lust and selfish voracity actually are turned around on occasion, making the trickster a compassionate and concerned protector of threatened maidens, a provider for his family, and a valiant fighter ridding humans of man-killing ogres (Bleek 1923: 45–46; Hewitt 1986: 1347–49; Guenther 1989: 149–51; Schmidt 1989, 2:82–107, 1993: 9–10, 1995: 164–65; Barnard 1992a: 258). He may also feel called upon to heal a person, or to revive someone who has died, or to proffer advice and extend help to someone in difficulty, in one case a Boer threatened by a poisonous snake (Bleek 1864: 11–13; Bleek and Lloyd 1911: 16–36). As for his outrageous cases of self-butchery, in most of the stories these acts are more self-sacrifice than self-indulgence: the food—his flesh, which he slices from his own body with shrieks of pain—is given to his wives and children, because he has failed as a hunter and provider (Guenther 1989: 102–104; Schmidt 1995: 88–92). That these tales may be more about the providential rather than the profligate trickster is suggested also by the fact that in them he usually has the shape of an agama lizard, a chameleon, or a frog—each a "rain animal" associated magically and symbolically with this life-giving substance (Schmidt ibid.: 214–15). The providential side to the trickster is perhaps more marked in the Khoisan mythological tradition than elsewhere in the world (Schmidt ibid.: 239). It may be a spillover from his other persona, as god.

True to his name, he delights, more than anything else, in playing tricks on the other beings of the veld and farms. These pranks are frequently obscene (Guenther 1989: 121–28, Biesele 1993: 171–79) and are expressed in such actions emanating from the nether regions of the body as fornication, flatulence, excretion, and "flashing." As noted in the previous chapter, another favorite trick the trickster may play on his wives is to serve them choice portions of his own flesh: his anus, testicles, entrails, or buttocks. His wife may return the favor by tricking him into eating her roasted labia as well as feces molded into an seemingly delectable and irresistible baby giraffe (Biesele 1993: 171–74). The last outrage not only flouts good manners but also confounds the opposite bodily functions of eating and excreting.

Trickster's pranks are usually carried out as nasty practical jokes that may do serious harm to their victims and may be accompanied with a strong dose of schadenfreude on the part of the perpetrator, voiced with boastful jeering. Yet, not infrequently his shenanigans will backfire, leaving the trickster the duped party, frequently hurt or injured, or even killed. Some of the tricks may have creative side effects that benefit nature and mankind, such as bringing fire and cooking to humans, as well as water and rain, medicines, healing potency, and the trance dance and state (Marshall 1962: 231; Schmidt 1977/78, 1989, 2:109–11, 125–36; Guenther 1989: 55–60, 121, 123; Biesele 1993: 105). His role as fire-bringer may be reflected in one of his designations among the /Xam, who referred to /Kaggen as "the old man 'Tinderbox-Owner'" (Bleek and Lloyd 1911: 13). In a palpably spicy tale, of which sections will be presented in chapter 6, the trickster figure Xau'gkiki is instrumental in bringing women and carnal knowledge to what were, in the beginning, male-only human communities (Guenther 1989: 62–63; for cognates see Dornan 1917: 78–79; Wagner-Robertz 1976: 542–43; Schmidt 1980: 21, 1989, 2:143–44; and Guenther 1989: 61, 63–64). Usually such creative acts are quite unintended, but not always; for example, Haiseb's creation, out of thin air, of a house and kraal full of cattle was a deliberate act of magic (Schmidt 1995: 70–71). Also deliberate was Haiseb's presentation of the stone game (*/hus*) to humans, on a rock surface, where (at Twyfelfontein in Namibia) one can still see the rows of holes Haiseb is said to have drilled into the rock (Schmidt 1995: 31). As argued by Schmidt (1974/75, 1995: 210–12), this "cloud game" was mystically linked to rain in Khoe Khoe thought, and the game—"African chess" or *mankala*—has this and other associations of fertility all over Africa, where it is a widespread, seemingly ancient game (Townshend 1976/77: 92–94).

An example from Nharo folklore will serve to illustrate the trickster's typical mode of creation—that is, through actions or effects that follow from some prank that has gone awry. The tale explains the origin of the riverbeds and water holes of the Kalahari:

> Pate walked and he saw a puffadder. She was sleeping in a hole in the sand with her young ones. He went over to the hole. He jumped over it and defecated on the puffadder and her young ones. He did this over and over again, until the puffadder thought she would teach him a lesson.
>
> And so when Pate came the next time and when he jumped, the puffadder bit him in the balls. They swelled up to a tremendous size, the size of boulders.
>
> Pate was in terrible pain and he ran all over the country digging holes to relieve his pain (by cooling his testicles). This is how every hole in the ground, the pans, rivers, caves and little depressions, were formed. (Guenther 1989: 121; a //Gana variant is noted by Tanaka 1996: 25)

The Trickster as God

One of the most enigmatic and complex aspects of the Bushman trickster is his relationship to god. He may be one with the main creator god—as among the //Gana, whose "fickle god Piisi/koagu is also allotted the status of the trickster" (Tanaka 1996: 25)—or he may be a second god, or a godlike being, standing in an oppositional, appositional, or parallel relationship to the creator god. As one might expect, the nature of that relationship is thoroughly ambiguous.

As already noted in part in the previous chapter, among some Bushman groups, such as the Namibian Ju/'hoansi, the trickster protagonist ≠Gao!na is at the same time the great god Hishe (Marshall 1962: 223). His name, as protagonist, may be Kaoxa; however, his divine name is usually reserved for his persona as god (Biesele 1993: 22). One of the other five names, and identities, of the great god Hishe/≠Gao!na is also //Gauwa, presented by Marshall as the "lesser god" of !Kung theology (Marshall 1962: 238–41). Yet, complicating matters further and adding to the ambiguity that attaches to this complex divinity, the Ju/'hoansi on the Botswana side of the border appear to employ the name *//gangwa* for the heavenly god, differentiating—not without some disagreement and confusion, it would seem—between the "great //gangwa" (*//gangwan!an!a*) and the "small //gangwa" (*//gangwa matse*) (Lee 1993: 113). While the trickster traits are much more developed in ≠Gao!na, //Gauwa's other being, the latter, "lesser god" also has certain trickster traits: //Gauwa is a "small man," yellow in color, thick-bellied, and of "small sense," who makes "many mistakes" and moves between heaven and earth, capriciously instigating good and evil deeds (Marshall 1962: 240). He is also the willful and wayward servant of the great god (Marshall 1962: 239). An earlier writer on the !Kung, Viktor Lebzelter (1934: 54–57), presents yet another reading of the nature of this complex divinity. As "/Nawa," he is the "great captain" of a host of smaller "//gaunab"s. While /Nawa is basically good and beneficent—especially to trance dancers, to whom he gives the power to heal, and to hunters, to whom he brings good luck in the hunt and from whom he receives offerings of meat after each successful hunt—his //gaunab underlings bring a great many diseases to humans. Like their master they live in the sky and tend their fires, visible as stars in the nocturnal sky.

The !Kung conception of //Gauwa is similar to the //Gãũwa of the Nharo and G/wi, who on the one hand is held to be a trickster, on the other a god, the "son of God," or a demiurge figure who competes with the creator, forever envious of the latter's greater creative powers (Guenther 1989: 50). The trickster imitates God in the act of creation, coming up, at every turn, with lesser and inferior, inverted or caricaturized versions of what God has made.

The Nama, linguistically and culturally similar to the Nharo and other "Central" Bushman groups, entertain the same dual concept of two opposed gods: the creator god Tsui//Goab and his adversary //Gaunab (Hahn 1881; Schapera 1930: 376–78, 396–97; Barnard 1992a: 257–60). This //Gaunab is not like the Nharo trickster //Gãũwa, however; in Nama supernaturalism the trickster is yet another figure, Heitsi Eibib. Like ≠Gao!na of the !Kung, this trickster-god has an alias when he appears in his guise as protagonist, namely Haiseb. However, once again there is no consistency on this point as Haiseb—laughed at and scorned in tales as fool, prankster, and man-eater—will also be referred to by storytellers as "the greatest being of the world . . . something like the Lord God" ("*das grösste Wesen der Welt . . . so etwas wie der Herrgott*") (Schmidt 1980: 9). In fact, some storytellers will substitute "God" for Haiseb, when telling a tale featuring the latter figure (Schmidt 1995: 20–22). Haiseb is the protagonist also of the oral literature of the Nama-speaking Hei//om Bushmen and Bergdama blacks (Schmidt 1986). Among the last group, the Bergdama (or Dama) //Gamab is different still: he appears to be the *only* supernatural being of the Dama belief system who combines within himself both life and death, as well as good and evil (making him an amoral spirit being), and who presides over a large village-like "heaven" to which depart the souls of the dead, in whose lives and affairs, while they were on earth, he frequently interceded (Schapera 1930: 397; Barnard 1992a: 260).

This complex and contradictory relationship of the trickster to divinity reveals that in Khoisan supernaturalism the former figure is more than the droll protagonist of oral literature, the role usually ascribed to him in other mythological traditions. He may also be a potent and well-defined divinity, or, as among the Bergdama, *the* divinity. ≠Gao!na is both the trickster Kaoxa and the great god Hishe. The same can be said of the Nama trickster Haiseb, who, as Heitsi Eibib (or even as Haiseb) was very much a god; indeed, according to Hahn (1881: 131–35), he was one with the creator god Tsui //Goab. He was worshipped at the various "grave" sites that people erected for him with heaps of stone, or on top of a certain tree to which he was carried by the wind, and was prayed to for rain, cattle, and good health (Schmidt 1993: 11, 1995: 201–205) and for success in the hunt (Schapera 1930: 398).

Help in hunting, especially after a succession of failed hunts, was one of the principal ritual functions of the trickster-god among a number of Bushman groups. //Kaggen was a "Master of the Animals" figure among the /Xam, who especially loved the game antelopes, especially the eland. This great antelope was the "centre-fold" creature in Bushman symbolism and religion (Vinnicombe 1976; Lewis-Williams and Biesele 1978; Lewis-Williams 1981, 1988; Guenther 1988). It was "God's favourite animal . . . lovingly created by the divinity and fed and groomed with honey-water" (Lewis-Williams and Biesele 1978: 120; also see Schmidt 1995: 192–94)—and it surrounded Cagn "in droves like cattle" (Schapera 1930: 181). Other favorites were the hartebeest (/Kaggen's "second favourite antelope"), gemsbok, and springbok (Lewis-Williams 1981: 5). The trickster-god /Kaggen employed a variety of ploys and ruses to distract a hunter from the prey animal he attempted to bring down; for example, he might turn into a louse to bite and torment the hunter and make him lose the animal's spoor (Bleek 1932: 120; Hewitt 1986: 125–28). As "chaser of game" he made animals, who were once as tame as oxen, wild and wary of men[4] (Hewitt 1986: 130–31; Guenther 1989: 160–61).

Similar attitudes and beliefs were held by other Bushman groups. In a ruse attributed to //Gãũwa by the Nharo he turns himself into a certain insect and approaches hunters, in order to spy on them as they plan out the hunt and to spoil its outcome (Guenther 1989: 116). If a Hei//om hunter abuses an animal or kills it against the wishes of //Gamab, the "Lord of Animals" will shoot the hunter with his disease- and death-arrows (Wagner-Robertz 1976: 540).

Reference has been made on several occasions to the trickster-god's healing role, as master of medicines and custodian of healing arrows in the context of the curing trance dance. We will meet the trickster-god in that capacity again, in chapter 8, where the trance dance will be examined in some detail. In chapter 7, we will meet //Gãũwa again in another ritual setting—passage rites—for both girls and adolescent boys. "Liking the women" even in his divine form, //Gãũwa is believed by the Nharo jealously to guard girls during menarche in order to keep away human rivals. As *//Gãũwassa,* his female guise, he is present when young men are instructed by their elders during male initiation.

As divinity, concerned with a variety of mystical matters bearing on the lives of the Bushmen—in particular hunting, healing, and passage ritual—the trickster-god, unlike his protagonist persona or counterpart, was thus capable of eliciting numinous sentiments in the Bushpeople. Among the "Maluti" Bushmen of Lesotho and the Orange Free State, the Mantis-trickster Cagn ('Kaang, or /Kaggen) was the "man (master) of all things," responsible not only for the animals—to whom he had given their special markings—and the hunt, but also for rain and the trance dance, performed for curing and prior to a raid (Schapera 1930: 180–81). He was prayed to and was "the object of a cult" (ibid.). His divine nature is revealed by his close association, or identification, with the double-gendered creator god 'Ngo. So numinous in portent was this dual deity that only the initiated men and healers knew of him and were allowed to speak his name (Schapera 1930: 181–82). /Kaggen-Mantis-God is described by one writer as "a pervasive, omnipresent, protean presence inhabiting the crucial areas of San life" and a "divinity who maintained the equilibrium between men and nature" (Lewis-Williams 1981: 124). While Nharo people may laugh and scoff at //Gãũwa in his personification as trickster, there is hushed silence at those moments in a trance dance or initiation rite when, as god, he is believed to be in the darkness of the wilderness outside the dance circle—or circle of old and young men at the initiation site. As for ≠Gao!na, who, as seen above, is one with the "great creator and controller of all things," the !Kung may only refer to god by that name because it is his "earthly" name and "less potent" than the other divine names (Marshall 1962: 223). The !Kung "'fear' to utter the names of the gods," to do so is "a death thing," and an explicit exhortation to children is the avoidance of any of the god's names (Marshall 1962: 227). Whenever reference is made to the gods it is with terms of respect (Marshall 1962: 226–27).

Although the two personas of their trickster-god are opposite in their mystical and moral character, as are the emotional attitudes extended to each, the Bushmen nevertheless merge the two personas. The reason, perhaps, is that both beings are creatures of the veld, and running through both their veins is the chthonian *élan vital* of nature, which brings, unpredictably and unaccountably, not only game, plant food, rain, and health, but also dearth, drought, death, and disease. Yet, having merged these two opposite beings—and having "insisted . . . that they are one and the same" (Marshall 1962 :233)—the Bushmen at the same time also differentiate between them, thereby creating vagueness and inconsistency (Marshall 1962: 235).

During storytelling sessions they approach the God from the "religious perspective" (à la Geertz 1966: 26–28) while laughing and scoffing at the Trickster, who may be derided for all his foolish and uncouth outrages. A rarer emotional response is to applaud and praise him for one of his good or providential deeds, or to pity him, in those tales that see him weeping over the death of a creature he loved. In his guise and demeanor, the trickster-god is usually depicted as a human; whereas the trickster protagonist is frequently grotesque, ogre- and animal-like. Yet, at the same time, a storyteller may remind his or her audience that, while he was a foolish and malicious prankster who harmed people—as in the story just told—he also helped humans, as he was, after all, also "something like god" (Schmidt 1980: 9; also see Schmidt 1986), indeed, even "exactly like god" (Schmidt 1993: 11). As god, the trickster receives prayers and is a trance dancer's directing spirit being. However, people may also rail at him: "Idiot! You have done wrong. You make me ashamed. Go away" (Marshall 1962: 239). Such may be the words toward //Gãũwa, especially of dancers who sense him near and seek him out once their bodies have collapsed in trance, to wrestle with him and force him into restoring health to people (Guenther 1986a: 271).

The grossly obscene, loathsome, and ludicrous attributes of the protagonist are bracketed out, however, when his divinity is stressed. Correspondingly, within tales the divinity aspect of the trickster's persona is generally absent, except perhaps at the beginning or conclusion of a tale, to remind everyone that, for all his outrages and obscenities, he is also the "greatest being" (Schmidt 1980: 9), that is, exactly like, or something like, god. Thus, while Megan Biesele's observation that the divinity aspect of the trickster's persona is absent from the tales (Biesele 1993: 181) may apply to Ju/'hoansi mythology—as well as reflect the general tenor of Khoisan oral literature—there are Khoisan mythological traditions wherein the moral nature of the double-faced protagonist is not so clear-cut. No matter which persona he adopts—vulgar, deceitful prankster of the stories, or protector of animals, dispenser of medicines, and guardian of rules at initiation—people never lose sight of the divine or earth(l)y counterpart to their trickster and god.

As revealed in Lorna Marshall's portrait of the protagonist ≠Gao!na, this merger of two opposite supernatural figures and emotional attitudes creates no small measure of confusion in the minds of the Bushmen, and a discrepancy—

"a forced and superficial verbal resolution"—between what they say and what they think and feel about their veld divinity:

> ≠Gao!na, we were told, was the oldest name of the great god. Through that name the !Kung identify the great god with an old *≠Gao!na,* the protagonist of many ancient tales. Some sense of logical necessity, I believe, compelled the !Kung to merge the two concepts so that they say, when they are asked, that the *≠Gao!na* of the tales and the great god are the same being, but this is a forced and superficial verbal resolution, for the two beings could hardly be more different. The people, I believe, really imagine them as different, and behave in quite a different manner as they speak of them. They tell the tales of the old *≠Gao!na's* doings without restraint, say his name aloud, howl and roll on the ground with laughter at his humiliations, whereas, when they speak of the great one in the east, they whisper and avoid his name. Yet they think that somehow in the rightness of things these two beings must be one, or so they are said to be. (Marshall 1962: 228)

Sigrid Schmidt (1986a: 242), differentiating between the trickster-god as he appears in folktales (*Volkserzählungen*) and folk beliefs (*Volksglauben*), notes a like contradiction and ambivalence in the sentiments of people toward Haiseb:

> With what keen merriment are the stories presented, how heartily people laugh about the foolish antics! There is no trace of this laughter or of the laughable in folk belief. There, what predominates is anxiety, fear, at the least awe. (Schmidt 1986a: 242, my translation[5])

As I have shown elsewhere (Guenther 1997c), it is only among the Christianized Bushmen—who have been introduced by missionaries to a dualistic notion of divinity which merges //Gāũwa with the wholly and unequivocally evil figure of Satan[6]—that the two godly beings become compartmentalized, morally and mystically. Yet, even so, the old ambivalence about the traditional trickster-god lingers on, in the feelings of even the most committed converts to the new religion. This is evident in a statement of the old farm Bushman Gaishe, a recent mission convert and the evangelist's church interpreter:[7]

> The oldest people did not separate these two men; they did not say this one is good and this one is not good. Now we are told that //Gāũwa is bad and only N!eri and his son Jesso Kreste are good. But we think that //Gāũwa is not so bad; he is, after all, under N!eri's control. And some things they do together; for example, to punish a bad person. N!eri will let //Gāũwa have him.

Across the border in Namibia, on one of the farms in the Gobabis District, a farm Bushmen put his own ambivalent thoughts on the question of the supposed identity between //Gāũwa and Satan somewhat differently, in terms that are not so much abstract-theological as *real*-political:

> I have often asked myself: "Who is Satan? He can't be //Gaua, as this one is all good and well-disposed towards us. What I think is that every bad Boer is a Satan! There is no other Satan that we !Kung of olden times would know." (Gusinde 1966: 22, my translation[8])

Yet, for all the doubt and ambivalence, as I will show below, there are also some—I think few—farm and mission Bushmen who have come to adopt the dualistic, compartmentalized view of divinity the missionaries have pressed on them. I will return to this matter—the relative success of the Christian mission among the Bushmen—in chapter 9.

Another Christian take on Bushman religion is the work of the Austrian Paters Wilhelm Schmidt (1933: 539–695) and Martin Gusinde (1966: 6–81), formulated in the context of the then (1930s) current and controversial "primal monotheism" framework for research in comparative religion. Being conceptually wedded to that scheme, the interpretation of these two cleric-scholars differs from that of the converted Bushmen and their missionary mentors. Whereas the latter would see Bushman religion as consisting of two gods—one good (=God), the other evil (=Satan)—the two scholars, true to the spirit of the monotheistic view they hold of Bushman religion, have identified //Gauwa not with Satan but with God, completely bracketing out this being's destructive, malicious, quixotic side. They locate evil within the trickster protagonist, whom they regard as a separate, possibly borrowed evil spirit being.[9]

Thus, to Pater Gusinde (1966: 75) //Gauwa the God is a "distinguished, impeccably moral personage" ("*vornehme, tadellos sittliche Persönlichkeit*"), devoid of "human urges" ("*menschliche Bedürfinisse*"), such as eating, drinking, sleeping—let alone sleeping with a woman. He is likewise without any "human inclinations" ("*menschliche Veranlagungen*"), such as excitement, anger, malice, and aggressiveness. Companionless and celibate, he lives in his caelial realm. He sees to it that each individual and group subscribes to "all laws that are in force and all exiting customs" ("*alle geltenden Gesetze und bestehenden Gewohnheiten*").

All this is as far removed as can be from the //Gãũwa of this chapter and, I submit, from the beliefs and myths of the Bushmen. What Gusinde has presented is a divinity arrived at through deficient ethnography[10] and filtered through a mesh of Christian theology. Gusinde's exegesis of //Gauwa confirms Sigrid Schmidt's (1986a: 228) astute comment (in the context of the Nama trickster-god Haiseb) that no scientific or theologically conceived paradigm can do justice to so complex a divinity. Gusinde's portrait of //Gauwa is a fanciful piece of ethno-fiction. Pater Gusinde's "creator and mighty architect of the universe" ("*Schöpfer und machtvoller Gestalter des Alls*") is about as remote from the veld god as the Abbé Breuil's "Isis-Diana of the Lesser Mystery of Egypt" is from the White Lady of the Brandberg!

The formulation of fanciful notions about Bushman divinity, and the dubious mental process of projecting Christian notions on Bushman belief are paralleled in reverse among some of the farm and mission Bushmen, in their notions about Christian religion, specifically the figure of Jesus Christ. Just as the Judaeo-Christian god is the a priori model of Pater Gusinde's //Gauwa, so the trickster-god guides the Bushmen's perception of Jesus Christ. Let us now turn to this latest addition to the gallery of tricksters in Bushman theology.

//Gãũwa Meets Jesus Christ

Given the ambiguity of //Gãũwa, and the ambivalence people feel toward this supernatural and mythological figure, it is not surprising that the trickster-god should be a "person of great difficulty" for those contemporary farm Bushmen who have had exposure to Christian beliefs (Guenther 1997c). The confusion derives from the dualistic theology of the new religion, which posits a God (along with his son) to be good and the devil to be evil. God is identified with N!eri, and //Gãũwa—or the equivalent trickster figure of other groups, such as Heiseb among the "Daman" Bushmen of northwestern Namibia (Lebzelter 1934: 10)—with the devil. The most recent reiteration of the latter conflation is the definition of "devil" and "satan" as *dxawa* (i.e., //ga[u]wa[11]) in the *Naro Dictionary*, currently compiled by the Summer Institute of Linguistics' cleric-linguist Hessel Visser.

Yet, as we just saw, in the view of farm and even some mission Bushman, //Gãũwa is "not so bad" and "under N!eri's control." From this follows the heretical, if logical corollary—which I have heard entertained by one or two farm Bushmen with whom I discussed these matters at and near the mission station at Dekar—that Satan, too, is probably "not so bad." To his severest shock, an early Rhenish missionary among the Khoekhoe was forced to confront the same abomination: having just asked his assembled congregation who it was that created them and all around them, the answer he received was, "the devil" (Schmidt 1973: 107).

However, more common was the conflation of //Gãũwa with Jesus Christ, or Jesso Kreste.[12] Sigrid Schmidt, who collected her Nama and Dama folktales from largely Christianized informants (Schmidt 1980: 241), reports a like process of conflation, of Jesus Christ with Haiseb, who was referred to as "our Jesus of old times."

The merger of these two figures is reflected also in the Christian glosses that some early commentators have given to some of the Haiseb myths. Sigrid Schmidt (1986a: 212–16) cites one example: Heitsi Eibib, after discovering a stand of ripe raisin berry bushes, asks his family to bury him in a shallow grave nearby. It is a ploy to enable him to eat up the succulent berries all on his own, an action he carries out as soon as the his family have walked away. He easily digs his way out of his grave and so gluttonously feasts on the berries that he has a violent attack of diarrhea. Schmidt points out that the tale, told with much glee, is about the trickster's obscene food greed and his refusal to share, and not, as the commentator Hahn has suggested, about the Old and New Testament themes of Adam eating the forbidden fruit and of Christ's resurrection. We have here another instance of "misapplied theology," akin to Gusinde's exegesis of //Gãũwa.

Among the Ghanzi farm Bushmen Jesso Kreste is featured in a number of origin myths, including imaginative, syncretistic cognates of the biblical creation accounts that may feature Addam and Effa as two of the "people of the

Early Race." In one story (Guenther 1989: 43–50) Jesso Kreste is one of the //gãũwas who supplies trance dancers with their curing arrows. The story featuring this //Gãũwa Jesso Kreste was presented to me by an old Nharo trance dancer by the name of //Ose, as a genuine *hua* ("a story of the old people"[13]). In it, Jesso Kreste lives in a house not far from the two termite-hill houses inhabited by Addam and Effa. They store bundles of healing arrows in front of their houses which Jesso Kreste will take and deliver to the //Gãũwani, his servants. They, in turn, will deliver the arrows to dancers who come to //Gãũwa's realm in trance. The story points to the mediating, providential role of Jesus Christ toward the dancers who, in entering the trickster-god's realm as spirits to obtain the healing arrows with which to treat the sick back in the villages, will no longer have to confront the trickster's spirit servants (the //gãũwani) directly. This they were previously required to do, at their gravest peril, before the arrival of Jessu Kriste on the supernatural scene. Like their master //Gãũwa, the trickster-god, the //gãũwani are capriciously dangerous, and the encounter with either //Gãũwa or any of his servants could cost the shaman his life. Jessu Kriste, a //Gãũwa himself—but one serene, passive, and strongly committed to healing —is far less dangerous.

Some of the notions entertained by other Christianized Bushmen, such as the Ju/'hoansi around Tshumk!kwi, show that there can also be a less serene side to Jesso Kreste. Like //Gãũwa, he seems to "like the women," being married to three wives (Volkman 1982: 9). His solicitousness toward the young, married Samaritan woman at the well, the text for the missionary's sermon delivered the Sunday before (Volkman 1982: 46; also see J. Marshall 1982), was seemingly mistaken as solicitation by the Ju/'hoan woman N!ai who attended the service. In her commentary (see chapter 6) after the sermon (Volkman 1982: 48) she noted that in his solicitous words to the woman Jesus was "fooling" her. Her comments suggest that N!ai had perhaps altogether misunderstood Jesus' intention, mistaking his interest in the Samaritan woman's spiritual salvation for carnal seduction. That is, she had, perhaps, mistaken him for a trickster.

The statements I obtained from the farm Bushmen in conversations about the new religion were frequently presented with the claim that Jessu Kriste is someone the old, old people have also known and believed in, that he is "definitely a Bushman person." He is of course nothing of the sort, but rather a new religious element about which there is evidently a good deal of confusion—the knowledge people have about him oftentimes being second-, third-, or fourthhand. Thus, the accounts I received varied widely. The degree of syncretism, or of the recognizability of Christian features, ranged from high (those in circulation among the "mission Bushmen") to low (many produced by the "farm Bushmen," such as //Ose's account referred to above). Many of the accounts I obtained had gone though a process of rethinking; the informant had cast the new supernatural figure in his or her own personal belief system. As a consequence of this process of redefinition and cultural and personal tailoring, Jesus Christ, in fact, is to many farm Bushmen Jessu Kriste, a trickster figure and the latest incarnation of the Ghanzi farm Bushmen's //Gãũwa.

In appearance, this Jessu Kriste differs from //Gãũwa in any of his other guises. He is fully human and not misshapen: a tall, thin person with a white face and beard. His abode is //Gãũwa's realm, the "good place" in heaven, where he lives as one of a number of other //Gãũwas (including Addam and Effa), among the souls of dead people. He lives on his own (although according to the Zhu/'hoan he has three wives), in a dwelling that is either a two-story "European house," or a tall termite hill. Most of his time is spent sleeping on a large "European bed"; sometimes he rouses himself to walk about and to perform a miracle or two. Because of his largely somnolent state, trance dancers are unable to summon him to the dance fire; instead, they have to go to him or to his servants themselves, as spirits in trance. It frequently happens that //Gãũwa, when in one of his vindictive moods, steals healing arrows from Jessu Kriste. This ill-intentioned act deprives trance dancers of one of their means of curing. Of all of the //gãũwani, the new //Gãũwa is the one most easily tricked.

Jessu Kriste's domain, the "good place" in heaven, is described as a "European place" (not unlike like Ghanzi town, the district capital). One rhapsodic account I received started out with the trucks that drive along gravel streets or are parked before tree-shaded double-story houses. People walk leisurely around with walking sticks,greeting each other in friendly fashion, or they sit on their front porches drinking creamed and sugared tea and chatting. At night they light their places by means of blazing coal oil pressure lamps that keep everything bright at night (and that show up as the nocturnal sky's bright stars). Cattle crowd everywhere, especially around the "dams" (water reservoirs) and windmill pumps, plump and ready to be milked and slaughtered. There are schools for children, hospitals for the sick, and a bank, opened to queues of people once a month by a clerk-//gãũwa who flies in by plane, bringing bags of money which he hands over to the people. The "bad place" is a burnt stretch of veld, with half-dilapidated grass huts that look abandoned and small. Scattered throughout are ember-lit, smoldering fires (the sky's faint stars); one great fire blazes in the center, in which bad people are burned. Wretched-looking, shivering people skulk about and cower by the fires, some of them munching on flies, the principal food item available to people in the "bad place."[14] The entrance to each place is guarded by two //Gãũwas.

We thus see Jessu Kriste within an extensively acculturated supernatural setting within which he plays a passive role. He has the appearance of a white man, and lives in a European house and sleeps on a European bed. These traits all reflect the ancillary and peripheral nature of this new //Gãũwa within the Bushman belief system. The features of the netherworld have a "cargo cult" ring to them, as they consist of all those European things—trucks, cattle, pumped wells, banks, hospitals, and schools—that contemporary Bushmen covet but never succeed in acquiring in their own lifetimes. This "candy-cane mountain" scenario reflects the people's state of economic depression and relative deprivation in modern Ghanzi society, a society dominated economically and politically by the Whites and Blacks, and rife with inter-ethnic tension (Guenther 1976a, 1979b, 1986b; Biesele, Guenther, et al. 1989). The netherworld traditionally might on occasion be depicted in like "milk-and-honey" terms; the eastern !Kung believed that the beyond held a "superabundance" of "honey, locusts, fat flies and butter-flies" in store for the dead (albeit, for consumption primarily by the "great captain" Huwe, rather than ordinary spirits) (Schapera 1930: 184). The notion that paradisal conditions prevailed at primal times, when the rocks lying on the ground were chunks of meat and fat, is also held by some Nama and Damara (though not by all; the opposite notion, that it was a place of want and hardship, is entertained by others) (Schmidt 1995: 150).

Moving from a description of the physical traits of Jesso Kriste to his metaphysical ones, we note that, like //Gãũwa (in some accounts), Jesso Kriste is held to be the son of God. His divine nature enables him to perform miracles, such as walking on water, feeding multitudes with just a small amount of bread and water, and healing or resurrecting people who are sick or who have died. While //Gãũwa has traditionally had such powers, the concept of miracle—as a discrete and deliberate display of supernatural power—is new within Bushman mystical culture. The term that has been coined to refer to this phenomenon is *aressa* ("making a thing that was never made before"). The Bushmen look at Jesso Kreste the miracle worker with some ambivalence: "he makes you believe a thing that is not," "he turns things around and makes them different from how they normally are." To one informant *aressa* is a "bad thing," akin to harming someone with witchcraft, "the sort of thing //Gãũwa might do to a person when he wants to kill him." Miracles are thus an addition to the trickster's bag of tricks; they are a species of deceit and another technique to bring about "topsy-turvydom," albeit for the most part with non-malicious ends.

A number of farm Bushmen are aware of the three central elements of Christology: the passion, resurrection, and ascension of Christ. Most of those "in the know" will also tell the story in recognizably Christian form. Others have not grasped this aspect of Jesus Christ and it is not part of their concept of Jesso Kreste. However, when I brought up this element in discussions and briefed informants on it, the story resonated with their own view of the //Gãũwa–Jesso Kreste paired being. They could make sense of it in the context of that view. Being beaten, torn apart, and killed is a plight also of the trickster, which he has suffered many times over whenever one of his misdeeds has backfired on him (sometimes bringing, in the process of his own suffering and death, boon to mankind—albeit, unintentionally so). And, after dying, he "resurrects" himself again, springing back to life. An informant similarly likened Jesso Kreste's ascension to //Gãũwa's power of flying up the sky, back to his place in heaven, or to his father, the creator god. The next time he is summoned by a dancer curing an afflicted fellow human, he will descend to be in the village among humans again, to bring to them curing medicines. Or, he will come down to the veld, to help an animal evade a hunter, or a hunter to kill an animal. The ascension element is part also of the !Kung's beliefs about the trickster: after his time on the veld as the trickster protagonist was over, he ascended the sky and became divine (Biesele 1993: 22). Thus, the basic plot elements and story line of the passion—the scorning, scourging, and killing of Jesus; his resurrection, ascension, and descent from heaven—are appreciated in a different mythological context, by persons who are outside the Christian fold and unaware of the theological and spiritual significance for Christians of Golgotha, Easter, and Pentecost.

In a number of ways Jesso Kreste deviates from the trickster, especially the protagonist of the tales. Jesso Kreste is more closely linked to the divinity trickster than to the veld trickster; thus, while he may perhaps "like the women"—and may even be married to three of his own—and while an element of trickery and deceit may be suspected in his miracles, he is never a prankster and vulgarian, but sedate and serene (as well as somewhat tired, rather than restlessly active, as is his Bushman counterpart). Also, his ritual role does not go beyond healing; while baptism is held to be a ritual equivalent to male initiation, he is not a presence at initiation rites. Moreover, he is not a protector of animals and helper of hunters. He is never anything but human in his guise, and is not associated with any animal; the Bushmen seem not have noticed the allegorical identification of Jesus Christ with the dove or the lamb.

The more religiously acculturated a Bushman is, the longer this list of divergent traits gets, and the more Jesso Kreste converges with Jesus Christ. The link to //Gāūwa of old is broken; instead, the trickster-god merges with the new savior's antithesis, Satan. The ambiguity of Jesso Kreste, and the emotional ambivalence farm Bushmen feel toward this new trickster being, in whom good and evil converge, give way to clarity. Jesus Christ, like his divine father, is wholly good and nothing but good, to Christianized Bushmen.

These tend to look with shocked embarrassment, or derisive laughter, at any Bushman who talks about Jesus Christ in the trickster idiom. Such talk is disparagingly dismissed as "lies of the old people," perpetrated by benighted, leather-clad, *kauka* ("backward") Bushmen of the veld (Guenther 1996c). Yet, even among this newest Christian flock, there are those—like the church translator Gaishe mentioned above—who still have their doubts about much of what they have learned from the evangelist. Much of its revolves around the figures of Jesus Christ, his God-father, and Satan-adversary, and the relationship of these new divinity figures to the trickster-god. All are "men of great difficulty."

The Abomination of the Trickster-God

We can assume that any other believing Christian would share the mission Bushmen's shocked reaction to what they have been led to view as heresy—Jesus Christ as trickster—or, by logical extension, as grand heresy—Jesus

Christ as Satan. Included in this category are Christian theology–oriented anthropologists, such as Pater Gusinde and his mentor Pater Schmidt, who likewise project the Christian scheme of thought and feeling onto traditional Bushman religion.

As I have argued elsewhere (Guenther 1997c), it is unthinkable for this scheme to countenance any association, let alone merger, of Jesus Christ with trickster, both because of the dualism and stoicism that constitute its philosophical framework, and because of the serenity, asceticism, and "blessed seriousness" (Rahner 1967: 38) that constitute the religious style and sentiment of mainstream Christians—primarily because of their abiding focus on "the tragedy of the crucifixion" (Trueblood 1964: 19). In a religion where "the very possibility of God laughing" is already blasphemy (Zucker 1967: 316), and where God is seen as the grand architect of order and structure, there is little room for tricksters (Hynes and Steele 1980: 17). Such a figure is the "personification of ambivalence" (Diamond 1972: xiii), the "embodiment of self-contradiction" and "the spirit of disorder, the enemy of boundaries" (Kerenyi 1972: 185). Such a figure is to be denied a place in the Christian *nomos* and *ecclesia,* which are, respectively, a system of knowledge and an institution of power with "little capacity for self-caricature and self-irony" (Cox 1970: 141). As for Jesus Christ, like his father he is deemed by certain ecclesiastics and homiletics incapable of laughing; at best he might smile, "with a spark of humour in his clear, deep eyes" (Cormier 1977: 12)—a far cry from the ribald mirth and laughter that surrounds his Kalahari counterpart.

Thus, to the Christian-minded scholar of Bushman religion, the Bushman divinity can only be understood in terms of the divinity aspect of the trickster-god. The trickster-deceiver-destroyer-hero is bracketed out and removed from the Bushman concept of divinity, the same way Satan is removed from the Christian God. And just as Satan is expelled from God's abode of heaven, so is his alleged Bushman counterpart dislodged from Bushman religion and culture generally. The figure is considered to be ancillary (a *Nebenwesen*, according to Gusinde), that is, deemed to have been derived from another culture, at some time or other in the past. Alternatively, it may be seen as an item of ethnographic misinformation, such as Fourie's alleged *Beobachtungsfehler* ("error of observation") about the !Kung trickster he calls Tji-Tji (see conclusion). Thus, in the context of a dualistic theological framework, which cannot contemplate and tolerate the conjunction of trickster and divine traits in the same god figure, a monotheistic theology is projected onto Bushman religion.

The same analytical strategy for cutting through the puzzling and—to the Western rational(ist) mind, unsettling—ambiguity of the trickster-god is also followed by some "secular" researchers. As suggested elsewhere (Guenther 1979a), this is none too surprising, given a common rationalistic, as well as dualistic, perspective that pervades both Western academic and theological thought. That is, like their theological colleagues, anthropologists and folklorists such as Hermann Baumann (1936) and Megan Biesele (1993) have analytically separated the protagonist of the veld and of the stories from the god of the sky and of belief, treating them as two distinct personas of the trickster-god, rather than integral aspects one of the other. They are depicted as separate supernatural entities, operating in distinct mystical spheres and eliciting opposed emotional responses.

The difference between the two versions of the rational, dualist interpretation of the trickster-god is the relative prominence and centrality assigned to either one or the other of his personas. For the two paters it is God, for the two professors it is the trickster.

Hermann Baumann offered his interpretation of the Bushman divinity as Pater Schmidt's contemporary, in the form of a critique and as an alternative to the latter's influential view.[15] To Baumann the basic framework of Bushman belief was not monotheism but "the mythic" (*Mythik*), and the basic supernatural agent not the one creator god but several *Busch- und Tierheroen*. These antic, magic-wielding, divinatory (rather than divine) "bush- and animal-heroes" are for the most part the trickster figures (principal among them is /Kaggen); they are the central element of the Bushman belief system which give to this religion its "absolutely unique position" ("*absolut besondere Stellung*") within the religions of Africa (Baumann 1936: 22). The reason the term "trickster" is not used by Baumann anywhere in his detailed comparative discussion of the figure—nor by his contemporary Schapera—is that the figure had not at the time been conceptualized as a mythological character or type.[16] The high and creator god, within Bushman as well as Khoekhoe religion, was viewed by Baumann as nothing more than a cultural borrowing," an adoption and adaptation at some remote time in the past "of the primal-negroid, animistic-atmospheric high god of the Bergdama" ("*lediglich . . . [eine] Umgestaltung des uralt negriden animistisch-atmosphärischen Hochgottes der Bergdama*") (ibid.: 22). Unlike the trickster figures who are richly represented and embellished within Khoisan mythology, Baumann remarks, the high god figure is almost never featured in myths.

In her recent book on Bushman folklore and religion, Megan Biesele (1993) offers an analysis of the trickster-god which, while better ethnographically based, more finely grained, and more sensitive to the perplexing nature of the trickster's duality, is similar to Baumann's. After noting the profound ambiguity of the Ju'/hoan trickster protagonist figure Kaoxa (≠Gao!na)—who consists of "two apparently different beings, one all too human, the other a god" (1993: 180)—and explaining one or another of the figure's traits as acculturational accretions, Biesele suggests that they may have been derived from two different historical strata. Moreover, she suggests that what is now merged and shares a common name may at one time in the past have been separate entities (Biesele 1993: 180–81). Thus, she is led to treat the "trickster incarnation . . . [as] an entirely separate realm of belief from that of the Ju/'hoan creator" (ibid.: 181). As did Baumann, she supports this dualistic appraisal of the divinity by pointing to the virtual absence in the tales of descriptions and details about the sky god, the lesser god, and the spirits of the dead. In this regard, she likens the Bushman god(s) to the gods of Greek mythology, who, as objects of cults, were found "only at the margins of the story, not its centre" (Havelock 1963: 171, cited in Biesele 1993: 181); the trickster's "earthly exploits," she argues, were kept distinct from the actions and being of his divine doppelgänger. As indicated above, this is largely, but not entirely, true of Bushman storytelling.

Even if Biesele's account were true and the god were indeed absent altogether from Bushman tales, the fact that Bushman individuals will, nevertheless, explicitly conflate the two figures in their beliefs and comments about the stories suggests that this separation is etic rather than emic. Biesele recognizes this—"Ju/'hoansi say he is the 'same' personage" (Biesele 1993: 22)—and throughout the book she refers to the figure as the "trickster-god" (ibid.: 17, 22, 36, 106), notwithstanding her analytical and heuristic separation of the two beings. Moreover, she suggests that one alternative way of viewing the trickster-god—"perhaps the best"—is "to see creator and trickster as two facets of a single important character" (Biesele 1993: 180).

Sigrid Schmidt is another researcher who is both equivocal and unequivocal in her interpretation of the Khoisan trickster, specifically the Nama and Damara Haiseb. While she argued in an earlier paper (1993) for the inherent unity of the protagonist and god—asserting that "Haiseb, the many-coloured trickster and Haiseb the god are one personality" (ibid.: 11)—more recently she appears to have separated the two figures (1995: 201–207, 229). She bases the distinction in part on the Khoisan mythological chronology of primal and present time. The trickster is placed into primal time, "a not yet complete world" (ibid.: 229) which is structurally in tune with his scurrilous antics, and the god into the present (i.e., pre-Christian) world, in which he oversees the lives of humans. In part her argument is phenomenological: the two figures are associated with two distinct regions of expressive and religious culture—folklore and folk belief (or religion)—and thus elicit distinctive emotional "perspectives" (ibid.: 206). People keep these regions distinct, and their responses—glee or awe—are relative to the context within which Haiseb is presented to them. Schmidt finds a parallel phenomenon in Western religion and folklore: the apostle Peter, who is on the one hand glorified with deep devotion, on the other made the butt of jokes (indeed, he is himself a trickster figure [Hynes and Steele 1980]). She applies this chronological and phenomenological perspective to explain the various contradictory elements of Haiseb, such as his guise as human as against Jackal, or as providential god as against cannibalistic ogre (ibid.: 215–24, 221–25).

Yet Schmidt admits that in the final analysis, such a separation is oftentimes "difficult" (1995: 229), and she sympathizes with the Damara student at the University of Namibia, who, after her guest lecture about Haiseb, asked with bewilderment, "so then, just who is he?" The problem of definition and distinction, Schmidt notes rightly, is especially marked with respect to the myths and stories about primal times, in which the protagonist is wont to become creator and divinity, sometimes within the same narrative. His "essential character" is "the kaleidoscopic interweaving of his many aspects" (ibid.).

For whatever—probably forever elusive—historical reasons, in the context of what Bushmen today appear to think and feel about their cosmology and their expressive and religious culture, contradiction is evidently and undeniably an integral element of the trickster-god's nature. Stemming from this conflation of two multiplex supernatural beings, numerous other opposed qualities converge, principal among them good and evil, the polarity most persistently kept apart and antithetical about the Khoisan divinity[17] (as of any divinity). As well as pervading his own nature, contradiction also permeated the mythological past—an inchoate world of incomplete, imperfect, unstable beings and states, with the trickster, that world's preeminent being, the most unstable. But not just the First Order, the world of myths, is ambiguous. The historical and contemporary world, the society and culture of Bushmen today, is shot through with like (anti)structural strains, of amorphousness, ambiguity, and ambivalence. These shape people's thoughts and feelings, their "moods and motivations," and provide the experiential basis and mental framework for the way a group or generation will read or gauge their trickster-god.

All this provides an analytical framework also for explaining why the Bushmen maintain their belief in and beguilement by this contradictory divinity protagonist rather than explaining away contradiction by establishing spurious (chrono)logical connections. Such was the framework Lorna Marshall had already considered over thirty years ago:

> I know nothing about the names *!Gara, Ganai ga,* and *≠Gaishi≠gai*", and nothing about the time or order in which the names may have been created by the !Kung, or adopted, or with which characteristics one or another may be associated. I *am* sure that current emotional needs and imaginations of the people who are now living have continued to be at work upon the image, interpreting it, recreating it, and bringing it to its present form. (Marshall 1962: 233, her emphasis)

Framing one's analysis in such terms—of the Bushmen's "current needs and imaginations"—the trickster-god's quixotic, ambiguous, multiplex, ludic nature make him the kind of protagonist, culture hero, and divinity that fits the social constitution and moral and mental disposition of the Bushmen. His protean plasticity enables people to address issues and concerns of the day—including exposure to the oppressive and exploitive *baas,* the bane of, but also the basis for, the farm Bushman's existence. The trickster-god is a wanderer both of the veld and of the farms; he is associated with the hunt and farm labor. At times he acts as a kind of patron saint to the hunter, and for the laborer he can become a kind of freedom fighter of the farms, who makes a dupe and cuckold of the baas (as he did before, on the veld, with respect to the Lion). As such his "activities are out lawish, out landish, outrageous, out-of-bounds and out of order," making him an "out person" par excellence (Hynes and Steele 1993: 3). Like the farm Bushmen today, the trickster is and has always been a "marginal man"; like him, they do not fit into the present-day social order of capitalist ranching and state government. To varying degrees and in different ways, through attitudes either of resignation and self-deprecation or of cultural revitalization and ethnic and political assertion, farm Bushmen, like the trickster, "accept rejection and reject acceptance" (Zucker 1967: 313). All the while, at the nearby mission station, //Gãũwa, the trickster-god, absorbs Jesus Christ within his being, thereby enhancing (as well as clouding) the farm Bushmen's understanding of the new religious order.

He is a mythological and spiritual being, in short, that suits the Bushmen eminently well. He, as well as the mythic and mystic beings and states that go along with him, are congruent with Bushman society and culture, in both traditional and historical times. The trickster-god is a divinity consistent with experience.

5

Stories, Storytelling, and Story Gathering: The Case of the Moon and the Hare

. . . "When I told the hare about it—knowing that his mother was not really dead but only asleep—the hare said, no, his mother did not sleep, but his mother had really died. It was this that I became angry about, thinking that the hare might say: 'Yes, my mother is asleep. . . . She lies sleeping; she will arise presently.'"

If the hare had believed the Moon we, who are people, would have come to be like the Moon: we should not die, altogether. The Moon cursed us on account of the hare's doings, and we die, altogether.

—DIA!KWAIN, /XAM BUSHMAN, MOWBRAY, CAPE PROVINCE, 1875

For darkness resembles fear, when trees do not stand in brightness so that people become afraid of the trees, the tress with darkness in them.

Angered he [the Moon] went up into the sky. He would make us lie in darkness. For there was no peace. The lion's spoor was there. We were always afraid in darkness. . . .

—//KABBO, /XAM BUSHMAN, MOWBRAY, CAPE PROVINCE, 1873

". . . I sit in the sun and listen to the stories that come from yonder; they are the stories that come from the distance.

For a story is like the wind, it comes from a far-off quarter, and we feel it. Then I shall get hold of a story from them, because they, the stories, float out from a distance. . . .

As my name floats along the road, to my place, so will I hear the stories following my feet's heels. I feel them because a story is like the wind. It is wont to float along to another place."

—//KABBO, /XAM BUSHMAN, MOWBRAY, CAPE PROVINCE, 1873 (CITED IN BLEEK AND LLOYD 1911: 299–305)

"Yes, of course some people tell stories one way, some another. Perhaps it is because people sometimes separate for a while and still go on telling stories. But in all these stories about the old times, people use different words and nouns for the same things. There are many different ways to talk. Different peoples just have different minds."

—!UNN/OBE, JU/'HOAN WOMAN, 1993 (CITED IN BIESELE 1993: 66–67)

The variability of Bushman belief is perhaps nowhere as striking as in their oral literature. This is evident when one delves into the corpus of folktales within one Khoisan group—the myth and lore, for instance, of the /Xam (Bleek 1875; Lloyd 1889; Bleek and Lloyd 1911; Guenther 1989), the Nharo (Guenther 1989), the Nama and Dama (Schmidt 1980), or the !Kung (Biesele 1993). They abound in versions and variants, "as uncountable as the grains of sand" (Biesele ibid.: 65), varying from storyteller to storyteller and group to group. It is all the more striking when one looks at Khoisan folklore as a whole. Taking that perspective,[1] the number and range of variation of tales can be dazzling, especially with respect to certain tale motifs.[2] The most widespread and varied stories are about tricksters, who are universal in Khoisan oral tradition; approximately four hundred trickster tales, versions, and variants have been recorded. The other pan-Khoisan tale is the myth of the Moon and the Hare, the topic of this chapter. Another, somewhat more restricted Bushman story, to which I will turn in chapter 7, is the myth of the "disobedient maiden," whose violation of proscription at menarche unleashes great dangers upon her and her people.

Apart from exemplifying, in dazzling fashion, the variability of Bushman belief, stories—and how they are told and acquired by the many men and women who participate in this expressive endeavor—are linked to the foraging ways of Bushman society. That link to the operational mode of foraging, and to its social relations and values, is the principal concern of this chapter. The analysis of the tale here featured will show that there is a connection between story gathering and storytelling, and foraging and its related social dynamics—specifically sharing and individualism—and will thereby reveal the presence and the workings within Bushman culture of a "foraging ethos."

My examination of the myth will consider its text and its performance, both marked by great variability, idiosyncrasy, and individualism. The analysis of these two aspects of the tale is couched in social-structural terms, within the framework of the foraging mode of production (which, as I will argue, is also a mode of thought). In view of the evident importance of this tale in Khoisan mythology and cosmology, and in light of the realization that its analysis in terms of function and process will not shed much light on why it might hold such importance, I will also attempt to probe its meaning. I will start with an outline of the myth in its most basic terms and survey its many prolific variants and versions among Bushman groups throughout southern Africa.

Textual Variation of the Myth

Approximately seventy versions and variants of this haunting myth of lost immortality have been collected in southern Africa over the past two hundred years, starting with Hendrik Jakob Wikar in 1779 (Schmidt 1989, 2:63, 1995: 152–55). Schmidt's catalog, in the section on this tale (ibid.: 63–70), includes virtually every Khoisan group; however, for reasons to be dealt with later, having to do with the linguistic and folkloristic work of some of the nineteenth-century missionaries who worked among Khoekhoe groups in Namaqualand north of the Orange, versions derived from this cultural province are represented especially fully. Because the myth thus appears to be particularly widespread in that region, some of the earlier writers regarded it as a "veritable Hottentot myth" (Bleek 1875: 10). However, Bleek was unable clearly to differentiate "Hottentot" from Bushman elements within the nine versions he collected (ibid.: 9) among the /Xam Bushmen (as well as the four versions that had been collected a decade earlier, at his behest, by the early missionaries [Bleek 1864: 69–73]). Indeed, as noted earlier, researchers today are unable clearly to differentiate between the two people, the Khoi and San (or Bushmen), as they have had a complex, two thousand year history of contact (Barnard 1992a: 28–36), such that in the nineteenth century, when Bleek and Lloyd recorded /Xam Bushman oral traditions, these had doubtless become permeated with Khoi elements.

On the question of ethnic authorship of the myth, one other contender must be brought up, namely such Bantu-speaking groups as the Zulu, Tswana, Pedi, and Herero, all of them neighbors to Khoisan peoples, all of whose folklore traditions have left their imprint one on the other (Biesele 1993: 31–17). Variants of the myth can be found in their mythologies as well (Bleek 1864: 74; Molema 1920: 173–74; Mönnig 1967: 46; see also Schmidt 1989, 2:63, and

Guenther 1989: 52), and some of the Khoisan versions appear to have Bantu elements (such as the chameleon messenger). This raises the question as to which of these two neighboring peoples are its author, the Khoisan or the Bantu speakers. For reasons gone into in an earlier chapter (chapter 3), I regard this as very much a moot question, in view of the centuries of contact between the two groups and the resulting difficulty of sorting out who got the tale, or elements thereof, from whom. Moreover, in the context of contemporary scholarship in the field of oral tradition, the question is of little analytical interest since folklore is treated as dynamic and changing, rather than in terms of static, museological labels or categories. As will be argued in the next section, a dynamic perspective on oral literature is especially appropriate when one looks at the myth and lore of a foraging group such as the Bushmen.

Here then is the tale of the moon and the hare, presented in stripped-down, generic, and composite form:

> The moon enjoins Hare to go to the village of the people to take to them Moon's message to humankind: that henceforth humans, when they died, would not die forever but would, upon their deaths, rise again. In this they would be like Moon himself, who dies at day's rise, only to rise again the following night. Upon arriving at the village of the people Hare distorted the message, telling humans that when they died they would die forever. Hare's distorted message cost humans their immortality and it brought them also the fear of death. Angered at Hare's lying, Moon split his mouth, creating the split hare's lip. Humans have hated the hare ever since and will kill it when they see it in the veld.

This basic plot is played out in endless variations which affect each and every one of its elements. Some accounts of it are truncated, others add further elements to the story. What is left intact, however, in almost every variant, is the cosmogonic, as well as emotional, core of the myth: that death was brought to humans because the magnanimous intentions that the moon—embodying eternal life—held for humankind were falsely conveyed to them by his mischievous messenger, the hare.

Some of the best-known versions, those told to Bleek and Lloyd by their /Xam storytellers, are truncated and leave out the messenger element (Bleek 1875: 9; Guenther 1989: 72–73; Schmidt 1989, 2:68–69). Bleek held these to be variants of the Bushman version, as against the Hottentot version that featured the messenger. This was the view also of Wilhelm Schmidt, in his own comparative analysis of variants of the tale (Schmidt 1933: 93–95). We now know that this assumption was incorrect and hasty, as it was based on too limited knowledge of Bushman folklore (which, in Wilhelm Bleek's case, was restricted almost exclusively to the /Xam, and in Schmidt's case consisted of only five variants).

In the alleged "Bushman" version of the tale Moon is seen to talk directly to Hare, who is bereft because his mother has just died. He talks to Hare-child, the "little orphan," either consoling or berating him and eventually threatening him, as he becomes progressively angered by the child's stubborn refusal to believe Moon's cryptic and paradoxical message about the non-death of his apparently dead mother. In one variant, by the narrator //Kabbo (LII.–6.664–677;[3] see Guenther 1989: 72–73), Moon's admonitions to the crying Hare are devoid of consolation and the message of resurrection; instead, in taunting and gloating fashion, Moon tells Hare-child to cry his heart out as his mother is good and dead, and forever so, while he, Moon, enjoys eternal life. The roles are reversed in another /Xam version, told to Lucy Lloyd by Dia!wain, wherein it is, in fact, Moon's mother who has died, leaving Moon the orphan. And Hare talks to the bereft Moon, telling him jeeringly what he just before told humans: that death is forever, even for Moon's mother.

Moving beyond the /Xam to other Bushman groups, one generally finds the same scene—a bereft child being consoled or hectored by the moon. Points of variation are the relationship of the principals to each other, their gender, or their ontological or vital state. Thus in a !Kung version the dead person is Hare's son. Moon reassures Hare that his son is not fully dead and that he will return to his father. Weeping, Hare states that his son is already undergoing putrefaction and he throws his body away (Schmidt 1989, 2:69). In a version recorded by Maack (n.d.: 34), possibly among the Hei//om, Moon is seen to be a young woman and the bereft party is male rather than female. Moreover, he is not an animal but a young boy. In his anger at the child's refusal to believe that his mother will live again—in the story, she appears not to be dead at all but merely unconscious—she splits the boy's upper lip and changes him from a human into a hare.

On the matter of the moon's gender, one should note that the female moon is rare within Khoisan mythology. The Hietshware told a tale which depicted the moon as a young and alluring woman who bathes at night and, in Lorelei fashion, brings doom to some nearby hunters who watch her voyeuristically (Dornan 1917: 80–81). More frequently and typically, the Bushman Moon is a man while Hare is a young girl or nubile maiden. She is such in a Nharo version of the lost immortality tale (Guenther 1996c). It was told to me by my most knowledgeable informant, !Khuma//ka, as a melodrama of lust and vindictiveness: Moon, a lecherous old man, lures the wary maiden into his lair and rapes her. To punish him for his vile act Hare-maiden first of all distorts the message about resurrection, underscoring its impact by adding the physical detail about the stench of the dead body (Guenther 1989: 53–54, 1996c). The last detail is found in a number of other versions, along with the taunting admonition that henceforth humans would have to bury their dead bodies because they will rot and stink (Schmidt 1989, 2:65, 66, 69). Next, she returns to Moon's place and throws her pubic apron on his face, after having first heated it on the embers of his fire to make it scalding and sticky. Thereby the dark side of the moon was created, as well as the blotches on his face, brought about by his attempts to scratch away the stinging, sticking apron.

The fact that Hare is usually cast as female, and especially as a young girl, disassociates the hare figure in the lost immortality story complex from the trickster persona which Hare holds in some Bantu tales, as well as some Bantu-derived Bushman stories (Schmidt 1989, 2:191–93; Guenther 1989: 191–93). The disassociation of the hare and the trickster in this tale applies especially to those versions that feature Hare as a nubile maiden, a figure that many a Khoisan trickster would typically lust after. For the trickster qua lecher to become such a figure himself would create a subject–object inversion (not that such would be impossible, given his ambiguous ontological state).

Yet, even some tales in the Moon and Hare set give to Hare something of the trickster's deportment. This is evident in two types of variants, those in which Hare is Moon's messenger and those in which Hare is the sole character of the tale. In the latter version Moon—or, in fact, God, introducing yet another variable dimension of note—is left out altogether as a force majeure determining the life or death of humans. Instead, in such tales it is Hare who, on his own whim, announces death to humans (Schmidt 1989, 2:68, 69). The stories that feature Hare as Moon's messenger to mankind cast the protagonist in one of the trickster figure's classic and universal garbs. In delivering the message, he usually (though not always) distorts the message out of mischief or malice—either wantonly, on a whim, or vindictively, because he is angered at some humans. The last may happen because the humans taunt him while he is delivering his message correctly, steadfastly refusing to believe the paradoxical conundrum he presents to them (the same way Hare, in other versions, disbelieves Moon). In another variant Hare is angry at the humans because they saw him naked as he was bathing (a variant, one wonders, of the above-mentioned Hietshware tale in which some men spy Moon-woman naked?) (Schmidt 1980: 6, 1989, 2:64).

The tricksteresque messenger element, in those versions that feature it, vary widely as well. The message may be conveyed either by one messenger, who is usually (though not always) Hare, or by two messengers. In tales featuring a second messenger, who is usually a small, slow, short-legged creature—such as a chameleon, a tortoise, a millipede, a louse, or a mouse—this second protagonist generally is the one sent out by Moon (or God) (Schmidt 1989, 2:63, 65). Being slow, the second messenger is usually overtaken by Hare who, again engaged in a classic trickster ploy, rushes to get to the people before the real messenger, and presents the distorted news. The versions vary as to Hare's motivation; in some cases, as indicated above, Hare intends mischief or malice, in others Hare has either misunderstood or forgotten the real message, because of his/her haste (Schmidt 1989, 2:63). In another spin on this plot element, Hare alters the message of the second messenger who has arrived before him/her, or contradicts the second messenger when he arrives after Hare and announces the message properly (Schmidt 1989, 2:65; Dornan 1917: 80). Yet another variation has the second messenger sent not by Moon but by Hare, who is unwilling to take Moon's message himself and so deputizes the other creature (Schmidt 1989, 2:64). Finally, there is a version in which it appears that the second messenger has altogether displaced the hare (Schmidt 1989, 2:68). Moreover, in this !Kxo tale, the recipient of the message is not humankind but Moon himself: the millipede announces to Moon that upon their deaths humans will be dead forever. Moon takes this pronouncement to heart so that, henceforth, humans suffer eternal death.

Some of the etiological details of the story, too, are variable. Virtually universal is the splitting of the hare's upper lip, at the end of the tale. This act is usually committed by the angered moon (or God), but in one version (Dornan 1917: 80) by the humans because of their rage against Hare. The instrument by which Hare's lip is split varies as well: stick, heated stone, axe, or shoe. In some versions the hare, who is a human when the story begins, becomes an animal at the tale's end (Maack n.d.: 34; Schmidt 1989, 2:67); moreover, he may acquire this animal's distinctive voice (Guenther 1989: 54). As an animal, he is pursued and killed by humans (Schmidt 1980: 5); however, his flesh may be taboo to humans who abhor the meat of a creature who has brought such calumny and calamity to humankind (Bleek 1864: 71; Schmidt 1989, 2:70). Or, the curse on the hare-animal may be that henceforth he shall be eaten (Schmidt 1989, 2:70). A cosmological notion of the /Xam which confers on the hare an especially ambiguous ontological state combines these two etiological outcomes: while the hare-animal is eaten by humans, the parts of his flesh that were never reversed when he was changed from a human to an animal and which have retained their human substance, are taboo (Bleek and Lloyd 1911: 75–81). Other versions state that it was not the hare who was subjected to change but the moon, who ends up changing his terrestrial abode, henceforth to be a stellar body (as happened to his relative or adversary, the sun, in a well-known /Xam tale [Bleek and Lloyd 1911: 45–55; Guenther 1989, 2:75–81]). In one version it was none other than Hare who brought this about; he decreed that the moon was to be the shoulder blade of a wild pig which would rise up the sky and illuminate the world (Schmidt 1989, 2:67; see also p. 66).

This survey of some (though not all) of the many twists and turns in the tale's text, through its almost six dozen versions and variants, reveals a remarkable degree of variation, especially if one considers the relatively confined size of this culture area. Some of the explanations for the qualities of fluidity, ambiguity, and variability that characterize Bushman mental culture in general and that were considered in chapter 3 also apply to this story and to Bushman oral literature generally. One is the isolation of Bushman groupings, which creates regional variation; another is the opposite—interaction with neighboring groups, with the Bushman as eager "foragers of ideas," adapting and adopting story material from others, including non-Khoisan peoples. The most important factor, however, is individual innovation, which is a function of oral transmission—dealt with in chapter 3.

There is evidence for individual innovation within the /Xam corpus, the most extensive collection of oral traditions in the field of Khoisan studies. It is evident in both text and texture (that is, the tale's verbal surface, which provides an indication of performative style). There are nine accounts of the tale in the /Xam collection, obtained by Bleek and Lloyd from four narrators (whose names were /A!kunta, //Kabbo, ≠Kasin, and Dia!kwain). Even though three of them were linked to each other by ties of kinship (Guenther 1995b), they presented narratives that varied extensively. Two of the variants, by //Kabbo and /A!Kunta, were devoid of the messenger element, and the rest featured the hare as messenger. In one of the two (//Kabbo's), Moon tells Hare that his mother is and will remain dead forever, while he gloats about his own immortality; in the other, as seen above, he consoles the hare; however, he does so with mounting anger at Hare's stubborn incredulity. The tales featuring the messenger, by the brothers-in-law ≠Kasin and Dia!kwain, vary in length and expansiveness and, as indicated above, reverse the roles of bereft and consoler played by Moon and Hare. This one tale does not provide enough narrative material to bring out the dimension of textual variation to any great extent. Yet, in looking at the entire /Xam corpus, and the hundreds or thousands of pages of narrative texts transcribed by Wilhelm Bleek and Lucy Lloyd for each storyteller, it is evident that each of the latter had his or her idiosyncratic rhetorical or performative style and own level of narrative competence (Hewitt 1986: 236–42, Guenther 1989: 27–29, 1995b). The result, in /Xam oral literature, was a remarkable degree of textual, textural, and stylistic variation, in excess, possibly, of what one finds in the folklore of other societies (in all of which variation is found, as it is the hallmark trait of oral tradition).

Although the Nharo sample of this one tale I collected is too small to detect individual (Guenther 1989: 22–25), performer-specific differences, on the basis of the overall body of tales I collected among the Ghanzi Bushmen, difference due to performer idiosyncrasy is a significant factor of variation in the oral literature of these people. Of the four narratives I collected of the myth of the Moon and the Hare, !Khuma//ka's version, which was briefly summarized above, was the most unusual and imaginative account of the story. Moreover, he was a most skilled and most appreciated storyteller who never failed to attract an audience whenever he sat down to tell a story. As I will elaborate below, what makes the text of this seasoned storyteller especially interesting is its "foraged" composition. It is an amalgam of more or less traceable plot elements, narrative bricolage—derived in part from his own Nharo culture; in part, from other Khoisan and even non-Khoisan sources—assembled in his stories in his own peculiar fashion, the hallmark traits of which are a spicy bit of eroticism and much melodrama.

Story Transmission and the Foraging Ethos

The way Bushmen obtain stories and how they tell them constitute one of the clearest exemplifications in Bushman culture of what might be called the "foraging ethos," or—a somewhat different concept (as I will argue below)—

the "foraging ideology" (Biesele 1993). Looked at from this perspective, we see foraging to be more than a subsistence mode or mode of production (à la Lee 1981), the dynamics of which are set by the environment and productive processes. Instead, foraging is viewed as a mode of thought (Barnard 1993), which, while remaining articulated within the infrastructural base, exists also apart from it, unbeholden to its concerns and constraints. The same dynamics—of mobility, flexibility, diversity, opportunism—that operate within productive foraging inform ideological foraging. Those social relations and values that are generated by, and that sustain, the foraging mode of production—openness, egalitarianism, sharing, reciprocity, and cooperation; and, standing in opposition to these communalist values and practices and held in balance by them, a strongly delineated sense of individualism (Barnard 1993: 33)—are at play also within the foraging mode of thought. Before turning to story transmission among the foraging society at hand, and how it exemplifies and sustains the foraging ethos, I will consider two theoretical implications that derive from moving foraging beyond the spheres of subsistence and the social relations of production.

The flexibility of foraging society—frequently attributed to ecological factors—can now be seen as reinforced by a parallel mental factor. What this suggests is that the parameters of foraging extend well beyond ecological considerations and the forces and relations of production. As Barnard (1993: 33) states fittingly, "Bushman [*sic*] are 'foragers' in many ways," even in the absence of a hunting-gathering subsistence mode; for instance, they "forage for relatives," in the terms of their system of kin classification and gift giving. Barnard thus "prefers to see the notion of 'sharing' defined in cultural, ideological terms," as independent from the society's mode of production (ibid.: 35; for different takes on the same notion see Ingold 1988 and Bird-David 1992b). Another expression of non-subsistence foraging is what, following Kirk Endicott (1979: 221), I referred to earlier (chapter 3) as "foraging for ideas," in the context of an assessment of outside influences on Bushman religion and expressive culture.

The last point suggests that relations with outsiders, with whom many Bushman groups (as well as most other hunter-gatherers) have had contact for centuries, can also be viewed in foraging terms. That is, the outsiders represent to the hunter-gatherers not so much another, morally equivalent fellow society, to encounter and engage economically, socially, and politically, on equal terms, but as yet another resource to be exploited—foraged—in terms of cost-benefit considerations. Here, the classic case that readily comes to the mind of the Africanist is the Mbuti, the "wayward servants"—and wary and canny ones—of the black villagers (Turnbull 1966). It is because of this sort of circumscribed incorporation of "'other people' as economic as well as social resources," Nurit Bird-David (1988: 30) notes (in counter-revisionist terms), "to be used for maintaining the hunter-gatherer way of life," that the social system of hunter-gatherers, who have lived for centuries near food producers, has remained fundamentally unchanged. These contacts and arbitrations with the outsiders are typically managed and negotiated shrewdly by the hunter-gatherers, with a view to serving their self-interests (ibid.: 26).

Turning now to storytelling, what links this expressive activity (as well as others) to the social dynamics of foraging is a basic characteristic, one derived from its oral performance mode and thus especially well defined within non-literate small-scale societies with well-established oral traditions. It is what the folklorist Barre Toelken has dubbed the "twin laws of folklore performance" (1979: 34). These "laws" enjoin the narrator to keep a balance between dynamism and conservatism as he tells a story. That is, the innovativeness and creativeness the narrator brings to her performance has to be held in check by the forces of tradition and orthodoxy that derive from the content and form of the narrative, as well as from the aesthetic and moral tastes of the audience. If the narrator becomes too creative, too idiosyncratic and avant-garde in her performance, she will lose her audience and her performance will fall short of its function as a communicative event, the sine qua non of storytelling. In a performance, a storyteller is thus, on the one hand, given free rein for individual expression, and, on the other, subjected to cultural restraints that reel the narrator back into the fold of tradition. This "law" applies to all forms of folklore, according to Toelken, although genres differ as to where they lie on the "spectrum of dynamism," some (like myths and proverbs) leaning more toward the conservatism end, others (like jokes and memorates), toward the dynamism end (ibid.: 35–36).

Where on the spectrum does the myth of the Moon and the Hare lie? To what extent do Bushman storytellers heed the "twin law"? Answering these questions will reveal some of the connections between storytelling and the foraging ethos.

Given the bizarre turns the story takes in its seventy-odd, profusely varied renditions, the first impression one gains is that in Bushman oral tradition the element of conservatism may well have been suspended. If this were indeed so, it would be all the more striking, in view of the tale's genre: myth. Conventional wisdom in the anthropology of religion holds that this tale type lies near the conservatism end of the variation spectrum, in view of its function. According to Toelken (1979: 36), this function "in most cultures is to provide dramatic experiential models of protected truths and laws, which would otherwise be very abstract" (Toelken 1979: 36). Thus, in contrast to other tale genres, myths as the "embodiment of dogma" are "usually sacred" (Bascom 1965: 4). Yet, the specimen before us is anything but; it is fluid and flighty and subject to much intra- and inter-group variation. As we saw earlier (chapter 3), this can be said of Bushman oral tradition generally; myths and all the other tale types, like the rest of Bushman expressive and mental culture, lie at a far remove from the conservative pole.

In view of the high degree of individual innovativeness in storytelling, the explanation that comes to mind in trying to make sense of this dynamic, nonconservative bent of Bushman religion and art is the individualism of the people, which, as seen in chapter 2, is especially marked in this society. To recapitulate the points made earlier about individual autonomy and individuation: a Bushman person is able fully to develop his or her personal capabilities and temperament, within a culture that is relatively transparent and undifferentiated so that each person can utilize and master all of its technical, social, and symbolic resources. This the individual does within a society which allows for such development because of its egalitarian makeup and because it contains few corporate institutions or structures that might absorb the individual within the collectivity. Moreover, the society is flexible in structure and has no rigid rules to constrain the individual. Given all this, it is not surprising that a man or woman turning to storytelling should do so in his or her own individualistic, idiosyncratic, inimitable fashion. In molding the tale's text and texture to her specific proclivities and temperament, and to her own creative designs, she finds in storytelling yet another expression of, or mechanism for, individuation. As intimated above, what stories are told, and how—textually and texturally, as well as contextually[4] (when, where, and to whom they are told)—all differs from person to person and from performance to performance. Factors of variation include individual ideas or whims; levels of interest, knowledge, or competence; as well as differences in temperament and life experience. In a society made up of assertive, autonomous individuals, the range of variation brought about by these factors could be virtually limitless.

With respect to the tale at hand, I have elsewhere (Guenther 1996c; also see 1989: 22–25) attempted to explain two of the strikingly different accounts of the myth of the Moon and the Hare I collected, in terms of biographical and personality traits of the narrators. The two narrators I considered were the above-mentioned master storyteller and raconteur !Khuma//ka, and Gaishe, another old and experienced Nharo man knowledgeable in Bushman myth and lore. Yet, despite the knowledge of *hua* ("old stories") each man held, and their narrative competence, in terms of content and style their accounts could not have differed more. In accordance with his easygoing, extrovert, playful temperament, !Khuma//ka dwelled expansively on a tale's droll, frequently erotic and scatological twists. He used dialogue extensively and imitated the voices and accents of characters—for instance, the Boer *baas* or English-speaking magistrate. His favorite stories were trickster tales. These were shunned by Gaishe, who self-consciously referred to such stories as "lies of the old people." What he liked were creation tales, especially "new stories" from the Bible, which he had learned from catechism classes and church services, after his conversion to Christianity a few years back. His narrative style is sedate and restrained, without any of the other man's Rabelaisian exuberance.[5] We thus see that the versions they tell of the myth reflect personality differences: the one's account is a tabloid melodrama, with bizarre and lascivious twists and turns; the other's is a sparse, sedate, straightforward etiological tale.

Megan Biesele was likewise struck by the high degree of individuation and individualism in Ju/'hoan oral tradition. "It is difficult," Biesele (1993: 66) writes, "to emphasize enough the great latitude for individual artistry granted among the Ju/'hoansi, whether in the folk tale form or in embellished narratives of everyday experience." One of the themes in this folklorist's perceptive study of !Kung folklore is explanation of the "richness and even apparent contradiction" of Bushman oral literature, brought on by the high degree of individualism and incumbent textual and textural variation. As already noted in chapter 3, Biesele's explanation is couched in terms of the rhetorical and communicative devices of orality (especially oral mnemonics).

Yet, the impression I gained of the Nharo storytellers and their audience was that this tolerance of individualistic creative latitude in the handling of a story is not limitless. It may even be a source of mild tension among narrators or between narrator and audience. I observed on several occasions how listeners would break into a storyteller's performance, expressing disagreement with one or another point in his rendition of the story, as well as adding or amending a point here and another there, in the course of its telling by the first narrator. Another thing I observed was that as soon as the first person had finished with his story, another would proceed to tell the same tale, in his own—at times widely divergent—version, with an introductory remark such as "that's not how I know this story," or, a bit less diplomatically, "no, that's not how the story goes; it goes like this. . . ." A case in point was !Khuma//ka's version of the tale of the Moon and the Hare, which he launched into as soon as Gaishe had finished his rather emaciated and low-key account of it, to which !Khuma//ka had listened, evidently with some impatience (Guenther 1996c, 1989: 53; also see pp. 59, 88, 117–18 for other instances).

Thus, as the Bushman storyteller tells a tale in her own fashion, the "twin law" will also curb her creativity and idiosyncrasy, lest she lose her audience with antic twists and turns which may deviate too much from the norms that define the creative parameters and perimeter of storytelling within her culture. The narrative challenge faced by the storyteller, of balancing personal innovativeness against collective standards, recapitulates the organizational challenge of her small-scale, fluid, foraging society: maintaining the balance between individual and communal interests. As discussed in chapters 1 and 2, this balance is precarious in such societies, in part because of the sometimes competing value sets of individualism and egalitarianism, in part because of the looseness of social organization. Yet, that critical balance is maintained because the values that underwrite these opposed organizational tendencies are also complementary; moreover, the looseness of Bushman social structure and values also renders society resilient and more tolerant of nonconformity and innovativeness on the part of its members than most cultures.

Because creativity and tradition, and individualism and conservatism are also opposed and balanced in storytelling, an expressive event of great frequency in the everyday lives of people, narrative performance becomes an important, ongoing mechanism for both individuation and social integration. The same can be said of the other principal expressive genre of contemporary

Bushmen—music—in both its religious and secular expression: as trance chanting and joint playing of musical instruments, the former by women, the latter usually by men. Writing of the trance song, Dorothea Bleek noted how, as the women chant the song and clap its rhythm, "the time is perfect but no two in a chorus seem to hit the same note, though the general burden of the tune is kept up" (1928: 22). Bleek's account of the women's performance conveys, on the one hand, the choir's collective expressive endeavor, which, through its joined voices and rhythm, is what allows the dancers to achieve trance and the ritual to reach its numinous climax. Yet, for all its collective power, the performance does not absorb, or drown out, the individual singer, who hits her own notes as she will, either in or out of tune with the rest. As often as not the individual's notes are out of synch, giving the trance chant its subtly cacophonous sound. To the Western ear this music sounds foreign and eerie, or even repugnant (as it does to some of the Ghanzi farmers, who are wont to ban "eeyia-eeyia"—or "hua-hua"—dancing at their farms, in part because of the noise, in part because such nightlong, exhausting events reduce their laborers' work performance the next day).[6]

On the subject of male orchestral music, Nicholas England describes how some !Kung men, joining another man playing his musical bow,

> will also draw upon [the same] melodic phrases, choosing whichever they desire at the moment and perhaps adding their individual embellishments and variations to the basic phrase designs. . . . This interchanging of melodic phrases is a common method of music making in Bushmanland, and it is a principle that, to my mind *epitomizes the Bushman way in general: it clearly reflects the Bushman desire to remain independent (in this case of the other voices) at the same time that he is contributing vitally to the community life* (in this case, the musical complex). (England 1967: 60, my emphases; quoted in Anderson 1990: 32)

What England calls "the Bushman way" is one part of what I would call the "foraging ethos." It is both the opposition and the integration—and thus the balance—of the processes and values of communalism and individualism, through, on the one hand, egalitarianism, sharing, reciprocity, sociability, cooperation, and consensus; and, on the other, each independent person's pursuit of his or her individual autonomy and agenda.

The telling and especially the gathering of stories—as of motifs for paintings and prints by contemporary artists, as described in chapter 3—is also like foraging with respect to the mode of foraging, rather than its social relations. It is intimately tied up with nomadic wandering, seasonality, and dispersal and concentration; with visiting, socializing, and "smoking." All this we find in //Kabbo's lengthy musing about homesickness for his people, the Flat People of the northwestern Cape, to whom he longed to return once his captivity was over. This he spent at the home of Wilhelm Bleek in Mowbray, on probation from the Cape Town jail; pressed into domestic service—"women's household work"—he plied his eagerly interested and prodding host and master and probation officer with stories (Guenther 1995b). At the beginning of the chapter I provided excerpts of this eloquent expression of the foraging spirit in Bushman stories and storytelling. Here is the full text:

> Thou knowest that I sit waiting for the moon to turn back for me, that I may return home to my place. That I may listen to all the people's stories, when I visit them; that I may listen to their stories, which they tell; they listen to the Flat Bushmen's stories from the other side of the place. They retell them along with the stories of the other people's own part of the country. They are listening to them, when the sun gets a little warm. So that I may sit in the sun and listen to the stories that come from yonder; they are the stories that come from the distance. For a story is like the wind, it comes from a far-off quarter, and we feel it. Then I shall get hold of a story from them, because they (the stories) float out from a distance. While the sun feels a little warm and I feel that I must now certainly go and visit my men friends and talk with them. For here I do work, women's household work. My men friends are listening to stories from afar, which float along; they are listening to stories from other places. As for me, I am here; I do not obtain stories because I do not visit. Thus I do not hear stories which float along. Here I feel I am with people of another place; they do not possess my stories. They do not talk my language; they visit people who are their like. . . . The Flat Bushmen go to each other's huts; that they may sit in front of them, smoking. This way they obtain stories at their places; because they are used to visit them in this way. They are smoking people. As regards myself, I am waiting for the moon to return back for me, that I may set my feet forward in the path [leading backwards to my home]. . . . I must first sit a little, cooling my arms; that my fatigue may go out from them while I sit. I just listen, watching for a story which I want to hear while I sit, waiting for it; that it may float into my ear. These are the stories I listen to intently; while sitting silently. I must wait, listening to stories behind me, as they travel towards me, following the same road. As my name floats along the road, to my place, so will I hear the stories following my feets' heels. I feel them because a story is like the wind. It is wont to float along to another place. (Bleek and Lloyd 1911: 299–305)

//Kabbo's description of how he acquires stories reveals one of the key foraging components within Bushman oral literature, the element of contingency. //Kabbo obtains "stories which float along" in the course of his peregrinations. Like himself, and the springbok he likes to hunt, the stories he gathers move around "like the wind," from "other places," "far-off quarters." Story gathering is akin to subsistence foraging in its open-endedness and opportunism; plants and game, which "come along" as the gatherer or hunter is out on a foraging excursion, result at the end of the day in a bag of *veldkos* or "game" that is never quite what it was on the previous occasion. The hunt, as observed by Rosaldo (1989: 129) among the Ilongot, holds unexpected surprises and requires of the hunter that he improvise and respond to the unexpected. Indeed, it is this very quality of contingency, which holds the element of suspense, that renders hunting suitable stuff for narrative (Rosaldo 1989: 129). Consequently, a hunt will yield both meat and a tale, to be told while the meat is cooking in the pots, or while the foragers are smoking after the feast.

As the foragers for food make do with what they find in the environment, so the foragers for stories put together their own assemblage of narratives, as "they retell them along with the stories of the other people," as they sit with others, visiting and "smoking." And when groups split up and "people separate for a while . . . they still go on telling stories," "with different words and nouns for the same things," as the Ju/'hoan woman !Unn/obe informed Megan Biesele (1993: 66–67; see chapter epigraph), all the while picking up new material from the other groups they contact while separated from their own band. !Khuma//ka's version of the Moon and the Hare was very much foraged in this way; as noted above, it was a shreds-and-patches admixture of elements, from various Khoisan sub-groups. They derive from his own sources, his own egocentric set of "men friends" (and, in his case, certainly also "women friends"), with whom he smoked and traded *huani* ("stories"), in the course of his life and travels through veld and farms.

In sum, storytelling and story gathering are linked to two elements of foraging: its structural dynamics and ethos, and its everyday practice. Regarding the first, a Bushman storyteller recapitulates in her performance the basic moral contradiction of her society, the tension between individualism and communalism. It is found within band societies because of the fluidity, mobility, flexibility, and lability that are the structural elements of the underlying social blueprint of such societies. The performance of storytelling draws the narrator into this contradiction. In telling her story and, while in the act, curbing the innovativeness and exuberance which, as a good storyteller she has and others expect from her and cherish, the narrator both experiences that contradiction and deals with it, by balancing it out. Story gathering, through which each narrator acquires his idiosyncratic repertoire of texts and performance styles, resembles hunting and gathering. Both are contingent, opportunistic, and innovative, yielding for each foraging expedition a bricolage of food items and stories.

Foraging Ideology or Ideology of Foraging?

How does this perspective on the ideological component of the foraging ethos differ from the reductionism of earlier Marxist-structuralist perspectives, such as Godelier's notion of "symbolic labor," which he applied to the belief and ritual of another African group of hunter-gatherers (namely the Mbuti[7])?

The latter position considers ideology merely in instrumental, adaptive terms—as a means by which to render subsistence and productive processes more efficient. Myths and beliefs in such a view are considered in terms of how they function as an ideology for the productive process of foraging. This is one of the approaches taken by Megan Biesele in her study of Ju/'hoan folklore, which, along with symbolic expression in general, she explains in terms of a metaphor taken from Bushman material culture: the carrying net by means of which people carry, in their heads, and share "adaptively significant information" (Biesele 1993: 43). The body of stories, Biesele submits, provides the !Kung with "a scaffolding upon which explicit information about resources can be vividly and memorably hung" (ibid.: 42). Specific stories serve as symbolic "pegs for adaptive information" (ibid.: 54).

The perspective on the notion of "foraging ethos" offered by the concept of "symbolic labor" differs from the one taken in this chapter. I see the foraging ideology, or ethos, as something more extensive and pervasive in forager culture than merely an ideological scaffold for production. I see foraging, in Bushman and hunter-gatherer society generally, as an ethos that pervades all systems and institutions of society, including religious and expressive culture, not just the ecological, techno-economic level. This has been an explicit theme of this chapter. It has also been an implicit theme in the chapters on Bushman society, which focus on such structural qualities of social organization as fluidity, flexibility, openness, adaptiveness, and diversity, and the basic value orientations of communalism and individualism, chief among them egalitarianism and reciprocity. They are the elements of the foraging or communal mode of production (Lee 1981, 1992) and they also constitute the foraging ethos. It pervades both society and belief.

As we move from foraging ideology in general to Bushman oral tradition in particular, we must ask, how apt is an analysis of its function and meaning that is cast in "symbolic labor" terms? To be sure, Bushman folklore does contain adaptive and productive elements. To some extent stories do indeed provide a scaffolding on which to peg information about resources. However, the resources so pegged are not just natural ones, but also social ones. Stories, in content and meaning as well as religious beliefs, practices, and symbols, are much more than just pragmatic, adaptive, or ecological knowledge, or symbolic hunting tools carried in the head rather than in a quiver (Ridington 1982) to complement and compensate for low-level technology. They are also social knowledge, and mystical knowledge of "other worlds"; in fact, I would contend that in the context of Bushman oral traditions, this is what constitutes the ideational core of Bushman folklore. Also, as I have argued elsewhere (1988), stories' epistemological thrust is not only "knowledge," based on evidence and objective, distanced observation of facts, but also "understanding," through intuition, empathy, or intersubjective encounter with the thing observed (typically an animal). So many of the stories, such as the one featured in this chapter, have nothing whatever to do with the food quest and contain no subsistence information; instead, they are concerned with a host of other matters—ethical, philosophical, cosmological, or aesthetic—frequently expressed in densely metaphorical fashion. This supererogatory focus is in evidence also on rock art panels; while many depict antelopes, the species rendered most frequently, and with the most lavish care, are those least commonly hunted, for reasons that are cosmological, symbolic, and aesthetic, rather than gastronomic (Guenther 1988: 194–95; also see Vinnicombe 1976 and Lewis-Williams 1981, two studies of Bushman rock art that consider social and symbolic explanations over subsistence).

As seen in this chapter, there is also a strong performative element to Bushman oral tradition. As suggested earlier, and shown compellingly in Biesele's study of Ju/'hoan folklore, the key values of Bushman society, especially reciprocity, equality, and sharing, are underwritten as much (if not more) by the oral performance of tales as by their plot and content.

As also shown by Biesele (1993: 79–87) in the same study, these values also pervade the Bushmen's principal ritual, the trance dance, in accord with its primary function of curing through trance and transformation. Curing, in its practice by Bushman trance dancers, is a communal ritual performance; its synergetic, solidarity-inducing mode of performance lends to the ritual a distinctly social stamp (this ritual will be examined in some depth in chapter 8). This outweighs the ecological, productive function that someone working with a materialist paradigm might be inclined to impose on this ritual pattern; for example, David Lewis-Williams (1982), in one of his earlier versions of the "trance hypothesis," sees the all-pervading theme of Bushman rock art to be trance dancing and curing. In this early paper, which is more materialist in its focus than his other writings, Lewis-Williams treats both the art and its central theme as symbolic labor, which "dealt with the reproduction of world order and the social processes of production."[8] The trance dancer achieves the former objective by manipulating the powers controlling rain and game; the latter through such tasks as curing disease, reducing tension, and, by means of extra-body travel, gathering information about the environment and about neighboring bands. In listing the social aspects of the ritual —curing disease and reducing tension—alongside the productive aspects, the impression is conveyed that they hold equal significance and equal explanatory power. They do not, in my view, as will be evident in my account of the ritual in chapter 8. There is, admittedly, an ecological dimension to the trance dance, which is linked through its curing function to such biological parameters as demography, health, and mortality, as well as to hunting, through the metaphorical link of the trance dancer to the hunter and to game animals. However, these are secondary elements of the ritual, overshadowed by such social, cosmological, and mystical concerns as transcendence and transformation, and social ones as solidarity, mutuality, political empowerment, and cultural revitalization.

Thus, while Bushman stories, as well as art and ritual, do all address themselves to ecological and productive concerns, they also move much beyond them, finding their fullest expression within the mental and social spheres of thought, feeling, and action.

The Text and Its Meaning

Let us now move beyond considerations of function, process, and context to return to the tale's content, specifically the question of what it might mean. The analysis so far does not address itself to this question, and without looking to answer it we would be unable to understand why this myth held center stage position within Bushman and Khoisan mythology and cosmology, as well as incorporating—for some peoples, such as the /Xam—numinous portent. This is a difficult undertaking (especially in this postmodern age of self-doubt and cynicism), as an exegetical foray into so culturally alien a story can readily lead to error or to unwitting projection of a Western meaning scheme upon a decidedly non-Western story. Yet, without the attempt, what is surely the most intriguing question about a story laden with meaning and significance to its tellers will remain unaddressed and unanswered.

The myth of the Moon and the Hare resonates with compassion and passion, and deals with existential and cosmological issues that are both universal and culture-specific. On the affective level, through which the tale lends itself especially well to dramatic performance, the story begins with an element of universally appreciable pathos: an orphaned, bereft, and disconsolate child being comforted by a fatherly or avuncular elder. The story ends on quite a different emotional note: the chagrin and rage of one of the protagonists and of humankind at immortality lost to humans as a result of an act of folly and pettiness. The former scene, of Moon consoling or hectoring Hare-child, is spun out extensively in one /Xam narrative. The storyteller (/A!kunta), presenting his tale to a large extent as a monologue by Moon, has him restating the fact of his own immortality—as against the mortality of the "creatures that walk the earth"—a total of seventeen times, each time by listing yet another creature that "must, indeed, die," while he, the moon, lives (see chapter 3, p. 77, for the text). Paradoxically, this rhetorical device has the narrative effect of enhancing rather than diminishing pathos and poignancy, as the repeated passages employ subtle differences in phrasing. Moreover, in speaking the part of the moon, the narrator employed special clicks that appear only in storytelling. This ethnopoetic device was used by a number of /Xam storytellers for the monologue or dialogue sections of their narratives, in which specific characters each speak with a distinctive click (Bleek 1936). In fact, the myth at hand employs this device for both of the protagonists. /A!kunta (as, presumably, /Xam narrators, storytellers, and listeners generally) was so intrigued by this narrative technique that he followed up his story with a lengthy exposition (to Wilhelm Bleek) on this narrative device (B XV.–1469–82).

Profound existential and cosmological themes ring through the myth. At its face value, the myth is a story about how humans obtained death, and the fear thereof, having previously enjoyed a state of immortality. This theme, of the greatest universal import to humans, is presented in a tale that is simple and moving, and accessible to both adults and children. Indeed, it appears that several of the narrators obtained the story, as many of the other stories they knew, from their mothers (Guenther 1995b). The myth offers an explanation, through a simple story, of how death—the ultimate "problem of pain"—entered human existence.

Its theme, of resurrection (in an inverse way), may have been what piqued the interest of the early missionaries in this particular myth. The very first versions of it were collected by such missionaries as Krönlein, Knudsen, Rath, and Priestley (Bleek 1864; Schmidt 1995: 153). One might conjecture that the missionaries eagerly pounced on the myth because it provided a basis within Nama religion for unfolding Christianity's version of resurrection—which, having lost in his own native religion, a convert might regain by embracing the new one. The story gave the missionaries an "in" on Nama religious belief, on a theological theme central to both religions. As pointed out by Sigrid Schmidt (ibid.: 153), missionaries did indeed confront this "superstitious idea," either by drawing a Nama or Damara who came forward with the old idea into heated disputation, "until they fell silent in shame," or by "singing and praying with them every morning and evening" (ibid., quoting from the writings, respectively, of the missionaries Schmelen and Moritz). Bleek's book on Khoekhoe folktales that contains the nine versions of the tale was widely read, having been published quite early, first in 1864 in English, and six years later in German. It may have led subsequent generations of missionaries venturing into the field to look for the myth among the Khoisan groups they were with, and to record it in their writings (in one case four times, into the same diary [ibid.]).

One might wonder at this point, is the prominence of the myth in the annals of Khoisan folklore simply a reflection of the importance attributed to it by Western missionaries, rather than a reflection of its salience within the Khoisan mythology? Is this another feature Westerners have "made" (up) about Bushman religion, along with moon-, mantis-, and devil-worship; an antelope cult; and primal monotheism? Probably not; my sense is that the myth was important to the Khoisan people in its own right, and it was and remains prominent within Khoisan mythology even without any prodding by missionaries.

In addition to addressing the explicit, weighty existential concerns already pointed out, the myth—at a deeper, more implicit level—is about division and separation generally. Apart from the separation of a mother from its child and of life from death, the myth deals with another elemental division: between the mythological First Order of existence, or primal time, and the legendary Second Order, set in historic time and the present. This, in Sigrid Schmidt's (1980: 242–43, 1995: 152–55) view, was the central cosmological theme and role of the tale, in the context of Nama and Dama mythology. She holds it to be the *Schlüsselgeschichte* ("key tale") of Khoisan cosmogony,[9] as the acquisition of death triggered the "great turning point," the transition of *Urzeit* ("primal time") into *Jetztzeit* ("present time") (Schmidt 1980: 6–7). Schmidt also notes that this pivotal myth was told to Nama boys at initiation (who henceforth had to refrain from eating the hare's flesh). This provides the myth with an experiential referent: male members of Nama society, as their own experience of separation from boyhood, symbolically recapitulate the separation of primal time from the present.

All of these separations—mythological past from historic present, life from death, child from parent, man from boy—are matters of the deepest existential and cosmological impact for humans at all times and places. The myth of the Moon and the Hare addresses itself to these portentous issues, in a culture-specific idiom. Further binary elements permeate the story, giving the theme of separation pervasive lateral roots: night (moon) and day (people's villages), and this opposition's incumbent polarities of dark and light, above and below, and cool and warm; solitariness (moon) and community (village); wisdom and maturity (moon); and folly and childishness (hare). The etiological twists at the tale's end, too, deal with the division of what was once whole: the were-hare (as it were) with human speech becomes an animal uttering a nonhuman vocal sound; the once uniformly light and cool surface of the moon has one half darkened and rendered hot; the hare's lip is now cleft.

Yet, it must be kept in mind that today's hare-animal also contains portions of human flesh, and the other half of the moon remains as it was in primal times. And one of the two protagonists, who appears in all of the variants of this seemingly binary tale, is a messenger figure reminiscent, in some versions, of the quixotic trickster figure, the central figure of Bushman mythology and the embodiment of anti-structure. As always, when coming across what appears to be a structuralist's structures within Bushman myth and belief, one must balance what one finds against the tangle of ambiguity that runs through and around Bushman religion.

These caveats cast a measure of doubt on the binary features this brief structuralist foray into the symbolic meaning of the tale has revealed. The next chapter, which will attempt an analysis of another theme of Khoisan oral literature along functionalist lines, will end on a like note of doubt and indeterminacy. The seeming inappropriateness or spuriousness of the two standard and stalwart, tried and tested theoretical approaches of the anthropology of religion, structuralism and functionalism, raises a number of conceptual questions. These will be dealt with in the conclusion.

6

Myth and Gender

Then the anteater [woman] says: "Springbok stand! The Lynx will kill you, the Lynx will kill you, for you are a springbok, a springbok that eats grass. . . . Lynx stand! You eat springbok. Springbok stand! The Lynx will catch you and eat you for you are a springbok. . . ."

Then the hyena marries the female hyena, for the hyena feels that he is a hyena, who eats people. He therefore puts his children into a burrow, because he has married a female hyena. . . . He brings to the hyena children, to the burrow, an ostrich. The hyena children then eat the ostrich. . . .

Then the jackal becomes a jackal. He marries a female jackal, for he is a beast of prey. Once he was a man. . . .

Then the silver-backed jackal marries a she-jackal. He puts the children into a hollow. The strandwolf puts the strandwolf children into a hollow. For the strandwolf feels to marry a she-strandwolf who lives in a hollow.

Then the aardwolf marries a she-aardwolf and because he realized that she lives in a cave he puts the aardwolf children into a cave.

—//KABBO, /XAM BUSHMAN, MOWBRAY, CAPE PROVINCE, 1871 (GUENTHER 1989: 84–85)

. . . While the men were with the women they just did not know how to live together with the women. They did not know how to get along properly with the women. And they were so dying for sex. But they did not know how to use their organ with the women. . . . They tried to find the right place, where to put it, they tried but they did not find it. There they were, everybody with his wife, everybody with his wife, everybody with his wife, everybody with his wife. . . . [T]hey placed their "rifles" everywhere—in the women's nostrils, in their mouths,

> *between their toes—trying to have intercourse. But they did not find the right place to put their part. . . . they tried but they did not find it.*
>
> *One day the women recognized the men's designs and they realized that the men did not know how to use their "rifles" and they said to each other: "One of us must go with a man and she must climb a tree and when she is high up in the tree the man must look up. . . ."*
>
> *And she climbed back down. And when she had come down he advanced to her and he used what he had seen with great pleasure: "Hi, this is the place we men can use for intercourse!"*
>
> *And they both went back to the village and the men all had intercourse and there was much pleasure. . . .*
>
> —!KHUM//KA, NHARO BUSHMAN, GHANZI, BOTSWANA, 1970 (GUENTHER 1989: 62)

> *. . . Women are strong; women are important. Zhun/twa men say that women are the chiefs, the rich ones, the wise ones. . . .*
>
> —N/ISA, A FIFTY-YEAR-OLD JU/'HOAN WOMAN (SHOSTAK 1981: 288)

In this chapter I return again to the topic of gender relations, examining this central facet of Bushman social organization in the context of their mythology, wherein it is equally prominent. I attempt an analysis along structural lines, in both senses—social and symbolic—of the term; I examine, on the one hand, the articulation of myth with social reality, and, on the other, the binary opposition—through gender—between those two cultural domains, and within one of them, myth. This chapter is very much an essay, that is, an exploratory, tentative examination of the problematic at hand. Another way to view the approach here taken is as a debate that advances at first the "aye" side, which argues in favor of a structural approach to this aspect of Bushman myth, and then the "nay" side, which adduces the evidence against. This sort of exercise allows one to test the explanatory potential, for Bushman religion, of these two key paradigms in the anthropology of religion, to see how far one might get with one or the other, or with both.

As I will show, the analysis this double-barreled structural approach presents seems apt on the one hand, yet on the other it seems to miss the mark altogether. The fact that my analysis of this matter both explains and obfuscates the examined aspect of Bushman mythology is further testimony to the ambiguity of this expressive domain of Bushman culture.

Gender Relations in Bushman Society

While the examination of gender relations in chapter 1 has revealed these to be fairly equal and in line with the general egalitarianism of the society as a whole, gender equality is nevertheless in some jeopardy in Bushman social organization. The inequity is found at the most fundamental and structurally significant social manifestation of gender within Bushman society, the division of labor by sex. On the face of it the apportioning of tasks seems equitable and in line with egalitarianism: gathering to the women, hunting to the men—each task with its recognized nutritional importance and its requisite, vast, and impressive body of knowledge and skills. Furthermore, most other domestic work is shared as well, more or less equally. Yet, on closer inspection, we find that there is actually less equity here than meets the eye: vis-à-vis woman the gatherer, man the hunter in fact holds more of what—given the centrality, the "fierceness" of egalitarianism in this society—one might consider to be his fair share of social, political, and religious significance, if not power.

One of the reasons for the elevated status of the hunter is the fact that the resources he provides—meat and animals—are greatly cherished, much more than are plant foods. Meat is something of a special treat—comparable, perhaps, to the Sunday roast in Western society of earlier, leaner years. Depending on the time of year, only about one-fifth to one-third of what people eat is meat; the rest of their diet consists of humdrum plant stuffs gathered by the women: roots, seeds, leaves, nuts, and melons, on occasion with a few click beetles, lizards, fledgling birds, or the odd tortoise thrown in, to round out the food groups. People covet and crave meat, and successful hunters returning home shouldering sides of meat might elicit so bucolic a scene as rushing, chanting, ululating, and dancing children and women. The joy is even greater if the animal is fat, as in Bushman culture animal fat is the symbolic cognate of honey and sex. Animals are food not only for the stomach; the mind, as shown in chapter 2, also feasts on beasts. Indeed, as we will see again in the next two chapters, animals are probably the Bushmen's prime food for thought, and—at the aesthetic, symbolic, and ritual level—they are the Bushmen's "significant others" with close mystical association to divinity, healing potency, regeneration, and sex (Guenther 1988).

Men usually hunt either as individuals or in small groups, three or four strong, and not infrequently they find themselves out on a hunt for days on end, roaming over wide stretches of terrain, in search of wary game or in pursuit of a large game animal—an eland or a giraffe—wounded with a poison arrow of slow lethal effect. This style of hunting establishes strong male solidarity among the men and demands of them physical and mental stamina, in contrast to plant gathering, where the quarry does not run away or charge you but is there for the picking or digging up. Hunting also forges political bonds with neighboring groups whose territory the men may enter in the course of a far-ranging hunt. The division of the meat from a large game animal by the hunter whose arrow caused its death is a band-wide, public affair; again this markedly contrasts with the division of plants by the woman gatherer, which takes place within her private domestic unit. The division of the carcass requires social finesse of the man in charge of the division and affords him the opportunity for discharging outstanding debts, as well as for indebting others to himself (Lee 1979: 243–48, 1993: 54–56). As we will discover in chapter 8, the trance dance, a potent ritual of "communal healing" (Katz 1981) that is symbolically and ritually linked to game animals and the hunt (Lewis-Williams 1981; Guenther 1988) features men playing the leading role.

As shown repeatedly in various places throughout the history of contact between Bushmen and encroaching and aggressive white or black colonists, the political potential for male power within Bushman social organization is capable of becoming actualized and full-fledged. In chapter 1 I described this process as it worked itself out in the Ghanzi veld, among the Nharo and ≠Au//ei. The same process could be witnessed a century or two ago in other parts of southern Africa: instead of the small, loose, pacifist bands of hunters of recent or contemporary times, one would have come across large, politically centralized, bellicose societies of warriors up to a thousand strong. They were led, ruthlessly at times, by a war chieftain into guerilla, hit-and-run raids against the colonists who, for almost a century, waged a brutal campaign of extermination against the Bushmen. At times they were mounted and armed not just with their hunting bows but with firearms; both these and the horses were stolen from the settlers.

Given the egalitarian makeup of Bushman social organization as a whole, the fact that the balance of power entailed in the economic division of labor tips toward the man constitutes a basic structural and moral contradiction of Bushman society. It is one that people seem to be aware of and that evidently grates on the personal lives of the women, as revealed in the two autobiographical accounts of the !Kung women N/isa (Shostak 1981) and N!ai (J. Marshall 1982; Volkman 1982). Both of the profiled women are seen, on the one hand, to be self-assertive and self-confident; they enjoy considerable independence and freedom of movement, and have the ability to initiate sexual activity as well as refuse sexual advances of men, including husbands. On the other hand, in their interaction with the men of their lives—fathers, brothers, lovers, and, especially, husbands—they begrudgingly and with no small amount of frustration recognize that ultimately it is the men "who have the upper hand" (Shostak 1981: 237). In her many, frequently stormy, escapades and several marriages N/isa is frequently the victim of bullying and abuse by insensitive and domineering lovers and husbands. N!ai's comment on the local missionary's sermon which she attended at the Dutch Reformed mission church at Tshum!wki reserve, in which Jesus asks a strange woman he meets at a well for water, reveals how, to a certain degree, this !Kung woman has internalized the notion of a husband's domineering control over his wife:

> Now really! Those two at the water hole had never even met before. How can a woman go down in a water hole with a perfect stranger calling himself "God's son"! It would have been very bad. Her husband would have punished her for being alone with such a man. That man was fooling her. (Volkman 1982: 48)

Gender Relations in Bushman Myth and Lore

Most of the narratives of Bushman mythology and folklore are about the First Order of existence—an inchoate early time when the boundaries separating beings and states were not fully set. As we saw in chapter 2, humans and animals of primal times were frequently merged into therianthropic were-beings; quite a few of these were not the big game or the predatory animals men hunt or dodge in the veld. Instead, they were small and obscure creatures, of the sort women might gather, along with roots, nuts, and fruit: mice, mongooses, songbirds, lizards, tortoises, beetles, as well as wasps and ticks. The central protagonist of /Xam folklore, /Kaggen (Mantis), was such an insect-man. He was one of the many and varied tricksters that roamed the mythical veld landscape of the Bushman. These trickster figures, as we saw in chapter 4, were beings of abiding ambiguity, a condition which, more sporadically, could also infect the "Early People," the humans of the First Order. They were wont to change back into animals (frogs, primarily, like the hapless prince of the Grimm tale), along with their material cultural objects—leather cloaks, arrows, or digging sticks which would change back into springbok, reeds, or branches. Humans, as yet, had "no customs," a state of affairs manifested, inter alia, in such profligate social behavior as incest, cannibalism, gluttony, taboo violations, boisterousness, and all-around boorishness. Once again, it was the trickster who could exemplify human flagrancy and folly in its most extreme form. Apart from the were-animals, there were also animals proper in the First Order; while these could be of all types, the species that predominated in the animal category were the game antelopes which the "Early People" hunted as eagerly as their descendants do in the second, contemporary order.

One of the central symbolic themes of the narratives about the First Order is gender. In the Bushman myth corpus this theme is set to the female key—a major key in the instance before us, not a minor one, as in the mythologies and cosmologies of so many other cultures (Guenther 1983, 1990b). Among the human protagonists in the myths and tales about the First Order, women outnumber and outshine men, and what men there are tend to be ineffectual and drone-like. The ultimate caricature of the man is the Trickster; as seen earlier, some of his most striking traits are such predominantly male failings as lechery and—its Bushman moral cognate—gluttony, as well as stinginess, boisterousness, and bullying. Women are consistently seen to show more resourcefulness and subtlety than men, as well as greater resolve and courage. Early Women are frequently called upon to display these characteristics in situations where they are accosted by lustful, coarse, and brutal men.

An example is the myth of Hare-maiden examined in chapter 5. After being wounded and violated by the Moon, an irascible—and, in one version, dirty—old man, she takes her revenge by setting alight her leather cloak and pubic apron. She throws the burning garments over Moon's face, thereby causing the dark blotches which remind humankind forever of Hare-maiden's plight and pluck. (Guenther 1989: 50–53, 71–74). The text of another example, featuring the trickster Pate and the woman and mother Puffadder, was given in chapter 4, p. 109. Because of her defensive action against Pate's coarse assaults on her and her brood, the water holes and riverbeds of the Kalahari were created by the man's testicles, into which she had buried her poison fangs. While in its narrative climax this act of creation is quintessentially male, nevertheless a woman is behind it and has brought it on. The third example is provided by the /Xam, in an unusual and engaging cautionary tale featuring a young Early Woman who is out alone in the mountains looking for lizards to eat. In the process she catches her breast in the cleft of a rock and she is immobilized. Two hungry, rogue Lion-men come across her spoor, and approach to take her as easy prey. However, she manages to keep her wits about her and to ward off the two lions (Guenther 1989: 111–14).

As seen from such narratives, women are not helpless victims in situations where they are confronted with threatening men. Not only are they able to hold their own, but they may actually get the upper hand, leaving the man duped and dumbfounded, or howling with pain. Another female strategy for maintaining safety and integrity is to keep men on as hirelings; for instance, women rear their own sons to be their beholden protectors against ogres and cannibals. Such an arrangement may persist in perpetuity when the women incestuously marry their menfolk—mothers their sons, and sisters their brothers (Schmidt 1980: 145–46). By thus keeping their own male kin to themselves they produce their own male issue to protect their own and future generations of sororal band groupings.

The emotional overlay to all of the stratagems and spoils that women take to and from their dealings with the men of the First Order is a fairly strong dose of gender antagonism; men are frequently at the receiving end of discomfiture, notwithstanding their brutish strength and aggressiveness. It is tempting to read this as the reflection, or projection, of resentment that real-life women feel toward real-life men, who hold dominance even though the moral setting of Bushman culture is one of equality and individualism.

Women can be dangerous in another, more basic, elemental way, not only to men but to humankind: they can cause the aforementioned transformation of humans into primal animals (as well as trees or stones) and cultural objects into their natural forms—simply by willfully refusing to abide by the social rules that apply to their womanhood. One of the key tale genres in the /Xam collection features this theme; possibly such stories were cautionary tales for nubile girls. As will be shown more fully in chapter 7, the tales all feature the "disobedient maiden" as the protagonist. Secluded from the rest of her group during menarche, she deliberately and repeatedly violates menstrual taboos. Her action is punished by the rain divinity !Khwa, and the punishment is the aforementioned awesome and portentous reversal of humans into animals, culture into nature, and order into chaos.

In a key /Xam cosmogonic myth a female figure, Anteater-woman, is also capable of bringing on the opposite process, of creative rather than destructive transformation. It affects a number of animals, whom she transforms ontologically from the therianthropic were-beings of the early order, to the animals of the present one. She changes not only their anatomical traits, but also their behavior, as regards feeding and habitation, as well as mating. At the opening of the chapter I provide an excerpt from this multi-versioned, at times extensively drawn-out myth.[1]

Some myths about another cosmogonic theme, the acquisition of fire, feature women as the protagonists, who either obtain fire from another party, or tend the first fire (Schmidt 1995: 156–58). Frequently these female custodians of fire are ostrich-women who keep the fire (an ember) underneath their wings/arms. In a !Kung myth fire was given to the first man by the first woman (Marshall 1962: 235). The ritual act at the end of the rite of menarche of some Bushman groups—lighting the fires in each of the hearths of the camp—resonates with this mythological theme. Yet another cosmogonic accomplishment of women, which I here only mention and will discuss more fully below, is introducing carnal knowledge to *man*kind. Just as in the !Kung fire myth, the first woman brings fire, so in a Nharo myth the first women give carnal knowledge to the first men (as seen in one of the epigraphs at the opening of the chapter). Sigrid Schmidt (1995: 158) suggests that fire and sex—the two "arts" men obtain from ostrich or human women—are symbolic cognates of each other, the first treasure kept by the ostrich-woman "under the wing," the second "under the apron." The fact that in the Nharo version of the latter tale (Guenther 1989: 62–63) the women are initially confused with ostriches by the men is consistent with this symbolic reading of the two tales.

Plants and gathering—the unsung, taken-for-granted food resource and subsistence role of Bushwomen—receive due recognition within the narratives. In one myth, women of the First Order throw the contents of their gathering cloaks up into the nocturnal sky, thereby creating the stars (Bleek and Lloyd 1911: 73–81). In an especially poignant tale a maiden impregnates herself by means of the juice of an edible grass she has chewed. The fruit of her womb turns out to be none other than the trickster (Heiseb, in this Nama tale), who shortly after his birth assumes the guise of a man and rapes his mother (Schmidt 1980: 39–40). After this incestuous assault he changes himself back into the baby; however, he is rejected by his mother who, understandably, has developed strong misgivings about her offspring. Apart from proclaiming the generative power of plants, this tale also expresses the themes of female autonomy: woman impregnates herself, with male issue, by means of a species of gathered food plant. Gender antagonism and male aggressiveness are other gender themes in the narrative, as well as woman's ability to cope with the problems these tensions entail.

Regarding the animals of Bushman myth and lore it is to be noted that the species featured most prominently are, to a significant extent, symbolical cognates of plants (Guenther 1990a). As noted above, rodents, small birds, tortoises, lizards, insects, and like small fry are a component of a woman's *veldkos*. In contrast to the "male" game antelopes and predatory felines that hold center stage in ritual and art, these "gatherable," small creatures are at times the important protagonists of the tales (such as Mantis, the !Khau lizard, or Hare). They underscore the female tone of Bushman myth, as against essentially male rituals such as the trance dance and male initiation rites, metaphorically or explicitly linked to hunting (and also expressed in art as its major theme). I return to this point in chapters 7 and 8 (also see Guenther 1990a, 1994).

Yet, even though they are quintessentially male, in both the socio-economic and the shamanic realms, game antelopes do also find their way into the female mythological domain. One symbolically pregnant way this comes about is through the "woman is meat" motif that reverberates through all of Khoisan folklore. It is a theme also in the female initiation rite, as we will see in chapter 7. In chapter 3 the basic plot line of this multivariable story was dealt with. A newly married man is repeatedly told by his kinsfolk that his wife, who recently joined her husband's group, "is meat," that he "has married meat." Incredulous at first, he is finally convinced and joins in eating his wife's flesh, after his kinsmen have killed her. Woman and marriage and game and hunting become symbolical equivalents; women are metaphorical game animals and thus not only the providers of plants but also the sources, ultimately, of meat. The belittling challenge to her economic importance as gatherer is defused through this symbolic transformation of women into game: plants and game both become the province of women, the former economically, within reality, the latter metaphorically, within mythology.

As it stands, the symbolic link between women and meat and sex and hunting might still be interpreted to favor the male as it is he who in the meat=woman and sex=hunt formula plays the active part. However, this is not necessarily the case. In the myth (as well as in real-life courtship) women may be the ones to initiate the sexual "chase"; thus, metaphorically, the woman can also be a hunter. They may take their lovers or husbands outright, as in the story mentioned above, wherein their mothers and sisters took their sons and brothers as husbands. And one comes across many a tale that features a husband dominated and controlled by his wife or wives, including Trickster, in spite of his great physical strength and magical powers (Guenther 1983; Schmidt 1995: 183, 197). Women's sexual pursuit of men may be carried out more astutely and elusively, through seduction rather than through forthright, or even forceful, action. This idea informs Barnard's (1980a: 112) interpretation of the eland dance that is performed at female initiation. As we will see in the next chapter, in that dance, which simulates eland courtship behavior, the men are the eland bulls, dancing behind the women, who also follow them in the circular dance. Barnard argues that, through their suggestive actions (lifting their skirts and exposing their buttocks), the women "'hunt' men by seducing them."

Two stories especially poignantly convey this expression of women's sexual power over men; one is a *hua* (an "old story"), the other a "new story" (Guenther 1989: 43–46, 60–63). In the first we see men teased and tormented out of their wits by women, and acting in a fashion that is as inane as it is impotent. Excerpts of the tale appear in one of the epigraphs of this chapter. In !Khuma//ka's rendition the tale is characteristically lengthy and spicy, and its climax is the bungling actions of the men. The tale is set in an early time of the First Order, when men and women still lived apart—men as hunters wearing leather things, women as gatherers, wearing grass skirts. The story relates the circumstances that brought them together and dwells on the consequences of this eventful meeting.

As the excerpt reveals, the men became very much "hot and bothered," being consumed by a desire they had never felt before—that is to say, lust. Their attempts to satisfy these unaccountable new appetites were laughably ineffectual. It was only after the women agreed among themselves to provide the bungling men with a crucial clue that they were able to have their way with the women. That accomplished, "there was much pleasure" in the village. To this day the men consider what they receive from the women "very nice food," "delicious fat," and "sweet as honey"—in a word, "meat."

To this day, it is also women who control and dispense sex. They may reject a man's advances, including their husband's (Shostak 1976: 272–74). But usually they do not, as they enjoy sex themselves, having engaged in sexual play since childhood and acquired sexual appetites as women that include the expectation of orgasm (Shostak 1976: 262–76; Lee 1993: 90–92). In the event that they are unsatisfied or unhappy with their partners, their experience and expression of jealousy and their acting out anger and frustrations on their partners or rivals are not any different from that of men (Lee 1993: 92). Moreover, they are not held back from taking other lovers any more than men are.

The recognition of what, deep down in Bushman society and cosmology, is an empowering and—for the men—life-sustaining fact made N/isa utter the statement about the importance, power, wealth, and wisdom of women that appears at the opening of this chapter. In full N/isa's statement is as follows:

> Women are strong; women are important. Ju/'hoan men say that women are the chiefs, the rich ones, the wise ones. Because women possess something very important, something that enables men to live: their genitals.
>
> A woman can bring a man life, even if he is almost dead. She can give him sex and make him alive again. If she were to refuse, he would die! If there were

> no women around, their semen would kill men. Did you know that? If there were only men, they would all die. Women make it possible for them to live. Women have something so good that if a man takes it and moves about inside it, he climaxes and is sustained.

As described by N/isa, female sexuality is to men what male healing potency—*n/um* or *tsso*—is to humankind. I will return to this observation in chapter 8.

In the second story we have just one female protagonist, who is strong and intractable, and whose willfulness and sexuality endangers herself and others (and who in this regard is reminiscent of the "disobedient maiden"). The woman is "Effa" (Eve), who (as seen in chapter 4), along with her mate and fellow //Gãũwa Addam, is a figure in the "new stories" told by farm Bushmen and derived, first- second-, or thirdhand from Christian missionaries, settlers, or converts. I collected a number of versions of this "new story" from Bushman storytellers (Guenther 1989: 43–50), including one from !Khuma//ka (Guenther ibid.: 47–49), which is drawn out and, once again, spicy at the appropriate spot in the narrative (predictably so, given the raconteur's Rabelaisian bent). He had heard the tale firsthand at catechism class when he lived at the Dutch Reformed mission station at D'Kar; however, he admitted that he "didn't understand a good deal about it very well" (see epigraph of chapter 9).

When he gets to the part in the narrative where God announces to the first couple the interdiction about eating from the one forbidden tree, !Khuma//ka generalizes from the actions of Effa to womankind as a whole, both those from Eve's times and women today:

> But the women of these people, if they are given instructions, they still want to do just as they please. They want to control just what is to happen. She came to him, wanting to control everything. And she controlled that man! (Guenther 1989: 48)

In the temptation scene—"Eh, taste this plant!"—she cuts short Adam's bleating protestations—"What did you do? This must not be allowed!"—saying, "No, man, don't tell me what to do!" Meekly he eats the fruit she hands him, and, suddenly realizing the nakedness of his body, and looking down at it, seeing "his penis standing up and looking at him," and, startled, thinking to himself that "everything is too complicated now," Adam runs off in a state of agitated befuddlement to hide from Eve in the bushes; at the same time she hides from him, having run off in the opposite direction. What they also hid, with leaves from the bushes, was their nakedness.

When admonished by their *//exa* ("headman"—in the biblical context, "Lord"), Addam points an accusing finger at Effa and says to God: "Here I am, and here is your wife [for me], who caused me to kill myself." As punishment, God announces that Adam's life will be "his sweat." As for Effa, she will henceforth be *sila* (literally, "to soften a leather skin"; figuratively, "vulnerable," "fragile") and *!gum* ("heavy," both literally and figuratively, as in "heavy thing" and "heavy heart"). "She will live in heaviness. That is all her life will be."

!Khuma//ka's narrative has the ring of his other story about men finding women and teaming up with them in marriage, after taking them from the veld to their villages, where the women soon took control. In both stories it was "their genitals" that gave power to women and caused men trouble and confusion. However, in the old story the complications are resolved and men and women live together, providing each other with meat—the former literally, the latter metaphorically. This is not the outcome in the new story, wherein the moral and cosmological tone concerning gender and sexuality rings with the somber sound of sin. This ring one never hears in any of the old Bushman stories, which are embedded in a different value system about sex, one that associates this "fat"- and "honey"-laden act as much with recreation as with procreation. The outcome of the old story about discovered sexuality has a sensuously joyous, Garden of Delights ring to it, in which both genders revel. The new story ends in gloom, doom, and toil. Addam and Effa, having first separated and hidden themselves from each other physically, are then separated socially and morally by God. The man becomes a hard, toiling worker, the woman a soft and "heavy thing." Her sexuality now burdens her down, with pregnancy, birth, and child care, and dependence on men. Before, it had given her independence from men, and power over them, when women were light and autonomous, not heavy and vulnerable.

The Equality of Bushmen and Women

This examination of Bushman folklore establishes, both explicitly and implicitly, that within the realm of myth and lore women are very much the prominent gender. They appear more frequently than men, are more resourceful than men, and are largely independent of men. In situations where they interact with men, women have at their disposal devices and stratagems for dealing with bullying, domineering male power and aggression. They hold awesome elemental powers over society and culture, and, through their life-sustaining sexuality, over men. It is tempting to regard this depiction of women, within the domain of culture that deals with mythological and mystical matters, as a social-structural mechanism for counteracting the male bias inherent in the economic and political domain of social reality. The physically, politically, and—potentially—militaristically powerful man of social life has his female counterpart in the astute, autonomous, and elementally powerful woman as she appears within the myths and tales about primal times. Thus, as in so many other cultures, Bushman myth might be seen to address and resolve the contradictions of social reality. It does so by means of the complementary opposition that holds between male and female dominance within society and myth, respectively.

At this point a simple but crucial question needs to be dealt with. Is the conclusion just arrived at—that symbolic-mythological female dominance holds in check economic-political male dominance—of any consequence whatsoever to the on-the-ground interpersonal relations between Bushmen and women? Stated differently, what, if any, bearing does the powerful woman of the myths have on "man the hunter" who reigns supreme, more or less, within the spheres of social reality or political economy? Leaving this question unaddressed is to render the revelations this chapter has suggested about myth, reality, and gender into nothing more than a merely plausible bit of functionalist and structuralist sophistry.

In the context of a functional analysis, there are some grounds for answering this key question, about the articulation of myth with reality, in the affirmative. For this oral culture and talkative people, storytelling is a much practiced form of expressive culture. For this reason myth and lore become highly salient features of everyday life. The tales can be expected, thus, to impact persuasively and pervasively the behavior and the values of the members of Bushman society.

To expand on this point, all anthropologists who have worked among the Bushmen are struck by the garrulousness of these people. Talking—*n//a*—is a means of communication and expression; it is both social and interactive, and individual and reflexive. Observers living among the Bushmen are struck by the "multi-channel" conversations that may run simultaneously, or by soliloquizing individuals, whose monologues seem to be addressed either to themselves, to another or others—though no one in particular—or to the group as a whole. Such are the "complaint discourses" of seniors—addressing all and sundry of the "entitlements" they are due from the younger generations (Rosenberg 1990) that seem to be directed primarily to themselves. As we saw in chapter 1, talking—frequently, fervently, freely—is an important device for inter- and intra-group interaction, decision making, and conflict resolution. Talking around the fire, either with one's own group or a neighboring band, is an event that happens virtually every night. Events of the day are discussed extensively, in several simultaneous conversations, and news and gossip are traded. Information is exchanged, in "debriefing" format—among people who were out on hunting or gathering expeditions earlier that day or week—on sightings of water, plant ripening, nut- or fruit-tree stands, animal spoors. Hunts are an especially favored topic, and in the retelling of the hunt that yielded the meat people are eating that evening, storytellers dwell on the exciting or uncanny things that transpired. Gossip is traded and family memorates may be recounted and, before long, the topic may be the "Early People." In this fashion, "talking" covers all of the bases of Bushman experience, from events and issues of the day and everyday, to those of the past and the world beyond. And the myths and tales are not just told to children—by their mothers and grandmothers as part of the socialization process—but they are also a central component of the narrative repertoire of adults. The fact that "virtually every old person (. . . perhaps forty-five or older) is able and usually willing to tell stories" (Biesele 1993: 18) attests to the cultural importance of stories in the people's lives. The fact that hours of leisure exceed those of labor in the social life of the Bushmen heightens the salience of stories in their lives.

Tales and tale performance sessions, with narrative material drawn either from myth and lore or from everyday life, are thus a pervasive, ongoing feature of Bushman life, and for this reason they form part of the symbolic and conceptual tool kit with which people make sense of that everyday reality. They become interwoven with the economic, social, and political actions people take, and this social reality provides the matrix of meaning for the tales. Through this close association of stories with everyday life, the domain of myth and lore stands in a dialectic relationship with society, each addressing and taking from the other. The stories, in short, provide significant input to the people's social construction of reality. As also illustrated by the myth featured in the previous chapter, the narrative, affective, and symbolic content of the tales resonates and articulates with social reality, as this reality provides the performance context and the matrix of meaning for the tales.

As we saw earlier, the tales are also remarkably resilient, and each generation readily and eagerly incorporates new and foraged narrative material. Their meaning-enhancing quality thus encompasses also the new life situations that provide additional grist for the narrative mill. And in grinding the new mythological and cosmological kernels, myth renders them culturally usable, palatable, and digestible. As we saw earlier, the pioneer farms of the trek Boers that were established in various stretches of Bushmanland in southern Africa are the setting for most of the Jackal-trickster stories; they feature Jackal as a Bushman farm laborer and Lion and Hyena as his Boer *baas* and duped fellow laborer, respectively (Guenther 1989: 115–16, 124–39, 150–51.) Missionary-derived stories from the Bible are creatively syncretized so that they fit into Bushman mythology (Guenther 1989: 41–50). The most common of these latter new narratives is the story of Adam and Eve, a tale whose gender theme, as indicated above, resonates with certain traditional stories. And most recently, paintings and prints, some of them explicitly narrative, feature some of the material, social, and political aspects of contemporary Bushmen's lives.

The fact that the much-told myths and tales featured in this chapter, that accord power and intelligence to women, have a bearing on people's ethos may explain why, in the final analysis, allowing for some regional variation (Barnard 1980a: 122), there appears to be something close to gender equality in Bushman society, "with no one having the upper hand" (Lee 1993: 92). Men are dominant, more or less, within the socio-political sphere; women, within the mystical-mythological sphere. Women also hold significant economic importance by virtue of their role as gatherers. The imbalance within the gender nexus which represents a basic and irksome contradiction of Bushman social organization and ethos has been redressed. Like the rest of Bushman society, egalitarianism and the principles of reciprocity, of give and take, end up also characterizing the relationship between men and women. Women, like men, have freedom of movement and may reach their own decisions about things, including whom they take as lovers and whom, ultimately, they will marry. Like men, they participate in public decision-making sessions convened whenever the group needs to plan a course of action, such as whether and when to leave a water hole. Women may even be headmen, and in the trance dance they perform the vital role of singing and clapping, providing the men with the active conditions for trance.

The explanation of gender equality in foraging societies has typically been couched by anthropologists in cultural materialist terms (Draper 1975; Leacock 1978; Lee 1979: 309–30, 447–53; Kent 1993b). That is, explanations (some of which were dealt with in chapter 1) are advanced in such positive terms as the empowering effects of female gathering (providing up to 80 percent of the food supply), the female solidarity–enhancing effects of daily gathering trips, the low birth rate (as well as the concomitant personal mobility of the woman, and the freedom to make her own reproductive choices), and social and spatial mobility. Alternatively, female egalitarianism may be explained negatively, in terms of the absence in Bushman and foraging societies of patrilineality and patrilocality, the bride price, the levirate, and other contractual arrangements between the spouse-exchanging groups that infringe on the rights of the wife-to-be. I would submit that such infrastructural and social-structural explanations do not tell the whole story, however. If they did one would be hard pressed to explain why there are some foraging societies with basically the same infrastructure, who do not accord equality to women (for instance, the Australian aborigines, the Ona of Tierra del Fuego, or the arctic Inuit). How gender relations are played out within the superstructural domain of myth and lore is the other part of the story, especially in a society where myth and lore are not ancillary but integral to social life.

The Limitations of Structural Analysis

I close this chapter with the same caveat that ended the previous chapter. In both instances I have presented an analysis of Bushman myth that is couched in social-structural and binary structuralist terms: in the first case, the myth of the Moon and the Hare, about life and death; in the present case, about female and male. When dealing with myth, especially myths on such portentous issues, both of these approaches come to the anthropologist's mind most readily—the former thanks to Malinowski; the latter courtesy Lévi-Strauss—and the respective analytical concepts, the "moral charter" and the "mythologics" (*mythologique*). Having here brought these analytical concepts to bear on Bushman myth, I now have the uneasy sense that my analysis obscures as much as it explains. Just as the structural foray into the meaning of the life and death myth presented in the previous chapter revealed binary patterns that only loosely fit the complex, multi-variant myth to which it was applied, so we find narrative and symbolic elements in the myths before us that fall outside the structural pattern applied to them.

For instance, while women certainly are key players in the myths, and give a strong female presence to Bushman mythology, the equally strong presence of the male trickster brings the opposite gender into this symbolic and cosmological domain as well. Likewise, while myth-animals are often small-fry, "gatherable" creatures, large animals, some of them game—gemsbok, kudu, springbok, elephant, ostrich—are on the scene as well. So are predatory animals—lion, hyena, jackal—although, in their moral and mental deportment, they may be "jackasses." This can be said especially of the lion, who in the form of the Boer *baas* is a frequent dupe of Jackal-trickster, his Bushman farmhand. It applies as well to the two lions who try to eat the young woman immobilized because her breast is caught in the cleft of a rock. "Mat" and "Belt," as they are called, are the two Laurel-and-Hardy-like dunces and laughing-stocks of /Xam folklore (Hewitt 1986: 107; Guenther 1989: 112). The fact that the girl's adversaries are none too bright somewhat diminishes the degree of accomplishment reflected in the young woman's ability to outwit them; imagine our own Little Red Riding Hood, stalked by Wile E. Coyote, rather than the Wolf. The character of the lion in the trance curing rite, as an animal of numinous portent (see chapter 8) is yet another of the many contradictions that are contained within Bushman belief.

As for women holding elemental, destructive, and creative powers, we must be mindful of the Kori Bustard of the !Kung, the creative equivalent to the /Xam Anteater-woman, who is a man. Biesele (1993: 97) sees his creative technique, of using fire to brand the First Order animals with the markings which they take into the Second Order, as a potent symbolic expression of his maleness. Underscoring his male gender is Kori's role as servant of Kaoxa, the !Kung male trickster. Indeed, in /Xam myth, as we saw in chapter 4, it is the trickster himself, /Kaggen, who may be the agent in the creative transformation of beings of the First Order. Indeed, in virtually all of the Khoisan mythological traditions we come across the trickster protagonist or god as creator.

Fire, which we saw above as another elemental element associated with women, as either its original owners, or the ones to bring it to humankind, is in other tales in the hands of men, usually a trickster. Or one may find other male figures as the original owners of fire, or stealers thereof—for instance, lions (Schmidt 1995: 16–17), animals linked with power and bullying, as well as hunting and shamanism, all matters imbued with maleness. Another deviation from the tale's common form is to feature a male ostrich as the original keeper of the fire, instead of the widespread female one (Guenther 1989: 58–60). This deviation creates contradictions in the tale (which did not bother any of the Nharo storytellers, however), for in the part of the story where the fire robbers also steal the ostrich's eggs to roast and eat, thereby discovering the cultural act of cooking, it is the cock ostrich who is seen to lay the eggs! Indeed, in another structuralist analysis, of Ju/'hoan folklore (Biesele 1993: 79–81), fire is unequivocally linked to maleness, through a pervasive series of metaphors (as against femaleness, the interpretation given to fire by Sigrid Schmidt, as noted above). The element symbolically linked to women, according to Biesele, is water. The moon, yet another portentous mythological being, who almost brought eternal life to humankind, is not female, as in most other cultures, but male (although, once again, not always). His adversary, Hare-maiden, as we saw in the examination of the many variants of this myth, is neither always female—in some accounts, "she" is even the male trickster—nor always triumphant over her lunar assailant, who may end up assaulting her and, after splitting her lip, making of her a creature of the wild, to be snared and eaten by humans. As for the pervasive and cosmologically significant symbolic identification of women with meat, I point to male versions of the tale, as noted in chapter 3.

Apart from specific elements of Bushman myths and tales, which allow for alternative explanation, one also needs to qualify the more general structural-functionalist analysis of the articulation between myth and social reality, offered in the preceding section. The closeness of this articulation, due to the prominence of storytelling in people's everyday lives, led to the classic functionalist conclusion about the ultimate egalitarianism of gender relations. In the context of Bushman society and cultures, a conclusion of this sort, couched in the analytical notion of myth as reflector and endorser of social institutions and values, does not quite ring true, however. For one thing, it overemphasizes the normative influence of folklore on the behavior of people, and overstates the didactic, philosophical—as against the ludic, recreational—impact stories have on Bushman tellers and listeners. For another, it suggests that the Bushmen are guided in their everyday actions and decisions by their myths and tales, rather than by practical, rational, and secular considerations. This is no more the case in this society than in most others. For instance, we saw in an earlier chapter that hunters, notwithstanding their culture's anthropomorphic view of animals, which is manifest in their folklore as well as their cosmology and ritual, are not held back from the task of hunting, killing, and eating them.

Given the surreal quality of Bushman myth, the link between myth and reality becomes all the more tenuous, selective, and arbitrary, as well as lighthearted and light-headed. Bushman myth, with a few exceptions (such as the one featured in the previous chapter), is either unconcerned, or only concerned in passing, with grave existential or social questions. The principal figure on the mythic landscape is the antic and ribald trickster—who is also a god—and the world he lives in is the inchoate First Order, with beings, states, customs all in flux. This setting for the stories, being fluid and flighty, is ill-suited as a repository of the culture's moral charter or for the expression of its deep structures of logic and order. While certain select myths or tales may address themselves directly to certain concerns of reality—for instance, the myth about the disobedient maiden may have served the /Xam as a cautionary tale for young women at menarche—most of them probably do not. Or if they do, the relationship may be only indirect and oblique, inverting or even perverting—in the case of trickster tales—real institutions and values. Some would argue—for example, Max Gluckman (1963) or Victor Turner (to whom I will turn in the conclusion)—that such inversion in myth and ritual in the end actually asserts order, rather than subverting it. This includes the trickster, who is held to "affirm by denying" and who, in the "very act of deconstructing, reconstructs" (Hynes 1993: 207–208; see also Toelken 1969 and Georges and Jones 1995: 293–99). Yet, in a society in which order is itself loose, labile, and surreal, one would not expect "anti-structural" myths or tales or protagonists to be anything other than what they seem.

I cannot readily detect in Bushman myths, with their myriad variations from storyteller to storyteller, group to group, and region to region, and with the pervasive aura of ambiguity that hangs over them, any narrative, emotional, or symbolic center, or ideational core. While female primacy is presented as such in this chapter, men, too, are encountered in Bushman myth, and I would probably be able to move a fair distance were I to attempt to prove the same hypothesis with respect to men as I just attempted for women. However, lest it be thought that I consider this chapter to have been a waste of time, I do regard the hypothesis and conclusion to be more valid for women than it would have been for men. Their justification is the *relative* centrality and frequency of the female motif in the myths, which is readily apparent. Also, the analysis and conclusion I offer makes structural sense as they resolve the social contradiction of one gender being less equal in a culture that stresses and maintains equality.

Yet, Bushman myth, like mythology or sacred texts universally, contains such a wide spectrum of ideas, beings, and events—many of them contradictory and impenetrable—that several opposed social, cosmological, or symbolic themes might be detected within it. In this chapter the cosmological and symbolic leitmotif was women, in chapter 3 it was animals, and in chapter 5 death was seen to be the theme of a prominent pan-Khoisan myth. And, as stated at the outset of this chapter, if the theme one detects and traces through the narrative and metaphorical tangle that is Bushman myth and lore is countered by another, or others, this mentally disconcerting realization confirms the hallmark trait of this expressive domain, and the others linked to it: ambiguity.

This chapter is thus disconcerting and inconclusive in its argument. It debates two positions: after hearing a carefully prepared case for structure and function from the "ayes," it resolves irresolutely that the "nays" have it. All this indeterminacy raises a number of important analytical questions for the student of Bushman religion, all of them revolving around our academic inability to conceptualize ambiguity. What do we do with those elements of the investigated field—in this case a tale or seemingly related tale complex—that lie outside the structural pattern we have identified, in a process of selection that seems arbitrary? Are those elements we have chosen to deselect merely metonymic noise? Can the explanation of the tales' meaning in terms of just the selected elements be anything other than incomplete and thus incorrect—notwithstanding its epistemologically commendable elegance and parsimony?

At this point I merely raise these questions, because they raised themselves in this and the previous chapter. I will defer my attempts at answering them to the conclusion.

7

Initiation Rites

Eland dancing is heavier and more deliberate than any other. It can perhaps be best described as a moderately slow, flat-footed run in which the body weight is allowed to settle firmly on each alternate foot as it is planted on the ground; indeed, at the moment of impact, all of the dancer's flesh sags toward the ground, graphically illustrating the direction of the weight. And her body ornaments follow the motion downwards, adding a small but clear clicking sound effect to the movement. The feet land flat and firm on each step, producing a thud in the sand. And all of this occurs at the moment of the sharp sound—"clink" describes it best in words—from the adze blades, for the dance step follows the beat of the /'aisi [adzes] exactly. The entire effect conjures a picture of the grandly muscular, fleshy eland, trotting along unhurriedly in the veld.

—ENGLAND 1968: 596, CITED IN BIESELE 1993: 197

Then she cut up the waterchild. She roasted it. Then the water hissed, because the fire felt that the rain was angry with her. So, when she lighted the fire, it went out.

Then a whirlwind came from behind. It swept around and gathered near the hut. The cold wind then drove along, lifting her up. The cold wind lifted her right up. She went up, sailing along the sky. And then she fell into a pond. She became a frog.

And the people who were seeking food, when they came they, too, became frogs. They dropped into the pond. The huts' bed mats became springbok and the sticks became bushes. The bedskins became springbok, because the people had become frogs. . . .

The karosses become springboks. They spring asunder and they shake out the water from their skins. The sticks become bushes and branches, while the arrows stand about all over, the quivers, too, stand about. The quiver skins out of which people have made the quivers become springboks. As the quivers stand about they get their ears. . . .

—/HAN≠KASSO, MOWBRAY, CAPE, 1878 (CITED IN GUENTHER 1989: 109, 111)

Initiation rites, especially those for girls, are symbolically rich and ritually elaborate in Bushman culture. This rite's transitional phase, which tends to be charged with metaphorical, liminal ferment in any culture (Turner 1970a), is protracted in the Bushman case, providing the symbolically appropriate arena for expressing the religion's and the society's fundamental (anti)structural theme, ambiguity. As with other facets of Bushman culture, this rite displays diversity, both within and across groups, attesting to the flexibility of the culture and to the individualism and creativity of its members, who formulate or forage the elements of their ritual and expressive culture in accordance with their mental, emotional, and aesthetic needs and tastes.

In my account of the rite I will describe, in truncated fashion (as detailed descriptions are available in the literature[1]), the ritual form and content of the female and male versions. I will also describe its variations, which are so extensive that in some of its forms the ceremony no longer looks like a passage rite. I will then turn to the transition phase in order to explore the symbolic dimension of the rite, examining in particular the extent to which it gives expression to ambiguity.

Female Initiation

While subject to considerable variation, in its basic form and content the female initiation rite was and is basically the same across Bushman tribes, from the /Xam of the Cape to the !Kõ, Nharo, and G/wi (Silberbauer 1965: 87) of the Kalahari. While modern !Kung ethnographers (Marshall 1959: 356; Biesele 1993: 134–36) refer to the rite, they present no detailed accounts of it. As in the case of my own fieldwork, which yielded only secondhand information on the rite, rather than firsthand observations (Guenther 1986a: 278–81), the scantiness of ethnographic data may reflect the intimate nature of one of the key events of the ceremony, and the sensitivity of the field-workers who might have been reluctant to pry. Presumably the rite for the !Kung follows the same pattern, as it evidently did among the !Kung-speaking ≠Au//ei, according to Dorothea Bleek, who likened their version of the ceremony to that of the Nharo (Bleek 1928: 23).

The women initiates, unlike their male counterparts, go through a classic rite of passage, which follows the tripartite scheme of separation, margin (or transition), and aggregation (or reintegration), à la van Gennep (1960) and Turner (1970a). Upon the commencement of her first menstruation the girl is secluded in a small grass hut built for her some distance from the camp. She stays in seclusion throughout her menstrual flow, as she is considered to be a danger to the men and even to the ground. This she should not touch with her feet when she leaves the hut to relieve herself; instead she is carried out, or wears sandals. The ceremony may continue beyond her menses, for several more days or even weeks, and it may be resumed at her next period, and the one thereafter. When in seclusion she is attended by two or three old female kinswomen, who feed her and give her water, both of which she takes in only small quantities. She is also informed of all of her duties as a woman and wife, and told of the many food taboos that she will have to observe, for varying lengths of time. Along with other dos and don'ts surrounding her menstruation, one of the things impressed on her is the danger this state holds for men and their weapons, as well as for the hunt. As we will see below, it was only in the context of this rite in its liminal phase, that these restrictions were lifted and she was allowed to touch (or even beat) men, as well as their weapons.

From the /Xam, whose folklore included an embellished cautionary tale about the "disobedient maiden" to which I will turn presently, one gets the impression that the girl's prolonged confinement, with all its restrictions and deprivations, might have been an occasion for physical and mental hardship for the girl (Hewitt 1986: 281). It was also one of potential danger, both to herself and to her people, resulting from violation of one or another of the many proscriptions that restricted her, in particular the one about fasting or food taboos. Another cause for anxiety and numinous portent was the presence of either the male trickster god (among the Nharo and !O !Kung) or the male rain divinity (the /Xam), attracted by the sexuality or the smell of the young woman. The /Xam girl tried to cover up the latter by daubing herself with *buchu* (Hewitt 1986: 285).

The culmination of the transition phase—which might occur on several occasions in the ceremony, as well as mark the onset of the festive aggregation phase—was the apparently pan-Bushman eland dance. Like the trance dance, the eland dance is performed at night; however, the dancers are primarily women, most of them old. Their buttocks bared, the women dance in a circle around the girl's hut or around the girl as she is sitting on a blanket, or they dance in two circles forming a figure eight. Usually one or several old men, the "bulls," will join in; they may be special relatives of the girl, such as (among the Nharo) her joking partners. They dance behind the women at the end of the circle, holding hornlike sticks to their heads, sporting tail-like appendages, and walking—their backs covered with a leather cloak—in hunched fashion. Their dance steps—a "moderately slow, flat-footed run"—simulate those of the eland; the dance routine of the "bulls" and the women is that of the courting eland. It includes mock fighting by the animated "eland bulls" (Heinz 1975c: 9, 11). I will present more details of this symbolically rich element of the dance later in this chapter.

The rite now enters its final phase, as the girl is brought back into the community and may be formally reintroduced to everyone as the new woman, impressing on her people and herself her new status. Another skill she may have to learn again is walking, taught by one of her old woman assistants on whom she leans heavily. She may also be expected to perform certain womanly tasks, such as rubbing people with *buchu,* or lighting their fires with a special stick. She may also be required to touch or handle men's weapons, as well as special bundles of medicine sticks. The !Kõ girl rubbed a bow and arrows with fat and shot them at a stretched gemsbok skin shield (Heinz 1975c: 9, 11).

She is the recipient also of a number of gifts, such as beads, necklaces, or skin blankets, that come to her from various relatives, especially male ones such as her father, uncles, and old joking partners. She has also incurred some obligations toward some of the people who attended to her during her initiation, such as the old woman who instructed her, to whom she will have to give an apron at some time in the future. Moreover, she may have to return some of the objects she used during her confinement, such as the pubic apron lent to her by an older female relative (Heinz 1975c: 10). Thus, as she enters adulthood, she is embraced by the spirit of communalism of her society, and its underlying ethos of sharing and reciprocity. Another element of her new status is that she may engage fully in sexual relations; if already married before her initiation, she may finally consummate her marriage. Whereas before her initiation she had played at sex with other boys or with her husband, sexual activity now has an added purpose, which, once it is realized through the birth of her children, will add a vital component to her new social status as woman.

Male Initiation

Male initiation took two forms in Bushman culture, one of which was found only among the northwestern tribes, such as the !Kung, ≠Au/ei, G/wi, Nharo, and !Kõ. The first was the "first-hunt," or more appropriately, the "first-buck" ceremony, performed individually for each hunter; the second, the "bush-camp" ceremony (called *choma* by the !Kung), performed for a group of boys (Lee 1979: 365, 366). The two rites might also be combined, as among the !Kõ, who normally incorporated a hunter's first-buck rite into the group ceremony (Heinz and Lee 1978: 107–108). The bush-camp rite was of restricted distribution; moreover, it has by now probably disappeared altogether from the ritual culture of the contemporary Bushmen.

The "first-buck" ceremony was traditionally carried out for boys in their mid- to late teens; however, more recently the age has gone up by a decade or more (Lee 1979: 238). It is not clear if the ceremony is, or ever was, obligatory. For instance, when visiting the !Kung of the Dobe–Nyae Nyae region in 1911, Hauptmann Müller (1912: 539) noticed that some men were without any of the tattoos resulting from the various magical cuts administered to the new hunter at initiation. When he asked an untattooed man for an explanation, the man questioned said that he didn't think it looked good! This suggests that, in addition to ritual prescriptions, aesthetic preference may have played a role in a person's decision about undergoing the rite (or that component thereof); again, we note the individualism and tolerance of Bushman culture.

One of the basic moral assumptions the !Kung held about male adulthood was that it commenced once a young man had killed his first large buck (Lee 1979: 236). As his ability to provide for a wife was predicated on that assumption in Bushman society generally, we may assume de facto that a man would go through the rite in his youth. We must note as well, however, that the ceremony did not mark any radical status change, as his first buck was not his first kill. In fact, it was not even his first buck, but his first *large* buck, drawn from a list of several eligible species, principally, among the !Kung and /Xam, the eland or the gemsbok (Biesele 1993: 94–98). By the time he embarked on his first-buck hunt the young man may already have been quite an experienced hunter, having acquired his skills by hunting and snaring smaller animals, under the guidance of his father or grandfather (Lee ibid.: 236). Another approach to the ceremony, usually taken by the older and possibly married hunter with children, would be to ask to be initiated post facto, that is, after he had been successful in bringing down a particularly splendid large-game antelope (Lee ibid.: 238).

While the details vary from group to group (some of which I note in a later section), a common element of the rite is the administration of cuts, which were rubbed with "medicine" that may have included fat from the killed buck. Another common element was the performance of a number of magical acts. Reflecting the concern about the balance and complementarity of gender, the !Kung performed two separate ceremonies, one for a female animal and the other for a male, in which the left and right side of the hunter's and the animal's body parts, respectively, were the focus of ritual attention. All of these observances were designed to improve the hunter's mental and physical skill at his hunting task. Thus, among the Nharo the vertical cuts between the eyes were assumed to increase the hunter's keenness of vision, while the horizontal cuts to his right side and back increased his speed at running (Guenther 1986a: 276–77). Other cuts were meant to increase the strength of the hunter's bow (Lee 1979: 238). The cuts left indelible tattoos, attesting permanently to the hunter's new status. Some of the magical acts that were performed on the boy constitute forms of sympathetic magic—such as rubbing the initiate with an antelope's severed ears so that it would "flap-flap" its ears rather than hold them up, thus facilitating the hunter's approach next time he stalked the animal (Lee ibid.: 239). As noted earlier (in chapter 3) and expanded on below, these magical practices are generally based on the assumption of a bond of sympathy between the hunter and the animal, a belief especially prominent among the /Xam (Lewis-Williams and Biesele 1978).

Apart from two or three common elements, the collective bush-camp initiation was a different type of ritual. What it had in common was the administration of cuts, for the purpose of improving the recipient's performance as a hunter, and the performance of hunts during part of the ceremony, which could last for several weeks (Lebzelter 1934: 6, 69–70). However, the chief purpose of this optional, and, among the G/wi, "not particularly significant ceremony" (Silberbauer 1965: 89), was to test the fortitude of the boys and young men who participated in it, as well as their ability to track and hunt animals. The elements of the former test included fasting, drinking very little, sleeping at night without clothing or blankets, or being beaten with sticks.

Additional elements, found in some but not all Bushman groups, were the instruction by the old men (who assumed a stern and authoritative mien for the occasion) in the social, domestic, and ritual obligations of manhood; the performance of dances; the encounter with //Gãũwa or Hise, whose presence the old (Nharo) men might simulate by whirring a bull roarer at night and leading the boys to a small grass hut one of the old men had secretly built out in the veld, and claiming that it was //Gãũwa's house (Lebzelter 134: 70; Guenther 1986a: 277). Among the Nharo the trickster-god could appear in female guise, and among the !Kõ his wives might make an appearance, lusting for the initiated men, only to be driven away with abuse by the men's living womenfolk (Heinz and Lee 1978: 114).

At the conclusion of the week- to month-long rite the men returned to their regular camp, from which they might have been only a few hundred yards distant, as its members had provided the men and boys with food and water throughout the ceremony (Lee 1979: 365). No ceremony marked the return of the Nharo young men, nor did their participation in the rite appear to have altered their social status in any appreciable way (Guenther 1986a: 278).

The exception to the somewhat rudimentary or fragmentary form of the group initiation rite are the !Kõ, who, as Barnard points out in his comparative work on the Khoisan, have "perhaps the most elaborate rituals recorded among Khoisan peoples" (1992a: 71). Here the ceremony, while flexible in its performance, was mandatory. It was an absolute requirement for the full social maturation of a man who, were he to skip the ceremony, would remain a "boy-child" for the rest of his life (Heinz and Lee 1978: 97). Whereas the rite was rather loosely structured among the rest of the Kalahari Bushmen, as well as lacking in one or another of the elements found in other groups, the !Kõ ceremony contained all of the elements, and followed the formal structure of separation and seclusion, transition and reintegration. In this respect the male rite paralleled the female one. In fact, the congruence of the male and female rites was evident in certain common ritual details; male and female initiates alike ritually shot a gemsbok skin shield and, upon their return to the camp after the conclusion of the rite, went from hut to hut to light people's fires and were reacquainted with each member of the community (Heinz and Lee 1978: 116).

Variations

Because of the male group initiation rite's loose and somewhat casual nature, as well as its limited distribution and the fact that, with one exception (the !Kõ), it was entirely optional for boys who could readily achieve their manhood without having participated in the rite, at least one researcher (Bleek 1928: 27) has suggested that it is not a Bushman ritual pattern, but a borrowing from neighboring Bantu-speaking tribes. This suggestion receives some support from the fact that in several cases—the Hietshware of eastern Botswana (Dornan 1917: 158–60) and the Kwadi of Angola (Almeida 1965: 32–36), as well as the Southern Bushman around the Drakensberg (Jolly 1996: 282)—one comes across an element of initiation that is definitely of Bantu origin: circumcision. This appears to have been an important aspect of initiation among the former group, being administered annually and collectively to both boys and girls, each in their own group. Among the Kwadi the operation, along with other Bantu-style mutilations, was performed only on boys. Girls' initiation ceremonies contained a number of other Blacks-derived features, such as the initiate's father killing an ox by suffocation after the girl's return to the village and other band members anointing the girl with butter and dressing her in new clothes (Barnard 1992a:132).

Another element that does not ring quite true culturally about the bush-camp rite is the excessively stern and authoritarian role the old men assumed over the young; among the Nharo, the men not only exhorted the initiates morally on the responsibilities that awaited them as adults, but also gave them harsh orders. Uncharacteristically, they even beat the young men with sticks, even though some of the youths were probably in their twenties, were married, and had children (Guenther 1986a: 277). The kin relationship between the youths and their stern taskmasters would ideally be a joking relationship, akin to the relationship between grandparents and grandchildren. Because of the joking relationship between members of alternating generations, the emotional quality of that relationship is at odds with the strictness and superordination of the old men over the young initiates. The fact that farm Bushmen today readily liken the */ri kaxu* rite of the old days to the Western school—an entirely foreign socialization concept to the Bushmen—and sometimes apply the same term to the modern school (including the missionary's catechism classes), further suggests that the rite is not fully attuned to Bushman society and culture.

There is also a structural reason why the collective male rite presents a basic problem for Bushmen: the requirement that boy initiates form groups, which should be as large as possible, goes counter to the nomadic and fluid movement and composition of camps. This means the rites can be held only during the winter aggregation phase, provided that there is enough food and water in a given area for enough people to get together. Richard Lee found these conditions to hold at intervals of between one and seventeen years; in one area they occurred in 1910, 1917, 1922, 1930, 1940, 1944, and 1950; in another region in 1920, 1921, 1928, 1934, 1942, 1943, and 1960 (Lee 1979: 365). Thus the mean frequency rate for the performance of the rite is only five-and-a-half years. Because of this relative infrequency, people in a certain area would sometimes be required to walk seventy to one hundred kilometers if they wanted to join an initiation rite (ibid.). All of these are practical complications, deriving from the Bushmen's nomadic lifeways and marginal environmental conditions, which militate against the smooth operation of the male group initiation rite. They confirm the suspicion that the "bush-camp" element of male initiation may have its source outside Bushman culture.

Yet, even though male group initiation rite might have been a cultural borrowing, as with other instances of cultural foraging, the people have adapted the rite to their own supernatural and ritual, as well as practical, concerns. For instance, the rite has assumed a strong emphasis on hunting, imparting to the hunter both the practical and symbolic components of the task of hunting, as well as requiring of him a display of physical fortitude and stamina. The divinity that is called up is the archetypical Bushman trickster-god and the dances that accompany the rite are of Bushman cultural provenance.

As regards the female rite, one Bushman group, the Hai//om, seem to have obtained much of this pattern from the Khoekhoe (Schapera 1930: 212, 285); as against the male rite, which seems to follow the Bushman, "bush-camp" pattern (Barnard 1992a: 215). In the former rite a most decidedly Khoekhoe element is the girls' touching the young men's scrota to ward off infection (Schapera ibid.: 285). This trait suggests to Schapera that it was "very probably" taken over from the Khoekhoe, whose male and female initiation rites show some fundamental differences (Schapera ibid.: 284–85). Yet, the Hai//om female rite also has some of the Bushman elements, such as her seclusion in a separate hut, the avoidance of contact with men, and the performance of a special women's dance (Schapera ibid.: 121). It is unspecified by Fourie, the chief ethnographer on the Hai//om (Fourie 1926: 57–59, 1928: 89–91), whether the last item is the eland dance.

As might be expected, there is considerable variation in the Bushman initiation rites even without any extraneous elements. Among the !Kõ, both the female and the male rite show extensive variation in detail, "as is so characteristic of many aspects of !Kõ ritual" (Heinz 1975c: 8). The male rite, despite its mandatory nature, is highly flexible and adjusted to the contingencies of each case, such that "no two performances are alike," some omitting or abbreviating certain elements (Heinz and Lee 1978: 114). There are no rigid rules pertaining to the sequence of the various events of the rite, the size of the "class" is variable, and the duration of the rite varies from one week to one month. Because of the "flexibility and adaptability" of the rite, it may include people other than !Kõ or Bushmen, such as the occasional Kgalagari or even the visiting anthropologist! The latter was Heinz himself, who underwent the initiation rite after experiencing a crisis of confidence that came after his !Kõ wife Namkwa informed him that, without the rite, he was, to her and her people, not a man but a "boy-child" (Heinz and Lee 1978: 97–102). To "do" him presented quite a challenge to the old men; yet they managed all of the problems his case presented:

> I was a white man, my language ability at the time was very limited, more suited to expressing my simple wishes than to understanding complicated discourse, though Thamae helped me tremendously. My foods and my cultural background were different, I hunted with a gun not with a bow and arrow; my stays with my friends were limited, so that they were unable to keep me under their guard or tutelage; there were those who were violently opposed to my being initiated. (Heinz and Lee 1978: 114)

Looking at Bushman initiation rites comparatively, in terms of regional variation, we find diversity in a number of its features. Within and across the different Bushman tribes the male rites vary in the degree to which they are preferred or prescribed, on a scale from mandatory to optional. Male and female rites vary in the degree to which they exclude males or children as spectators, again spanning the full scale from exclusive to inclusive. Indeed, in one case (the G/wi), the male may undergo a quasi initiation himself in the context of a girl's initiation, in the event that he is married to the initiate. During her confinement, at the admonition, hair-cutting, and tattooing phase of her rite, he joins her and undergoes the same ritual procedures that also include the mixing of blood from one another's cuts (Silberbauer 1965: 84–86). Other elements vary as well, such as the age of the male initiates, which ranges from the mid-teens to the mid-thirties, and their marital status. For girls the age is everywhere early puberty, signaled by first menstruation, except among the Hei//om, whose girls start the ceremony before puberty. This enigmatic Bushman people deviate from the normal pattern in another way: they begin the girl's rite on a collective basis, in its prepubescent phase, and only individualize the rite when a girl starts her first menses (Barnard 1992a: 210). The duration of both sets of rituals varies, from a day (such as a contemporary !Kung's first-buck ceremony) to a month or longer, among groups who repeat the (female) ceremony the second or third month. The eland in the female dance may be replaced by another animal, such as the gemsbok or an unspecified bird, as among the ≠Au//eisi (Bleek 1928: 23). While cuts are administered widely among the Kalahari Bushmen—with the option to decline open to individuals—they seemed to be absent from the rites of the southern /Xam. At least one group, the G/wi, cut not only their male and female initiates, but also the apprentice trance dancer (Silberbauer 1965: 99).

Male Initiation or Hunting Magic?

Whereas the female pattern, in all of its variant forms, falls in line with the etic tripartite structural model of passage rites, a number of the male variants so deviate from that scheme that one is hard-pressed to recognize them as exemplars of this ritual type. For instance, following Barnard (1980a: 17; also see 1993: 60–61), I have elsewhere (1986a: 275) suggested that the Nharo bush-camp rite should be regarded as a formal rite of passage in only a loose sense, primarily because it did not mark any clear status change. The participant was frequently neither a boy, nor a non-hunter, nor single; thus his optional participation in the rite constituted no passage from one social state and status to another. Like Barnard, I would treat the Nharo case as an instance not of initiation but of hunting magic.

The other male rite, too, can be seen to deviate, in a number of formal ways, from the structure of passage rites generally. As evident from Lee's (1979: 238–40) case study, the !Kung initiate undergoing his first-kill rite was the thirty-year-old, married man Debe, who had hunted on many occasions before. Moreover, upon completing his ceremony, he was still five years away from the adult man's privilege of having assigned to himself the cherished "men's portion" of meat whenever a carcass is divided. For this privilege he would have to wait, as it is age rather than hunting accomplishment that confers this right on a man (ibid.: 240). Thus, the rite marked no clear status change for the initiate. Moreover, that the !Kung rite is more a case of hunting magic than initiation is suggested by the fact that a hunter, when he is down on his luck, may have old cuts opened and new medicine rubbed in. Alternatively, he may again experience one or several of the five ritual performances that an initiate undergoes. They would be part of a series of other magical acts he might perform to improve his hunting luck, such as rubbing blood from a small kill on his bow to enable him to make a big kill next, or searching his mind for any taboo violations that might have occurred.

Yet, within the kaleidoscope of Bushman male initiation patterns across southern Africa there are also those male rites that are clearly rites of passage, such as the bush-camp rite of the !Kõ and the first-kill rite of the /Xam (and of the !Kung, according to Lewis-Williams and Biesele [1978], on the basis of a comparative analysis). Formal and substantive parallels to the female passage rite among the !Kõ have been noted above. Similarly, an old /Xam man would build a special grass hut for the first hunter the evening after he had wounded his first buck with his poison arrow. He treated the boy as though he were ill, cosseting him and kindling his fire; among both the /Xam and the !Kung, "the boys' eland first kill rituals," Lewis-Williams and Biesele (1978: 126) suggest, "are in some ways a mirror image of the girls' puberty rituals."

Thus, in view of all this regional variation, once again we run into difficulty in attempting to apply Western academic categories and analysis to the fluid and varied field that is Bushman religion. There are instances when the academic rite of passage category fits and there are instances where it fits only partially, or not at all.

Transition and Transformation

The anti-structural tenor of Bushman religion and belief is given free rein within the transition phase of Bushman initiation rites, which are exceptionally complex ritually and symbolically. It is prolonged and texturally embellished and the female rite, in its seclusion-transition phase, provides the occasion and setting for a much-told myth within the oral literature of some Bushman groups. The transition phase's most prominent presence—in a sense not only metaphorical and spiritual, but also palpable—is an animal. This animal is almost always the eland—or some other cognate big-game animal—the Bushmen's fat- and symbol-laden antelope of antelopes. Some researchers (Vinnicombe 1976; Lewis-Williams 1981; Lewis-Williams and Biesele 1978) hold it to be the dominant symbol of Bushman culture, which interrelates, multivocally and inextricably, "natural phenomena, human experience, cosmic events and divine activity" (Vinnicombe 1976: 397).

The female ceremony especially is subject to such symbolic and ritual embellishment. As noted above, it is the more elaborate of the two rites—mandatory for each young woman and indispensable for her social maturation, and as a consequence, universal within Bushman and Khoisan culture. In it, all of the symbolic and affective stops—of liminality, inversion, celebration—that accompany the transition phase generally are pulled out, creating a ritual performance of great emotional intensity and symbolic density, akin in this regard to the trance dance.

In the transition phase of the female rite liminality is achieved, in part, through the suspension of certain standards of decorum, and in part through the inversion of certain social categories. When the women expose their buttocks during the eland dance they are in violation of a defined standard of Bushman "public decency," as it is that part of the female anatomy that is considered erotic in Bushman culture and thus is required to be covered at any other time. "It is a dance of an intimate nature," Dorothea Bleek (1928: 23) noted of the Nharo, which "they certainly . . . would not wish to perform . . . before strangers."[2] This may have been a reason why at the transition phase of the rite all men and boys had to leave the site or even the village (Bleek 1928: 23). Another erotic element is that the dance is a dance of courtship—the men, dancing in hunched-up position behind the women, evidently wooing them. However, inasmuch as the courtship routine of the dancers simulates eland mating patterns, performed rather sedately, with heavy, deliberate steps conjuring up "a picture of the grandly muscular, fleshy eland, trotting along unhurriedly in the veld" (England 1968: 596), the eroticism of the dance is decidedly muted. It is ludic—explicitly so when the "bulls" engage in playful jousting—rather than lascivious. The latter was the moral gloss attributed to the dance by some early observers, such as Dorothea Bleek. Having witnessed a performance that seemed to have been toned down—"kept in moderation" (perhaps for her benefit)—Bleek ventured the somewhat gratuitous opinion that "it might easily be very indecent, probably would be so among wild clans" (Bleek 1928: 23).

The social categories to be inverted are those of age and gender. The eland dance is an event at which the old act like the young. The performers of the eland fertility dance are usually (though not always) old men and women whose own procreative power and health are on the wane. The gender inversion is evident in the female initiate's touching (Silberbauer 1965: 86), or even handling men's weapons and medicines, and acting as a hunter when she shoots (as among the !Kõ) arrows at a stretched, suspended antelope skin (Heinz 1975c: 9). Another hunting "implement" the /Xam maiden was required to handle is her father's hunting dogs, whom she had to subject to ritual treatment lest they "play with the game," rather than bring it to bay (Hewitt 1986: 283). Moving to a more metaphorical level, yet another male "implement" the Hai//om (as well as Khoekhoe) maidens are reported to have handled at initiation was the testicles of the adolescent men in the camp (Schapera 1930: 121, citing Fourie 1925/26: 58), in order to prevent their swelling in the event of some future contagion with menstrual blood. Female control over males is evident also when the !Kung girl hits the adolescent boys of the band filing by her, with a stick daubed in ochre (Lewis-Williams 1981: 51).

Another aspect of the male domain that the female initiate assumes contact with and control over, one symbolically linked to hunting, is curing. Among the !Kõ she carries medicine sticks on her back at one phase in her initiation (Heinz 1975c: 9) and the !Kung and the /Xam regarded a "new maiden" to be the source of *n/um* (or */k'ode*), the healing potency normally associated with the male trance healers (Lewis-Williams 1981: 51–52). Fat and rain, two potent metaphors for *n/um*, were also symbolically linked to her; in the words of the /Xam informant Dia!kwain, "When she is a maiden, she has the rain's magic power" (Lewis-Williams ibid.: 52). Indeed, it was the scent of rain that exuded from her which, so Lewis-Williams suggests (ibid.), attracted !Khwa to her confinement hut.

Still at the level of metaphor, the woman's assumption of the male hunting role is evident also in the !Kung circumlocution for menstruation, "she shoots an eland" (Lewis-Williams 1981: 51). Lewis-Williams notes that her association with hunting may in fact be quite direct, as a girl at menarche is linked to elands by means of a bond of sympathy through which she can affect the success of a hunt (ibid.). Indeed, during the liminal phase, the girl's status is paradoxical; as Lewis-Williams points out, "she is spoken of as if she were a hunter *and* as if she were an eland" (ibid.). Yet, in the wider context of Bushman cosmology and mythology, her status as the hunted game animal is, in fact, not paradoxical. It is an expression, in the ritual context of menarche, of the theme of women as meat, of meat eating as sex, and of hunting as marriage, which, as seen in chapter 3, are central themes in Bushman mythology and cosmology. Her being readied for sex and marriage through her rite of passage, and her metaphorical transformation into a game antelope and meat are symbolically consistent in the wider context of Bushman cosmology.

This brings us to the two ontological categories which become inverted in the Bushman initiation rite, those of human and animal. The boundaries between these two categories of beings get blurred extensively, in both the female and male rite. Regarding the first, apart from the principal of the rite being metaphorically transformed into an eland at certain moments during the transition phase, the participants, too, are so transformed in the course of the dance they perform—the women as receptive eland cows, the men as rutting bulls—dancing out their gracefully deliberate steps with intense absorption. Rubbing the girl with eland fat orectically intensifies as well as concretizes the metaphor so that it strikes not only the mind but also the senses. A similar effect is achieved by the dancers through the courtship choreography of their dance, underscored by bulls' "horns" and tail, and by the clinking of the women's ornaments and the axes and knives, at the same rhythm to which the eland moves its clicking hooves (England 1968: 596; see chapter epigraph). As suggested earlier, so absorbing may the performance of this mimetic eland dance routine be for the participants that it may actually come close to a transformation experience, from human to antelope.

It is at this point in the rite that transition comes close to being, or in certain instances or for certain moments actually being, transformation. At such a point, the Bushman rite moves beyond the themes enacted universally in initiation rites: suspension of social status and the consequent liminality and inversion of social and moral categories and rules. What we find transpiring—and what we will see happening also during the trance dance—is the actual ontological transformation, mimetically and symbolically, of the neophyte, and those around her, into animals. It is an ontological transformation even more radical than what Turner means when he talks about "growing" a girl into a woman, rather than moving her, ontologically intact, "an unchanging substance," "from one position to another by a quasi mechanical force" (Turner 1970a: 96). The transformation undergone by Turner's Ndembu girl, for all its ontological implications, still moves along a human, cultural trajectory. That of the Bushgirl and her companions is more radical; she is jumping from the human–culture track to the animal–nature track. Yet, as noted in chapter 1, inasmuch as these two lines of track frequently converge within Bushman cosmology, this is less a quantum leap than it would be in many other cultures. Transition rites represent one of a number of crossing stations between human and animal, like the trance dance, and certain motifs in rock art and myth.

One of these myths actually addresses itself directly to the theme of menarche and its powers of ontological transformation. It is a theme in /Xam myth, and, to a lesser extent, art (Lewis-Williams 1981: 42–43); the transformation it describes is more radical yet than what has been described so far. It is a permanent reversal, of the girl and all of her people, not into the charismatic, kindred eland, but into frogs. Indeed, among the /Xam this ontological transformation or reversal can be so extreme that not just people change to animals, but artifacts of culture revert back to the beings of nature from which they were made. The epigraph at the opening of this chapter provides one text of this important myth, which exists in sixteen versions in the Bleek and Lloyd collection (out of a total of about a hundred narratives) (Hewitt 1986: 78). The folklorist Roger Hewitt (ibid.: 80) outlines the basic story as follows:

> A young woman who is submitted to ritual seclusion leaves her hut each day when all the people have gone out to collect food. She goes to a waterhole and

catches a Waterchild [usually a calf-like bovine or antelope-like creature] which she kills, takes back to the camp and eats. She then returns to her hut. When the people return from the hunting ground the girl's mother brings her food, but, because the girl is already full, her appetite is small. Her mother suspects that she is getting food from elsewhere and takes steps to discover what is happening. However, before her mother confronts her daughter !Khwa [the rain divinity, see chapter 3] is so angered by the girl's behavior that he carries her, her *xoakengu* [old women attending her during seclusion], and her mother and father off in a whirlwind, depositing them in a pool where they become frogs. Their possessions also fly to the same pool and return to their natural forms.

The protagonist, or antagonist, of this portentous drama of transformation and reversal is the "disobedient maiden," who through her defiance of the rules and proscriptions placed on her during her dangerous, "betwixt-between" phase, unleashes elemental forces of destruction on her and her people's heads. The story attests to the power of the Bushwoman, which is especially acute at menarche; while she occupies this liminal state, the rules and categories that give her social shape and substance are suspended.

In the male initiation rite, the forces and dangers of liminality and of social and ontological inversion or transformation, are all considerably more muted. As regards the *choma*-style male ceremony of the !Kung and other northwestern Bushman groups, the liminal and transformative elements of this quasi passage rite are inchoate or absent altogether. The one component to convey an aura of the liminal, along with the numinous, is the presence of //Gãũwa or Hise, an ambiguous divinity that imbues the ritual site of one or two groups with his or her preternatural and ambivalent presence. However, this phase may be lacking altogether from the rite or, among those groups that include it, may be an optional feature of the ceremony. Its impact on the week- or monthlong ritual is thus too limited for it to inform the rite as a whole with a liminal aura.

Where one does find liminality and transformation, among certain groups, is in the first-buck ceremony. As seen above, this rite and the menarcheal rite, especially among the /Xam, share a number of similarities in ritual form and content, and in basic symbolic content. What was impressed on the young, new hunter, in his public status change from a non-hunter to a hunter, were the observances and rules of respect and sympathy for the game antelope he set out to hunt. As seen in chapter 2, these were an integral component of hunting among the /Xam. As seen in chapter 3, they referred to them as *n!anasse*; Lewis-Williams and Biesele (1978) found a similar notion among the !Kung (see also Lee 1979: 239). The animal targeted by the young hunter ideally was the symbol- and sentiment-laden eland; however, as shown by Richard Lee (ibid.: 230), among the !Kung gemsbok, kudu, wildebeest, roan antelope, hartebeest, and giraffe would also fit the bill. He would be enjoined to direct the full battery of respect and sympathy practices in his pursuit of this game animal, at every phase of the hunt. For instance, having wounded the antelope, he had to refrain from certain actions which, by virtue of his identification with the animal, might confer on it strengths and abilities that would impede its death from the arrow poison; for example, by walking fast he would give it speed, or by sleeping on soft grass he would allow it to fall into invigorating sleep (Lewis-Williams and Biesele 1978: 124–28). The practice of painting the eland's forehead mark, a tuft of coarse red hair, on his own forehead and nose renders poignant and graphic the !Kung boy-hunter's identification with his eland quarry. Because of the comprehensiveness and intensity of these ritual observances, the young hunter's attunement to and identification with the prey animal would become all the more intense.

The bond with the eland reaches its pitch after the killing, butchering, and cooking of the animal (Lewis-Williams and Biesele: 128–30). The old men then subject the young hunter to the "eland ritual," which, through a variety of contagious, physical acts, establishes a palpable bond to the animal. Cuts are administered into which eland medicine is rubbed. It is made, in part, from the *n/um* rendered from those parts of the animal that contain concentrations of the healing potency, such as the throat and collar bone. Like his female counterpart, he is covered with eland fat, which is flicked over his body with the animal's tail, forelock, ears, and the hairy skin of its dewlap. Placed on his temples is the hair from the eland's ears. One of its forelegs—the left if the killed animal is female, the right if it is male—is used to make hoof prints on the blanket upon which the young hunter sits, as well as the characteristic clicking sound made by the animal's hooves when it walks (another parallel to the female rite). The hoof prints encircle him, in order to help the hunter, in future eland hunts, locate the animal's tracks, as well as prevent the animal from going off in any direction.

The effect of this ritual, along with the preceding observances of sympathy, may be to create moments where, at the experiential level, the hunter may feel one with the animal. Such is the description of the experience provided by an ethnographer who, in a trance state that led to his own antelope transformation, "emulated the game animal by voicing deep grunts and . . . rapid arm movements and stomps" (Tanaka 1996: 27). David Lewis-Williams (1981: 65) suggests compellingly that the moment of transformation of the young hunter into his antelope quarry may be the meaning behind certain depictions of therianthropic figures on southern Bushman rock art panels. An example is the scene on the Burley I panel at Barkley East (ibid.: 49), which shows two antelope-headed, cloven-footed hunters leaving behind them eland footprints, and striding alongside a herd of eland.

Transformation, Anti-Structure, and Egalitarianism

We have seen in this chapter that initiation rites are another arena of Bushman religion within which the anti-structural undercurrents of Bushman society and culture find expression. One of the most persistent and poignant manifestations of anti-structure in Bushman cosmology is the ambiguity of humans vis-à-vis animals and, more generally and in a different ontological mode, of culture vis-à-vis nature. Anti-structure and ambiguity culminate in the radical reversal of terrestrial humans into aquatic frogs, and of their karosses, mats, arrows, bows, and sticks into bucks, reeds, and bushes. This transpires in the narratives about the menarcheal rite, unleashed by the disobedient maiden.

The rite itself—as well as, to some extent, its male counterpart, the first-buck ceremony—culminates in the mystical identification of humans with the animals of the hunt, the significant nonhuman beings in Bushman cosmology that contribute such a strong force to the formation of self-knowledge on the part of the Bushman people. This knowledge and bond, which men hold by virtue of their subsistence role as hunters, comes to be experienced also by women (as well as old men, who no longer hunt), through the culture's initiation rites. The boundary between human and animal becomes exceptionally fluid during the transition phase, and the border opens up widely into the animals' world. In dancing the eland dance, young women, old women, and old men jointly sojourn in the animal's inner world. They still the "longing for other blood," which this hunting people, who live in and from nature and in cheek-to-jowl proximity to animals, appear to hold more strongly than other folk—agricultural or industrial—who have distanced themselves so much farther from nature.

Through the ambiguity acknowledged and celebrated during the liminal phase of the transition rites, which reverberates through all of Bushman religion, belief, and society, polarities are suspended, between men and women, old and young, human and animal.

And suspended as well are the tension and animosity that stem from polarity and opposition. As I will develop more fully in the conclusion, this anti-structural bent pervading Bushman culture and society may very well constitute the structural basis for the relatively low degree of conflict and high degree of egalitarianism and tolerance of autonomy and idiosyncrasy within relationships among men, among women, between young and old, between the individual and the community, and between humans and animals. It infuses Bushman society with the quality of *communitas*, the embrace of which is wide enough to corral into the community of humans those animals they sense to be significant others.

I turn next to the trance dance, the other important Bushman ritual. Underlying the ritual's goal and method, curing through trance, are the same sociological and cosmological themes that we find in initiation rites: equality, mutuality, fellowship of humans of either gender, and the fellowship of one human, the dancer or the initiand, with animals.

8

The Trance Curing Dance

N/um is put into the body through the backbone. It boils in my belly and boils up to my head like beer. When the women start singing and I start dancing, at first I feel quite all right. Then, in the middle, the medicine begins to rise from my stomach. After that I see all the people like very small birds, the whole place will be spinning around, and that is why we run around. The trees will be circling also. You feel your blood become very hot, just like blood boiling on a fire, and then you start healing.

—UNIDENTIFIED JU/'HOAN TRANCE DANCER (LEE 1993: 115)

Trance medicine really hurts! As you begin to trance, the n/um slowly heats inside you and pulls at you. It rises until it grabs your insides and takes your thoughts away. Your mind and your senses leave and you don't think clearly. Things become strange and start to change. You can't listen to people or understand what they say. You look at them and they suddenly become very tiny. You think, "What's happening? Is God doing this?" All that is inside you is the n/um; that is all you can feel.

—N/ISA, A JU/'HOAN WOMAN AND HEALER (SHOSTAK 1981: 299)

. . . But I was under water! I was gasping for breath, I called out, "Don't kill me! Why are you killing me?" . . . The two of us struggled until we were tired. We danced and argued . . . for a long, long time. We did it until the cocks began to crow.

So, my friend, I sang that song and sang it and sang it until I had sung in the daybreak. . . . Yes my friend. Now up there in the sky, the people up there, the spirits, the dead people up there, they sing for me so I can dance.

—KXAO GIRAFFE, A JU/'HOAN TRANCE DANCER (BIESELE 1993: 70–71)

The author, too has experienced the trance-like state of being melted away into the other world as he emulated the game animal by voicing deep grunts and delved into the dance with rapid arm movements and stomps.

—TANAKA 1996: 27, N.2

The trance dance is the central ritual of Bushman religion and its defining religious institution. The farm Bushmen of Ghanzi regard the *tsso n≠a,* the medicine dance, as the quintessential "Bushman thing," and the *tsso k"au,* the trance dancer, the ultimate Bushman. They contrast trance dancing with the divinatory séance and the witchcraft complex of the black *nkaba* ("diviner"), the clinic or hospital of the European *suster* or fly-in *doktor,* and the black evangelist's or Afrikaner *predikant*'s mission church service (Guenther 1986a: 240–41, 1992).

According to Megan Biesele (1993: 74), the !Kung Bushmen of the Kalahari hold the trance dance to be an ancient part of their culture. This appraisal is borne out by centuries-old rock paintings in many parts of southern Africa that are replete with the trance motif (Lewis-Williams 1981; Lewis-Williams and Dowson 1989; Dowson and Lewis-Williams 1994). It is depicted either figuratively, through metaphorical or mystical images of trance, or literally, through bent-over, collapsing, or collapsed dancers who bleed from the nose and dance to chanting and clapping. The fact that trance dances are described by all writers who have visited the Bushmen, even nineteenth-century ones, further attests to the ubiquity and antiquity of this key Bushman ritual. Wilhelm Bleek's /Xam informant Dia!kwain described what appears to have been a trance curing dance, in the context of an explanatory commentary he was asked to give of a rock art panel that depicted a dance scene (Bleek 1935: 11–14; also see Hewitt 1986: 29). Andrew Smith's account of his 1834 trip to the Bushmen around Kuruman even contains an illustration, by expedition artist Charles Davidson Bell, of what appears to be a trance dance (Smith 1975: 133). Arbousset and Orpen, in the 1840s and 1870s, described a nightlong, "circular" dance in which dancers collapse and cure by touching the sick with hands they have put under their armpits (Stow 1905: 119; Schapera 1930: 180–81; Schmidt 1933: 549–51). All of this sounds very much like the trance dance as it is performed by contemporary Kalahari Bushmen (although the earlier dance contained additional elements evidently not found in the later versions, such as the use of charms and the equal participation and trance collapse of women).

In view of the numerous and, in part, readily accessible accounts of the trance dance among all of the major Bushman groups,[1] I will not offer any detailed description of the ritual. Instead, I will focus on the two key experiential processes at work in this morally charged and symbolically pregnant ritual that are germane to the theme of this book. These components are also the reason for the paramount importance of this ritual, at a personal, social, and cultural level.

The first process is the mental or psychological experience of altered states of consciousness; the second, the moral, social, "synergetic" (Katz 1982) process of curing and the collective and emergent sense of fellowship. The latter affects primarily the non-dancing participants and attendants; the former, the principal—the trance dancer. While the audience and the performer are interconnected, and interact and reinforce one another, they are also distinctively different, moving along separate psychological and symbolic channels, entering different ontological realms. The first, individual-focused process alters reality, drastically and dramatically imbuing it with flux and ambiguity. The second, group-focused process, instead of altering reality, enhances it, through an intense sensation of fellowship among the people present. In the context of that setting, the solidarity generated within the ritual can translate, among contemporary, non-foraging Bushmen, into ethnic identity. Thus, as we will see, the second process of the dance can also become a force for social and political change. As such, what is altered is not the experiential reality of the people at the dance, but cultural reality.

Because of its impact on reality at the individual psychological level, as well as at the collective social and cultural levels, the trance dance is as important a religious institution today as ever. Unlike the initiation rites, which for men have disappeared and for girls have faded in social significance, the trance dance is a ritual as much for contemporary Bushmen as it was for traditional ones. It attests to the resilience and adaptability of Bushman religion at the level of ritual.

Liminality, Transformation, and Transcendence

The objective of the curing dance is to achieve the state of trance (which the !Kung call *!kia*) and thereby transcend ordinary life and reality. Mind-altering drugs play a negligible role in inducing this state of altered consciousness. It seems that in the past indigenous hemp might have been employed sporadically by the G/wi (Eibl-Eibesfeldt 1980: 68), and the use of an unidentified hallucinogenic powder has been reported among the contemporary Hai//om

(Schatz 1993: 12); however, the Nharo vigorously deny any connection between *dagga* and the trance ritual. Instead, trance is achieved through the vigorous, sustained, and physically exhausting activity of dancing around a nocturnal fire, to the chanting of women—both the fire and the chanting producing hypnotic effects. The physical strain and the frenzy the dance reaches at its climax, the rhythm of the chant, and the clapping hands of the women seem to be sufficient conditions for inducing trance, especially in experienced performers.[2] Depending on the level of experience, it may take a dancer from one to several hours to reach trance, and he may be able to repeat this grueling experience more than once during a single nightlong curing session.

The trance phase, the emotional and mystical climax of the ritual, is oftentimes preceded by a less serious, playful phase, consisting of clowning acts by the dancers and non-dancers—including women and children, who may all join the dance circle to play at the dance. The celebratory tone of the dance at its initial phase stands in marked contrast to the portent that follows. It sets the stage for the liminal and transcendent phases that ensue, as the dance gathers numinous momentum in its long dawn-to-dusk progression.

The reason children like to be part of a trance dance performance is that trance singing and dancing is part of their play repertoire; indeed, every child (especially boys) aspires to become a "master of *n/um*." Play trancing includes the utterance of the "death-shriek" (Eibl-Eibesfeldt 1974: 247); the fact that this intensely awesome and dead-serious element of the ritual should find its way into the play actions of the children underscores the quality of moral and emotional ambiguity that seems to attach to the curing rite. Trancing is a goal about half of the boys and one-third of the girls will achieve when they are men and women (Katz 1976: 284; Lee 1993: 117).

A trance dance may actually be initiated out of such a play context, at a small play fire near sunset, around which girls may sit and clap and chant, and boys dance (Heinz 1975a: 28, 1975b: 7). The !Xõ call such child's dance-play "calling their elders" (Heinz 1975b: 7). In the course of the evening, elder children and teenagers replace the smaller children, and as evening progresses into night, women and men take over. Initially they, too, may continue for a bit in the playful vein, adding elements of sexual banter (Eibl-Eibesfeldt 1974: 245, 251) or some of the scatological antics that may also mark the opening phase of dancing by the star dancers (Guenther 1986a: 256). Thus, the dance proper usually gets under way only after the younger generation, as well as women and non-dancers, all have had a chance to play at the dance, in a ludic, non-trance fashion. It is at this phase more than at any other that the dance is an "occasion for great fun, flirtation and hilarity," engaged in not for the purpose of healing but "for the sheer fun of it" (Biesele 1993: 74–75).

Dancers try to prolong the pre-trance state, during which their actions and words grow more and more intense, disassociated, erratic, and even destructive. This describes the trance routines especially of the younger and less experienced dancers, who may try to throw themselves in the fire, throw embers over their chests and heads, tear down huts, or rush at, grab, and even bite bystanders. I once saw a man in this state wrest a small child out of its mother's arms and swing the terrified, wailing child over his head, dodging the mother and others who tried to take it away from him. On another occasion the target of the frenzied trance dancer's attack was the anthropologist present at the ritual performance: he came rushing at me wielding a heavy stick, minutes before trance collapse and after an attempt to tear down a nearby grass hut, shouting "I see //Gãũwa!" However, before he could reach me he was subdued by his assistants and spectators.

It is at this point in the dance that a dancer's healing potency, called *n/um* (*n/om*) by the !Kung and *tssõ* (*tcõ*) by the Nharo, heats up in his stomach, pouring forth from his body in the form of sweat. Being the exudation of *n/um,* the trancer's body sweat is held to be therapeutically efficacious. The curer copiously rubs his sweat over the "patients," the sick persons sitting or lying near the dance circle, on whose behalf the curing ceremony is held. Having treated them in this fashion, he tries to rub or touch with his healing hands as many of the onlookers as his power permits, for palliative reasons or to ensure good dreams. The reason for prolonging the staying power of healing during this manifestation of his trance state is that it allows him to accomplish his calling with maximum effect.

A Nharo informant likened the ability to extend this pre-trance, pre-collapse curing phase to the "staying" power of a man during lovemaking. Both are evidence of potency, of either the healing or the sexual kind. This observation by the Nharo informant resonates with Richard Lee's comment that among the Ju/'hoansi *!kia,* trance, appears to be "connected with sexual arousal and orgasm" (Lee 1993: 120). It may also explain why among the same people "the women really like the healers" and why aging healers, whose sexual and healing potency are waning, will look wistfully at a young dancer in trance, saying to themselves, "Think of the sex the guy's going to get" (Katz 1982: 186). His willing partner after the dance would likely be one of the women from the chanting circle, or two of them, "one on his left side, another on the right" (Katz ibid.).

Before the climactic event of trance a dancer may have been in a liminal, disassociated state for a whole hour or longer. Although he dances and cures in ever more labored and erratic fashion, his words and actions are nevertheless such that throughout he conducts himself like an active, purposive, conative member of his everyday social community. He cures and touches people, and his words—contrary to some writers who probably did not properly understand them because of the strained voice in which they were uttered—are sensible and coherent, presenting a boosting commentary on his actions: "I am imitating god," "I am doing the work of a healer," "I am the dancer Garia Pek," "I am a dancer, I am numba o'wann" ("number one"). As seen in chapter 1, another line of commentary may deal with the moral deportment of members of the camp, consisting of exhortations to stop quarrels and restore peace in the group. Frequently the dancer's words and phrases are directed toward the women, in order to beseech them to sing well so that he may trance (Wiessner and Larsen 1979; Eibl-Eibesfeldt 1980: 68–69; Guenther 1986a: 258). The lyrics of songs sung by a trance dancer when playing his thumb piano (which a number of them do) resonate with some of the same themes that define his song texts while he is trance dancing, such as sickness, suffering and death, dreaming, god, //Gãũwa, and ghosts and mothers (Biesele 1975b).

The closer he gets to the moment of collapse, the more erratic his actions become, as he sways and stumbles, no longer in step with the rhythm of the dance (Eibl-Eibesfeldt 1974: 247). His words become incoherent and incomprehensible and his gaze turns more and more blank and seemingly inward looking. Yet, even now, moments before his trance "death," he may turn outward again, to the people and events around him in the "real" world. While seemingly oblivious to the things around him, his gaze may become suddenly alert and his actions fully attuned to ordinary reality again. This was once borne out strikingly at a trance dance performance I attended. It was held at a farm whose owner had explicitly forbidden its performance, after having earlier on been asked for permission to dance that night. He was one of those Ghanzi farmers to whose ear and mind Bushman trance dancing is "just noise" that is likely to impede the farmer's family's sleep and his Bushman laborers' work efficiency the following day. At one point in the dance, when the dancer was well along his way to trance and my eyes were on him and his intense face, which stared into the darkness beyond the circle lit by the fire (where //Gãũwa is believed to lurk), I noticed how his facial expression suddenly changed, from its blankly staring gaze, to startled alertness. His actions, too, became swift and coordinated, as he bolted away, just when the farmer stepped into the circle grim-faced, bringing the chanting to a sudden end.

The dancer's ambiguous, betwixt-between altered state before trance collapse, when one foot and eye are still in the here-and-now while the other are set to the spirit world beyond, abruptly changes to an alternate reality at the moment of his collapse. While he is now quite "out of it," he still keeps himself connected spiritually to the normal reality on which he has temporarily turned his back. This he accomplishes through his task of healing, discharged not visibly and bodily now, but mystically, in spirit and through spirits.

Underscoring the separation aspect of this moment, the Nharo (and !Kung) liken trance collapse to death, and all the pain and suffering incumbent on dying are held to be part of the trance dancer's experience at this point. Everyone's fear is "that he may never come back" (Katz 1976: 290), that the "half-death"—*//abe* or *//o !gei* in Nharo, meaning literally "dead-awake"—of trance may turn out to be full death.

He enters this "death" state most dramatically, uttering a piercing "death-shriek," which the !Kung call *kow-he-dile* (or *kaohididi*), accompanied by convulsive shaking of his body, and followed quickly by the dancer's collapse (Lee

1993: 115; Biesele 1993: 75). Eibl-Eibesfeldt (1974: 247) provides a clinical description of the shriek, which he considers, rightly, to be stereotyped and practiced (starting, as noted above, as child's play): "long-drawn out, moaning shrieks, which trail off in a tremolo, are followed by sharp, short shrieks which are accompanied with strong convulsions of the body" (my translation[3]). This eerie, Dante-esque sound is also accompanied by retching and spitting; according to the !Kõ this is caused by the sickness and "evil" the dancer has absorbed in the course of healing (Heinz 1975b: 8).

The death-shriek and collapse mark the turning point of the ritual, from the physical plane of curing within the realm of ordinary reality, to the mystical plane within the preternatural reality of spirits and the spirit world.

As he passes through the state of trance and nears trance collapse, and then collapses and goes through whatever experiences may await him on the spiritual plane (which are beyond the anthropologist's grasp), the trancer undergoes a process of personal transcendence, which significantly alters his "sense of self, time and space" (Katz 1976: 288). And the fact that this self-transcendence takes place in the context of the social community—as the curing dance is a classic "rite of solidarity" and an instance of "community healing" (Katz 1982)—adds a vicarious, public element to the trancer's personal transcendence. In the Bushman spirit of sharing, the onlookers partake of the dancer's altered and alternate state, as they watch him now lying alert, being massaged and revived by his assistant, then shakily getting up either to start dancing again, or to tell people what his spirit saw and did. His report of what he experienced and learned about the spirits and curing is communicated with urgency and listened to with rapt attention, as many regard it as an "important piece of truth" (Biesele 1993: 70). His personal experience brings "transcendence into ordinary life and ordinary life into transcendence" (Katz 1976: 284). As Megan Biesele puts it:

> The trance dance involves everyone in the society, those who enter trance and experience the power of the other world directly, and those to whom the benefits of the other world—healing and insight—are brought by the trancers. (Biesele 1993: 70)

In the fashion of shamans all over the world, the trance dancer, by means of altered states, enters the spirit world and obtains from it the wherewithal to restore the health of sick fellow humans. In the Bushman's view, there are basically two mystical techniques for bringing this about (with details varying among different Bushman groups): transformation into an animal and extra-body travel. The latter the trancer does in the form either of an animal or of a spirit, seeking out and confronting the spirit being or beings who caused the disease. He may do so by walking or running through the veld, following or guided by a spirit or spirit animal, or by flight, the people around him becoming "very tiny," "like very small birds" (Lee 1993: 115; see illustration at chapter opening).

Transformation may be into such animals as lions, leopards, and snakes—that is, predatory animals which hunt (underscoring yet again the symbolic, shamanic link between the trance dancer and hunter). Among Kalahari Bushmen, the lion was a trance dancer's most common spirit incarnation (Katz, Biesele, and St. Denis 1997: 24–25). It is an animal that is a ready candidate as the trancer-spirit's vehicle or companion, in view of the relationship of respect and collegiality that holds between the two like-minded, evenly matched hunters (see chapter 2). Moreover, lions are out in the night, beyond the firelit circle, likely watching the proceedings of the people with interest, as is their habit at all times (and that of their human fellow hunters, vis-à-vis the lions). They might even roar, as not infrequently they do at night, especially if the people they watch do something untoward. Their roars add to the sense of awe and dread that hangs over people at this moment in the dancer's experience, as it complements mystical peril from spirit beings with potential real danger from actual animals (whose beastly otherness, as we saw above, is especially evident to the !Kung when the animals roar, as people, according to Marshall-Thomas, do not understand the language of lions).

The "lion-experience" can absorb the dancer so thoroughly that it may be held by both himself and the people watching to be an actual transformation. As described by the Ju/'hoan trance dancer Tshao Matze: "When I turn into a lion, I can feel my lion-hair growing and my lion-teeth forming. I'm inside that lion, no longer a person. Others to whom I appear see me just as another lion" (Katz et al. 1997: 24). He might crawl on all fours, just prior to collapse (Eibl-Eibesfeldt 1980: 72–73), and after "death," his spirit may run out into the night as a lion to mingle with lions in the veld, possibly forever, never to return to the community of humans (Heinz 1975b: 8). Were he to really die—as some trancers have, so I was told—his having joined the lions may be one explanation people have for his death. The /Xam told Lloyd that lion's hair came out of the back of dancers who were lion-afflicted, which their assistants would rub with fat and pull out. In such a state the shaman might also roar and bite people and would have to be forcibly restrained by people around him (Bleek 1935: 2, 4). Apparently one way for the /Xam medicine man to bring on a lion transformation was to "snore" (suck?) the same creature out of the sick person. Like other animals (owls, butterflies, springbok), the lion could enter a person and, to cure him of the invasive animal disease, the medicine man had to suck the spirit creature into himself, sneeze it out of his body, and cast it away. As a lion, a trance dancer represented a danger to his fellow dancers and the spectators at the dance, whom he might rush at and chase into the darkness where other lions or spirits might lurk. This was the case especially with respect to young or inexperienced dancers, or, among the /Xam, ones improperly attended by fellow dancers, who were in danger of "slip[ping] into the feared form of the 'angry' lion" (Lewis-Williams 1981: 97; see also 1982: 436).

Another animal the /Xam dancer could become on the spiritual plane was the antelope (this reportedly was Jiro Tanaka's own experience, as seen in one of the epigraphs). As argued by Lewis-Williams (1981: 91–100, 1982: 435; also see Guenther 1984: 48–51, 1990a: 239), the antelope-man motif of Bushman rock paintings—some of which depict not only the animal's cloven feet but also wings that take the figure heavenward, or laterally across the landscape—depict nothing other than dancers in trance. Thus, unlike the lion transformation of the /Xam shaman just referred to, which are associated with danger or sickness, the antelope-trancer transformation represents curing in its most potent form.

More dangerous even than any unruly lion-shaman, for the Nharo, Hai//om, or !Kung trance dancer, is his confrontation with //Gāũwa, //Gaunab, or the //gangwasi, as the !Kung call the spirits of the dead and principal agents of disease (Lee 1993: 113–15). He may reach the spirit(s) by moving just outside the lit circle where the trickster god can be expected to lurk close by, watching the proceedings (Guenther 1986a: 261) and, according to !Kung and !Kõ belief, inducing trance and curing power in the dancers (Heinz 1975a: 28; Eibl-Eibesfeldt 1980: 245; Biesele 1993: 70–71). Alternatively, his extra-body journey may take him great distances across the nocturnal landscape (Lewis-Williams 1982: 436–37). He may be guided by an animal, such as an antelope, or ride on its back, to a *Lebensbaum* ("tree of life"), up which the Hai//om "shaman" will climb, entering the celial domain of the spirits via this archetypical shamanic route (Wagner-Robertz 1976: 541–42). Another shamanic means of traveling between the real and spirit world is by "the thread of the sky," up and down which the !Kung dancer's spirit might climb (Biesele 1993: 72).

The reason for the dancer's quest, the confrontation with the spirit(s) at its destination, and the danger, is that his mission requires him to plead with the spirit(s), and if necessary fight with him, her, or them, or shoot arrows at them or at their own disease arrows, in the fashion of a mystical "star wars" (Wagner-Robertz 1976: 539; Eibl-Eibesfeldt 1980: 68; Guenther 1986a: 272; Biesele 1993: 72). Another danger might be that of being drowned by a spirit, while attempting to obtain the curing dance song from him (Biesele 1993: 70–72; see epigraph). As noted earlier, so dangerous is the trance dancer's spirit mission to the nether realm that it could change his half-death into permanent death, so that his inert body would never rise again. I heard from the Nharo about dancers dying—"really," "fully"—at a trance dance, for that very reason; indeed, in the resigned view of dancers I interviewed, such was a dancer's ultimate fate. The spirit(s) may be ill-disposed and malevolent, as well as strong and not easily vanquished. Among the Hai//om, the danger may be of a different kind, emanating not from //Gamab, but his wife, a one-legged, nymphomaniacal harridan named Kaindaus. She may present herself to the dancer's spirit alter ego as a seducing enchantress and, in the event that he should refuse her advances (as he must), "hell's fury" is loosed on his head by the spurned woman-spirit, in the form of torture and dismemberment (Wagner-Robertz 1976: 536–37). The Hai//om shaman /Garugu //Khumob (alias

Joel) attributes the four-day-long, near-death illness that afflicted him after a cure to a thrashing he had received from Kaindaus on that occasion (Schatz 1993: 8).

The other preternatural source of danger and pain, and, potentially, death to the trance dancer, is the healing potency (*n/um* or *tssõ*) that boils up in his stomach. This is its ultimate ambiguity: it can bring both death and life; like medicine everywhere, it can cure and it can kill. *Tssõ,* in Nharo, is the term for medicine and one of the terms for poison; among the linguistically related Kxoe, the concept of *tçõ* describes a force that is both curative and harmful, being more associated with disease and death than with healing (Köhler 1978/79: 26–29). It has assumed the latter values also among the sedentary farm Nharo of Ghanzi, as well as among the !Kõ, whose concept of */oa* is referred to unambiguously by Heinz (1975b: 7) as an "evil force" of !Kõ supernaturalism. Ilse Schatz (1993: 15) reports that the above-mentioned /Garugu //Khumob was as much dreaded as a sorcerer by the farm Hai//om as he was respected and acclaimed as a healer. In the former role he was believed to abuse his powers of healing and to bring disease or death to enemies, by means of the same invisible arrows which he used to shoot down disease. Among the farm Nharo *tssõ* has become a concept of witchcraft, freshly minted with acculturative borrowings from the witchcraft complex of neighboring Tswana and Kgalagari. For those living in dense and permanent village communities rife with tension and "village politics," witchcraft and sorcery accusations have become a new source of social conflict and a new category of disease which the Bushmen address by drawing concepts from groups among whom twhey are well established, and blending them with concepts of their own (Guenther 1992a; also see 1979a: 175–76, 1986a: 60–67, 273–74; and Vorster 1994, 1995). Such new social conflicts and diseases and the reconceptualizations of traditional concepts of medicine have heightened the inherent moral ambiguity of the traditional Bushman concept of healing potency among some farm Bushman groups.

Among the more traditional !Kung, on the other hand, *n/um* has been characterized by writers first and foremost as a healing force (Katz 1982; Lewis-Williams 1981) and as a substance and power that, being a "gift from God," is thoroughly and unequivocally positive (Katz 1982: 152–53, 242–45). Yet, here too, dark and dangerous elements—pain, the unknown, the //gangwasi, death—surround what appears to be inherently beneficial. The pain may be so intense or disconcerting to a dancer that he or she may stop curing altogether. As N/isa stated:

> Lately, though, I haven't wanted to cure anyone, even when they've asked. I've refused because of the pain. I sometimes become afraid of the way it pulls at my insides, over and over, pulling deep within me. The pain scares me. That's why I refuse. Also sometimes after I cure someone, I get sick for a while. That happened not long ago when I cured my older brother's wife. The next day, I was sick. I thought, "I won't do that again. I cured her and now I'm sick!" (Shostak 1981: 303)

Richard Lee (1993: 117–19; see also Katz 1982: 119) discussed this dark side of *n/um* with his Ju/'hoan informants, adding to the list of dangers what he himself experienced at his one attempt at entering *!kia,* "an acute fear of loss of control" (Lee 1993: 117).

The zero-sum formula that underlies the act of curing in Bushman medicine is another fundamental reason trance dancers feel ambivalent about the culmination and climax of their vocation: to restore health to a sick person is to sap the health of the healer, bringing him yet another step closer to his own death. If *n/um* doesn't burn you, and *!kia* or the lions that your spirit merges or mingles with don't half kill you, the spirits and their arrows to whom you expose yourself at every trance will get you. Another reason, given by the Nharo, is the growing deterioration and weakness of the healer's body, as a result of taking each person's sickness up, allowing it to spend itself in a body pervaded and strengthened with *tssõ* (Guenther 1986a: 268–71).

Another element of anxiety in the trance dance is the people's realization that the outcome is unpredictable, in view of the imponderable will of the god who dispenses the medicine, or the uncertainty of the outcome of a wrestling match between a dancer and a spirit. In the words of N/isa, yet again:

> N/um is powerful, but it is also very tricky. Sometimes it helps and sometimes it doesn't, because God doesn't always want a sick person to get better. Sometimes he tells a healer in trance, "Today I want this sick person. Tomorrow, too. But the next day, if you try to cure her, then I will help you. I will let you have her for a while." God watches the sick person, and the healer trances for her. Finally, God says, "All right, I only made her slightly sick. Now, she can get up." When she feels better, she thinks, "Oh, if this healer hadn't been here, I would have surely died. He's given me my life back again."
>
> That's n/um—a very helpful thing! (Shostak 1981: 301)

As I reported earlier, the farm Bushmen have recruited Jesus Christ as their newest //Gãũwa spirit being in order to mediate between the dancers and the disease spirits, as the former attempt to secure curing arrows from the latter. This can perhaps be seen as a mythical mechanism for reducing the unpredictability that surrounds trance curing.

While many men, and some women, strive to become healers, they also dread this ominous decision and may struggle against it. This ambivalence is reflected in the career of Tsau, the great !Kung dancer among the Ghanzi farm Bushmen at the time of my fieldwork:

> Tsau knew that he would be a dancer when he was a young boy. He received some of his early training from his father who was himself a dancer. His grandfather had been a dancer as well; he treated Tsau when he was a young man and suffered from a serious sickness. He contends that this sickness caused his death during that portentous night that his grandfather treated him. After his grandfather had revitalized him, he trembled violently for a

> long time. In the morning he awoke to the crowing of a cock and rose up to be a doctor. The trembling had been N!eri's sign to him to be a dancer. He was sick one other time and was treated by his uncle. Since then, sickness has forever afflicted him as it is the lot of the dancer to take the sicknesses of all the people into his own body. He states with grim resignation that his body will ultimately be so weakened by all of the accumulated sicknesses that it will succumb and he will die. (Guenther 1986a: 268–69)

The remarkable song texts of the Ju/'hoan musician and trance dancer Jack recorded by Megan Biesele (1975b) reverberate with the same spirit of self-sacrifice and of resigned acceptance of suffering, disease, and ultimately death, which is the trancer's lot.

Apart from the moral ambiguity that surrounds healing potency, and the emotional ambivalence of healers toward it, this force is enigmatic in other ways. It can manifest itself in ways other than as healing potency or medicine. *N/um* can refer also to a "special skill or anything out of the ordinary," such as "menstrual blood, African sorcery, herbal remedies, a vapor trail of a jet plane, tape recorders, and travelling in a truck at high speeds" (Lee 1993: 115). As noted above, the equivalent Nharo term has been blended with the Tswana concept of witchcraft, and its Kxoe cognate, *tcõ,* has been folded into a new chronological category, Sunday, among the missionized Kxoe at Andara. The term for this day of the week is *tcõ-/'e* ("the day of *tcõ*-power"). According to Köhler (1978/79: 27) the reason for holding Sunday to be charged with this formidable power is the belief that the mission somehow, at some time in the past, had contact with bad and destructive *tcõ* on that day of the week, henceforth rendering Sunday ill-fated and unsuitable for the performance of any work throughout its quotidian course. The negative gloss on this new day and new word may be a reflection of the misgivings the Kxoe hold about the mission operation in their land (an issue to which I will return in the next chapter).

To sum up, the trance dance is a ritual of transformation and transcendence that alters the performers' and participants' sense of reality. It takes the dancer into the realm of the spirits and may transform him or her, spiritually or metaphorically, into an animal. Like the beings of the First Order in mythic time, the dancers of today may shift their ontological state, crossing back and forth between boundaries that separate them from spirit and animal beings, and from life and death. At one phase of the dance, before the moment of collapse, they stand on the threshold of both realms, in the full view of spectators and participants, who witness the dancer's intense experience of disassociation. Preceding this numinous phase is a ludic celebratory one that draws in children; their playfulness and hilarity stands in contrast to the deeply serious and supernatural events that follow. The disjuncture of this moment provides the threshold, the transition from ordinary to altered, alternate, and transcended reality. It also gives to the trance dance an element of emotional ambivalence, derived from the opposition of ludic hilarity and numinous portent. Abiding or fatalistic ambivalence may be the trance dancer's emotional frame of mind, in view of the dangerous and imponderable nature of his or her business. It is due to the unpredictability of his mystical sources for medicines and curing power, of the gods and spirits in the darkness beyond, and of the healing potency inside her stomach.

The Trance Dance and Cultural Revitalization

The trance curing dance is performed with somewhat greater frequency among Ghanzi farm Bushmen than among their "veld" counterparts in other parts of the Kalahari. Instead of being performed primarily during the aggregation phase and sporadically for the rest of the year, the trance dance has become a year-round ritual that may be held several times a month or week, drawing many participants and spectators. The intensity and duration of performances has also increased, individual dances sometimes lasting not only through the night but possibly through the next day and night, for as long as two or even three days and nights.

Moreover, there has been a proliferation of different types of dances, each with different songs, created by one of the many trance curers who move across the farms in itinerant fashion (Guenther 1986a: 254). As noted recently by Richard Lee, the same can be said of the Ju/'hoansi in the Dobe region where, in addition to the standard curing dance consisting primarily of male performers, the Giraffe Dance, a "women's dance" (the Drum Dance), has become so popular that "it has taken on the character of a social movement, gaining new converts every year" (Lee 1993: 119). Women may introduce their daughters to the dance when they are small girls and "train" them for trance by giving them a root to eat that they hold to contain psychoactive properties (Shostak 1981: 298, 301–302). In this female variant of the trance dance the two roles are reversed, the women going into trance (though not necessarily performing cures) and the men providing the music, by means of a long drum. In addition, a Ju/'hoan man introduced a brand new dance in the late 1960s, the above-mentioned Trees Dance, based on the Rand mines dances performed in the mining compounds every Sunday (Lee 1993: 121).

Yet another new type of dance, performed by schoolchildren of all ages in Botswana,[4] is "traditional dancing" (as it is billed by the various troupes and their mentors and sponsors, when they perform at annual events or competitions). A troupe may have a repertoire of several dance numbers, which are versions of different traditional ritual or recreational dances. Some of them have names and songs pertaining to the new economic and social reality; for instance a favorite number of the preschool dancers at Dekar, and an award-winning hit, is a dance called "B.M.C." (Botswana Meat Commission). The dance is performed to the repetitive chanting of those three initials. The performers wear "traditional dress"—leather loincloth or skirt—or "undress," as chests are bare. The exception at the daylong event I witnessed in July 1994, that featured dance troupes—including many comprised of black children—from all over Ghanzi and Ngamiland Districts, was one troupe whose top-covered female performers received a few boos from the audience. Thus, the dancers subscribe to the image of "veld Bushmen" held by members of the wider Botswana society, and they attract a wide audience wherever they appear. At the event I observed the Bushchildren competed against Tswana, Kgalagari, and Herero schoolchildren, who were fully clad in school or scouts' uniforms. Their dance routines consisted primarily of rather stiff and severe military-style stick- or baton-wielding, marching, and drill exercises. By comparison, the Bushman performance was novel, fluid, and graceful; in fact, the dancers were the decided favorites of the audience, whose numbers tripled (to about six hundred) when the "Basarwa" dancers were on stage (in part, I suspect, because of their exotic appearance and appeal). The judges were evidently as impressed as the audience, giving most of the awards to the Bushman dancers.

In tandem with the increased incidence and intensity of trance dancing and the proliferation of the trance dance and dancing in general is the professionalization of the dancer. Whereas in traditional times trance dancers were indistinguishable from other members of the group, half or one-third of whom may themselves have been dancers, in the modern farm context trance dancers may take on special forms of dress and "insignia of office." An example is the Hai//om farm Bushman and shaman Joel, who, when performing the trance ritual, will wear a certain type of leather apron, several glass and ostrich eggshell bead necklaces, a Plains Indian–style headband stuck with ostrich feathers, and a "medicine drum" strapped around his neck (Wagner-Robertz 1976: 537; Schatz 1993: 11). Quite unlike traditional trance dancers, he used what appeared to have been a mind-altering powder, which he burned in the fire, and his curing routine included such actions as singing in !Kung (a language people do not understand, whose speakers, especially the ≠Au//eisi, are held to be strong curers, as well as sorcerers), sneezing, handling fire brands, doing push-ups over the embers, and rushing into the bushes when in trance (Schatz 1993: 11–15). Moreover, this renowned shaman (who died in 1987) was distinguished mystically from non-shamans by the long list of food taboos he had to observe (Wagner-Robertz 1976: 538–39); so many and varied were his meat taboos that, when this food item was handed out by a farmer after slaughtering, he was given leave to pick his own choice pieces (Schatz 1993: 16). Gusinde (1966: 134–35) reports a similar state of ritual embellishment and professionalization among the Hukwe (Kxoe) ritual specialists of the lower Okavango, describing the process as the development of an *echtes Schamanentum* ("true shamanism"), as against its incipient form among other Kalahari Bushman groups.

Among the Ghanzi farm Bushmen, the *n/a k"au* likewise has become a highly specialized ritual expert who possesses prestige and influence; thanks to the fees he charges for his services, he is, by farm Bushman standards, a man of wealth. His clients may include Blacks, who may turn to Bushman doctors for help with certain illnesses, or white farmers, who may hire a Bushman shaman to perform a "rain dance" or two, during a particularly trying drought period (Gusinde 1966: 21; Guenther 1986a: 254).

The latter performance once again reflects the plasticity, as well as the opportunism, of Bushman belief: the Nharo do not have any ritual concept of rain dance and I have heard them express strong skepticism about claims that such magical dances can have any effect. Yet, when called upon by a farmer to do the Bushman "rain dance thing," which the latter holds to be a Bushman's unique esoteric skill, the dancer, who may be one of his laborers, will generally oblige him. The reason, in part, is because the request comes from the *baas;* thus, it would not be in the Bushman's interest to decline and to attempt to enlighten his employer about the benighted notions about the Bushmen he holds in his head. Yet, the Bushman's yielding to the boss's request does not constitute any act of apostasy; beliefs and convictions are plastic and tolerant enough to allow him to go through the charade without compromising his beliefs. Also, since the farmer will usually pay the dancer some remuneration for his dance, there is "money in it" for him; indeed, in the old days, I was told by Ghanzi Bushmen and farmers, alleged "rain dancers" moved from farm to farm during drought periods, offering to do their esoteric service for a fee.

Incidentally, another client for a Bushman dancer's expert services might be the anthropologist: Pater Gusinde had his fieldwork activities "cleared" with //Gauwa by a !Kung dancer. In trance, the latter sought out the spirit to ask him about the matter. He was given the go-ahead: it was the determination of the dancer that what Gusinde was doing was deemed "something good" by //Gauwa (Gusinde 1966: 21). Like the Bushman rain doctor hiring on with the *baas* farmer, this is another instance of the Bushmen's opportunistic exploitation of outsiders, as a resource to be foraged.

There are many trance dancers in Ghanzi who are ranked by the people with respect to their power as healers. The esteem in which they are held ranges from low-ranked, little "G. P."s to doctors of renown, whose prestige comes close to that enjoyed by a Western screen star or star athlete (Guenther 1986a: 262–69). They move from farm to farm, performing the curing ritual usually at the behest of specific individuals who have fallen ill. Drawing heavy fees for their services, which they may convert into cattle, the trance dancers of renown have become some of the most affluent farm Bushmen (their wealth derived from "their own work," rather than labor done for Whites). They are on the move all year long and their trance dance performances may draw onlookers and participants who may number in the hundreds.

A similar development has been reported in recent years among the Dobe !Kung—as well as those at /Kae/Kae (Katz, Biesele, and St. Denis 1997)—where the professionalization of healers has created strains in interpersonal relations and contradictions within Bushman ethos. As reported by Richard Lee:

> In the past *n/um* was freely given and the rewards to the healers were manifold and diffuse. Personal satisfaction, the love and respect of family, and the

> gratitude of those they had "saved" are some of the positive themes mentioned by healers in interviews. But the interviews contain another theme, a recurrent complaint about other Ju/'hoansi: they are *chi dole* (bad, strange) because they take the medicine for granted and don't pay for successful treatment. ≠Toma zho, a famous /Xai /xai (/Kae/Kae) healer (see Katz 1982: 177–95), has started to make regular trips to the Ghanzi farms to cure and dance because at /Xai /xai "people haven't paid me anything. (Lee 1993: 123)

It might be noted, parenthetically, that ≠Toma zho's expectation about being paid by his Ghanzi clients was possibly a touch too optimistic. When I was doing my fieldwork in the late 1960s a favorite topic of conversation, and of complaint, for some of the healers was people reneging on their payment of fees (Guenther 1986a: 264, 268).

As I have shown elsewhere (Guenther 1975, 1976a, 1976b, 1979b, 1986a: 50–68, 287–89), there are several reasons for the increased stature and status of the modern trance dancer. The mounting incidence of disease and the general state of economic and psychological depression of the farm Bushmen have led to a rise in the demand for the trance curer's services. It has also increased the extent of his esoteric knowledge, as evidenced by the proliferation of songs and dances mentioned above. One new element of ritual and medical knowledge are the imported diseases: organic ones such as smallpox, tuberculosis, and venereal diseases, and psychosomatic ones such as witchcraft and sorcery (Guenther 1992a). While the farm Bushmen have distinguished these conceptually and practically, allocating the first to the European settlers and their medical experts and the second to the Bantu-speaking experts (Guenther 1986a: 273–74), some of the younger, more ambitious healers will also take on one or both of these non-Bushman disease types (Guenther 1992a: 85). They may employ Bantu divinatory techniques for diagnosing a suspected case of witchcraft, or take a patient's pulse or listen to his chest, in the manner of the clinic nurse. Alternatively, a Bushman healer may co-opt the medical expertise of the other two systems and healers, by insisting that a Bushman patient also seek out the services of the nurse or diviner, alongside the treatment offered by himself. The explanation impressed on the patient is that treatment would only be effective if it were taken in the context of the Bushman's own curing dance.

However, apart from his highly effective role as healer (Guenther 1986a: 272–74), there is another reason for the elevated social position of the trance dancer among contemporary farm Bushmen: the political role as agent for social change and cultural revitalization that he has been cast in by so many farm Bushmen.[5] As we saw in chapter 1, in the "traditional" context, the trance dance may be performed during a time of social conflict; in the course of a performance the trance dancer may pointedly address himself to issues of tension in the group, and berate individuals or the group collectively for their quarreling and urge them to reconcile. Thus, alongside his explicit esoteric and ritual role as curer, he may play an implicit political role, as arbiter of intra-group conflict. In the modern life situation, beset with oppression, deprivation, and frustration, some people again turn to the trance dancer and the dance with political, rather than—or alongside—religious expectations.

As a synergetic rite of intensification that engenders a strong sense of fellowship and moral well-being in its participants, and resolves any conflicts that there may be among them, the trance dance is a suitable vehicle for cultural revitalization. And the dancer, the star performer at this socially and culturally charged event, is a suitable catalyst for political mobilization. Apart from "embody[ing] the values of egalitarianism and tolerance, and reinforc[ing] the idea of mutual effort against misfortune" (Biesele 1993: 76), in the modern social context of multi-ethnic conflict, the trance dance acts as a mechanism for instilling a sense of collective ethnic identity.

The dance is the ultimate "Bushman thing" (to use Nharo parlance). Significantly, the Ghanzi farm Bushmen believe that //Gāũwa, who is attracted to a trance dance, strongly disapproves of "shiny European" objects, such as knives, tin cans, or flashlights, as well as tobacco. As I suggested elsewhere (Guenther 1975: 164), this detail is one of a number of symbolic "boundary markers" whereby the Bushmen, the *n/oa kwe* ("red people") assert their collective identity vis-à-vis the other ethnic groups within the pluralistic society of Ghanzi.

The trance dance is morally and physically invigorating, it is acknowledged; sought out as a potent curing rite by Bushmen and non-Bushmen alike, it confers wealth and prestige on its practitioner. In the late 1960s, when Bushman deprivation and despair were at a peak, I talked to farm Bushmen who looked to the charismatic, rich, and powerful *n≠a k"au* as something close to a prophet-leader, who could take them out of their present state of misery to their "own place," a farm or stretch of land to be secured "for Bushmen" by the District Commissioner and the government. The process of cultural revitalization set in motion by the trance dance held the potential then of becoming a revitalization movement, spearheaded by the trance dancer (Guenther 1975, 1976b). The reason this did not happen may be the fact that in the following two decades the government introduced a number of development measures that improved the economic prospects of the farm Bushmen, including the establishment of several Bushman settlements, away from the oppressive farm block (Guenther 1986a: 296–314).

Flexibility, Adaptability, and Variability of Bushman Ritual

The changes the trance dance has undergone among the farm Bushmen of Botswana also demonstrate the flexibility of this pattern of Bushman religion. What the trance dance demonstrates as well, quite strikingly, are the correlate properties to flexibility, resilience, and adaptability. Like the rest of the institutions and patterns of Bushman culture, ritual, too, is seen to be adaptive, by virtue of the same (anti)structural qualities that pervade all of Bushman society and culture, amorphousness and ambiguity. The ritual has undergone considerable change in form and content, especially as a result of the process of professionalization, in the hands, oftentimes, of flamboyantly individualistic performers.

Yet, there is also a certain degree of uniformity to the trance dance—more so, perhaps, than for any other component of Bushman belief and ritual, including initiation rites. While to some extent this may be due to the fact that we have here, at last, an element of religion that is not so much "thought out," as are elements of belief, as it is "acted out"—in fact, "danced out." The trance dance is ritual par excellence, performed in the morally charged public arena of the congregated camp, or the multi-band group, or the farm village, whose members are all present and give to the ritual their rapt attention. It is held at night, around a brightly lit fire, at the center point of the gathered assembly. In this it differs from the more variable initiation rite, which is a secretive, gender- and age-segregated passage rite, at which the ritually and symbolically most significant events happen during the transition phase, in or around a dark, door-less, secluded hut, or out in the veld, away from the camp or village. The public setting of the trance dance may be a factor of the stability and uniformity of this ritual; its public, transparent, and participatory nature may act as a curb on Bushman religion's strong penchant for variation, very much as did the audience on the storyteller, as seen in chapter 5.

Its uniformity is derived also from the trance dance's cultural status within the multi-cultural setting of the Ghanzi farm Bushmen as "a Bushman thing," in fact, *the* Bushman thing. In it converge key mystical and mythological notions uniquely held by this people: trance, potency, the trickster-god, therianthropic transformation.

Yet, being a Bushman thing, it is also flexible and variable, ambiguous and multiplex (such is the nature of things Bushman). This is the case especially today, due to the professionalization of the dance, which has proliferated the dance's variable traits (Guenther 1986a: 262–70), as well as introduced new versions of a dance, or altogether new dances, both for curing and for recreation (a development that was discussed in chapter 3). Dancers today, especially those of "star" quality, each have their own dance routines at the various phases of the dance, their own visions of the spirits, and, while a certain popular dance may dominate his or her repertoire, new dances, with new songs and new animal "sponsors," appear all the time. Regarding the last point, I came across such trance dance animals—other than the most common species, the giraffe—as gemsbok, duiker, antbear, polecat, and ram. There is indication of some regional variation of the dance also in traditional times, before its professionalization (however, to a considerably lesser extent, it would seem, than in initiation rites, and even less than in belief, myth, and lore). For instance, Mattenklodt (1931: 214–15), on his brief sojourn through the Dobe–Nyae Nyae area in 1917, describes a Ju/'hoan trance dance in which the women stood upright outside the circle while delivering their song to the dancing men, rather than sitting inside the circle, the "normal" Ju/'hoan dance pattern. I observed the same pattern among the G/wi outside the Ghanzi farm block in 1969, and the above-mentioned illustration in Andrew Smith's 1834 account of the Bushmen of the northern Cape depicts the dance in like fashion. Hahn (1870: 121) describes a trance dance at which music was produced with a water-filled drum. Lebzelter reports seeing !Kung curing dance performances in northeastern Namibia in which men accompanied the chanting women on one-and-a-half-meter-tall drums they had received in trade from the Okavango people to the north (1934: 48).

In closing, I once again bring up Dorothea Bleek's perceptive observation about the delivery of the women's trance song that was raised in chapter 5, in a discussion of the balanced interplay between individual creativity and collective standards of form, content, and aesthetics set by tradition in Bushman expressive culture. "The time is perfect," writes Bleek (1928: 22), "but no two in a chorus seem to hit the same note, though the general burden of the tune is kept up." This statement likewise sums up the blend and balance between flux and stability, and variability and uniformity that we find in this ritual (as well as pointing to the important contribution of women to the ritual, thus balancing another polarity). As argued in chapter 5, this is the expressive equivalent to the social dichotomy of individualism and communalism which runs also through all the other expressive, symbolic, moral, and institutional spheres of Bushman culture.

9

Missionaries and Bushmen

"Ik kan niet meer, the Bushmen have worn me out and I have been constrained to leave them."

—JACOB LINKS (SHAW 1841: 274)

If the Bushmen would settle down, our reform work would not be so difficult. Under the present circumstances a regular influence over the Bushmen is impossible. If we could get the Bushmen to settle down and to learn agriculture we could prevent them from dying out and educate them in the Christian faith.

—WUST 1938: 329, CITED IN GORDON 1992: 144

. . . He has no religion, no laws, no government, no recognized authority, no patrimony, no fixed abode . . . a soul, debased, it is true, and completely bound down and clogged by his animal nature.

—TINDALL 1856: 26

He knows no God, knows nothing of eternity, yet dreads death, and has no shrine at which he leaves his care or sorrow.

—MOFFAT 1842: 59

I understand that some of them have a confused idea of a Great Being, and actions which they consider it impossible for man to effect they ascribe to the Being, but they have no knowledge that they are possessed of souls any more than beasts; of course they have no knowledge of a future state of existence.

—CAMPBELL 1822: 314

Was not John the Baptist a Bushman? Did he not dwell in the Wilderness? Was he not clothed with a leather girdle, such as they wear? And did he not feed on locusts and wild honey? Was he not a Bushman?

—PHILIP 1828: 13

And now I don't quite know how I can explain this [i.e., how man was created]. Because what happened is rather unusual and it seems to me that they were "just like stories" [i.e., lies]. That is all I know. I don't know how men were created. Hey, [laughs] I don't know which story I should tell. . . . I don't know. Regarding the Adam and Eve story, well, I don't know, I didn't understand a good deal of it very well. Yes, there is a lot I didn't catch about those two. But [laughs], I hear that there was a field somewhere and in the middle of that field there was a tree. . . .

—!KHUMA//KA, FIFTY-FIVE-YEAR-OLD MISSION BUSHMAN, GHANZI, 1970

Those are the lies we heard. Those are the lies we were told by the old people.

—GAISHE, SIXTY-FIVE-YEAR-OLD MISSION BUSHMAN, GHANZI, 1969

It is ironic that the lies the old "mission Bushman" Gaishe alludes to are not the benighted comments of the early missionaries cited before him, but the beliefs, myths, and rituals of his own people, prior to the arrival of any missionary. It is ironic as well that the truths they brought to the Bushmen, about matters of the soul and the divine, would cause the Bushmen who received them so much doubt and self-consciousness about what they had previously believed, along with some confusion about what they were asked to believe instead. This is evident from the comments by the second cited Bushman, !Khuma//ka. In view of his consummate skill as a storyteller—in which role we met him in chapter 5—he is never at a loss for words; yet here we see him stumbling for words as he attempts to zoom in on the "new story" he had heard some time before, at catechism class.

This chapter will examine the impact of the missionaries who have contacted the Bushmen over the past two hundred years. As we will see, this contact, despite its long duration, has been sporadic and "low-key" (Barnard 1992a: 261), leaving no deep or lasting impact on the religion of the Bushman. By contrast, missionization has been extensive and intensive, and of lasting effect among most other ethnic groups of southern Africa, including the related

Khoekhoe (Barnard ibid.: 261–63). Indeed, in the nineteenth century, with an "occupation rate" (ratio of mission station to population) of between 1:9,600 and1:3,500, southern Africa was considered, after Oceania, to be the "best occupied portion of the heathen world" (Du Plessis 1909, 1911: 404). All the time and manpower available to missionaries in the southern African field allowed for "long conversations" between themselves and the native population, and for rebuttals and counter-rebuttals on either side (along the famous lines of Livingstone and the Kwena rain chief). This resulted in the implanting of Christianity within the religion of such people as the Tswana, and the "colonization of their consciousness"—the ultimate measure, according to the Comaroffs (1993), of the success of a mission enterprise among a proselytized people.

No such long conversations took place between the oftentimes restless and otherwise preoccupied missionaries and their restive Bushman flock; their consciousness remained uncolonized, and the occasional seed that was implanted by the occasional missionary withered as a seedling. By the above standard, the Bushman mission was a failure.

Why, in the midst such earnest and comprehensive mission activity, did the missionaries neglect the Bushmen (a charge leveled by a number of writers in the field of South African missiology, such as Hahn [1870: 153] and Marais [1939: 30])? Why was the mission enterprise among the Bushmen a failure? What were the barriers and obstacles that prevented the Bushmen from entering the Christian fold, as had so many of the other peoples of southern Africa?

I will examine these questions in two time periods and regions, the nineteenth-century Cape and the present Ghanzi District of Botswana. As throughout this book, the "present" refers to the 1960s to 1970s, when I did the bulk of my fieldwork, most of it at a mission station. I will spend more time on the earlier period, in part because more happened at the mission front in the previous century than in the present one, in part because it is a little-known and neglected area of Khoisan ethnohistory. Because of the issues it raises for the student of Bushman history, religion, and culture it is a field of study that deserves more attention from Khoisan researchers. The fact that these missionaries—such as Pastor Vedder, the Reverend Dornan, and Paters Estermann and Gusinde—have been such a presence further underscores the need to understand the effects of the missionary enterprise on the Bushmen.

Because of the obscurity of this aspect of Bushman ethnohistory, this section of the chapter contains a fair amount of historical documentation, presented in straight historical narrative. The intention is to fill an information gap in Bushman studies, as well as to stimulate others toward more research in the area.[1] My approach to the contemporary Bushman mission scene in the section following is intensive rather then extensive. That is, instead of attempting a survey of all of the various mission endeavors (the task in the historical section), it will look in somewhat greater depth at just one recent station.[2]

The Bushman Mission in the Cape in Colonial Times

The Bushman mission in colonial Cape Province was part of an extensive proselytizing enterprise that was well established and at its peak in the last year of the eighteenth century, when the first Bushman mission was set up. Mission activities had started about the middle of the preceding century, at first in the Portuguese territories by Jesuit and Dominican missionaries (DuPlessis 1911: 7–18). The first isolated missionary efforts among the pastoral Khoekhoe were by Petrus Kalden, who was clergyman at the Cape from 1695 to 1707, followed by two Danish missionaries in the early part of the eighteenth century (DuPlessis ibid.: 47–49; Müller 1923: 23). The Moravians established the first well-funded mission stations among Khoekhoe in 1737 (Du Plessis ibid.: 50). The London Missionary Society (LMS), the mission group most involved with the Bushmen, began operations in southern Africa in 1795 (Du Plessis ibid.: 50–60). The Dutch Reformed Church appeared on the scene around the same time and expanded throughout the nineteenth century (Dutch Reformed Church 1912; van der Merwe 1936); one denomination or mission society after another was establishing missions in rapid succession.

Among the hundreds of mission stations that had been and were being set up by the colonizing settlers among the indigenous peoples of the colonized territories, one finds evidence for only a few that were missions to Bushmen. With the exception of the first, all opened in the nineteenth century and none lasted for more than a few years. Given the early and extensive coverage of the subcontinent as a whole, one must wonder why contact with the Bushmen should have been so sparse, so recent, and so ephemeral. The fact that this particular African people were so salient in the European imagination adds further weight to the question. No other native group of colonial southern Africa were as much written about as the Bushmen, in terms and tones that ranged from racist vilification to rhapsodic vindication (Guenther 1980, 1986b).

The record left by early missionaries, travelers, and historians gives clear evidence for seven (see map 2)—and unclear evidence for another three—attempts at mission activity that targeted the Bushmen, either exclusively or primarily.[3] In addition to carrying out mission work specifically among Bushmen, they practiced a more indirect style of missionization among them. This was to extend mission activities to those Bushman individuals or family groups that happened to live near a non-Bushman station (Szalay 1983: 217).[4] These contacts tended to be superficial because the Bushmen, as nomadic people, would only reside at the mission settlement sporadically and for short periods of time. Moreover, the dominant African people among whom the missionary labored tended to discourage their activities among a despised, enserfed group of underlings (Hepburn 1895: 91–95; Dornan 1917: xx).

The first and best-documented Bushman mission scheme was the LMS station at the Zak River in the Hantam mountains, just beyond what was then

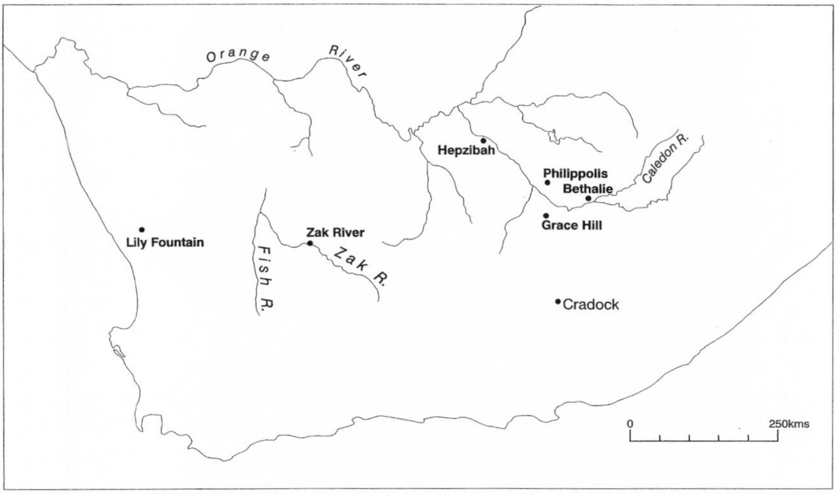

Map 2. Nineteenth-Century Mission Stations to Bushmen.

the colony's northern border. Optimistically christened "Happy Prospect," it was set up by the Reverend John Kicherer, and it soon became well known to colonial settlers and officials. This was because the station received repeated visits, possibly, because it was the only rest-over place for miles for travelers through this remote frontier region. A number of them reported on the place in their writings (Barrow 1801: 51–53; Collins 1809: 23–24; Lichtenstein 1811: 229–37), and Kicherer himself wrote a widely read and much-cited "narrative" of his experience just after he had abandoned the place in 1803 (Kicherer 1804). At the time he deserted the station it had become a sizable settlement of between five and six hundred inhabitants, an undetermined number of whom were probably not Bushmen, however, but Korana or Khoekhoe. The initiative to set up the station had apparently come from the Bushmen and Korana themselves, who, on the advice of a local Dutch frontier farmer, had come to Cape Town in 1798 to request a missionary for their region (Strassberger 1969: 66). Kicherer arrived at the Zak River the following year and, with the help of three assistants and a base herd of sixty oxen and two hundred sheep, which he had succeeded in subscribing from local Dutch settlers, he set up an agricultural mission station. Its principal target group were to be the Bushmen of the surrounding area; however, from the start Khoekhoe and Korana also arrived and set up their residences at the Zak River settlement.

The farming component of the mission was evidently never developed to the extent anticipated by Kicherer and expected by the LMS officers. Kicherer's priority seemed to be to preach the gospel and to engage the Bushman residents in "fervent prayer" (Kicherer 1804: 8–9), something noted disapprovingly by one of the visitors to the station who remarked that Kicherer appeared "wholly to forget that mankind was destined to work as well as to pray" (Lichtenstein 1811, 2:230). Kicherer's attempts to secure moral and, especially, material support from local farmers were unrelenting. They became increasingly reluctant to provide voluntary contributions, forcing the missionary to undertake long treks from the Colony's periphery to its center at Cape Town, in an attempt to procure stock, tools, and clothing.

Notwithstanding so earnest a display of commitment on the missionary's part, the Bushman mission residents soon became disillusioned and began to leave the station. Others became hostile toward Kicherer, and it would seem that several attempts were made on his own life and those of his assistants (Kicherer 1804: 13, 21, 38; Hahn 1870: 153). The missionary's weakness, all along, was that he "failed to keep up the necessities of life by instructing the native in agriculture and animal husbandry" (Lichtenstein 1811, 2: 231). In defense of "this restless man" (Marais 1939: 30) it must be said that the missionary had to contend with a host of serious obstacles, all of which undermined the economic viability of the station. Bushmen plundered the station or poisoned its wells during one of his absences, lions killed the mission cattle, and ever more antipathetic or even hostile Boer settlers became increasingly opposed to the missionary's activities (Kicherer 1804: 28, 31, 41; Hahn 1870: 107). The protracted drought of 1804 was the final blow. Kicherer abandoned the project and went to Graaf-Reinet to accept the call as minister of the Dutch Reformed Church (Spoelstra 1902: 18).

When he left he placed the station under the care of a lay missionary–farmer by the name of Christian Botma. However, over the next two years the settlement disintegrated. The Bushman residents had all deserted the station and only some forty "Hottentots" and "Bastard-Hottentots" had stayed on. The morale at the station was low and the lives of the mission's residents were deemed by one contemporaneous writer to have become "wholly useless and abandoned to sloth" (Lichtenstein 1811, 2:236). In consequence, the *Landdrost* (District Commissioner) of the district threatened that, unless conditions improved at the station, its converts would be forced to do public work in Tulbagh (Lichtenstein ibid.). Moreover, the colonial authorities sent a commission to inspect the LMS stations north of the Orange River because "reports had been received to the effect that a community hostile to the colony was growing up there" (Theal n.d.). The commission presented a report similar to Lichtenstein's, stressing the low morale at the Zak River station. It did not, however, consider the mission to constitute a threat to the settlers.

The second LMS venture was started in 1801 at the Hex River, at the request of the Griqua, the people laying claim to this region of the northern frontier of

Cape Colony. This new operation was set up as an extension of the Zak River station, the core members of which initially were Bushman converts from the nearby, earlier station. Its leader was a previous partner of Kicherer's, the missionary Kramer. For a while Kicherer joined his colleague at the new station; however, he left soon, finding conditions no better than they had been at his own station. The Hex River settlement floundered for a few years and then dissolved (Burkhardt 1877: 107).

The third and fourth attempts, again by the LMS, were undertaken at Toverberg on the Seacow River, not far from the Orange, in the northern reaches of the district of Graaf-Reinet. The first was called "Gracehill" (and was known also as "Thornberg"). It was founded in 1814, at the recommendation of the missionary John Campbell after a visitation to the region (Campbell 1815: 325–38, 348–49). Four years earlier Major Collins had been commissioned to tour and report on the northern regions of the Colony. One of his recommendations for the development of the northern frontier had been the establishment of a mission at the site (Collins 1809: 23; Orpen 1908: 117). Two missionaries (Smith and Corner) preached the Gospel to as many as five hundred Bushmen. Two years later the missionaries split up and Corner moved a "three-day's journey" northwest where he established the second station. He named it "Hepzibah."

Both of these stations enjoyed a most encouraging beginning. Uplifting the missionaries was the ready reception they and their gospel received from the Bushmen when they arrived at the site. As will be seen presently, the local white settlers were less enamored of the two missionaries. Another hostile group were some of the nearby Xhosa, who sometimes wandered through the stations' vicinity and threatened their peace and security (Wright 1971: 30). However, with respect to the Bushmen, the people at the center of the missionaries' concern, all went well and the two men made conversions with ease and in great numbers. The missionaries were as delighted as they were relieved, as some of the local Bushmen had initially greeted them with wary suspicion because they were of the same skin color as the local farmers whom the Bushmen resented for their oppressiveness (Hahn 1870: 153; Burkhardt 1877: 108). Economic conditions, too, proved fortunate as there was a good supply of ground water. Thriving gardens and fields soon surrounded the stations with crops of grain, maize, pumpkins, potatoes, watermelons, and vegetables. At Gracehill even grapes were planted and construction was started on a grain mill (Szalay 1983: 218).

However, despite these encouraging beginnings, the stations dissolved four years after they were founded. Their dissolution was as abrupt as it was radical, for reasons that were more than anything political. The Landdrost of Graaf-Reinet ordered the stations' closure after reaching the conclusion that the mission was "enticing tame Bushmen from the service of the Colonists and created enmity between the missionaries and the inhabitants of the Colony" (Williams 1967: 13–14). The reason for this view and action was complaints received from the local Boer farmers about the two missionaries. They were based on concerns that the stations offered a "haven of safety" for unruly, indolent, and thieving Bushmen.[5] It appears that some of the Bushmen had actually fled from farms in the region and deserted their posts as farm laborers. Moreover, a few had evidently used the mission as a base from which to rob and rustle neighboring farms. However, some of the charges against the missionaries appear to have been fabrications: in particular, the accusation that the missionaries had equipped the Bushmen with firearms and were engaged in fomenting rebellious attitudes or armed resistance against the colonists. After the dissolution of the two stations, some Boers allegedly moved into the missionaries' houses in order either to kill or to take into forced farm labor those Bushmen who had stayed behind at the mission (Hahn 1870: 155). The station at Toverberg was ceded to a local Boer settler, for the purpose of erecting a colonial church at the site (Philip 1828: 284).

Seven years after the closure of the two missions, in 1825, an unsuccessful attempt was made by the influential Cape Town cleric and LMS missionary Dr. John Philip to reconvert the remnants of the Gracehill and Hepzibah congregations and to revive the two stations. The impetus for these efforts derived from emotional reports and appeals by various philanthropically minded travelers through the region from the last years of the first through the early years of the second decades of the century, about the pitiful condition of those converted Bushmen who had stayed on at the stations. They were reported as faithful stalwarts who, despite the gravest adversities, continued to grow plants on the mission ground, and to sing hymns and offer prayers, in fervent hopes of the eventual return of a missionary (Philip 1828, 2:27).

The next station appeared in 1823 in Griqualand, again as a result of the efforts of John Philip (Szalay 1983: 216, 219, 227–28). For the first two years of its existence Philipolis—as it was called, in its founder's honor—was run as a mission to Bushmen. After being closed down for a year it was reopened, this time as a mission to the Griqua, having been handed over to their chief, Adam Kok II, in 1826. Throughout its short life as a Bushman station it had lingered on, and only in its last year was mission work carried out with any degree of commitment on the missionary's part (one James Clark). The principal reasons this mission attempt was aborted were, on the one hand, the Griquas' incursions into the region, and on the other, the local white farmers' general lack of support and recognition of the settlement as a mission. The white farmers grazed their cattle on the mission pastures, in willful disregard of the mission's claim to ownership to the land (Szalay 1983: 277–78).

The sixth attempt at mission work among Bushmen was begun in 1829, once again by the LMS missionary Philip, near the mouth of the Caledon River in Griqualand. Its two missionaries Clark and Kolbe enjoyed the generous support of the Griqua chief Kok, who also offered material assistance in the form of cattle, goats, and sheep. However, the Caledon River station, known later as Bethulie, proved unviable and failed throughout to attract and convert Bushmen. Consequently, in 1833 the LMS handed the mission over to the Paris

Mission Society, who turned it into a mission to the Tswana (Burkhardt 1877: 110; Richter 1922: 276; Kirby 1940, 2:84–85; Wright 1971: 30).

The seventh attempt at Bushman mission work came to a tragic end. In 1818 Jacob Links, a Khoekhoe lay evangelist who had been trained by the Methodist missionary Barnabas Shaw, was appointed "Assistant Missionary to the Bushmen" by the Church Conference in Britain. Links applied himself wholeheartedly to his assigned task. His style of evangelizing was quite unique for a missionary of his time: he adopted the nomadic way of life of his charges, and wandered with the Bushmen and lived on their food. However, this technique of participant proselytizing proved too strenuous; after an undisclosed period of time (perhaps a year or two), reduced to hunger, and to wearing skin clothing, he appeared back at Shaw's station at Lily Fountain, gasping the "Ik kan niet meer" utterance that appears in one of this chapter's epigraphs. However, in 1824 he once again resumed his labors, this time in the company of two colleagues, the missionary Threlfall and another Nama lay missionary. In the following year, while journeying into Bushmanland by oxcart, the trio was attacked and murdered by a party of Bushmen (Harcombe 1928; Birdwhistle 1966). The case received much attention and may be one reason for the stridently negative views this particular missionary, Shaw, held about the Bushmen (Shaw 1841: 28–27; see also Guenther 1980: 130).

In addition to these fairly well recorded mission undertakings, there are obscure references in a few of the nineteenth-century sources to three other attempts at Bushman mission work. Campbell (1837: 188–89) mentions two stations along the Cradock River which he passed on his follow-up journey through Griqua- and Koranaland in 1820. Both stations were evidently small-scale, precarious LMS ventures run by converted Khoekhoe evangelists, on sufferance of the Griqua chief Adam Kok. At one of the stations, named Konnah, Bushmen were taught agriculture. This mission was troubled by landless Griqua who, through "vicious speeches," turned the Korana, the owners of the land on which the station was located, against the missionaries. The other station, Ramah, experienced much trouble in its efforts to bring the Gospel, along with agriculture, to the "wild" and especially unruly Bushmen there. Campbell found that the interest of these Bushmen in Christian teachings was low. Stow (1910: 201–203) makes mention of a small mission station for Bushmen between the Black and White Kei Rivers. It was founded in 1839 and dissolved with the Xhosa wars. It appears that the Bushmen, under the leadership of their missionary Joseph Read, fought on the side of the white colonists. The land the mission had operated on was annexed to the Xhosa, forcing the Bushmen and the missionary to vacate the station (Szalay 1983: 229).

The Failure of the Cape Bushman Mission

All of the mission stations set up among the Bushmen within and beyond the Cape's colonial boundary ended in failure, after some encouraging beginnings for about half of them. All were short-lived and most were aborted well before the religious, economic, and social impact of the mission could have pervasively and lastingly affected the lives of the Bushman residents and converts. The survey of the various efforts reveals a number of historical and structural problems, evident both at a practical and at an ideological level. The historical problems are those specific to the time; the structural problems have to do with the social organization and ethos of Bushman society. They bedeviled the mission venture in the nineteenth century, and continued to beset missionaries in the twentieth century. I will consider this set of problems in the next section, in the context of an examination of a recent mission venture among a contemporary Bushman group.

In the nineteenth century missionary activities were carried out against an ideological backdrop of notions and stereotypes entertained by the white settler society as a consequence of two centuries of Bushman contact and persecution. The general view of settlers, colonial officials, clergy, travelers, and writers was that the Bushmen were a "doomed people" who would soon disappear from the northern, mountainous, or arid periphery of the colony, where they made their "last stand." Their "melancholy history" was coming to an end, and the "last and failing remnant," in the Cape province, "are erased from off the great world's face," as one nineteenth-century poet put it (William Scully, cited in Du Plessis 1911: 256) in a rhapsodic elegy about the Bushmen that summed up the general view of the period.

In retrospect, this assessment of the Bushmen as a people whose end was near and inexorable was unfortunately correct, as far as the Cape Bushmen were concerned. The "*fin tragique*" (Ellenberger 1963) of the indigenous hunting nomads, who fiercely competed with the settlers' stock for the same, vast ranges of pasture land (Schott 1955), turned out to be irreversible. The sorry fact that they had been pursued relentlessly throughout the previous century, as well as the century during which missionaries began to turn to them, was brought home to the settlers and their colonial government by the report presented to Parliament at Cape Town by L. Anthing. He had been commissioned to carry out an investigation of rumored atrocities by settlers against Bushmen in the northern frontier, and the report he presented confirmed and exceeded the rumors. What had gone on, and was continuing, was at times out-and-out, unadorned genocide, just as had happened the previous century:

> The killings of the Bushmen were not confined to the avenging or punishing of such [cattle] thefts, but that, with or without provocation, Bushmen were killed—sometimes by hunting parties, at other times by commandos going out for the express purpose. (Anthing 1863: 4; also see Marais 1939: 27–30 and Hewitt 1986: 43–44)

There is a large literature on this sorry chapter in white (and black) settler–Bushman history, that describes the killing of three, possibly even four, thousand Bushmen, -women and -children, and the de facto enslavement of those not killed, as farm laborers (from nine to twelve thousand in number) (Szalay 1983: 258).[6]

Given its wide currency (Guenther 1980), the doomed-people view was likely shared by the missionaries and mission societies of the time. On the one hand, it may explain why missionary activity was approached by some (such as Philip) with ardor and relentless effort, as though to give a doomed people one last chance. On the other hand, the pessimistic resignation entailed in the tragic and romantic notion of a doomed people's last stand may explain why the labors of others were not more persistent and why most gave up after a few years. It is true that there were a number of very difficult and trying problems—more trying, perhaps, than those experienced by missionaries working in other regions and with other ethnic groups. I will turn to these presently. However, one may wonder whether the key reason for what seems, by comparison, a somewhat low-key and halfhearted mission enterprise, was not a gloomy sense of futility about laboring among a vanishing people. This appraisal applies not so much to the individual missionaries who, in the few years that they did spend among the Bushmen, appear to have applied themselves wholeheartedly to their task, in one unique case by assuming the nomadic lifestyle of the target people. Most had demonstrated a high degree of resolve and commitment. The appraisal is more applicable to the sponsoring mission society, which, in the case of their Bushman operations, dissolved a station, or handed it over to another organization, with a surprising degree of readiness.

Apart from the "doomed people" stereotype, there was another, more negative and pernicious component to the image Europeans held of the Bushmen at the time: that of the "brutal savage" (Guenther 1980). Just as this image provided justification to settlers and administrators of the time for their equally brutal actions of genocide, expropriation, enslavement, and enclosure (Guenther ibid.: 135–36), so did it justify the missionaries' neglect of the Bushmen. On the other hand, the stereotype might also have been used to justify the failure of their efforts to convert them (Lewis-Williams 1981: 117). This rationalization is predicated on the basic notion that the Bushmen had no religion whatsoever, nor any capacity for religion, because of a state of spiritual benightedness. Thus, once again, the task required of the missionary or missionary society would be a futile one. To bring to them religion, especially, it was held, such a spiritually demanding and historically developed faith as Christianity, would necessarily fail, as there was no point of departure or anchorage within Bushman culture for the Christian faith (or for any developed religion).

Such colonialist thinking is the spiritual counterpart to the other notion entertained by colonial settlers and administrators about the Bushmen: that, for these people, hunting and nomadism are bred in the bone, that the Bushman "by his nature is more carnivorous than graniverous" (n.a. 1877: 7; also see Guenther 1977a). In short, the Bushman is no more capable of converting to Christianity than he is of adopting civilization (Du Plessis 1911: 269). Such a view derived from the implicit sociological-theological view of nineteenth-century missionaries that Christianity was an integral component of society, rather than an "autonomous" domain (Russell and Russell 1979: 100–101). Its effect was the linking together of Western religion with Western civilization, resulting in the concurrence, in nineteenth-century mission work, of two gospels, that of the "Word" and that of the "White Shirt."

While there is no reason, nor evidence (with one exception), to suggest that the specific missionaries who ventured into the Bushman field entertained any pejorative sentiments about the Bushmen, it is a matter of public record—a fragment of it provided in the chapter epigraphs—that more than a few other missionaries working in southern Africa subscribed to the racist notions of the day, about the religious and cultural backwardness of the Bushmen. One of them was, in fact, John Kicherer himself. From the account he gives of the Bushmen in his "Narrative" (Kicherer 1804), it appears that the experience had indeed embittered him and that he perhaps needed to justify its failure to himself and to his society (both the LMS and society at large). The way he went about this task of self-vindication and sour-grapes rationalization was to paint a portrait of the Bushmen so defamatory that the conclusion of their unsuitability for the Gospel becomes a self-evident truth, thereby resoundingly justifying his failure at the set task of shepherding them into Christianity's fold. The portrait he presented, as shown more fully elsewhere (Guenther 1980: 126–27, 135–36), stands as the most pernicious character assassination of the Bushmen on record. They are depicted as porcine, pongid, filthy, lazy, morally degraded, infanticidal, vicious, and violent creatures, "on a level with brute creation." Kicherer's description influenced the attitude toward the Bushmen of a number of his contemporaries, several of whom, in their own writings, cited verbatim Kicherer's most defamatory passage (Guenther ibid.: 126–27).

The Reverend Kicherer's portrayal of the Bushmen appears to have left its mark on a number of his missionary colleagues. Their own comments about the Bushmen echo Kicherer, albeit in more constrained fashion. It is also clear from their pronouncements that they deemed the Bushmen's "Christianity-potential" to be low. Thus, Wilhelm Posselt, who did mission work among the Xhosa in the mid-nineteenth century (Pfitzner and Wangemann 1891), described the Bushmen he happened across at the Kei River as "semi-human goblins" and expressed his serious doubt as to their possessing an immortal soul. Barnabas Shaw (1841: 28–29), whom we met earlier, expressed much the same idea, as did Eugene Casalis (1889: 154). The views of the missionaries Moffat and Tindall about the benighted state of the Bushmen with respect to God and eternity, his fear of death, and his debased soul are sampled in one of the epigraphs (see also Lewis-Williams 1981: 116–17). One might add to these pronouncements that of Holub, who in his encounters with the Bushmen reports that, while he "did not notice any evidence of religion" among them, he did notice "a kind of esteem for a certain snake" (Holub 1881: 5, cited by Lewis-Williams ibid.: 117). Other non-divine objects of Bushman worship that were mentioned in chapter 2 were the moon and the mantis. Indeed, for some writers, the next logical step, in the minds of the theologically benighted and spiritually debased Bushmen, was a belief in the devil himself (Schmidt 1973: 107; Guenther 1980: 129;

Lewis-Williams 1981: 118). In short, Nature, so declared the colonial poet William Scully, had failed to provide the Bushmen with "ears to hear and eyes for seeing"—except in a physical sense, in keeping with their "animal nature" (Du Plessis 1911: 256).

Those writers who report detecting evidence of religion among the Bushmen were wont to explain its presence in terms of borrowings from other, more developed peoples (Fritsch 1872: 427). As mentioned earlier, a like explanation was proposed by Abbé Breuil for the complex, sophisticated, and evidently religious, "White Lady" panel of the lower Brandberg, which he explicated in terms of ancient Egyptian cults, brought to this remote outpost in the southwest African desert by ancient Egyptian traders (Guenther 1984: 15). There was general doubt about the proposition that any of this evidently complex and sophisticated religious art could have been created by the Bushmen, as these people even today, according to a German settler, "occupy so low a rung on the human ladder that they are unable to draw even the simplest of figures" (von Eckenbrecher 1907: 180).

The last two examples, about Bushman art (which, as we saw earlier, is a component of Bushman expressive and ritual culture), have taken us into colonial German South West Africa, where the same racist views prevailed about Bushman and Khoekhoe religion. Gusinde (1966: 73) reports how these shocked the Protestant mission inspector Burkhardt when he encountered them on his tours of inspection. They considered the religious beliefs of the "Hottentots" to be "extraordinarily deficient" ("ungemein mangelhaft"), as they had "no conception of a higher being, and a small, crawling insect, called 'Mantis,' which they are afraid of killing and which they fear, and which they beseech for temporal favors, is almost the only object of their superstitious adoration"[7] (my translation).

For the sake of fairness and balance, we must not forget those missionaries and other writers who spoke out against this defamatory representation of the Bushmen. Some were, in fact, highly sympathetic to "these poor waifs upon Creation's skirts" (Scully, cited in Du Plessis 1911: 256), who, for all of the atrocities they may have committed against the white settlers in their struggle for survival, were a people "more sinned against than sinning." They were referred to in biblical terms—for instance, as the "wild Ishmaelites of the South African desert." Perhaps this was a rhetorical device used by clerical writers well versed in Christian hermeneutics for eliciting sentiments of sympathy in Christian readers, through a basic appeal to their religion's universalist doctrine of the "spiritual unity of mankind." This view was also linked to the proposition entertained by some pious writers and settlers that the Bushmen and Khoekhoe might have been the Lost Tribes of Israel, who left monuments—the "*Haitsi-Eibib*-graves," piles of stone probably marking Khoekhoe burials—on their circuitous route to Canaan (Barnard 1992a: 263). And, as we saw at the head of this chapter, Dr. Philip reminded his readers that "John the Baptist was a Bushman"! Yet, such charitable pleas were issued[8] too infrequently to displace the uncharitable, pejorative view of the Bushmen. It was not until well into the current century that the Rousseauian trope gained the upper hand in the writing of missionaries, travelers, novelists, and anthropologists (Guenther 1980; Barnard 1989).

Apart from these ideological problems which jeopardized the success of any mission enterprise among the Bushmen of the nineteenth-century Cape, there was also a list of obstacles of a more concrete nature. One was the difficulty of access to the Bushmen, who lived in the most remote regions of the colony, and frequently beyond its boundaries. Travel was by ox wagon, allowing for an average speed of at most twenty-five kilometers per twelve-hour day (Lee and Guenther 1993: 206), provided the oxen were not sick or lost, the wagon's wheels or pole did not break, or the guides did not get lost—all frequent mishaps that could delay the weary traveler at one spot for days. There was also danger, especially when the route left the relative security of the colony and entered the "bad lands" beyond the frontier which were inhabited not only by hostile Bushmen, but also by other colonial outcasts and outlaws—escaped convicts and slaves, army deserters, indigents, many of mixed blood—leading lives of brigandage (Dunn 1872, 1873; Guenther 1986b: 32–33). The murder of the venturesome Links and his two associates galvanized the apprehension a missionary might have felt about the perils of traveling through these remote regions.

A very real practical problem that hampered mission work throughout was communication. The Bushman click languages were virtually unintelligible to the missionaries and difficult to learn (then as now). Indeed, many a colonial European held the Bushman tongue to be quite unlearnable. One element of the Bushman stereotype was that their language was unfitted to convey symbolic meaning. Bushmen give "utterance to no articulate sound," according to the Reverend Wood (1877, 1:242), author of a popular Victorian book about "the uncivilized races of man in all countries around the world" which is a repository of every conceivable pejorative notion about the Bushmen, as of other tribal peoples. Bushmen were thus forced to supplement their vocalizations with extensive gesturing, virtually eliminating any conversation in a Bushman horde after nightfall!

Lacking in linguistic facility, missionaries working among the Bushmen invariably used interpreters. These were usually Khoekhoe, who also spoke a click language (albeit one different from that of most of the Cape Bushmen). Alternatively, they might employ "tame Bushmen" as interpreters; that is, second- or third-generation Bushmen in the service of European settlers. The problem with the latter arrangement was that such individuals were evidently frequently treated with suspicion by their "wild" compatriots, who, it is reported, tended to harbor a deep-seated hatred toward such "renegade" Bushmen (Hahn 1870: 84).

Mistranslation, always a problem in cross-language communication with interpreters, could be particularly confounding in the context of a prayer session or sermon led by a missionary, especially one with a penchant for metaphorical or allegorical parlance. James Chapman reports on mistranslations from services he witnessed among the Orlam Khoekhoe at Gobabis in the early 1860s:

> The difficulty in pronouncing many words in the Hottentot language, so that the sense is not made ridiculous, is so great that one can easily say, "our springbucks which art in heaven." I have known a missionary to excite the risibility of a whole congregation, or cause women to blush, or others to beam. (Chapman 1971, 2: 209)

One way out of the communication problem which was as simple as it was ineffective is reported wryly by Lichtenstein (1811, 2:230) from the Zak River station: to dispense with the Bushman tongue altogether and to preach in one's own language. "Even though it was a language of which they understood not a word," Lichtenstein comments, "their instructor [Kicherer] thought it sufficient to learn the scriptures by heart, hoping that thus they would learn the language, and then understand the prayers how mystical soever they might be."[9]

The most serious practical problem, one that jeopardized not only the viability of a station but also the physical survival of the missionary stationed beyond the frontier, was economic. It was brought about by the policy, subscribed to by the mother church or society (especially the LMS), that a missionary be sent out with very few provisions. Consistent with this policy was the fact that he was paid the most meager of salaries. The directorate of the LMS maintained that a missionary ought to be able to support himself right away from the mission's land, if he was issued the right agricultural equipment and a few months' provisions. Ideally, he would also start with a small herd of cattle and small stock, provided to him by local farmers. This position became one of the central principles of the London Board. The effect on the missionary was that he faced the alternative between "trading or starving," and was forced as well to entreat local white settlers for stock and food donations (Du Plessis 1912). The extremely low amount of funds allocated to a missionary exacerbated his economic plight. There was never enough money to pay for the buildings that had to be built and for the stock that had to be bought, over and above what was "subscribed" from the regional settler community, with increasing reluctance. Economic hardship thus forced the missionary also to be a farmer, for the sake of his station's economic viability, as well as his own subsistence needs.

Practicalities aside, the establishment of agriculture also had a strong ideological element. According to LMS policy, there was a double component to the missionary's mission: "the Word" and "the Plough." This was clearly stated in the 1817 Annual Report by the directors of the LMS: "we take a plough with us. Let it be remembered that in Africa the Bible and the plough go together" (Szalay 1983: 218). Other symbols of civilization—as of Christianity, as noted above—were European clothing and rectangular stone houses (Szalay ibid.)

One of the ecological conditions required for the "Edict of the Plough," the proper climate and soil, was usually anything but optimal in the marginal land stretches inhabited by the Bushmen. These adversities forced the missionaries into a position of dependence on the largesse of local settlers and of friends and church members at the metropolitan church, who were canvassed for money or who would knit "little caps and stockings for the heathens, who have no inkling of what a head-covering is and whose soles are as hard as shoe leather" (as wryly put by Theophilius Hahn [1870: 155]). The missionary's approach to the settlers was usually hat-in-hand solicitation; another approach was bartering or performing work for the farmer, or having it performed by mission residents. In two cases (Caledon and Philipolis) the stock of resentful settlers was actually subscribed to the station by government decree (Szalay 1983: 233–34). As was seen above, Kicherer was forever on the move, in pursuit of either vagrant Bushmen or provisions.

The economic problems of a missionary at his mission farm thus made "the mission of the Plough" a matter not just of ideology, but also of necessity. In order to maintain the economic viability of the mission farm, and allow it to feed its congregation of Bushmen, the congregants had to work. This they were most reluctant to do, and a missionary's attempts to exert pressure in this regard usually resulted in the Bushmen's departure. And, adding insult to injury, they might even laugh at the missionary, as peevishly noted by the Rhenish missionary Kremer, at Gaub to the north in Namibia in 1893, after he had tried to get his !Kung charges to grow crops at the mission farm! (Gordon 1992: 64)

Some missionaries—for instance Wust, cited in one of the chapter epigraphs—explained this problem in cultural terms, that is, emphasizing the incompatibility of the nomadic, hunting way of life and the sedentary, agricultural ways of European and Christian folk. Likewise, the Reverend Dornan had earlier explained the "small interest in Christianity" of the Bushmen, and its lack of impression upon them, in terms of their "unsettled and wayward manner of life" (1917: 40). The first step, and the missionary's greatest challenge, was thus to rein in the wanderers and get them settled down and set up for agriculture.

In addition to a nomadic cultural tendency, there was also a historical reason for the Bushmen's reluctance or refusal to work on the mission farm. In the latter third of the nineteenth century most of the Bushmen in the frontier regions where the missionaries set up shop had at some time or other, and for varying lengths of time, worked for white farmers; indeed, the ethnohistorian Miklos Szalay estimates that already by the 1820s at least three thousand Bushmen worked on the farms in the northeastern frontier region (1983: 240–41). Some spoke smatterings of Dutch and had received, from the farmers for whom they worked, European names such as Silvester, Lustig, Dragonder, Bartman; or David Husar, Klaas Katkop, and Jantje Tooren—the Dutch names of Bleek and Lloyd's storytellers Dia!kwain, ≠Kasin, and //Kabbo (Szalay 1983: 256; Guenther 1995b). The "encirclement" of Bushmen by the Boers and trek

Boers in the second half of the century affected virtually all Bushman groups within and even beyond the frontier, drawing the Bushmen into a dependency relationship with the farmers, that is, into a labor relationship (Szalay ibid.: 245; also see Dunn 1872, 1873; Guenther 1996b). Thus, it can be assumed that more than a few of the Bushmen reported to have shunned work at their missions did so not because of some innate cultural tendency, derived from their nomadic ways. They had sought out the mission station to begin with to get away from farm labor and its oppressive, exploitative conditions (Szalay ibid.: 241, 248–56). If any "foraging" tendency was at work in this decision it was the calculating, exploitive, maximizing weighing of alternatives, in tune with the foragers' tendency, noted earlier, to treat outsiders as economic and social resources. Thus, the mission Bushman asked by a missionary to work would likely not have deemed the request an "optimal foraging strategy."

It is conceivable also that the Bushmen realized then what historians studying the Bushman–settler contact at that time realize now (for instance Szalay 1983: 240–42, and Gordon 1993: 64–71, 239–40, in the context, respectively, of the colonial Cape and South West Africa): that their being settled at a mission station engaged in agricultural and domestic labor could—and, as shown by Szalay and Gordon, frequently did—become merely another means of "taming" Bushmen to be well-trained laborers who, after their conversion, education, and training at the mission, would be all the more assimilable into the local farm labor pool. In Szalay's estimation, some of the Cape missions were the country's precursory "Bantustans," labor reservoirs where local farmers could get workers and return them when they were no longer needed, that is, when they were old, sick, and spent (1983: 167).

So, many left the mission station or, if they stayed, turned into a source of ongoing frustration to the missionary. To replace those that left, or to find mission residents willing to work, other local native groups might join the mission, gradually displacing the Bushmen. Having once been displaced, it was difficult for the Bushmen subsequently to rejoin the mission community. As seen above, in a few instances the latter may in the meantime have officially changed from a "mission to Bushmen" to a "mission to Griqua" or Tswana. Such a turn of events confirmed the wariness and hostility with which the missionaries had been received by Bushmen residents from the start (for instance, Smith and Corner, as well as the missionaries at Philipolis and Ramah). Given the oppressive, at times and in places genocidal, treatment the Bushmen received from the white settlers in recent times, it is surprising that more missionaries did not suffer the fate of Jacob Links and his two associates.

Thus, the two chronic, mutually reinforcing problems faced by the Bushman missionaries were a precarious economic state and, stemming from it, tension with both the Bushman mission residents and the local settler community, whose members the missionary unrelentingly pressed for work or for donations. Apart from the irritation and the drain on their own resources, the farmers were wary and unsympathetic toward the missionaries for other reasons. In some cases, the mission settlement was perceived as a haven for lazy and mendacious Bushmen. This perception was not altogether groundless, as some of the Bushman mission residents or converts were indeed runaway former laborers or slaves, whose settlement at the mission and acceptance of baptism offered the hope of escape from toil and oppression. Another concern of the settlers was that teaching the Bushmen reading and writing might "spoil" them for farm labor, rendering "the heathen too wise by instruction" (Kicherer 1804: 42).

The settler–missionary antagonism was not just one-sided. The missionaries sometimes held the "boors" or "trekkers" to be almost as spiritually benighted as the Bushmen. The former found the settlers' simple, patriarchal piety unsophisticated and their attitudes and actions toward the Bushmen reprehensible, on religious grounds. On the first point, one early "liberal" writer scoffs at "trek boer" piety as nothing more than "a kind of feeling or religious intuition" based on "all kinds of dreams or visions," rather than on the Bible (which many of them were unable to read). The Bible was taken so literally by these extreme fundamentalists that they believed the actual physical book—"exactly as it stood, border illustrations and all"—rather than just the Word it contains, to have been derived from the apostles and prophets (Russell and Russell 1979: 103).

The second point of moral and theological divergence between the missionaries and the settlers, on "race relations," was based on fundamental doctrinal differences between the established "settler congregation" and the expatriate missionary. As suggested by Russell and Russell (1979: 101–103, 112–15), the former, in the course of generations of association with the indigenous tribal people, came to eschew the "universalistic injunction" of Christianity—i.e., the brotherhood, in Christ, of all men—in favor of a particularist theology that justifies the exclusion of "the natives" from the Christian fold. Members of such settler congregations behaved, so the Russells argue (ibid.: 101), "on the whole with phenomenal indifference to the spiritual fate of the natives." This common attitude among Whites in (former) colonies of settlement is especially well defined in situations where the Whites are Calvinists, especially arch-Calvinists (as were the South African trek Boers), as this denomination has a "theological predisposition to exclusiveness in the doctrine of election and predestination" (ibid.: 103). Moreover, apart from the content of their theological beliefs, what also differentiated the missionary at the South African frontier from the settler congregation was its style, characterized by the Russells (ibid.: 101) as "proselytizing zeal." This was channeled especially to the cause of universalism, about which the settlers felt so ambivalent or which they rejected.

In sum,

> settler congregations regarded them [missionaries] with suspicion and hostility, seeing them as agents of agitation and disturbance, creators of new social problems with which settlers would have to contend. (Russell and Russell 1979: 102)

Or not: as we saw earlier, the termination of the three mission stations run by Botma, Smith, and Corner was influenced, if not initiated, by antagonistic, sabotaging white settlers. The ideological and political tensions between the settlers and the missionaries also undermined the economic viability of the mission stations, which, as noted earlier, depended largely on settler donations of stock and other material resources. The resultant economic plight of the mission forced missionaries to enact the "mission of the Plough," triggering an exodus among those Bushmen who had come to the mission and overcome the sense of wariness and hostility commonly extended to the missionaries, by virtue of their affiliation with the oppressive settler society and people. Additional practical problems were inaccessibility and difficulty of travel and communication, danger, and deprivation. All of this stood under an ideological cloud that rendered tentative and tenuous the mission enterprise among the Bushmen: the perception of the Bushmen, on the one hand, as a people whose doom and extinction was foreordained and, on the other, as people who were unequipped culturally, morally, and spiritually for adopting European civilization and religion—the Word and the Plough (and the White Shirt), which the colonialist ideology regarded as inseparably linked.

Given all of these problems, it is difficult to conceive how the mission to colonial Bushmen, at the Cape and elsewhere, could have ended in anything other than failure.

Contemporary Missions to Bushmen

At the time I lived there, the Gereformeerde Kerk mission at Dekar in the Ghanzi District of Botswana consisted of around a hundred souls. The mission settlement was run by two lay missionaries: one a black evangelist whose primary role was to preach and teach the Gospel; the other a white, Afrikaner farmer charged with managing the mission farm and herd. The operation had been founded in 1965 as a "mission to Bushmen" by a congregation in the Namibian town of Aranos, not far from the Botswana border. After Botswana gained her independence in 1968, the mission was enjoined to change its mandate from targeting just one ethnic group to serving all ethnic groups, in line with the democratic, multi-racial policies of the government. It did so in the course of the following decades, attracting to the settlement also Kgalagari, Tswana, Herero, and "Coloured" residents.

In the mid-1980s the mission changed direction again, becoming a predominantly secular, highly active, and effective NGO for which proselytizing had become merely one of about a dozen activities. Since the early 1990s a Dutch missionary-linguist (Hessel Visser) has lived at Kuru, endeavoring, under the auspices of the Summer Institute of Linguistics, to prepare a Nharo orthography, literacy, and language-acquisition program (Visser 1994, n.d.), as well as a translation of the Bible. Dekar also changed its name, to Kuru Development Trust (*kuru* being the Nharo word for "do" or "make"). It is still, ostensibly, open to all of the region's RADs, or Remote Area Dwellers, the bureaucratic term the government introduced in the 1970s as a non-ethnic designation for the country's economically underdeveloped tribal minorities. Insofar as these are primarily Bushmen, Kuru is, in fact, a development center for Bushmen.

My headquarters for my doctoral fieldwork from 1968 to 1970, and a follow-up study in 1974, was the village attached to the mission farm and church, which the Bushmen called /Oaxa. My next-door and next-to-next-door neighbors were farm and mission Nharo Bushmen, the latter converted or about-to-be-converted members of the mission church, who constituted the core of /Oaxa's Bushman population. Most attended catechism class and the weekly church service on Sundays (which I attended as well), conducted by the black evangelist-missionary. My comments on the structural and ideological problems of mission work among the Bushmen is based on the conversations I have had with these neighbors. In my discussion I will deal with only those problems that are structural in nature and stem from the contradictions and disjunctures between the religions and cultures of the "sending" and "receiving" peoples. There were also a host of other problems of a contingent nature, having to do with such things as the personality of the two missionaries or of certain other prominent mission residents; specific doctrinal details in the mission policy, specifically of the Gereformeerde Kerk; or inter-ethnic tensions among the Bushman and non-Bushman residents. I have discussed the effects of these specific problems on the mission Bushmen elsewhere, as well as problems deriving from the wider society of Ghanzi (Guenther 1973, 1977b; also see Russell and Russell 1979: 99–115).

As noted at the beginning of the chapter, the emotional and intellectual attitude of many of the mission—as well as farm—Bushmen with whom I discussed the new religion, was one of confusion, self-consciousness, and ambivalence, as well as of disagreement. There were those who were strongly drawn to what they heard from or through the black evangelist, and gained, so it seemed to me, moral and spiritual comfort from some of the Christian teachings. Repeatedly I heard Bushmen give testimonials as to how much such spiritual notions as resurrection, divine love, and redemption meant to them.

Others, probably most, doubted and were skeptical about what they were told: for instance, their own alleged sinfulness as human beings or the alleged evil of //Gãũwa (alias Satan). Some were unsure about whether they had properly understood what they had heard at catechism class or at the church service and sermon. An illustration, not from Dekar but the mission at Tshum!kwi, is N!ai's commentary about the missionary's sermon on Jesus and the Samaritan woman at the well, which was cited above (chapter 4, p. 117). The passage suggests that the Bushman church member mistook Jesus' solicitousness for solicitation!

As at the Cape, this lack of proper understanding resulted in part not from the implicit theological difficulty or complexity of the new faith, but simply from communication difficulties. Neither of the missionaries at Dekar spoke Nharo. Regular services and catechism classes were translated from SeTswana into Nharo. Whenever the minister from Aranos visited to administer the *nagmaal* (communion)—which, at that time, was given separately to Whites and Bushmen, each in their own church building—translation was usually through two interpreters, from Afrikaans, to SeTswana, to Nharo. Some of the local, third-generation Afrikaners who were fluent in Nharo, as well as SeTswana, appreciate the distortions this creates:

> Interpretation never works properly. It goes from Afrikaans to Setswana and from Setswana to Bushman, then it's quite altered. It's no longer what the *predikant* said. I know, because I know all three languages, and my wife also. (Russell and Russell 1979: 107)

Even those Whites who have fluency in the Bushman language admit defeat when it comes to translating "things of the Lord" (ibid.).

Another reason for the low understanding and commitment of some of the mission Bushman was the discrepancy some perceived between the expectations they held when joining the mission settlement and what was delivered, as well as what was expected of them. It is clear that many of them were drawn to the mission not so much by spiritual prospects and needs but practical ones. Some found employment at the mission church and farm, men as farm laborers or assistants and interpreters to the evangelist; women as domestic servants in the two missionaries' households, or as sales clerks in the small mission shop-cum-café. This was the reason others, who had lost their jobs and could find employment at no other farm, came to Dekar, in hopes of also finding employment at the mission. Only a few did, as the small number of jobs available at the mission station were soon filled. Others came because they had kin at /Oaxa and wanted to stay for extended visits, bringing along their donkeys and goats to graze on the mission pastures. The amenities of the mission, such as the school and the clinic, attracted yet others. The mission clinic sometimes looked after chronically ill people, dispensing long-term treatment (for instance, for tuberculosis). Some of the parents of the schoolchildren stayed at Dekar village in order to be with their children.

The basic and minimum expectation the mission placed on the residents was regular attendance at catechism class and church; moreover, they were urged to send their children to the school at the mission compound, as well as to "help out" voluntarily whenever the missionaries needed extra assistance. Some found these requirements irksome. Another issue some found to be a problem was the large number of people at the settlement and the interpersonal tensions this created, especially vis-à-vis the black section of the mission village, which progressively increased in numbers.

In view of the benefits and problems residence at Dekar entailed for the mission Bushmen, for many the decision whether to stay at the mission settlement or to leave depended on the ratio of those benefits to costs. Some left temporarily; others left for good. Thus, a number of residents viewed the spiritual side of the mission—its own raison d'être—as a means toward one or several practical ends which held priority in their own lives.[10]

One way the Bushmen dealt with their doubts about elements of belief of the new religion was to relate a new element that was clouded in doubt to their own beliefs. Earlier we saw examples of this creative process of syncretic integration of two sets of beliefs, involving Jesus Christ and Adam and Eve. The integration of these scriptural personages operated at different degrees of explicitness; for example, Jesus Christ's association with //Gãũwa was explicit in the ideas of some Bushmen, whereas Eve/Effa's becoming a cognate of female protagonists of primal time, such as the woman who brought carnal knowledge to the men or the disobedient maiden, was implicit.

Such processes of personal and cultural syncretization may well increase the convert's understanding of the new belief which, by this process, may have moved from a peripheral or ancillary position on his spectrum of personal belief to a more central one. However, the meaning of the syncretistic form of the belief may deviate widely from its meaning in the original Christian theological idiom. This matter was discussed in chapters 3 and 4 and illustrated with examples; for instance, Jesus Christ and Adam and Eve as //gãũwani guardians of trance healing arrows or the sacrament of baptism as a modern version of the bush-camp male initiation rite.

However, the kind of doubt I most frequently came across at /Oaxa and other farm Bushman communities was skepticism—not about the new religion but the old; that is, self-doubt. The self-conscious qualification of "what I will tell you now, or have just told you, are lies of the old people" was attached as a rider to many a narrative. This denigrating, critical, condemning view of Bushman traditional beliefs added a further element to the collective sense of inferiority generally held by the farm Bushmen.

Yet, there were also individuals who were assertive and positive about their religion. Some accepted the cultural integrity and mystical power of the Bushman divinities, either //Gãũwa or N!eri, as well as the efficaciousness of Bushman healing, by means of the trance dance (see chapter 8). In fact, it was that ritual, and its performer, the *n/a k'au,* that people felt most positive about, including Bushman converts who, with the missionary's reluctant approval, participated at the trance dances so frequently held in the village. One of the two missionaries was especially uneasy, deeming the trance dance a species of magic, tainted with sorcery. Given the morally integrative and wholesome quality of this curing ritual, such a conflation would never occur to a Bushman, nor to any other non-white native African, in view of the radically different form and content of these two patterns of magic.

The overall impression I gained from my—occasionally long—conversations with mission Bushmen was that their grasp of the new religion, as well as their commitment to it, were both rather tenuous. The reason has of course nothing whatsoever to do with spiritual benightedness, the explanation popular among the Cape colonialists, as well as some of the Boers of Ghanzi, reflected in comments such as " the Bible is too far above him, too complicated" (Russell and Russell 1979: 108). It is partly a matter of inadequate teaching or understanding, a lack of the sorts of "long conversations" the missionaries had engaged in with the neighboring Tswana. It is also partly the lack of practice of the new religion. Without the collective experience of the religion, culminating in the Sunday service and, in the Gereformeerde setting of the mission church, the *nagmaal,* the religion remains an empty abstraction. Its teachings and tenets lack the component of meaningful action, an anchoring point in experience, and thus their meaning remains abstract.

And, to the convert, new at the game, they are also abstruse; the new religion is altogether "too complicated"; it gives people "much difficulty" (for example !Khuma//ka, as noted at the chapter opening). According to Russell and Russell (ibid.: 108–109), the Ghanzi Boers' dismissal of the concept of a Christian Bushman, especially as a fellow *Dopper* (as the practitioners of the Gereformeered branch are called), derives from their implicit understanding of this principle of Durhkeimian and Geertzian sociology or anthropology of religion. Being kept outside the Afrikaner community, society, and culture, through centuries-old barriers of exclusion, the Bushman converts are deprived of membership in the religious collectivity through which the new religion would gain meaning and become real to its new practitioners. To deny that the Bushmen can be Christians at the spiritual level is to deny that they can be Europeans at the social level. Expression of the first notion in forceful terms provides ideological reassurance that the second will never come about.

The problem of settler hostility toward the local Bushman mission of course never reached the extremes in Ghanzi that the same problem acquired in the Cape, over a century earlier. While I found a few white settlers who were genuinely in favor of the mission and its "good work," most looked at it with a sense of unease, bordering on antipathy in a handful of cases.[11] The grumblings sounded similar to what the Cape settlers felt, that the mission attracted *skelms* (scoundrels) and deserter laborers who had left their previous farm jobs under a cloud. There was also the notion that the mission "spoiled" Bushmen and made them "uppity," and taught them abstract things beyond their grasp, rather than what they should and could know, practical farm skills. But there were no thoughts, let alone actions, about closing down the mission, and the evangelist's requests to be allowed to preach at a farmer's Bushman village were always granted. Presumably, their tolerance of the mission was based ultimately on the fact that its establishment in their region, by a faraway congregation, constituted no financial burden to the local farmers, as it had done to their Cape predecessors who were forever hounded by the missionary or even the government for "subscriptions." Its funding and supervision was not "their problem." Moreoever, the socio-political setting of the Ghanzi farmers, a multi-racial black democracy, would contribute to the muting of any expression of antipathy toward spreading the white man's religion among one of the country's non-white peoples.

The exclusion of the christianized Bushmen from the established congregation of the same denomination points to the key problem in the failure of the Bushman mission, not only in the one instance at Dekar, but at all of the other mission stations of the nineteenth-century Cape we surveyed before. It is the inability of converted Bushmen to come together in a congregation of like-minded believers. Being excluded from the congregation of the white *Doppers* meant that they had to establish a congregation themselves. Such indigenous congregations appeared among other tribal groups, sometimes through mass conversions by chiefly fiat (as among some Tswana tribes), or, more commonly, through the training and permanent placement within the native community of an indigenous evangelist. The eventual ordination of the evangelist into a full-fledged minister and the formal recognition of his church and congregation by charter rounds out this process of the "indigenization" or "inculturation" of African churches that is found all over Africa. It resulted in the eventual establishment of like-minded, independent African churches and sects, led by black ministers and "Bantu prophets" (Sundkler 1961, 1962; Hillman 1990).

No such process ever happened among the Bushmen, of either the past or present. The reasons have to do with Bushman social organization and with ethos. The amorphousness and fluidity of social groupings militates against the establishment of so cohesive a group as a congregation, and the individualism and idiosyncrasy of belief militate against like-mindedness.

Perhaps the most fundamental barrier against Christianity—the hapless Jacob Links would likely have agreed—is the nomadic way of life of the Bushmen. The structural foundations of the settler's religion is sedentism. A church, both in the physical and social sense, as building and congregation, is inconceivable for nomads. The additional infrastructural elements of a mission—the farm, pasture, herd, school, and clinic—further implant the church on its plot of land. Those white frontier settlers who, in the past, opted for a nomad's way—the "trek Boers"—had to accommodate, or resign themselves, to this structural requirement, by receiving *nagmaal* from an itinerant *predikant*. Alternatively, they might shun the church and its minister altogether, venturing forth northward, just themselves, their Bible, and their beasts, in the culturally acclaimed spirit of self-reliance and independence (van Onselen 1961; Russell and Russell 1979: 103–104).

While in present-day Ghanzi the onetime trek Boers of the district (Russell and Russell 1979: 10–26) have now settled down and founded their church and congregation, the Bushmen have not. The farm Bushmen were almost as mobile and restless when I was in Ghanzi as presumably they have always been, creating today the same problems of Christianization as was noted by the missionaries Wust and Dornan a century ago. Nomadism today is brought on by unemployment, landlessness, search for employed kin with whom to stay for a few weeks or months, search for wild plant foods and game in remote regions of the farm block, and other reasons having to do with their destitution and marginalization within Ghanzi society (Guenther 1976a: 124–35, 1977a, 1986a: 129, 146–56; also see Sylvain 1998 for an examination of the same processes among farm Bushmen in the Omaheke District of Namibia). This applies also to the mission village of /Oaxa. Monthly censuses revealed a high degree of fluctuation, from a low of about thirty to a high of about 120, in the composition of the six "bands" that made up the village (Guenther 1986a: 185–87). The lack of constancy of the domestic groups of the mission residents was an ongoing concern for the missionaries. The evangelist tried to meet it by following his scattered flock about once every month when he left the mission settlement for a week or two to hold services among the Bushmen at various farms. However, given the distances different family groups or individuals were scattered, each in another direction, it was impossible for the missionary to see all of them. Those most remote were never seen and gradually they and the missionary would lose contact with each other altogether. Some greeted this development with indifference while others grumbled, with some bitterness or disillusionment, how the *moruti* (minister) and the church had forsaken them. The comment of the minister from the mother church in Namibia about the Bushman mission at Dekar is a virtual replay of comments of his nineteenth-century counterparts: "The Bushmen don't stay in one place, they move out, they move around everywhere. There's one of our members in Gaborone [the capital of Botswana, some six hundred kilometers away]" (Russell and Russell ibid.: 109)

The moral and ideological prerequisite for forming and sustaining a congregation—like-mindedness—is conspicuously absent from Bushman belief. As seen throughout this book, belief is highly flexible and variable, subject to virtually every single individual's personal interpretation. Bushman religion lacks a common center and is devoid of orthodoxy. It is my sense that people implicitly value this central and essential attribute of their religion, as it conforms ideologically with the principles of egalitarianism and individualism that constitute the moral pillars of their society. As suggested in chapter 3, the other quality of Bushman religion—its elusive and enigmatic ambiguity, as well as its beguiling polyvocality—also appeals to the people, at some unconscious, spiritual, and aesthetic level, as it conforms to the basic fluidity and amorphousness of their social structure (as well as to the ludic bent that is evident in their social interaction and expressive performances).

Because of these fundamental ideological and epistemological qualities inherent in Bushman religion, the mission enterprise among its adherents over the past two hundred years would likely have failed, even had it been free of the sorts of problems described in this chapter. The Bushmen would be unlikely ever to take to Christianity, unless their religion and society were to change in a number of fundamental ways. In one way, its qualities of fluidity and resilience, especially the aspects of adaptability, openness, and tolerance to the beliefs of other groups, including non-Bushmen, could work to the advantage of a missionary trying to draw the Bushmen into his religion. The Bushmen have rarely rejected outside beliefs; instead, they have foraged for them eagerly and drawn them into their own corpus of ideas, practices, and myths.

What would likely soon turn out to become a problem for the missionary, however, is that once adopted, the new beliefs are also adapted. In the context of Bushman religious and expressive culture this second step of remolding the received beliefs would likely produce ideas that a missionary would locate on a spectrum from antic fancy to grand heresy, causing him feelings ranging from uneasy bemusement to alarm and outrage. The latter response, as we saw in chapter 4, is elicited by the Christ–trickster conflation, or worse yet, by the trickster's kinship to //Gãũwa, who may be identified with Satan, resulting in hybrid who would be an unthinkable, intolerable abomination to the missionary.

The religious openness of the Bushmen, an advantage to the missionary initially as it would gain him entry into the community and beliefs of the Bushmen and permit their conversion, might, later on in the proselytizing process, turn into a disadvantage. Once converted and admitted to the new church, the new members would be expected to stay faithful to the creed that they adopted. Yet, given their foraging ways, such a "monogamous" marriage to the new church might soon experience the strains of adulterous heterodoxy. Bushman Christians might well pick and choose from other religions that come their way. An example is the repeated consultations of a black diviner by converted Bushman residents at /Oaxa, who suspected that they were the target of a witchcraft or sorcery attack. It was inconceivable to both missionaries, who were both deeply concerned about such actions, that a Christian could get himself into such a situation (which is frequent enough in African villages all over sub-Saharan Africa). Another extra-Christian store of mystical, mythical, and ritual beliefs and practices from which converts continue all the while to draw is their own religion, especially the trickster protagonist-cum-god and the trance dance (both, as noted above, elements of traditional religion the evangelist at Dekar deemed especially pagan and "anti-Christian," because of their perceived connections to the devil and magic, or even sorcery).

Two Incongruous Belief Systems

This survey of mission activities among the Bushmen in colonial and recent times has adduced the many and varied reasons why "the notion of radical conversion through religious experience would be largely inapplicable to the Bushmen" (Barnard 1992a: 261). In part it was the halfhearted, unsustained attempts of the missionaries, many of whom, in the Cape, were dubious about the whole enterprise from the start, in view of the negative estimation in which they held the Bushmen and their capacity for Western religion and civilization. In part it was a large number of recurrent practical and structural problems that seemingly defied solution.

The key problem, however, is the fundamental ideological and metaphysical incongruities and incompatibilities between the two religions. On the one hand, we have a religion that emphasizes divine reason and operates by means of a set liturgy performed by staid priests; on the other we have tricksters and trancers, transformation and altered states. The first declares itself the one true faith which it transports to every corner of the world so that it might supplant the religions found there. The second is a religion that is fluid and variable and thus has no conception of such a thing as one faith, let alone one true faith; instead of taking their religion to others, Bushmen will take from other religions that happen to cross their path whatever suits their spiritual fancy. Finally, Christianity regards humans as singular beings because they mirror God, and, on that basis, declares the universal brotherhood of humankind, whereas the Bushmen regard humans not so much as one with God and unique and united as a result, but as kindred to the animals because each developed from the other.

At the most basic level what separates the two religions is the same thing that separates the two societies and cultures. They are fundamental structural principles, antithetically opposed: fluidity versus fixedness, lability versus stability, liminality versus structure, *communitas* versus society, inclusivity versus exclusivity, polyvocality versus orthodoxy, ambiguity versus clarity. Each of the cultural sub-systems examined in this book—from subsistence patterns, social institutions, and processes, to belief, ritual, and expressive forms—has demonstrated one or more of these anti-structural tendencies, revealing Bushman society, culture, and religion to be profoundly different from their counterparts in the West (and in most other parts of the world).

Once again, I point to the problem this raises for the anthropologist of religion: the difficulty of studying a domain of culture informed with all of the anti-structural traits on the left side of the list, given that as researchers we subscribe to an epistemology that is derived primarily from the right side. I will address this question in the conclusion.

Conclusion: Bushman Religion and the Tolerance for Ambiguity

The laws of logic which ultimately govern the world of the mind are, by their nature, essentially invariable; they are common not only to all periods and places but to all subjects of whatever kind, without any distinction even between those that we call the real and the chimerical; they are to be seen even in dreams. . . .

—COMTE, CITED IN LÉVI-STRAUSS 1963: N.P.

Just as Nasrudin looks for the key not where it is lying—in darkness—so anthropologists as a whole study religion—a "dark" phenomenon—within either the open arena of social interaction, or the mind, lit up by its inherent logic and rationality. . . . [U]nless we look in the darker domains of culture, our search for the key to religion will continue to be an exercise of futility.

—GUENTHER 1979A: 127

Twenty-five years ago I concluded an article I wrote about Bushman religion with the above remark. The paper dealt with the limitations of the theoretical tool kit available to the anthropologist of religion when he set out to understand and explain the religion of the Bushmen. It led also to a critique of the anthropological study of religion in general, through a process of extrapolation I would not attempt today (in view of the distinctiveness of the case at hand, and the society and culture that embed it). My basic conclusion then was that this study has serious limitations, because of an ingrained inability of anthropologists to deal with ambiguity. It is unacknowledged as an element of religion (or any other domain of culture), and argued away in some fashion or other. For deep-seated epistemological reasons we anthropologist-academicians cannot tolerate ambiguity, I argued then. It would seem, alas, that I have not learned much since writing this paper, as shown by this book and especially this chapter, which is on the same issue: our anthropological, Western-intellectual penchant for structure and rejection of anti-structure. And the conclusion reached is much the same as well, except that it is more limited in scope: that this penchant for structure and order can lead to a distorted understanding of certain cultural domains, in particular religion, and especially the religion of the Bushmen (and societies like them, that is, hunter-gatherers).

The Bushmen, as seen throughout this book, appear to have no lack of tolerance for the ambiguity inherent in their belief system. They seem untroubled mentally and emotionally by such cosmological and logical incongruities as humans merging identities with the animals of myth and veld, or god being both creative and destructive—the source of disease and death, but also of healing, along with a physiological-mystical bodily potency. With respect to religious sentiment, these people blend the numinous with the ludicrous, as reflected in the merger of trickster with god and the clown with the shaman (in the early phase of the trance dance). The contradictions in their "religious attitude," their theology, and their cosmology—of which they may be made aware only by the probing questions of resident anthropologists—do not cause them intellectual unease. They seem not only unperturbed by the great variation in beliefs and myths, as well as the narrative accounts thereof which they hear from other people, but actually seem aesthetically to cherish the interpersonal idiosyncrasies of ideas.

None of this is to suggest that the Bushmen are irrational and "pre-logical" people, incapable of clear thinking. Quite the contrary is the case, as revealed, for example, by the extensive and highly efficient knowledge and know-how they display in their subsistence activities. Subsistence activities are very prosaic and pragmatic, carried out with little magic and divination. This applies especially to gathering. The hunt, while for the most part an efficient, instrumental act based on a store of empirical knowledge, also brings an element of sympathy and moral and affective attunement to the prey animal to bear on hunting at certain of its stages. Such empathetic attunement of the hunter to the prey may also enhance the efficiency of the hunt, as instrumental knowledge about animals is complemented by intuitive understanding. White employers frequently remark on the adeptness farm Bushmen display with machines, such as wind pumps, diesel engines, and trucks (Russell and Russell 1979: 103; Guenther 1986a: 132). As we will see below, a number of anthropologists have characterized the Bushman worldview in general as being of "prosaic" bent.

I differ in my explanation of the Bushmen's tolerance for ambiguity from the likes of Lévy-Bruhl also in that I do not couch it with reference to some dualist, mentalist-mystical propensity, such as primitive irrationality as against Western rationality. Instead, following Evans-Pritchard's dictum that "religion is what religion does," I ground mental patterns in social reality, as well as in "experience" (in line with Evans-Pritchard's colleague Lienhardt). For ecological, social, and historical reasons, that reality, in the Bushman case, also is ambiguous—loose, fluid, labile, resilient, adaptable—in its structure, institutions, and ethos (as well as being pervaded with a sense for the ludic). One reason Bushman social organization is ambiguous is because it is small-scale and simple, that is, lacking in social segmentation, status differentiation, and minutely defined jural rules. As Turner (to whom I will turn again below) has argued, simplicity in social structure has the effect of liberating the human propensity for structure. This liberating effect plays itself out especially in the realm of myth, ritual, and symbol, and it affects the individual and his or her relationship to the group. As we saw in chapter 2, Bushman society produces individuals who do and think their own thing, in a context of egalitarianism. As shown in chapter 3, this fosters a fragmented, heterogeneous worldview, with a wide range of ideas and practices, expressed and transmitted by socially equal and culturally individuated men and women. The ambiguity of Bushman belief is thus not a matter of some innate psychological propensity, but a matter of a complex blend of social structure, the ecological and historical circumstances that shape it, and the individuals that act through its institutions and values.

The tolerance for ambiguity we find in the minds and the culture of the Bushmen is not found among anthropologists, however. It is an a priori assumption of academe that there is, there must be, structure. The reason for this intellectual reluctance, if not inability, to accept what on the face of it seems Bushman religion's essential characteristic, is the entrenched rationalism and scientism of classic academic anthropology. As discussed more fully elsewhere (Guenther 1979a: 114–19), this Western intellectual mold appears in two main versions in mainstream anthropology, functionalism and structuralism. I have recently argued elsewhere, in a position paper on the anthropological study of African ritual (1997b), that these two paradigms are still alive and well in that field, and that most of the recent studies are branches off either a functionalist or a structuralist trunk.

In the context of the anthropological study of religion, the former paradigm, in the robe of "functionalist pietism," argues that religion is the social grease and glue of tribal society, its core institution. This paradigm's high priest is Malinowski, who deems myth to be no idle tale but a "hard-worked active force," a "pragmatic charter of primitive faith and moral wisdom" (Malinowski 1948: 101). The latter, in its garb of "structuralist stoicism" (à la Lévi-Strauss), argues for a deep-seated rationality within belief and ritual. Myth is treated as a culture's "meta-theory," containing logical components that are based on binary oppositions and that operate through complex, chainlike metaphorical transformations and inversions. "Laws of logic" are at work in myths—notwithstanding the latter's "chimerical" and dreamlike propensities—which are invariable and universal, and inform "all subjects of whatever kind," in the words of Auguste Comte, whose rationalist credo is summed up at the opening of this chapter (and appears on the frontispiece of Lévi-Strauss's book [1963] on the totemism debate, as its guiding analytical principle).

The mind-set underlying these two paradigms predisposes ethnographers toward structure and order, which, if not obvious at the surface (as it rarely is), is assumed to be there all the same—subterranean, oblique, transformed and inverted—to be searched for strenuously until it is found. And if unsuccessful today—because of inadequate data—the search, it is assumed confidently, will yield the looked for patterns of order and structure in the future, once the quantity and quality of data have improved.

Such were the caveats some of the earlier writers, such as Schmidt, Gusinde, and Schapera, added to their explanations, wherein the evident and startling inconsistencies and ambiguities of Bushman religion were attributed to the "obvious inadequacies" in the reported data (Schapera 1930: 190). Explanations thereof thus had a tentative ring to them. Today the volume of data has greatly increased and its quality is likely as high as is possible, given the methodological limitations that attach to the task of empirical, reliable, objective ethnographic data gathering at any time and any place (especially on the cultural domain of religion)—of which anthropologists are today more aware than they have ever been. In our attempts to make sense of Bushman religion, we can no longer blame data to justify the presentation of provisional explanations and defer the task of explaining ambiguity to a future point.

How have Western students—theologically and anthropologically minded ones—dealt with the evident ambiguity which met their eyes when they looked at Bushman religion? What are their various takes on the ambiguity of a cultural domain that is presumed to be functional and structural, pragmatic and rational, notwithstanding appearances to the contrary? How do these a priori assumptions hold up in their analyses of a religious complex all writers describe with such adjectives as "ambiguous," "incoherent," "muddled," "contradictory," "ambivalent," "inconsistent," "confused," "variegated," "diverse," "fluid," "scattered," "amorphous," "diffuse"? These are the central questions for this chapter.

Another question to be dealt with pertains not to Bushman religion, but to the matrix which embeds this domain, society. Just as religion has caused head scratching among anthropologists over its "dark, unlit" face of ambiguity, contradiction, and variability, so has society, over corresponding structural characteristics. And just as some of the more extreme writers on Bushman religion have offered the dubious proposition that what Bushman have by way of supernatural or preternatural doings and inklings is, in fact, not religion at all, so some hunter-gatherer theorists have suggested that what Bushmen (and people like them) live in are not societies.

Coping with Ambiguity

The basic strategy students of Bushman religion have employed to deal with its ambiguity is to identify what is perceived as its core, preferably looking at more than one instance (Bleek 1911: xxx; Schapera 1930: 395–99; Gusinde 1966: 75; Biesele 1978, 1993: 15–23; Guenther 1989: 33–36; Barnard 1992a: 252; Schmidt 1995: 152), and then to treat this disembodied complex of beliefs and practices as capturing the essence and meaning of Bushman religion. This core is then presented to the reader clearly and in summary fashion, with the rough edges and contradictions edited out (creating thereby the misleading impression of coherence). There are two elements of variation to this basic, essentialist strategy; one concerns the selection of elements to include in the core, the other the treatment of those elements that lie outside it.

The definition of core elements is guided primarily by one consideration: the relative frequency with which they recur, from one Bushman band and tribe to the next, across southern Africa. This was basically the methodological and analytical approach followed by Barnard (1992a), as he defined the core of Bushman (and, at the same time, Khoekhoe) religion, as well as of all the other cultural domains. Through a careful and comprehensive study of regional comparison he felt able to isolate an underlying "Common Bushman" "structure of structures" (Barnard 1992a: 3–7; also see 1988). In studies that deal with the religion of only one Bushman group, the core may be defined in terms of the more agreed-upon features of belief. This is what guided me, in my attempts to formulate an integrated picture of Nharo religion (Guenther 1986a: 217). In Raymond Firth's (1964) terms, I presented what he calls the "core" of beliefs ("firmly held in its essentials and usually simple to state"), and I left aside some of the more variable dimensions of belief—ancillary and fluctuating personal variations, and what Firth calls the "periphery" of belief ("vague, involving either difficulties of formulation or certainty of conviction").

In addition to this rather straightforward "statistical" approach to identifying the essential core of Bushman religion, there are other approaches, which are more selective and less neutral theoretically. Here the analyst's theoretical and ideological orientation will have a bearing on the selection of elements, as well as the evaluation of these elements with respect to their denotative and connotative meanings. Of these there have been several in the course of the history of Khoisan studies.

One of the two Christian-oriented approaches was either to question or deny that Bushmen worshipped God and that they subscribed to religion, the racist view of some of the early missionaries mentioned in the previous chapter. The opposite view, held by Pater Wilhelm Schmidt and his disciples, as well as others (such as Vedder and Estermann), was to define Bushman religion in theistic terms which were familiar to the researchers, mainly as a primal and pure form of monotheism. Exegetical accounts of Bushman religion were built around this core concept.

A rival view, which had been formulated by the previous generation of anthropologists and continued to have its adherents in Schmidt's time (such as Bleek and Lloyd) and was vigorously opposed by the latter (Gusinde 1966: 79–80), argued that the Bushmen worship not God, who appears as a remote and vaguely defined supernatural entity in Bleek and Lloyd's account of Bushman myth and belief, but the moon, along with other stellar bodies (Bleek 1911: 435). In support of this Müllerian scenario for Bushman supernaturalism, Bleek probed Bushman oral literature for sidereal tales, the importance of which he ended up exaggerating (Hewitt 1986: 91; Guenther 1995b).The assignment of prominence to this relatively minor element of Bushman myth and lore is the more surprising in view of the prominence of the trickster figure Mantis in /Xam mythology, which Bleek's daughter Dorothea clearly recognized (Bleek 1923). This suggests that the junior Bleek's judgment on this point might indeed have been theoretically clouded.

It was this latter figure, and "bush and animal heroes" ("*Busch- und Tierheroen*") like him, that another writer deemed the central element of Bushman religion. As discussed in chapter 4, Hans Baumann (1932), a contemporary of Schmidt's, presented his "animistic" interpretation of Bushman religion as a corrective to the latter's "theistic" one. In Baumann's view conceptions of god are vague and otiose, and they stand as a foreign element within Bushman supernaturalism, derived long ago from the black Bergdama (Gusinde 1966: 79). Moreover, magic and divination are elaborate ritual elements in Baumann's view of Bushman religion. An ethnographic case that falls in line with this magic-animistic portrayal of Bushman religion is Köhler's sketch of Kxoe religion, which is presented as rich in a magic generated by a "preanimistic, motivating force" ("*präanimistische motivierende Kraft*"). As for the Kxoe god, (s)he is a bisexual being defined only vaguely, being a personification of the collective world of ancestral spirits, akin to a "manistic half-god" ("*manistischer Halbgott*"). Magic, along with "Mantik," were the themes also of popular books on the Bushmen and their religion (Holm 1965), especially those of Laurens van der Post (Barnard 1989), which treated the mantis not only as "the god of the Bushmen of southern Africa" (van der Post 1961: 18) but also as a kind of Jungian archetype of renewal and redemption (ibid.: 221–33), capable of touching the spiritual sensitivities of people as remote from the Kalahari as New Yorkers in an apartment on Park Avenue South, at Christmas (van der Post 1975).

Diametrically opposed to this animistic, magico-religious portrayal of Bushman religion are those accounts that emphasize the "prosaic" quality of the Bushman worldview, in which magic and "superstition" play a minor role, being confined to a religious domain that is more or less autonomous, impinging little on the people's *world*view (Heinz 1978b; Blurton-Jones and Konner 1976). Earlier (chapter 3) I discussed how Blurton-Jones and Konner were impressed by the extensive body of knowledge the !Kung had of animals and by the clear-minded, inductive way whereby they communicated that knowledge. While some "non-rational beliefs" were entertained about some animals—for instance about a giant baboon "of remarkable sexual appetites" (the !Kung !King !Kong!?) threatening women on gathering outings—such notions played a negligible role in the !Kung's everyday life (ibid.: 343–44). What makes women cautious when they are out gathering are threats more realistic than any baboon rapist, according to Blurton-Jones and Konner (ibid.: 343). Instead of depicting the Bushman as a *homo religiosus,* what is asserted is that "the Bushman is the original scientist" (Heinz 1978b: 148), "a realist, pragmatist and proto-scientist" (ibid.: 159). (S)he walks through life and the Kalahari veld with the positive outlook of the positivist, displaying none of the elements of "fear, intimidation or haunting" that trouble so many other tribal folk (ibid.: 160). If he fears something there is sound and solid reason for fear, in the form not of spirits, ghosts, or demons, but snakes and scorpions, leopards, lions, and elephants, and drought or food shortage. She has a religion, nevertheless, and a God; however, she will turn to God only in situations that defy her "wealth of factual knowledge" and baffle her "inquiring mind"—catastrophes such as droughts. He resignedly, and humbly, accepts such events as "the will of his God" (ibid.: 160). It is tempting to think that the background in biological sciences shared by these three authors may have flavored the accounts they render of Bushman cosmology.

Lewis-Williams's "trance hypothesis" is a recent formulation of the essence of Bushman ritual and belief. This feature is expressed within Bushman culture in vivid, symbolically pregnant form primarily through rock art, as well as myth and, of course, ritual. Altered states of consciousness of the trance dancers, and their mystical, cosmological, and therapeutic dimensions, are seen to constitute the emotional and symbolic center of Bushman "shamanic" religion. Richard Katz's (1976, 1982) and Dagmar Wagner-Robertz's (1976) work on the !Kung and Hai//om, respectively, complement this representation of Bushman religion. The former focuses on its ritual, healing side; the latter on its cosmological, hunting side, especially the core concepts of the Spirit Keeper of the Animals and the shamanic life-tree.

Recently Megan Biesele (1993) presented an account of Bushman myth and ritual in which the theme of the equality and complementarity of men and women is seen to be the dominant symbol of Bushman cosmology and ritual. This binary pair pervades a wide range of other existential, social, and cultural spheres and is symbolically mediated through ritual, the circular dance path, and the central fire.

Each of these explanatory paradigms—theistic, sidereal, animistic, prosaic, shamanic, gender-symbolic—does indeed explain one or another, or several, of the many facets of Bushman religion. Because of its ambiguity, the field of Bushman religion is wide and open, encompassing enough to admit of approaches from a variety of theoretical denominations. However, none encompasses the field in its entirety, despite the claims to the contrary of most of the students cited above.

Two ways of handling the elements that are, or appear to be, ancillary and peripheral to the core can be distinguished in the studies of Bushman religion. One is to bracket these elements out of the analysis altogether, acknowledging that the analysis is limited, as well as allowing for the possibility that, were the excluded, hidden dimension to be added to the analysis, the outcome might be a different reading of Bushman religion. Such focused, qualified, and modest studies are relatively few in Khoisan studies (as in anthropology generally). An example is Megan Biesele's just mentioned work on Ju'/hoansi folklore and ritual. She points to the fact that her study deals with only a small selection of her total corpus of (fifty) tales, which itself represents only some of the main story groups. She also admits that the gender polarities which provide the symbolic key to her analysis of !Kung myth and belief form a scheme into which some of the stories, the ones selected, "can be fitted." Her interpretive paradigm, she says, is "*one* possible way of understanding a complex, multi-faceted tradition" (Biesele 1993: 83, my emphasis).

For the most part studies of Bushman religion address themselves also to the elements lying outside the core that has been defined. They do so in two basic ways. The first is to treat what lies outside as "noise," that is, as elements extraneous and incidental to the symbolic and cosmological center that has been defined through the stipulated core. The elements are explained (away) either as "survivals" from a remote and now irrelevant past, or as more recent or present-day accultural accretions from external, culturally alien religious traditions. This approach was entertained by some of the earlier writers, such as Schapera (1930: 168–70, 10–95) and Marshall (1962: 221–22), especially in their attempts to sort out what is perhaps the most confused feature of Bushman religion: the multifarious names and attributes of divinity. It was especially popular among the early German-language writers, reflecting the culture-historical, diffusionist bent of German anthropology.

Regarding this approach to the non-lore elements, Walter Hirschberg (1933: 134) sees Bushman culture as a "gathering place of temporally highly diverse time elements" ("*Sammelstelle zeitlich sehr verschiedener Zeitelemente*") and its various elements as "the last ruins and remnants of primeval hunting cultures" ("*die letzten Trümmer oder Reste uralter Jägerkulturen*"). It is a shreds-and-patches amalgam of cultural survivals from various phases in the past, and, more recently, of cultural borrowings, diffused from hither and yon or foraged from neighboring cultures. As noted in chapter 3, in the section discussing the accultural factor in Bushman religion, the latter tendency is especially apparent in Bushman religion, striking one of the German writers as revealing a special "penchant for acculturation" (Köhler 1978/79: 13) and another as a manifestation of an "innate tendency" of the Bushman people for adaptation to, and mimicry of, the beliefs of other, neighboring peoples (Gusinde 1966: 55[1]).

Thus, in the view of these earlier workers, one part of Bushman religion, what they deem the core, is their "very own possession" ("*ureigener Besitz*"), while the other consists of elements derived from the past and from other cultures. The symbolic and cosmological fit of the latter with the former is not only loose but also creates a hotbed for confusion and contradiction within the native belief system, as the obsolete and derived elements clash with those of the core. Thus, for instance, the core creator god postulated by Gusinde for

!Kung religion is made to confront extraneous, archaic, or recently borrowed elements of belief and ritual: animistic notions of mantis and moon worship, or shamanic elements of curing, hunting magic, and divination. Such extraneous "magical" elements are then added, by an adaptation- and mimicry-prone people, to a "religious," monotheistic belief system and a ritual form in which prayer and thanksgiving were the prime objectives. To Baumann, on the other hand, as noted above and discussed more fully in chapter 4, it was the "bush and animal heroes" who were the core supernatural agents; god was derived from the outside, a version of the high god concept of a black neighbor group (the Bergdama) (Gusinde 1966: 79).

These early researchers saw their principal task as differentiating between the "essential" (*tiefgründig*) core of Bushman religion and the "incidental" (*nebensächlich*) survivals or accretions (Gusinde 1966: 18), and in this fashion

> to loosen up the convoluted complex of the belief system of the "yellow people" of south Africa and to draw out its historical development in a straight line. (Gusinde 1966: 79, my translation[2])

After this exercise of historical chaff and primal wheat differentiation, what appears initially as an off-centered, "convoluted complex," is now seen to be "straight lined." The uniquely Bushman religious core (ibid.: 18) has been revealed. Ambiguity has given way to order.

The other analytical way of handling the elements of Bushman religion that lie scattered beyond the core is to link them to the same, instead of disassociating them from it. That is, instead of viewing the scattered elements as symbolically and substantively extraneous to Bushman religion, they are seen as an integral component of its core elements. The basic argument is that their contradictory makeup is more apparent than real, that at the subsurface, structural level they are logically linked to the core, through the symbolic machinations of inversion and transformation. A key process in these logical operations is metaphor.

Thus, Lewis-Williams and his followers, in invoking his "trance hypothesis" as the key to all Bushman rock art (including, perhaps, Upper Paleololithic cave art [Lewis-Williams and Dowson 1989]), subsume what others have classified as altogether different representational motifs—hunting magic, domestic scenes, portrayals of women and of plants, striding figures, narrative scenes of mythological or real events, such as raids or commando pursuits by mounted British redcoats—under that one interpretive umbrella. Metaphor is the key concept underlying the reasoning behind this position. Lewis-Williams posits a long chain of trance metaphors—game antelopes, bovines, water, rain, honey, bees, perspiration, nasal hemorrhage, infibulation, *buxu*—by means of which he is able to corral a wide range of images into the trance hypothesis. Also included are the enigmatic abstracts and "geometrics," which are held to be representations of "entoptic" phenomena produced by the retina or optic nerve in an altered state (Lewis-Williams and Dowson 1988). The decision as to the trance component of one or another representation is deemed by some to be arbitrary and is the key element in what has become one of the most enduring and interesting controversies in Khoisan expressive culture.[3]

Recently Barnard (1992; also see 1988) has presented an argument in favor of structure within Bushman religion (and social organization and culture as a whole), in a cogently argued and meticulously researched book (Guenther 1992c). The structure he identifies is made up of the core elements of Khoisan religion (Barnard 1992a: 252), not unlike the summary of that religious tradition presented above, in chapter 3. Along with that structure Barnard also recognizes fluidity, as the second characteristic of the religion; however, in his view, fluidity does not preclude structure. Instead, "fluidity in religious belief functions as an indigenous creative and explanatory device and as a product of linguistic and social circumstances, both within broadly defined structural frameworks" (Barnard 1992a: 262). The constituent elements of the structure of Bushman religion may be held constant, be transformed, or be inverted, through time and over ethnic boundaries (ibid.). Structure imposes "constraining rules" over the second characteristic, fluidity, and its "generative principles" that create diversity. In combination, these rules and principles keep fluidity, diversity, and ambiguity in check, and structure ends up prevailing, even though that structure "is sometimes difficult to define in precisely structural terms" (ibid.: 263). In its recognition of fluidity (and with it diversity and ambiguity) as one of the two characteristics of Bushman religion I find myself in agreement with Barnard's position. My objection is that it overemphasizes structure,[4] which it assumes and imposes, and for all of its acknowledgment of ambiguity, this analysis ends up falling into the same order-structure mold of the other explanatory approach.

I very much agree with Barnard's statement about the creative and explanatory capacity of fluidity and the linkage of fluidity to language and social organization. His first point is consistent with my argument that ambiguity creates salience, rendering the ambiguous entity an object of beguilement and intellectual and aesthetic elaboration. As argued in chapter 3, the example that best illustrates this for Bushman cosmology is animals. Moreover, I would hold that fluidity is a mainspring for creativity and explanation also because of its being cut loose from structure; it operates beyond structure, in a liminal, antistructural never-never land.

However, while I agree with the linkage of fluidity to social organization, Barnard's argument that by virtue of that linkage there is structure strikes me as logically flawed. Inasmuch as social organization is itself pervasively fluid (as Barnard recognizes [1992a: 262]), one must ask how structure could be derived from such a connection.

Barnard qualifies his Whorfian thesis about belief and myth gaining structure from their link to language, which he argues specifically in the context of the complex notion of divinity of the Nharo (ibid.: 254–55), by saying that belief "is to some extent independent of language" (Barnard ibid.: 255). This is because religion is to a large measure an "inner state"; there is an experiential dimension to belief, argues Barnard, that lies beyond language and thought and that is intrinsically untranslatable. It is this ineffable, preverbal, non-semantic quality of religion, utterable only through metaphor, which I hold to be the characteristic expressive and conceptual mode of Bushman religion. Indeed, as argued elsewhere (Guenther 1979a), I hold it to be the mode of expression, feeling, and thought of religion generally, although in the religions of more complex state societies, myth and ritual frequently are co-opted by the holders and institutions of power, to express and serve—clearly and explicitly—their temporal, prosaic, and pragmatic designs.

With respect to the extent that the grammatical rules of Bushman language also impinge on belief—an arguable position, well argued by Barnard—I again wonder how much structure would be conferred to belief by virtue of this relationship. The reason is the highly metaphorical nature of some Bushman languages, such as G/wi (Silberbauer 1981: 130) and !Kung (Biesele 1993: 23–27). As noted in chapter 3, Megan Biesele, perhaps the best !Kung speaker among the troop of anthropologists who have studied this linguistic group, points to the pervasive presence of metaphor and "metaphorical play" in Ju/'hoan language, everyday conversation, and "expressive life," which renders the same "highly oblique, indirect and allusive" (ibid.: 23). Just as it is difficult to conceive of religion and belief gaining structure by being linked to an amorphous social system, so would it strike one as unlikely for belief to gain structure through a linkage to a language that is oblique and metaphorical.

In sum, given the high degree of fluidity in Bushman religion and throughout the social reality within which it is embedded, I would caution against overemphasizing the element of structure—or worse, holding structure up as the defining quality of Bushman religion, society, and culture. While it is unlikely, perhaps impossible, for any of the latter three domains to be devoid of some structure, in the case at hand structural elements are no more than minimal (except during times of stress and upheaval, when Bushman band society can become politically organized and socially structured, a point to which I will return later). What we find is a society, culture, and religion wherein fluidity and amorphousness are integral, rather than peripheral or antithetical elements of form and structure. As shown in the preceding chapters, what structures society and ethos is the "foraging way" of people, in the context not only of their subsistence economy, but also of their society and ideology. The open-endedness, opportunism, maximization, and egocentrism that mark the subsistence economy extend also to patterns of social interaction and individualism, and define the society's basic institutions and values, such as joking-avoidance relationships, modes of exchange, decision making, reciprocity, sharing, and egalitarianism. And in religion, belief, and myth it is ambiguity that is the ontological and conceptual substance of the beings (shamans, tricksters, therianthropes) and states (trance, transformation, the inchoate First Order). And many of the infinitely varied ideas people hold about their culture's store of beliefs and myths have been "foraged" from other groups, bands, and tribes, in the course of a life of ceaseless wandering. The performance of these expressive forms emphasizes individualism and innovative artistry, whereby each performer gives new textual, textural, and metaphorical twists to the tale, song, or dance performed.

Looking at Bushman society in these terms brings to mind Victor Turner's (1969) seminal concepts of "communitas" and "anti-structure." Let us examine their applicability to the Bushman case.

Bushman Society and Religion as Communitas and Anti-Structure

Bushman social organization has many of the classic elements of communitas, as delineated by Turner (1969: 97–145). Groupings are small, consisting of autonomous individuals rather than norm-governed social personae (they fit in Buber's I–Thou modality for interpersonal relationships). Mobility and organizational simplicity and fluidity are the basic structural attributes. Social organization of social groupings of the communitas mode is marked by egalitarianism and statuslessness, territorial and social openness, absence of property and corporateness, patterns of universalistic kinship and of loose marriages, sensitivity to conflict and its casual measures for resolving intra-group tension. Moreover, in relation to the wider, encompassing or encapsulating society, the Bushmen hunter-gatherers are socially marginal and inferior. All these traits we recognize in Bushman society.

Another basic element Bushman society shares with communitas-style societies is that an inverse relationship holds between social structural simplicity and ideological complexity. Looseness of social structure permeates social institutions and roles, and results in the suspension of the constraining effects of structure on the expressive and religious domain. These can unfold, are given "free rein":

> Rules that abolish minutiae of structural differentiation in, for example the domain of kinship, economics, and political structure liberate the human structural propensity and give it free rein in the cultural realm of myth, ritual and symbol. (Turner 1969: 133)

This process of "liberation" of society from the strictures of structures, and the resultant liminality, is a society's principal force of creativity and font of culture. It brings about the envisioning—beyond the given structures—of new possibilities, creating a "'more than this' dimensionality of existence" (Hynes and Steele 1980: 28). The contradictions and ambiguities generated by such a state of liminal foment are, according to Barbara Babcock-Abrahams, "creative negations" that beget a *mundus inversus* that "reinvents life with a vigour and a *Spielraum* [an area of playful inventiveness] attainable (it would seem) in no other way" (1978: 32, cited in Hynes 1993: 213). As noted by Turner, a key player—indeed, a deep- or meta-player (Hynes ibid.: 214)—in this seminal, liminal world of topsy-turvydom is the trickster, who "breaks the cake of custom and enfranchises speculation," thereby bringing on a "promiscuous intermingling and juxtaposing of categories" (Turner 1969: 213; also see Hynes 1993: 211–14).

As we have seen throughout this book, the trickster is the prominent figure of Bushman myth, lore, and religion, injecting into these areas of Bushman culture creative ferment, along with laughter (as well as moral outrage and rectitude, thereby also reaffirming the system of values and beliefs, along with disassembling and deriding it). The world he inhabits, the dreamlike "First Order," along with its surreal inhabitants, is likewise an instance of creative dissolution of the order of things. Turning to the real world, we see the shaman-dancer, who through his experiences of trance and transformation, enters alternate states of consciousness and being and opens up another path toward another world, of inversions and possibilities. Expressive performances are also prominent and embellished elements of Bushman social life. There is the much noted readiness of people for laughter and playfulness, which enters even the serious business of politics, wherein leaders with ambitions to power are ridiculed and conflict is resolved by ludic ploys or antics. (Although here one has to beware of rose-colored romanticism; as noted in chapter 3, laughter may also hide tension in Bushman society.)

Yet, Bushman society and religion differ from Turner's model of communitas and anti-structure in one critical way: everything else being equal—that is, in the absence of oppressive "external circumstances" that mobilize society and rationalize its ideology—anti-structural conditions in traditional Bushman society are permanent, rather than preliminary or liminal. Turner, notwithstanding his sustained focus on the processual and liminal dimension of social and symbolic states, in the final analysis remains wedded to the order-structure doctrine of academic anthropology. In his view, communitas and liminality are but temporary oscillations of society and religion, held in check by structure and order, the dominant and regnant state of affairs (Turner 1969: 127). After a due amount of time has lapsed, communitas and liminality are reabsorbed into society's orderly march. Society ends up actually being strengthened by the reaffirmation of order made possible through this lapse into disorder.

To Turner, ultimately and everywhere society is order, consisting of such structural elements as rigidity, segmentation, property, authority, and the suppression of individuality. This applies to "all societies, past and present," including the "simplest societies." The view of thinkers such as Rousseau, Marx, and Morgan that simple tribal societies allow individual liberty and choice, and are without power and property, Turner considers to be an erroneous instance of "state-romanticism," entertained by "structurally superior" members of society (Turner 1969: 130). Even in these simplest of societies communitas is merely juxtaposed to society—as a temporary, dialectical social modality—rather than being considered one with society.

The Bushman case suggests that anti-structure is capable, in fact, of being a prevalent, if not permanent, state of society and ideology in some societies, rather than a temporary or incidental one. It suggests that anti-structural and anti-nominal forces may, in fact, be capable of generating a modus vivendi for people, free of the tempering and towering presence of social structure. As developed in chapter 1, organizational fluidity does not mean organizational anarchy. While individuals are autonomous and "uncommitted" to others, and pursue their self-interest, the ecological and moral context of the egocentric networks that constitute Bushman social organization is defined by reciprocity, sharing, and egalitarianism. This draws the individual into the community and individual action effectively becomes communal action. As for the explanatory capability of ambiguity, I have shown throughout this book how this all-pervasive element of Bushman expressive culture—which is exceptionally rich, as it contains intra-cultural variation and extra-cultural accretions—generates such mental qualities as symbolic salience, intellectual and aesthetic beguilement and tension, and heterodox tolerance of the ideas of others. Thus, organizational and explanatory capacity can be found within fluidity and amorphousness.

However, it must be added that along with these anti-structural proclivities of social organization, Bushman society and ideology contains elements of social structure of the classic, functionalist mold. As seen in chapter 6, social organization contains a potential for male political power and property, as well as the structural potential for multi-band organizations with centralized, even militaristic leadership. While incipient during "normal" times—that is, when relatively isolated foragers are organized in autonomous band societies—this structural potential could become actualized quite readily in crisis times. The change from communitas to social structure is radical indeed, when an egalitarian band becomes a bellicose chiefdom. Such structured bands either stayed that way until they were exterminated by the invading settlers against whom they mobilized their political capabilities, fully but fruitlessly, or they returned to the foraging, communal mode of existence. This we saw happening among the Bushmen of the Ghanzi District: after their subjugation, as a politically and even militarily organized quasi chiefdom, by the BaTawana and Orlam Namas in the latter half of the nineteenth century, the structural mode of their society became once again that of the foraging band; they fell back into the processual whirl of communitas. The historian Richard Elphick traced such (at times cyclical) oscillations, from wealthy and politically organized and militaristic cattle herders to simple hunter-gatherers, among Khoisan groups of the Cape (1977: 30–41).

Another fate was to be subjugated, to become an enserfed underclass of the conquering group. In this state their society once again fell into the communitas mode; however the structural reasons here were social marginalization, rather than the foraging lifeways of autonomous band societies. As shown by Turner (1969: 94–130), and before him by Park (1928), Dunning (1959), and Dickie-Clark (1966), the social organization of "marginal men" living in the "marginal situation" is also informed with communitas. Another structural difference between the marginal Bushman and the foraging one is the former's attachment, however loose, to a political master and his involvement, however desultory, in herding and/or cultivating. These political and economic features, absent from the foraging band, confer an element of structure to the marginal situation not found in the foraging one. All this is a theoretical plank also in Wilmsen's (1989) revisionist view of the allegedly contrived nature of the foraging, egalitarian Bushman.

Thus, viewed diachronically, over the past two or three centuries, Bushman society, too, can be seen to have oscillated between anti-structure and structure. However, the relationship between the two modes differs from Turner's conception of it. In the Bushman case the shift from communitas to social structure is historical and contingent; in Turner's it is systemic and dialectic—the two social modalities, in the latter case, being counterpoised, with structure holding the upper hand and communitas being a temporary aberration, which society allows. It does so because of a "human 'need' for ritual liminality," which, to Turner, is once again counterpoised with the even stronger need for the opposite modality, for structure and order (Turner 1969: 203).

This study of Bushman religion and society could be seen as an endorsement of the first of these "needs" within social man, for liminality. And, in addition to confirming the reality of communitas within one specific non-Western society, it also shows the organizational capabilities of this anti-structural modality. Classic functionalists associate this with chaos and anarchy and see it as the antithesis to society; they thus find it irreconcilable with social structure. Processualists like Turner (as well as Gluckman and others of the Manchester School) see it as a dialectic, complementary component of social structure, which it inverts and deconstructs, and thus asserts and re-constructs.

What this study of Bushman religion and society suggests is that the people under discussion, and other hunter-gatherers like them, live in societies that are profoundly different from societies like our own. As so eloquently argued by Pierre Clastres (1977), they are egalitarian "societies against the state," with systemic and effective controls against accumulation and power (the workings of which we examined in chapter 2). Yet, as suggested by this account of Bushman society and belief, their difference is even deeper than that: such societies are not just against the state and hierarchy, but against structure and order; they are not just egalitarian societies, but liminal ones, and are not just acephalous, but amorphous. The difference between the two types of society lies at a social-structural level deeper than the organizational and institutional plane of power and politics.

Yet, such societies also contain within their organization the seeds of the order and structure one finds in the other type of society. They are kept dormant during times of stasis and germinate rapidly in times of crisis. Whether these structural seeds have lain in the subsoil of their foragers' band society since time began for the Bushmen, or whether they were implanted in the course of historical time, through their clashes and brushes with passing or settling state-based outsiders, is the question of the day for students of the Bushmen and of other hunter-gatherers.

Do the Bushmen (and Other Hunter-Gatherers) Have Societies?

When the social scientist considers the features of structural fluidity and lability of Bushman society, as well as the lack, for some groups, of political and cultural autonomy, the question is raised whether a social grouping so thoroughly fluid and, in certain instances, encapsulated or enserfed, and without any evident capacity for social reproduction, would not fall outside the definition of society. There are those—for instance, Tim Ingold (1990), in his comment on the revisionist controversy surrounding the question of the isolation and autonomy of the !Kung in recent historic times—who exclude hunter-gatherers such as the Bushmen and other small-scale, "immediate-return" foragers from that fundamental social category. What makes such groupings different from society, argues Ingold, is a distinctive "quality of relatedness" or "sociality" based on trust and "relations of incorporation," rather than on "dominion" and "relations of exclusion," the corresponding social principles in a society (Ingold 1990). In another discussion the same analyst (Ingold 1988) points to the subsistence mode of hunter-gatherers as another distinguishing feature, with the insistence that hunting and gathering be treated not so much as an instrumental technique of subsistence procurement than as an instance of social action. Putting the two notions together, we see that hunter-gatherers follow lifeways and live in organizational patterns altogether different in type from those that constitute society (a view which, in some form or other, has been held in hunter-gatherer studies since Steward). Society, as a "level of social integration" or a "social formation," and as a category of social thought, is reserved for other people, basically those with food-production and state formations.

Researchers today are generally less absolute about the two categories at issue, expanding or modifying either "hunter-gatherer/forager" or "society," and blurring the conceptual boundaries classic anthropological theory has drawn around each. Recently Ernest Burch (1994: 447–51) revisited the old social theory question of what sort of thing does or does not constitute the "functional prerequisites of human society," and he tailored the definition of society to the fluid, egalitarian, symbiotic dynamics of hunter-gatherer society in such a way that "band societies" and "industrialized societies" could be encompassed within the same definition. I would also advocate an expanded definition. As argued in the section above, while they differ in fundamental ways, the distinction between structured state-based society and unstructured band-based non-society is nevertheless also specious because each societal type contains elements of the other. Bushman band society contains the structural potential for power, hierarchy, competition, and aggression. As for state societies, communitas and liminality (and, in that mode, also equality or inferiority) can be seen to "break" in at every point in the society's structure:

> Communitas breaks in through the interstices of structure, in liminality; at the edges of structure, in marginality; and from beneath structure, in inferiority. (Turner 1969: 128)

There are those who, instead of expanding the category of society to include also the foragers' "band society," prefer to expand the category of hunter-gatherer, taking its key parameters beyond the subsistence criterion of foraging, to include low-level horticultural societies. An example is Robert Kelly, who in a recent comparative study of the lifeways of about 120 foraging societies, includes a number of tropical horticultural ones (Kelly 1995). The reason for extending the category of "foraging society" in this fashion is in part because for Amazonian, African, and South-East Asian horticulturalists hunting and gathering is an important, supplementary subsistence component (just as marginal food production is a secondary subsistence mode for a number of "primary" foragers). But the chief reason for encompassing both types of "foraging societies" within one category is sociological rather than ecological: they both have low levels of wealth and power accumulation, and are very much "egalitarian societies" (Woodburn 1982; also see Clastres 1977), with a mode of production that is no longer merely "foraging," but "communal" (Lee 1992); indeed, such societies are exemplars of "primitive communism" (Lee 1988).

Still others take the hunter-gatherer category even further, beyond study of aboriginal and isolated "band societies" in marginal land stretches that pursue an arguably archaic foraging lifeway, to include such other "hunter-gatherers" as Japanese or European whalers or fishermen (Iwasaki-Goodman and Freeman 1994; Smith 1987) and socially marginalized, "urban nomads" such as vagabonds, beggars, panhandlers, street people, and gypsies. The German researcher Aparna Rao (1993) refers to this category of people as the "peripatetic niche," and identifies a number of formal attributes shared by all of its diverse members (including hunter-gatherers), such as a nomadic life style, opportunistic foraging, low-level trade or sporadic work, social and economic dependency, low social status, personal autonomy, loose connection of the individual to the collectivity. She adds a criterion not often noted by students of tribal hunter-gatherers, although it is frequently present (including among the farm Bushmen): that such peoples are deemed by members of the wider society to hold ritual power, for which they are either esteemed and sought out, or demonized or criminalized (Rao ibid.: 503–509). (As a parenthetical aside, Julienne Hanson [1995], tongue in cheek, includes yet another member for inclusion in the category of urban peripatetics, Western academics. The sexual division of labor within academe sees male academics engaged in "research/hunting" and female academics in "teaching/gathering"—the former the exalted and exciting, high-risk and low-return academic subsistence activity; the latter the humdrum, low-status, low-risk, and high-yield one.)

Broadening the perspective on hunter-gatherers in this fashion shifts the category far beyond cultural ecology and ethnography into the field of sociology, specifically the conceptual and substantive realm of such topics as class, ethnicity, labeling theory, relative deprivation, and—as noted in the section above—marginality (see Gmelch 1986). As a consequence of this disciplinary shift the analysis and the theoretical models of hunter-gatherer studies are altered radically. This is especially noticeable in the current revisionism debate, where theoretical notions from sociology are combined with others from political economy, world systems theory, and post-structuralism, as well as from archaeology and history.

All this conceptual rethinking and retooling around the basic question on hunter-gatherer society (and history), along with the general, discipline-wide postmodernist cynicism and self-doubt about the basic enterprise of ethnography and anthropology which has hit Kalahari studies with a special vengeance, has raised doubts and misgivings in some researchers' minds about the subfield of hunter-gatherer studies. One recent researcher suggested glumly that, given the conceptual vagueness and fluidity of the hunter-gatherer category, it may be no more than a "mirage" and no longer "a useful category for theoretical purposes" (Burch 1994: 454). Richard Lee (1992) has recently spoken of a "crisis of representation," and has suggested ways of resolving the disagreements and contradictions that have split the field into three camps, with one of them, the revisionists, the most vitriolic and unaccommodating. Other researchers (Kent 1992; Shott 1992; Guenther 1996a), too, have recently suggested fruitful ways of reconciling or synthesizing the latter paradigm with the research directions of hunter-gatherer studies generally.

Thus, for all the dismal soundings of current and recent researchers (Arcand 1981, 1988; Barnard 1983: 208–209), the field continues to have a future, especially in the areas of applied or advocacy anthropology. The Bushmen, like most other "post-foraging" hunter-gatherers all over the world, are now in the process of reconstituting their cultural integrity, as well as organizing politically and securing their territorial and economic base and their rights as citizens in their respective nation states. Many have become people with the cultural resources and the political resolve to resist and prevail, by whatever economic, social, or cultural means they have come to adopt, whether through circumstance or choice. It is these means, circumstances, and choices that could and should constitute the principal agenda of researchers working among today's and tomorrow's hunting-and-gathering ethnic minorities. (See Myers 1988: 266, 274–76; Burch and Ellanna 1994: 311–12.)

The Analytical and Methodological Challenge of Ambiguity

I have perhaps been overly critical of past and present writers' attempts at getting a handle on Bushman religion. It is a slippery and nebulous field and a will-o'-the-wisp that eludes the academic anthropologist's grasp. Perhaps what religious scholars and anthropologists have done to explain those isolated aspects of Bushman religion that lend themselves to academic analysis and to bracket out the rest, is all that can and should be done. It provides a point of focus, a center, for a madly and maddeningly ambiguous field within which no clear referent is defined. Such a referent is provided by the discourse set by academic anthropology, functionalist or structuralist, and to go beyond those recognizable elements on which we have a fix is to be cast adrift in an analytical sea of unsignified signifiers. The result could be one of those exercises of "jejeune cabalism" which, Clifford Geertz (1966: 42) warned, can arise whenever ethnographic studies become too particularist and arcanely emic, when descriptions become excessively "thick," and when etic analysis and academic inscription become jettisoned altogether. Such an approach could have resulted in a book, in the case at hand, entitled something like *The Teachings of Ou /Oma* or *!Khuma//ka Speaks,* in the romantic modernist style of 1960s hippy anthropology. Alternatively—and not, in my view, preferably—such a book might fall in line with its postmodernist, cynical, yuppy successor, offering a crafted, contestable, multi-layered, and multi-vocal text on the subject—disjunctive and discursive in style, and dense and impenetrable in analytic structure and intent.

Yet, not to take one's exploration of Bushman religion beyond what the spotlights of functionalism and structuralism reveal about the field is to gain understanding that is as limited as it is misleading. I took a double-barreled, functionalist-structuralist shot at a couple of features of Bushman myth in chapters 5 and 6, and concluded that the analysis it allowed, while arguably elegant, obscured as much as it explained. The impression this sort of analysis conveys is that what is analyzed, Bushman religion, is an integral, integrated core institution of Bushman society and culture and that its beliefs and myths are logically consistent and symbolically integrated. However, this is largely untrue, as shown throughout this book. Bushman ritual is relatively undeveloped, and belief hovers above social reality, vague and diffuse.

The methodological problem is that, because of its ambiguity and its open, fluid, "foraged," shreds-and-patches contents, the "wonderful muddle" that is Bushman religion contains every conceivable trait and pattern, permitting of every conceivable analytical or interpretive approach. It also contains structure and structures; like any ambiguous field one might look at—say the stars or clouds in the sky, or the surface of the wall of a rock shelter—patterns will readily be detected by an eye and brain that suffers from "ambiguity overload." Constellations become twins, a virgin, a bull or scales; clouds whales or elephants; and cracks, fissures, and depressions the outlines and bodily texture of an animal about to be painted. Such structural patterns are spurious, however; they may even be fleeting, as are the cloud-elephants, which shift their shape the next minute, due to the currents of the wind. The cloud example is analogous to Bushman religion, which is ambiguous and fluid, at any one time offering a different constellation of ambiguity.

The challenge is to find a structure that is not some spurious, isolated, imposed pattern but an integral, integrating, central element of the overall field. And if that is not found—as I submit it is not, within Bushman religion—the first challenge is to admit defeat, instead of doggedly continuing to search the culture, prodding and pestering informants with questions. Such a search is likely to yield what is searched for, thanks in part to self-delusion, and in part to misinformation proffered by tired-out informants.

A case in point was Louis Fourie's Dama informant Apollo, who, exasperated by the doctor-anthropologist's persistent questioning about !Kung religion, shouted out what Fourie transcribed as *gus tji-tji*. Allegedly this, in shortened form (Tji Tji) was entered into the ethnographer's notebook, as one of the names of the Bushman god //Gauwa. It is so inscribed in Fourie's account of !Kung religion (Hahn et al. 1928: 104) and in Schapera's book on the Bushmen (1930: 190, 195). What came to light some two dozen years later (Gusinde 1966: 23–24), when Apollo worked for the equally dogged Pater Gusinde, was that what the informant had said to Fourie that day, irritated by the latter's irksome questions, was "you asshole!" Apollo confessed his deceit to Gusinde who, on the basis of this "worrisome inaccuracy" ("*bedenkliche Ungenauigkeit*"), now felt called upon to express doubt as to the reliability of the rest of Fourie's ethnographic work (wherein an ontologically and morally ambiguous portrayal of the !Kung divinity stood diametrically opposed to Gusinde's scheme). It remains an open question whether or not the information Gusinde received on that matter from the same informant was any more reliable.

Once the presence of ambiguity within the observed entity is admitted, the second challenge is to attempt to gain understanding thereof, in its own terms, ideally going beyond the postulation of mystifying truisms, such as some innate mental propensity toward muddled, pre-logical thinking.

This book is an attempt to go beyond such facile explanations. Treating the anti-structural contents of Bushman belief and myth—and, to a lesser extent, ritual—as a given, I have first of all tried to convey its elements of ambiguity and variation, by presenting a detailed account of the fuzzy contours of Bushman religion. In this I focus primarily on the central figures of myth and of ritual, the trickster and the trance dancer, whose pervasive ontological ambiguity is underscored by their actions—respectively, transformation and trance—forever altering or transcending each figure's being.

Next, I have grounded the ambiguity of belief and myth within social reality, a field that is seen to be fluid and open as well. The two cultural domains are variations on the theme of ambiguity, religion playing the melody, society the accompanying harmonies, on many instruments. As far as the analysis of society is concerned I have drawn from ecological and sociological theories that emphasize individual agency and decision making, such as behavioral ecology, as recently summarized by Robert Kelly (1995), in a work that attempts to explain the diversity of hunter-gatherer lifeways. And, moving from economic patterns to social ones, I have made use of the processual approaches of

Frederic Barth—which are applied to Bushman social organization by Ornulf Gulbrandsen (1991)—and of Victor Turner (1969, 1974). Turner's ideas on symbolism have appeared in several places in my analysis of elements of religion, especially in the context of the transition phase of passage rites (1970a, 1970b).

The reason the Bushmen are not perplexed by the ambiguity of their beliefs, nor driven by any "need" to put order into their mythological and cosmological realm, is this prevailing contrapuntal relationship between religion and society. In form and substance their religion defines for them a perception of nature, the cosmos, and divinity that is in concert with a life of nomadism and hunting and gathering, of close attachment to nature, of individualism and equality, of loose social attachment to a small community to whom each is morally tied through bonds of reciprocity, and whose company each seeks in the interest of physical survival and aesthetic gratification. With its qualities of ambiguity and interpersonal and regional diversity that attach to all of its supernatural elements, and its tolerance toward and interest in the beliefs, stories, and songs of others, Bushman belief can be regarded as an ideology consistent with the mobility, openness, fluidity, flexibility, adaptability, and unpredictability of the foragers' life.

To the extent that it is a charter, in its formal attributes Bushman religion provides the ideological underpinnings for the foraging way. This is not meant in any narrow sense, as "symbolic labor" endorsing or replicating a specific subsistence task, although, in a way that element is there as well, inasmuch as the beliefs about the sympathy bond between human and animal, as well as the prominence of game antelopes in art and myth, could be seen as enhancing the subsistence task of hunting. Foraging, as argued earlier, is an ideology, a basic ethos, which interacts dialectically with social organization. Akin to Weber's "Protestant ethic," it is an ideological component of foraging work that shapes not only the processes of production but also the way the people relate to each other socially and how they give meaning to their life and world.

Finally, I return to the qualification I applied earlier when discussing the anti-structural nature of Bushman society and religion, as it provides further confirmation of the dialectical relationship between religion and society. In situations of political upheaval (which, as we saw in chapter 1, for the Bushmen, has always meant contact with encroaching, hostile settler groups), looseness and amorphousness of social and political organization gives way to tightness and structure. And as we saw in chapter 3, accompanying this alteration of social structure is a simplification and rationalization of belief, and differentiation and professionalization in the status and role of the trance dancer. The anti-structural forces of Bushman society and culture which had reigned freely before are now reined in, as the institutions and processes of society, and the beliefs and practices of religion are brought to bear on the crisis at hand. This process, of a fluid society assuming structure in a situation of change and upheaval, is the reverse of the more familiar lapse into disorder undergone by ordered societies in like times, pointing, once again, to the conceptual difficulty of drawing a categorical distinction between the society of foragers and non-foragers.

The ultimate conclusion to be drawn from such comparisons of the effects and the significance of anti-structure in simple and loose band societies such as the Bushmen's, and in complex and integrated state societies is, simply, that ambiguity, liminality, and communitas are elements of society and culture everywhere. While varied from society to society, as well as within a society and throughout its history, in the degree to which the forces of anti-structure and *a-nomos* are given free reign, such forces, as noted by Thomas Beidelman in the context of a study of the trickster figure of the East African Kaguru, are the "essence of social life." "We should remain suspicious," writes Beidelman,

> of approaches that allocate ambiguity, contradiction and conflict to the periphery of society. Contrary to being indications of change, dysfunction, or 'cognitive dissonance', these phenomena under scrutiny represent the essence of social life. (1993: 191)

The case at hand, a society and religion in which these anti-structural phenomena represent not the essence of social life but its substance, underscores the aptness of this observation. Both also underscore the need for anthropology to acknowledge ambiguity as an integral quality of society and culture, and to move the same from the discipline's epistemological periphery closer to the center.

Notes

Introduction

1. With the exception of a book and television series on contemporary Bushmen (titled *Testament to the Bushmen*), which van der Post presented late in his life, many years after writing his Bushman books (van der Post 1984).

2. Recently a retrospect was undertaken on the work by Richard Lee and the "Harvard group" of associated researchers working among the Ju/'hoansi (!Kung) of Botswana and Namibia, spanning a period of three decades (Lee, Biesele, and Hitchcock 1996). Of the eleven categories of ethnographic work the authors distinguished, six are in the area of cultural ecology (ecology, demography, genetics and medical research, ethno-archaeology, child rearing and infant development, aging and care giving, exchange networks). The remaining five categories are social organization; history, social change and contemporary problems; film studies; communicating knowledge to a wider public; and rituals, beliefs, music, and dance. Three of the four monographs cited in the latter category appeared in the 1990s (England 1992; Biesele 1993; Marshall, n.d.); the fourth is Richard Katz's study of !Kung trance dancing (1982).

3. As well as the late Harald Pager (1971, 1975, 1989), whose monumental work on the rock art of the Brandberg in Namibia is continued by Tilman Lenssen-Erz (1989, 1994) and his associates at the University of Cologne.

4. This excellent book—a sequel, a generation later, to Katz's 1982 monograph on Ju/'hoansi trance dancing and dancers—appeared after the completion of this book. Consequently, I have been unable to incorporate the information and insights provided by the new study into my own discussion.

5. In his essay on "the psychology of the trickster figure" in Radin's book on the Winnebago trickster (1972), Carl Gustav Jung draws the same parallel, between trickster and shaman, in a comparative religion context (see also Campbell 1959: 274, who views the trickster as a "super-shaman"). In his study of North Amerindian trickster, on the other hand, Mac Linscott Ricketts (1993) considers these parallels to reflect not a kindredness between trickster and shaman, but a "radical opposition," basically that between sacred and profane, the former embodied by the shaman, the latter by the trickster (who also parodies the shaman).

6. A recent volume, derived from the work of the "Trickster Myth Group" within the American Academy of Religion and assembled by William Hynes and William Doty (1993), reflects the growth of interest in and research on the trickster, since the figure's first conceptualization by Radin over forty years ago. Significantly, there is no reference anywhere in the book to any of the Bushman tricksters.

1. Bushman Society

1. The book was recently translated by Edwin Wilmsen and Klaus Keuthmann (Wilmsen 1997).

2. I should here note that I never came across this gloss on the name in my fieldwork among the Nharo; the latter employ that designation as their term of self-reference. They also are aware of the term //Aikwe, meaning the "home area people," as an alternative to Nharo.

3. And toned down somewhat, after a stinging criticism by Passarge's contemporary Gustav Fritsch, in a review of *Die Buschmänner der Kalahari* in the *Zeitschrift für Ethnologie* (vol. 38, 1906: 71–79). Fritsch, who had never traveled through Ghanzi and whose own book on the Bushmen (1872) was based on groups further to the south and west, saw Passarge's Bushman *Reich* as a figment. He deemed Bushmen incapable of such complex social formations, and accused Passarge of fabrication and his Nharo informant of prevarication. In his heated rebuttal, Passarge (1906: 411–15) suggested that ≠Dukuri's realm did not extend over all of the Ghanzi veld, and that there were other, fairly confined "state-like" associations in this vast land.

4. The term here used by the Nharo narrator was *//exa,* which today would be translated as "headman" rather than chief. However, it is also the term for "chief," of olden times. In the context of the narrative the term could have been used in both senses. Tsabu is presented as "the Chief of the Nharo," rather than as headman of a specific band; however, the sphere of his actions in the reported incident seems to be a band at a specified locale. Discussion of the story with its teller revealed that Tsabu was leader of more than one band.

5. For instance, one narrative tells of a farmer, who, in retaliation for the magistrate's murder, allegedly killed thirty Bushmen—by poisoning their wells—near the site of the murder. In turn, the Bushmen "put a curse" on the farmer and his house, which consisted of rendering his two daughters lifelong spinsters. It worked: neither of them ever married. This grim, Grimmian scenario led the distraught father to so desperate a measure as to write to none other than Adolf Hitler in the fatherland, pleading with the Führer to send two strapping German men to *Süd-West,* as husbands for his ill-fated daughters. (The fact that one of them bore the proud name of Brunhilde may be the reason Hitler responded, in the form of a sympathetic letter; however, no husband!)

6. See also Barnard 1980c for a comparative account of three diverse types of Nharo communities.

7. June Helm (1968), in describing the social organization of the Canadian subarctic Dene, differentiates in similar fashion among three types of groupings, the "task group," the "local band," and the "regional band." Looking at Western subarctic groups generally, the late Stanley Hunnisett found this tripartite scheme among a number of other groups (Hunnisett 1993: 97–99).

8. Eine Vergnügtheit herrschte hier, die an Tollheit grenzte. Das Lachen klang so herzerfrischend, dass man unwillkürlich mitlachen musste.

9. I present my account from descriptions I obtained from Nharo informants and an old Ghanzi farmer. I never myself observed this "game" as a full-fledged, complete performance. Instead, what I saw were truncated versions of it, such as abuse turning to laughter, as others gleefully surround two quarreling individuals.

2. Values and Individuals

1. For a critique of this paradigm see Paine 1974; Kapferer 1976; and Weiner 1996: 1064–65.

2. See Wilmsen 1989: 16–24 for a critical review of this paradigm.

3. Also see Woodburn 1982: 440–41, for examples from the Hadza and Mbuti, and Boehm 1993: 230–31, for widely cross-cultural examples.

4. A generation ago Goldenweiser noted a similar process in the conversation styles of "primitive folk" in general:

> When the executive speaks, words emerge from his lips not unlike mechanical tools which, having established contact with those spoken to, make them go through their paces. Such words are brief, as precise as possible, and thoroughly impersonal. . . . But we also speak to reveal content, inviting the one spoken to to participate in our ego. . . . Here personality comes to the fore, time flows easily, what counts is the enhancement of the moment through psychic interplay . . . such was the conversation of primitive folk . . . here folklore thrived and mythology took form. (Goldenweiser 1931: 108–109, cited by Diamond 1963: 92)

Hierarchy is another element of social structure contained in, or absent from, the speech patterns of speakers in these two types of society. Megan Biesele explores this element in the exchange of information among the Ju/'hoansi, in terms of her concept of "sapiential authority" (Biesele 1993: 43–44).

5. See Woodburn (1982: 448) for a similarly ambivalent, not to say dismal, report on the moral constitution of the Hadza. For an extreme, and, to some critics (Barth 1974; Heine 1985), a methodologically and ethnographically suspicious, version of the same see Turnbull's (1972) monograph on the Ik of Uganda.

6. While reported with the hyperbole characteristic for writers of that period, John Campbell's description of the child-rearing practices of the Bushmen he observed at the Orange River (in Griqualand) resonates with contemporary accounts:

> Their [children's] only employment is to fetch water for the family. Their parents only teach their children how to act in war, and counsel them to be faithful to each other. They very seldom chastise their children, but when they do, even the least of them will resist by throwing stones at their parents. (Campbell 1815: 315)

7. As is obvious from my discussion, I use this term quite differently from the usage of Carl Gustav Jung, in whose psychoanalytical scheme individuation was a key concept, which to him meant the psychic wholeness of an individual achieved, usually late in life, through reconciling within his personality its different contradictory elements (Georges and Jones 1995: 242).

8. This position continues as an axiomatic and somewhat ethnocentric and state-centric assumption in the writings of writers on complex societies, such as Louis Dumont, who, in *Homo Hierarchicus* (1972: 42) writes: "As opposed to modern society traditional societies . . . know nothing of equality and liberty as values . . . know nothing, in short, of the individual . . ." (cited in Béteille 1986: 122).

9. But note Sharp (1968: 160), who argues a case for the analytical utility of the role construct in foraging societies.

10. Also see Ingold's (1986: 130) insightful comment on this point.

11. Whether or not foraging bands (of the simple type, rather than complex one, à la the American Northwest coast) are instances of "society" is currently a subject of debate among anthropologists. I will deal with this question in the conclusion.

3. Bushman Religious Belief and Cosmology

1. An arguable point: Sigrid Schmidt, the leading contemporary expert on Nama mythology and folklore, while noting underlying "common themes" and a "clear picture of the world" in Nama myth and belief, also emphasizes its inherent qualities of contradiction, multifariousness, and denseness (1995: 152, 166–67).

2. For the same reason, the notions cf moon- and mantis-worship also entered the writings of nonanthropological writers of popular travel books or novels. Laurens van der Post's work is a prime example, especially his 1975 novella *A Mantis Carol* (Barnard 1988). Another is Erik Holm's 1965 book on Bushman religion, consisting of the three elements of "mythic, magic and mantic," with the last element—*Mantik*—at its center. An entire chapter is devoted to explaining the elevated status of the insect in terms of its biological peculiarities (also see Schmidt 1973: 103).

3. A similar process, of imperious Boer settlers plying their Bushman laborers with religious information that denigrates the Bushmen and, on a spiritual plane, "keeps them in their place," was brought to my attention by some of my Bushman informants. Its theme was not god but creation; the cosmological assertion being that the Bushmen were a caricature of the baboon, created as such by //Gāūwa (Guenther 1979b: 158, 1989: 50).

4. "Die . . . [Buren] . . . sagten uns, der Gott, der Schöpfer Himmels und der Erde, sei unser Gott nicht; sie [zeigten] uns eine Art Fliege, die die [Buren] Hottentotten-Gott nennen, und sagten: "Sehet da euren Gott!!" Wenn sie am Sonntag etwas beteten, und wir wollten einmal am Fenster horchen, dann jagten sie uns gleich weg; ihre Religion, sagten sie, wäre nicht für uns. So blieben wir dann gänzlich in Ungewissheit. . . . Man sagte uns, nach dem Tode sei alles aus mit uns, und da wir unter den [Buren] in diesem Lande so viel litten, so wünschten wir den Tod, um von allem Elend erlöst zu sein."

5. Among the Eastern Arctic Inuit the symbolic correspondence between male sexuality and hunting (as well as soapstone carving, another male activity) is explicit, according to Nelson Graburn (1976: 49). The same terms describing certain phases of the hunt are applied to symbolically equivalent sexual behavior (and to carving). Thus *qinirkpuk* describes "the right kind of game" and refers also to "a willing woman," and *pinasuakpuk,* "the animals; with active excitement, with shooting and the animal succumbs" refers also to "the woman; exciting activity, the woman succumbs, relief."

6. The archaic English word "venery" suggests that this symbolic equivalence, of hunting and sex, is an element also of Western thought. The two glosses in *The Concise Oxford Dictionary* for the term are "hunting" and "sexual indulgence."

7. An insightful comment on this point by the Namibian–South African researcher Helmut Reuning makes evident that this ambivalent, slightly disorientating and disjunctive attitude may be shared by Kalahari travelers other than the Bushmen. He states:

> Wenn man in der Kalahari zu Fuss unterwegs ist, kann es passieren, dass man unerwartet einen Springbok oder Gemsbok—im Drakensberg ein Eland—auf kurze Entfernung vor sich sieht. Man hat dann sofort das Gefühl: "Ich bin nicht allein hier—so wie ich ihn, kann

der Bock mich beobachten." Und, falls man 'für den Pott' schiessen *muss,* muss man sich zwingen umzudenken und das Tier also Ziel anzuvisieren. Mir ist es jedenfalls so zumute gewesen; und ich glaube nicht, dass jemand sich leicht darüber hinwegsetzen und einfach losballern kann . . . (When walking along on foot through the Kalahari, you may unexpectedly find yourself face to face with a springbok or gemsbok—or, in the Drakensberg, an eland—a short distance from yourself. Immediately one gets the sensation: "I'm not here alone—just as I am watching him, so the buck may be watching me." And, should one be *forced* to have to shoot "for the pot," one is forced to rethink and to sight the animal as target. At least, that's what I've felt; and I don't believe that anyone can easily bracket out any of this and simply start shooting. My translation). (pers. comm., 26 Jan. 1994)

8. Robert Tonkinson (1978) has examined the connection between orality and myth, and explained the fluid and variable character of the latter in terms of the former, among the Australian Mardudjara.

9. According to Biesele (1993: 33) the source of these types of power-extolling tales is west and central Africa, whence they spread to the less hierarchical Bantu-speaking societies of southern Africa. One might note that African art, in the same west and central African region (the heartland of African art), served the same hegemonic ends as oral literature (Fraser and Cole 1972; Szalay 1986; Fardon 1991).

4. The Bushman Trickster

1. It is once again difficult and fruitless to take a "two peoples" approach to this complex figure, that is, to differentiate in any clear-cut fashion between the Bushman trickster and his Khoe Khoe counterpart. The protagonist-divinity figures of the two Khoisan peoples are the same in form and substance, in some groups (such as the Nharo or Hei//om) sharing the same name and appearing in stories identical in narrative from and content. One significant difference, reflecting the key socio-economic distinction between the two Khoisan peoples (although not all of them, nor any specific Bushman or Khoe group at all times [Barnard 1992a: 259–60]), is that the Khoe trickster Heiseb is associated with cattle—indeed, was born a bull-calf (Schmidt 1993: 9, 1995: 200)—in a number of tales (although he is associated with veld foraging and roaming in an even greater number). In a close comparison of the Nama and Damara trickster figure Haiseb with those of the !Kung, /Xam, and Maluti Bushmen, Schmidt (1995: 226–33) concluded that, while different in details and emphases, the trickster figures and stories about them are basically cut of the same cloth. The convergence on this element of Khoisan religious culture is consistent with its general unity, leading one researcher refer to it as the "Khoisan religious tradition" (Guenther 1989: 33–36; see also Schapera 1930: 395–99).

2. See Guenther (1997c) for a discussion of the trickster elements of the Devil in medieval European folklore. Also see Russell (1984: 62–91) and Schmidt (1986a: 241, 1991, 1993: 15–54).

3. There is a body of folklore scholarship in North America, dating back to the previous century, that applies the same notion—of the trickster (Br'er Rabbit and John) as a black folk hero pitted against the white slave owner and master. See Roberts (1989).

4. It is not certain whether this character is actually another trickster figure. Appearing in only one /Xam narrative, and seemingly absent from the stories of all the

other Khoisan groups, the figure is not sufficiently defined to allow for any clear characterization. The mixture of antic mischief and custodial concern in the welfare of game animals is tricksteresque (see Guenther 1989: 160–61).

5. Mit welch grosser Heiterkeit werden die Geschichten vorgetragen, wie herzhaft lacht man über die Dummheiten! Nichts von diesem Lachen oder gar Lächerlichen gibt es im Volksglauben. Dort überwiegt Angst, Furcht, zum mindesten Ehrfurcht.

6. The merger of the //Gāūwa figure with "the evil being" and Satan appears to go back to early Christian–Khoisan contacts, having first been applied by missionaries to the Nama //Gaunab, and afterwards extended to other manifestations of the Khoisan trickster-god, such as that of the !Kung (Fourie 1928: 103; see also Schapera 1930: 191, 386–87; Lebzelter 1934: 57; Barnard 1992a: 252; and Schmidt 1995: 205).

7. Elsewhere (Guenther 1996c) I have presented a portrait of Gaishe as a "mission Bushman" which focuses on his endeavors to reconcile some of the contradictions between the new beliefs he has recently embraced and the old ones he feels compelled to eschew.

8. "Oft habe ich selbst mich gefragt: 'Wer ist Satan? Er kann nicht //Gaua sein, weil dieser ganz gut und uns wohlwollend ist. Ich glaube, jeder schlechte Bur ist ein Satan! Einen anderen Satan kennen wir !Khung von alther nicht.'"

9. See Gusinde (1966: 6–81) for a review of the earlier versions of the monotheistic interpretation of Bushman religion, as well as his own view. The latter, based on his own recent, and quite scanty, fieldwork, is a strong endorsement of Pater Schmidt's notion of primal monotheism. Another ethnographer to present Bushman data in support of Schmidt's theories was Viktor Lebzelter (1934: 54–56).

10. See Köhler (1978/79: 48) for a critical comment on Gusinde's fieldwork, which he faults for its brevity and for the ethnographer's inadequate language skills.

11. In order to facilitate the acquisition of literacy among Nharo schoolchildren—some of whom receive their early schooling in Nharo—the orthography developed in the Nharo literacy scheme at Dekar (of which the dictionary is one project) uses consonants to designate clicks, instead of the conventional linguistic designations.

12. A similar conflation, of Jesus Christ with the local trickster figure, has been noted in North America; for instance, among the Winnebago, the trickster Hare can become so merged with Jesus Christ in the minds of some Indians that they will state that they have no need for Jesus Christ, "as they already [have] Hare" (Henderson 1964: 104–105). Similarly, the conflation of Jesus with the Algonkian hare-trickster Nanabush—the former's "living equal"—is the theme of a recent (1993) play (entitled "If Jesus Met Nanbush") by the native Canadian playwright Alanis King-Odjig.

13. The full text of this highly and imaginatively syncretistic myth is found in Guenther (1989: 46).

14. Among the Bushmen of Ukuambi in northwestern Namibia, by contrast, flies—"big" ones—form the sole diet of the sprits of the departed in the "good place," the heavenly mansion owned and presided over by the divinity !Khuwa (Lebzelter 1934: 13).

15. See Gusinde (1966: 79–80) for a primal monotheist's rebuttal of Baumann's critique of Pater Schmidt.

16. The key work that conceptualized this figure in the study of world mythology and comparative religion, Paul Radin's *The Trickster,* was not published until 1956.

17. For instance, Alan Barnard, in a structuralist analysis of the Khoe Khoe and Nharo beings, differentiates these along the axes trickster–god and good–evil (1992a: 256–60).

5. Stories, Storytelling, and Story Gathering

1. In my discussion of this tale I will draw extensively on Sigrid Schmidt's comprehensive, two-volume *Catalogue of Khoisan Folktales of Southern Africa* (1989), a vast compendium of texts deriving from virtually every known Khoi and San group, neatly catalogued and cross-referenced, allowing for comparative analysis of genres, types, motifs, versions, and variants. In my discussion of the myth I have also included some versions not found in the catalog, mostly because they surfaced after its publication.

2. As one might expect in a culture area consisting of regionally isolated and linguistically disparate peoples, there are also tale types of more restricted circulation, such as the /Xam tales about Dawn's Heart and the rain "divinity" !Khwa, or the !Kung Elephant Girl stories.

3. The numbers refer to the cataloging system used by Bleek and Lloyd, as well as the Jagger Library, University of Cape Town, that owns the collection.

4. Discussions among folklorists about the distinctions between text, texture, and context (especially in a performance sense, wherein the context is essentially the "performance event"), as well as about the relative analytical merits of a textual as against a contextual approach, or a plea for treating the two as complementary, have gone on over the past three decades, and have resulted in an extensive literature. Key works, or summary position papers, are Dundes (1980), Ben-Amos (1972, 1992), Murphy (1978), Toelken (1979: 8–9, chap. 2), Bauman (1984, 1992), Georges and Jones (1995).

5. In recently rereading Paul Radin's book on the trickster, I noted that he, too, had met two storytellers (the brothers Sam and Jasper Blowsnake) whose different temperaments left their imprint on the text and texture of the stories they told (Radin 1972: 121–24). Even more interesting is the coincidence that those differences in personality and narrative style correspond, respectively, to those displayed by !Khuma//ka and Gaise. See Georges and Jones (1995: 269–88) for a general discussion of the biographical approach to the study of folklore.

6. The recent work of the French ethnomusicologist Emmanuelle Olivier (1997), which treats Ju/'hoan music as a semiotic system, traces both the structural rules underlying that music and the sequence of rules performers have to learn informally (in part through stories).

7. Godelier discusses in particular the Mbuti crisis ritual, the *molimo* rite. Later, in my discussion of the Bushman curing rite, the trance dance, I will examine the applicability of Godelier's approach to the Bushman case. For a similar recent investigation of Pygmy hunting ritual, that focuses on the ritual role of women in the failed hunt, see McCreedy (1994); for a critical evaluation of the Godelier-inspired notion of ritual and belief as mechanisms that intensify processes of production, see Myers (1988: 266–69).

8. Lewis-Williams's analysis of the Bushman trance dance echoes Godelier's analysis of the Mbuti *molimo* ceremony (1977: 9–10, 51–61), which is seen, in the final analysis, as "an intensification of the processes of production" (Morris 1987: 27). Inasmuch as this rite addresses as one of its key existential concerns the failed hunt, its analytical treatment along cultural materialist lines might hold more promise than in the Bushman context, wherein this is not a key concern.

9. This point can be argued. While I would not question this interpretation of the myth in a Nama and Dama context, its applicability in quite those terms to other

Khoisan mythological traditions is somewhat questionable. There (for example, the mythologies of the /Xam, Nharo, or !Kung), the bearing of the myth of the Moon and Hare on the reversal of the First to the Second Order is, at best, oblique. There are other tales, such as the "Anteater's Laws" or the Branding of the Animals by the early people, that deal directly with the reversal theme.

6. Myth and Gender

1. For the full text of one of the shorter versions see Bleek and Lloyd (1911: 199–295) and Guenther (1989: 83–85); for a composite summary see Hewitt (1986: 116–17).

7. Initiation Rites

1. For the !Kung see Lee (1979: 238–40, 365–66), Biesele (1993: 134–36), Lewis-Williams and Biesele (1978); for the !Kõ see Heinz (1975c) and Heinz and Lee (1978: 94–97, 100–20); for the /Xam see Lewis-Williams (1981: 41–68), Lewis-Williams and Biesele (1978), Hewitt (1986: 75–88, 279–86), Guenther (1989: 105–11); for the Nharo see Bleek (1928: 23–25), Lebzelter (1934: 69–71), Barnard (1980a), Guenther (1986a: 274–81); for the G/wi see Silberbauer (1963, 1965: 83–89). For general comparative summaries see Schapera (1930: 118–26) and Barnard (1992a: 59–61, 71–72, 112–113, 130–32, 154–55, 215–16).

2. For this reason the recent exposure of this "exposed" ritual dance by an ethnographic filmmaker—Paul Myburgh, in *The People of the Great Sandface*—raises some justified concern about professionalism and ethical responsibility. See Gordon (1990) and Guenther (1990a).

8. The Trance Curing Dance

1. For ethnographic accounts of the !Kung trance dance see Lebzelter 1934: 47–49; Gusinde 1966: 135; Marshall 1969; Katz 1976, 1982; Katz, Biesele, and St. Denis 1997; Lee 1967, 1968, 1993: 115–19; Biesele 1993: 74–81, 93–98; on the Nharo see Guenther 1975, 1976b, 1986a: 253–74; Barnard 1979, 1992a: 153–54; on the /Xam see Lewis-Williams 1981, 1982, 1983; Lewis-Williams and Dowson 1989; Dowson and Lewis-Williams 1994; Hewitt 1986: 292–94; on the G/wi see Silberbauer 1965: 97–101, 1981: 175–77; Eibl-Eibesfeldt 1980; on the !Kõ see Eibl-Eibesfeldt 1974; Heinz 1975b.

2. In her study of the Ghost Dance revitalization movement of some of the Plains and Great Basin Indians of North America—which, like the Bushman curing rite, contained the element of altered states—Alice Kehoe (1989: 101) likewise attributes the inducement of the dancers' trance experience to a variety of physiological factors, rather than mind-altering drugs, which were absent from the ritual repertoire of the dancers. Citing Rybak (1977), Kehoe describes trance-inducing factors that are similar in kind to those at work among Bushman trance dancers: alternating the speed and volume of speech rhythms, with attendant change in the rapidity of heart beats; alternating high and low voice pitches, inducing subconscious mood changes in the listeners; hypnotic gestures by speakers or singers; hyperventilation and mental disassociation through frenzied dancing.

3. "Auf langgezogene, stöhnende Schreie, die in ein Tremolo übergehen, folgen spitze, kurze Schreie, die von starken Konvulsionen des Körpers begleitet sind. . . ."

4. Richard Lee provides a brief account of the Ju/'hoan troupe from /Xai/xai, the /Gwihaba dancers, in the Dobe region (1993: 177–81).

5. The situation here described applies to the late 1960s, my most extensive fieldwork period. Since then, the political actions of the farm Bushmen of Ghanzi, who represent a new, more educated and politically aware generation, have become more direct and more "rational." Some of the modern developments are mentioned in chapter 1. Katz, Biesele, and St. Denis (1997) report a similar process of politicization among the Ju/'hoan trance dancers at /Kae/Kae in their study of the same in 1989. The dancers transferred their mystical powers and their knowledge of the world and the dangers beyond, to the contemporary political and economic arena. A number of them were effective and articulate spokespersons for the community on political issues.

9. Missionaries and Bushmen

1. The historical survey I offer in this chapter is no more than a preliminary step, as it is derived not from primary sources but from published ones. Many of these are by missionaries, and contain, necessarily, biases of different sorts. Three good recent studies by an ethnohistorian, an historian, and an anthropologist, on the situation in the Cape, the northern Cape, and Namibia, are—respectively—Szalay (1983: 215–34), Penn (1991: 11–21), and Gordon (1992: 64–65, 143–46).

2. A brief word about recent or contemporary missionary activities in other regions: in Ghanzi (and, to my knowledge, Botswana) Dekar is the only mission specifically directed to Bushmen. Other churches, such as the Rhenish (Lutheran) church of Namibia and the London Missionary Society (LMS), send missionaries or evangelists to or through Ghanzi to preach primarily to Coloured or black Africans. In the process they might also contact Bushmen, some of whom are attached economically or through marriage to the other groups (Guenther 1979a: 97–98). In Namibia the prime targets for Bushman mission work, all by missionaries from one or another denomination of the South African Dutch Reformed Church, are the ≠Au//eisi of Gobabis District, and the Ju/'hoansi and Hei//om, at Tshum!kwi (Tsumkwe) and Tsumeb (Budack 1980; Volkman 1982: 9, 46–49; Gordon 1992: 177–79), respectively. In the 1960s the Catholic mission order Les petits frères de Jésus worked for some years among the !Kung of northern Namibia and northeastern Angola (Budack ibid.) There is also one Dutch Reformed mission enterprise operating in South Africa, at the temporary tent city of Schmidtsdrift, where some four thousand Angolan !Kung and Namibian Khoe have been patriated. They are the soldiers, or former soldiers, of the South African army, and their families, who took the option given them to follow the departing South African military to South Africa (Le Roux 1995a).

3. It should be recognized that the distinction between "Bushman" and "Hottentot" (Khoekhoe) was often not clearly drawn by the early writers (see Marks 1972; Szalay 1983: 68–69; Guenther 1980: 13–31, 1986a; Barnard 1992a: 7–12). Thus, some of the mission stations identified in the early writings as "Bushman" may, in fact, have been occupied by Bushman only partially, along with such other Khoisan or Khoisanoid groups as the Khoekhoe, Griqua, or Korana.

4. For instance, Casalis and Ellenberger among the Sotho of Basutoland (Casalis

1889: 62; How 1962); Hepburn among the Tswana of Bechuanaland (Hepburn 1895: 76–78, 168–69); Shaw in Little Namaqualand among the Nama (Shaw 1841; Richter 1922: 281); Vedder among the Nama and Herero of South West Africa (Vedder 1922; Vedder and Unterkeller n.d.; Olpp 1922).

5. As reported by Robert Gordon (1992: 64, 65, 71), the same complaint was made by German settlers in colonial South West Africa (for instance at Kremer's mission station Gaub, near Grootfontein).

6. For further historical studies of the plight of the Cape Bushmen in colonial times see Hahn 1870; Stow 1905; Ellenberger 1963; Wright 1971; Marks 1972; Szalay 1983; Penn 1996.

7. ". . . keine Vorstellung von einem höheren Wesen, und ein kleines kriechendes Insekt, 'Mantis' genannt, das sie zu töten sich fürchteten, und es um Verleihung zeitlicher Bedürfnisse anriefen, war fast der einzige Gegenstand ihrer abergläubischen Verehrung."

8. For example, by MacKenzie (1871: 511–12) and Livingstone (cited in Maler-Sieber 1978: 24).

9. The opposite undertaking, of using a Bushman language to communicate the Christian message to Bushmen, is reported by Gordon (1992: 178), with respect to a South African Afrikaner missionary working among Ju/'hoansi at Tsumkwe in Namibia. The missionary has embarked on an ambitious project to translate the Bible from Afrikaans to !Kung, which strikes Gordon as "one of the most eccentric examples of idealism," in view of "the small number of Ju/'hwasi readers, and the fact that all schooling was in Afrikaans."

10. A somewhat extreme version of what I saw at /Oaxa is reported by Toby Volkman for Tsuhm!kwi (1982: 9; also see Gordon 1992: 178–79 and p.64 for another expression of the same issue). The Dutch Reformed Mission at Tshum!kwi, founded in 1961, failed for the first ten years to attract any !Kung converts. In the early 1970s some Bushmen came to the church and this stirring of interest culminated, in 1973, in a "mass conversion" of two hundred. This apparent dramatic turnabout was based on the expectation, on the part of the Bushmen, that upon conversion each of them would be given a white shirt. This misunderstanding was derived from an allegorical ritual drama the Dutch Reformed Church missionary had performed that involved washing and untying a dirty and blindfolded man, bound hand and foot, and dressing him with a white shirt, to illustrate the transformative power of Christianity (Volkman 1982: 9). The expectations this performance had raised not being met, attendance at church plummeted, standing, a year later, at twelve church members. The year following church services were suspended. The mission reopened in 1978; however, no Bushmen were counted among its members in 1980.

11. When conducting a survey of ten Afrikaner- or German-owned farms in Gobabis District in 1994, I heard much the same sentiments expressed toward the missionary working among the farm Bushmen there. In fact, while I was there one farmer had forbidden the missionary access to his farm, blaming him for problems of labor unrest among his workers.

Conclusion

1. This view was not held by all of the early German ethnohistorical writers. Instead of ascribing resilience and acculturational "readiness," Rüdiger Schott (1955) presented

the Bushmen of the colonial Cape as resisting (oftentimes with force) any of the incoming settlers, because of a deep-seated economic and social structural incompatibility between the foraging way of life and agropastoralism.

2. ". . . den verknäuelten Komplex des Glaubenssystems der 'yellow Peoples' in Süd-Afrika aufzulockern und in seiner historischen Entwicklung geradlinig zu zeichnen."

3. See Dowson and Lewis-Williams (1994) for the most recent update on the controversy. It includes critical evaluations of the trance hypothesis (including one by myself; see also Guenther 1984). For other discussions of Lewis-Williams and his followers' interpretive paradigm see Lewis-Williams 1981, 1982, 1983, 1988; Lewis-Williams and Dowson 1988, 1989; Solomon 1992, 1994; Jolly 1996).

4. This objection, not surprisingly, is the reverse of Barnard's criticism of my own view (as argued in my 1979a paper): namely, overemphasis of fluidity (Barnard 1992a: 262).

References Cited

Almeida, A. de. 1965. *Bushman and Other Non-Bantu Peoples of Angola*. Johannesburg: Witwatersrand University Press.
Anderson, R. L. 1990. *Calliope's Sisters: A Comparative Study of Philosophies of Art*. Englewood Cliffs: Prentice Hall.
Andersson, C. 1856. *Lake Ngami*. London: Hurst and Blackett.
———. 1875. *Notes and Travels in South Africa*. London: Hurst and Blackett.
Anthing, L. 1863. "Cape Parliamentary Papers: Report A39." Cape Town: Government House.
Apte, M. L. 1985. *Humour and Laughter: An Anthropological Approach*. Ithaca: Cornell University Press.
Arcand, B. 1981. "The Negritos and the Penan will never be Cuiva." *Folk* 23:37–43.
———. 1988. "Il n'ya jamais eu de société de chasseurs-cueilleurs." *Anthropologie et Sociétés* 12: 39–58.
Arnold, R. 1987. *Märchen aus Namibia*. Hanau: Verlag Müller and Kiepenheimer.
Atkinson, J. 1992. "Shamanisms Today." *Annual Reviews of Anthropology* 21:307–37.
Babcock-Abrahams, B., ed. 1978. *The Reversible World: Symbolic Inversion in Art and Society*. Ithaca: Cornell University Press.
Baines, T. 1864. *Explorations in South-West Africa*. London: Longman, Roberts, and Green.
Bank, A., ed. 1998. *The Proceedings of the Khoisan Identities and Cultural Heritage Conference Organized by the Institute for Historical Research University of the Western Cape, South African Museum, Cape Town, 12–16 July 1997*. Cape Town: Info-Source.
Barclay, H. 1993. "Comment." On Boehm, pp. 240–41.
Barnard, A. 1978. "Universal Systems of Kin Categorization." *African Studies* 37:67–81.
———. 1979. "Nharo Bushman Medicine and Medicine Men." *Africa* 49:68–80.
———. 1980a. "Sex Roles among the Nharo Bushmen of Botswana." *Africa* 50:115–24.
———. 1980b. "Kinship and Social Organization in Nharo Cosmology." Paper presented at the Second International Conference on Hunting and Gathering Societies (CHAGS 2), Laval University, Quebec.
———. 1980c. "Basarwa Settlement Patterns in the Ghanzi Ranching Area." *Botswana Notes and Records* 12:137–50.
———. 1983. "Contemporary Hunter-Gatherers: Current Theoretical Issues in Ecology and Social Organization." *Annual Reviews of Anthropology* 12:193–214.
———. 1985. "A Nharo Word List, With Notes on Grammar." Occasional Papers no. 2. Durban: Department of African Studies, University of Natal.

———. 1988. "Structure and Fluidity in Khoisan Religious belief." *Journal of Religion in Africa* 18:216–36.

———. 1989. "The Lost World of Laurens van der Post?" *Current Anthropology* 30:104–14.

———. 1992a. *Hunters and Herders of Southern Africa.* Cambridge: Cambridge University Press.

———. 1992b. "The Kalahari Debate: A Bibliographical Essay." Occasional Papers no. 35. Edinburgh: Centre for African Studies.

———. 1993. "Primitive Communism and Mutual Aid Kropotkin Visits the Bushmen." In C. M. Hann, ed. *Socialism.* London: Routledge, pp. 27–42.

Barrow, J. 1801. *An Account of Travels into the Interior of Southern Africa 1797 and 1798.* London: Stratham.

Barry, H., I. Child, and M. K. Bacon. 1959. "The Relation of Child Training to Subsistence Ecology." *American Anthropologist* 55:481–98.

Barth, F. 1966. "Models of Social Organization." Occasional Papers no. 23. London: Royal Anthropological Institute.

———. 1974. "On Responsibility and Humanity: Calling a Colleague to Account." *Current Anthropology* 15:99–103.

Bascom, W. R. 1965. "The Forms of Folklore: Prose Narrative." *Journal of American Folklore* 78:12–31.

Bauman, R. 1984. *Verbal Art as Performance.* 2nd. ed. Prospect Heights: Waveland Press.

———. 1992. "Folklore." In R. Bauman, ed. *Folklore, Cultural Performances, and Popular Entertainments.* Oxford University Press, pp. 29–40.

Baumann, H. 1936. *Schöpfung und Urzeit im Mythus der afrikanischen Völker.* Berlin: Dietrich Reimer Verlag.

Beidelman, T. O. 1993. "The Moral Imagination of the Kaguru: Some Thoughts on Tricksters, Translation and Comparartive Analysis." In Hynes and Doty, pp. 174–92. [1908]

Ben-Amos, D. 1972. "Toward a Definition of Folklore in Context." In A. Paredes and R. Bauman, eds. *Toward New Perspectives in Folklore.* Austin: The University of Texas Press, pp. 3–15.

———. 1992. "Folktale." In R. Bauman, ed. *Folklore, Cultural Performances, and Popular Entertainments.* Oxford University Press, pp. 101–08.

Bender, B. and B. Morris 1988. "Twenty Years of History, Evolution and Social Change in Hunter-Gatherer Studies." In Ingold, Riches, and Woodburn, pp. 4–14.

Béteille, A. 1986. "Individualism and Equality." *Current Anthropology* 27:121–34.

Biesele, M. 1975a. "Folklore and Ritual of !Kung Hunter-Gatherers." 2 vols. Ph.D. diss., Harvard University.

———. 1975b. "Song Texts by the Master of Tricks: Kalahari San Thumb Piano Music." *Botswana Notes and Records* 7:171–88.

———. 1976. "Aspects of !Kung Folklore." In Lee and DeVore, *Kalahari Hunter-Gatherers*, pp. 302–24.

———. 1978. "Religion and Folklore." In Tobias, pp. 162–72.

———. 1993. *Women Like Meat: The Folklore and Foraging Ideology of the Kalahari Ju/'hoansi*. Johannesburg, Bloomington: Witwatersrand University Press/Indiana University Press.

Biesele, M., R. Gordon, and R. B. Lee, eds. 1986. *The Past and Future of !Kung Ethnography: Critical Reflections and Symbolic Perspectives. Essays in Honour of Lorna Marshall.* (QKF 4). Hamburg: Helmut Buske Verlag.

Biesele, M., M. Guenther, R. Hitchcock, R. B. Lee, and J. MacGregor. 1989. "Hunters, Clients and Squatters: The Contemporary Socio-Economic Status of Botswana Basarwa." *African Studies Monographs* 9:109–51.

Bird-David, N. 1988. "Hunter and Gatherers and Other People—A Re-examination." In Ingold, Riches, and Woodburn, pp. 17–30.

———. 1992a. "Beyond 'the Hunting and Gathering Mode of Subsistence': Observations on the Nyaka and Other Modern Hunter-Gatherers." *Man*, n.s., 27:19–44.

———. 1992b. "Beyond the 'Original Affluent Society': A Culturalist Reformulation." *Current Anthropology* 33:25–48.

Birdwhistle, N. A. 1966. *William Threlfall.* London: Oliphants.

Birket-Smith, K. 1959. *The Eskimos.* London: Methuen.

Bleek, D. 1923. *The Mantis and his Friends.* Cape Town: T. Maskew Miller.

———. 1927. "Buschmänner von Angola." *Archiv für Anthropologie* 21:47–57.

———. 1928. *The Naron: A Bushman Tribe of the Central Kalahari.* Cambridge: Cambridge University Press.

———., ed. 1931–1936. "Customs and Beliefs of the /Xam Bushmen (from Materials Collected by Dr. W. H. I. Bleek and Miss L. C. Lloyd between 1870 and 1880), Parts I-VII." *Bantu Studies* 5:167–79; 6:47–63, 233–49, 323–42; 7:297–312, 375–92; 9:1–47; 10:131–62.

———. 1936. "Special Speech of Animals and Moon Used by the /Xam Bushmen." *Bantu Studies* 10:163–99.

Bleek, W. H. I. 1864. *Reynard the Fox in South Africa.* London: Trübener and Co.

———. 1875. *A Brief Account of Bushman Folklore and Other Texts.* London: Trübner and Brockhaus.

———. 1911. "Dr. Bleek's Report, etc., Regarding Photographs Sent to England by Government December 23, 1871. Notes to Accompany the Photographs." In Bleek and Lloyd, pp. 434–39.

Bleek, W. and L. Lloyd. 1911. *Specimens of Bushman Folklore.* London: George Allen and Co. Ltd.

Blurton-Jones, N. and M. Konner. 1976. "!Kung Knowledge of Animal Behavior." In Lee and DeVore, *Kalahari Hunter-Gatherers*, pp. 325–48.

Blurton-Jones, N., K. Hawkes, and P. Draper. 1994. "Differences between Hadza and !Kung Children's Work: Affluence or Practical Reason?" In Burch and Ellanna, pp. 169–88.

Boehm, C. 1993. "Egalitarian Behaviour and Reverse Dominance Hierarchy." *Current Anthropology* 34:227–54.

Brearley, J. 1988. "Music and Musicians of the Kalahari." *Botswana Notes and Records* 20:77–90.

Bredekamp, H. 1994. "The San, Social identity and Historical Consciousness in Post-Apartheid South Africa: A View from the Cape." Paper presented at the conference on People, Politics and Power: The Politics of Representing the Representing the Bushmen of Southern Africa, Johannesburg, 4–7 August.

Briggs, J. 1982. "Living Dangerously: The Contradictory Foundations of Value in Canadian Inuit Society." In Leacock and Lee, pp. 109–32.

Budack, K. 1980. "Die Völker Südwestafrikas." #18 "Vom Völkerhass zur Nächstenliebe." 26 September. #23 "Der Tod des Magistrats von Gobabis im Kampf mit 'Buschleuten.'" 10 December. *Allgemeine Zeitung* [Windhoek]

Burch, E. S. 1994. "The Future of Hunter-Gatherer Research." In Burch and Ellanna, pp. 441–55.

Burch, E. S. and L. J. Ellanna, eds. 1994. *Key Issues in Hunter-Gatherer Research.* Oxford: Berg.

Burkhardt, E. E. 1877. *Die evangelische Mission unter den Völkerstämmen Südafrikas.* Bielefeld and Leipzig: Velhagen and Klassing.

Campbell, John. 1822. *Travels in South Africa.* London: Black and Berry.

———. 1837. *A Journey to Lattakoo.* London: The Religious Tract Society.

Campbell, Joseph. 1959. *The Masks of God: Primitive Mythology.* New York: Viking.

Casalis, E. 1889. *My Life in Basutoland.* London: The Religious Tract Society.

Cashdan, E. 1980. "Egalitarianism among Hunter-Gatherers." *American Anthropologist* 82:116–20.

———. 1986. "Hunter-Gatherers of the Northern Kalahari." In R. Vossen and K. Keuthmann, eds. *Contemporary Studies in Khoisan,* vol. 1. (QKF 5). Hamburg: Helmut Buske Verlag, pp. 145–80.

Chapman, J. 1868. *Travels in the Interior of South Africa.* 2 vols. London: Bell and Daldy.

———. 1971. *Travels in the Interior of South Africa, 1849–1863.* 2 vols. Ed. E. Tabler. Cape Town: Balkema.

Childers, G. W. 1976. "Report on the Survey/Investigation of the Ghanzi Farm Basarwa Situation." Gaborone: Government Printer.

Clastres, P. 1977. *Society against the State.* New York: Urizen Books.

Collins, Colonel. 1809. "Journal of a Tour to the North-Eastern Boundary of the Orange River and the Storm Mountain by Col. Collins in 1809." In D. Moodie, ed. *The Record,* Part V:1–38. Cape Town: National Library.

Comaroff, J. and J. Comaroff. 1993. *Of Revelation and Revolution. Christianity, Colonialism and Consciousness in South Africa*, vol. 1. Chicago: University of Chicago Press.

Cormier, H. 1977. *The Humour of Jesus.* New York: Alba House.

Cox, H. 1970. *The Feast of Fools: A Theological Essay on Festivity and Fantasy.* New York: Harper and Row.

Diamond, S. 1963. "The Search for the Primitive." In I. Galdston, ed. *Man's Image in Medicine and Anthropology.* Monograph 4, Institute of Social and Historical Medicine. New York: International University Press, Inc., pp. 62–115.

———. 1972. "Introductory Essay: Job and the Trickster." In P. Radin. *The Trickster.* New York: Schocken Books, pp. xi-xxv.

———. 1974. *In Search of the Primitive: A Critique of Civilization.* New Brunswick, New Jersey: Transaction Books.

Dickens, P. 1994. *English–Ju/'hoan /Ju'hoan–English Dictionary.* (QKF 8). Cologne: Rüdiger Köppe Verlag.

Dickie-Clark, H. F. 1966. *The Marginal Situation.* London: Routledge and Kegan Paul.

Dornan, S. S. 1917. "The Tati Bushmen (Masarwas) and their Language." *Journal of the Royal Anthropological Institute* 47:37–112.

———. 1925. *Pygmies and Bushmen of the Kalahari.* London: Seeley, Service and Co.

Doty, W. G. 1993. "A Life-Time of Trouble-Making: Hermes as Trickster." In *Mythical Trickster Figures.* Tuscaloosa: The University of Alabama Press, pp. 46–65.

Doty, W. G. and W. J. Hynes. 1993. "Historical Overview of Theoretical Issues: The Problem of the Trickster." In Hynes and Doty, pp. 13–32.

Dowson, T. and D. Lewis-Williams 1994. *Contested Images.* Johannesburg: Witwatersrand University Press.

Draper, P. 1975. "!Kung Women: Contrasts in Sexual Egalitarianism in the Foraging and Sedentary Contexts." In R. Reiter, ed. *Toward an Anthropology of Women.* New York: Monthly Review Press, pp. 77–109.

———. 1976. "Social and Economic Constraints on Child Life among the !Kung." In Lee and DeVore, *Kalahari Hunter-Gatherers,* pp. 199–217.

Dumont, L. 1972. *Homo Hierarchicus.* London: Paladine.

Dundes, A. 1980. "Texture, Text and Context." In A. Dundes, *Interpreting Folklore.* Bloomington: Indiana University Press, pp. 20–32.

Dunn, E. J. 1978. "Through Bushmanland." In A. M. Lewin Robinson, ed. *Selected Articles from the Cape Monthly Magazine (New Series 1870–76).* Cape Town: Van Riebeck Society. [1872, 1873]

Dunning, R. W. 1959. "Ethnic Relations and the Marginal Man." *Human Organization* 18:117–22.

Du Plessis, J. 1909. "The Determination of Unoccupied and Partially Occupied Territory." *Report of the Proceedings of the Second General Missionary Conference.* Bloemfontein, July 1909. Cape Town: Townshend, pp. 31–71.

———. 1911. *A History of Christian Missions in South Africa.* London: Longman, Green and Co.

———. 1912. *The Evangel in South Africa.* Cape Town: Cape Times.

Durkheim, E. 1964. *The Division of Labour in Society.* Trans. G. Simpson. New York: The Free Press. [1893]

Dutch Reformed Church. 1912. *Missions of the Dutch Reformed Church of South Africa.* Stellenbosch: Office of the General Mission Secretary.

Eibl-Eibesfeldt, I. 1973. "!Ko-Buschleute (Kalahari)—Trancetanz." *Homo* 24:245–52.

———. 1980. "G/wi-Buschleute (Kalhari)—Krankenheilung und Trance." *Homo* 31: 67–78.

Ellenberger, V. 1963. *La fin tragique des Bushmen.* Paris: Amiot, Dumont.

Elphick, R. 1977. *Kraal and Castle: Khoikhoi and the Founding of White South Africa.* New Haven: Yale University Press.

Endicott, K. 1979. *Batek Negrito Religion.* Oxford: Oxford University Press.

England, N. 1967. "Bushman Counterpoint." *Journal of the International Folk Music Council* 19:58–66.

———. 1968. "Music among the Zu/'wa-si of South West Africa and Botswana." Ph.D diss., Harvard University. (Published as *Music among the Ju/'hoansi and Related Peoples of Namibia, Botswana and Angola.* New York: Garland Publishing, 1992.)

Estermann, C. 1976. *The Ethnography of Southwestern Angola, Volume I: The Non-Bantu Peoples; the Ambo Ethnic Group.* Ed. G. D. Gibson. New York: Africana Publishing Company. [1956]

Evans-Pritchard, E. E. 1937. *Witchcraft, Oracles, and Magic among the Azande.* Oxford: Clarendon Press.

Fardon, R. 1991. *Between God, the Dead and the Wild: Chamba Interpretations of Ritual and Religion.* Edinburgh: Edinburgh University Press.

Firth, R. 1964. "Religious Belief and Personal Adjustment." In *Essays on Social Organization*. London: Athlone Press, pp. 257–93.

Fourie, L. 1926. "Preliminary Notes on Certain Customs of the Hei//om Bushmen." *Journal of the South West African Scientific Society* 1:49–63.

———. 1928. "The Bushmen of South West Africa." In H. P. Smit, ed. *The Native Tribes of South West Africa*. Cape Town: Cape Times, pp. 79–105.

Fraser, D. and H. M. Cole. 1972. *African Art and Leadership*. Madison: University of Wisconsin Press.

Fritsch, G. 1872. *Die Eingeborenen Südafrika's ethnographisch und anatomisch beschrieben*. Breslau: Ferdinand Hirt.

———. 1906. "Die Buschmänner der Kalahari von S. Passarge." *Zeitschrift für Ethnologie* 38 (1906): 71–79.

Gardner, P. 1991. "Foragers' Pursuit of Individual Autonomy." *Current Anthropology* 31:543–72.

Geertz, C. 1966. "Religion as a Cultural System." In M. Banton, ed. *Anthropological Approaches to the Study of Religion*. (A.S.A. Monograph 3). London: Tavistock Publications, pp. 1–46.

Georges, R. A. and M. O. Jones. 1995. *Folkloristics: An Introduction*. Bloomington: Indiana University Press.

Gluckman, M. 1963. *Custom and Conflict in Africa*. Oxford: Basil Blackwell.

Gmelch, S. 1986. "Groups that Don't Want in: Gypsies and Other Artisan, Trader, and Entertainer Minorities." *Annual Reviews of Anthropology* 15:307–30.

Godelier, M. 1977. *Perspectives in Marxist Anthropology*. Cambridge: Cambridge University Press.

Goldenweiser, A. 1931. *Robots of God*. New York: Knopf.

Goody, J. 1992. "Oral Culture." In R. Baumann, ed. *Folklore, Cultural Performance and Popular Entertainments*. Oxford: Oxford University Press, pp. 12–20.

Gordon, R. 1990. Review of "People of the Great Sandface," by Paul Myburgh. *CVA Review* (Commission on Visual Anthropology) (fall): 30–34.

———. 1992. *The Bushman Myth: The Making of a Namibian Underclass*. Boulder: Westview Press.

Graburn, N. 1976. "Eskimo Art." In N. Graburn, ed. *Ethnic and Tourist Art*. Berkeley: University of California Press, pp. 39–55.

Guenther, M. 1973. "Farm Bushmen and Mission Bushmen: Social Change in a Setting of Pluralism and Conflict of the San of the Ghanzi District, Republic of Botswana." Ph.D. diss., University of Toronto.

———. 1975. "The Trance Dancer as an Agent of Social Change among the Farm Bushmen of the Ghanzi District." *Botswana Notes and Records* 7:161–66.

———. 1976a. "From Hunters to Squatters: Social and Cultural Change among the Ghanzi Farm Bushmen." In Lee and DeVore, *Kalahari Hunter-Gatherers*, pp. 120–33.

———. 1976b. "The San Trance Dance: Ritual and Revitalization among the Farm Bushmen of the Ghanzi District, Republic of Botswana." *Journal of the South West African Scientific Society* 30:45–5

———. 1977a. "Bushman Hunters as Farm Labourers." *Canadian Journal of African Studies* 11:195–203.

———. 1977b. "The Mission as 'Sample Community': A Contemporary Case from Botswana." *Missiology* 5:457–65.

———. 1979a. "Bushman Religion and the (Non)Sense of Anthropological Theory of Religion." *Sociologus* 29:102–32.

———. 1979b. *The Farm Bushmen of the Ghanzi District, Botswana.* Stuttgart: Hochschul Verlag.

———. 1980. "From 'Brutal Savages' to 'Harmless People': Notes on the Changing Western Image of the Bushmen." *Paideuma* 26:123–40.

———. 1981. "Bushman and Hunter-Gatherer Territoriality." *Zeitschrift für Ethnologie* 106:109–20.

———. 1983. "Bushwoman: The Position of Women in Bushman Society and Ideology." *Journal of Comparative Sociology and Religion* 10:12–31.

———. 1984. "The Rock Art of the Brandberg of Namibia. An Interpretive Analysis." Wilfrid Laurier University, Research Paper Series no. 8465.

———. 1986a. *The Nharo Bushmen of Botswana.* (QKF 3). Hamburg: Helmut Buske Verlag.

———. 1986b. "Acculturation and Assimilation of the Bushmen of Botswana and Namibia." In R. Vossen and K. Keuthmann, eds. *Contemporary Studies on Khoisan.* (QKF 5). Hamburg: Helmut Buske Verlag, pp. 7–51.

———. 1986c. "From Foragers to Miners and Bands to Bandits: On the Flexibility and Adaptability of Bushman Band Society." *Sprache und Geschichte in Afrika* 7: 133–59.

———. 1986d. "'San' or "'Bushman'?" In Biesele et al., *The Past and Future of !Kung Ethnography,* pp. 347–73.

———. 1988. "Animals in Bushman Thought, Myth and Art." In J. Woodburn, T. Ingold, and D. Riches, eds. *Property, Power and Ideology in Hunting-Gathering Societies.* London: Berg, pp. 192–202.

———. 1989. *Bushman Folktales: Oral Traditions of the Nharo of Botswana and the /Xam of the Cape.* (Studien zur Kulturkunde 93). Stuttgart: Franz Steiner Verlag Wiesbaden.

———. 1990a. "Covergent and Divergent Themes in Bushmen Myth and Art." In K. Kohl, K. Muszinski, and I. Strecker, eds. *Die Vielfalt der Kultur.* Berlin: Dietrich Reimer Verlag, pp. 237–54.

———. 1990b. "Gender Symbolism in Bushman Expressive Culture." Paper presented at the Sixth International Conference on Hunting and Gathering Societies, Fairbanks, Alaska, May–June.

———. 1990c. Review of "People of the Great Sandface," by Paul Myburgh. *CVA Review* (Commission on Visual Anthropology) (fall): 44–45.

———. 1992a. "'Not a Bushman Thing': Witchcraft among the Bushmen and Hunter-Gatherers." *Anthropos* 87:83–107.

———. 1992b. "Comment." On Wilmsen and Denbow, pp. 509–10.

———. 1992c. "'The Pattern is the Thing': Diversity and Uniformity amongst the Khoisan." Review article on *Hunters and Herders of Southern Africa*, by Alan Barnard. *Current Anthropology* 20:185–235.

———. 1993/94. "'Independent, Fearless and Rather Bold': A Historical Narrative on the Ghanzi Bushmen of Botswana." *Journal of the Namibian Scientific Society* 44:25–40.

———. 1994. "The Relationship of Bushman Art to Ritual and Folklore." In Dowson and Lewis-Williams, pp. 257–75.

———. 1995a. "Contemporary Bushman Art as Counter-Hegemony." Paper presented at the Annual Conference of the American Anthropological Association, Washington, D.C., November.

———. 1995b. "Attempting to Contextualize /Xam Oral Tradition." In J. Deacon, ed. *Voices from the Past.* Johannesburg: Witwatersrand University Press, pp. 75–97.

———. 1996a. "Hunter-Gatherer Revisionism." In D. Levinson and M. Ember, eds. *The Encyclopedia of Cultural Anthropology*, vol. 2. New York: Henry Holt and Company, pp. 622–24.

———. 1996b. "From 'Lords of the Desert' to 'Rubbish People': The Colonial and Contemporary State of the Nharo Bushmen." In P. Skotnes, ed. *Miscast: Negotiating the Presence of the Bushmen.* Cape Town: University of Cape Town Press, pp. 225–38.

———. 1996c. "Old Stories/Life Stories: Memory and Dissolution in Contemporary Bushman Folktales." In C. Birch and M. Heckler, eds. *The Aesthetics of Story Telling.* Little Rock: August House Publishers Inc., pp. 177–98.

———. 1996d. "Diversity and Flexibility: The Case of the Bushmen of Southern Africa." In S. Kent, ed. *Cultural Diversity among Twentieth-Century Hunter-Gatherers: An African Perspective.* Cambridge: Cambridge University Press, pp. 65–86.

———. 1997a. "'Lords of the Desert land': Politics and Resistance of the Nineteenth-Century Ghanzi Bushmen." *Botswana Notes and Records* 29:121–41.

———. 1997b. "African Ritual." In S. Glazier, ed. *Anthropology of Religion: A Handbook.* Westport, Conn.: Greenwood Publishing Group, Inc., pp. 161–90.

———. 1997c. "Jesus Christ as Trickster in the Religion of the Contemporary Bushmen." In K. Koepping, ed. *The Games of Gods and Men: Essays in Play and Performance.* Hamburg: LitVerlag, pp. 203–30.

———. 1998. "Farm Labourer, Trance Dancer, Artist: The Life and Works of Qwaa." In Bank, pp. 121–34

Gulbrandsen, O. 1991. "On the Problem of Egalitarianism. The Kalahari San in Transition." In R. Gronhaug, G. Haaland, and G. Henriksen, eds. *The Ecology of Choice and Symbol: Essays in Honour of Frederik Barth.* Bergen: Alma Mater Forlag AS, pp. 81–111.

Gusinde, M. 1966. *Von gelben und schwarzen Buschmännern.* Graz: Akademische Druck- und Verlagsanstalt.

Hahn, C. H. L., H. Vedder, and L. Fourie. 1928. *The Native Tribes of South West Africa.* London: Frank Cass and Co. Ltd.

Hahn, T. 1870. "Die Buschmänner." *Globus,* 18:65–68; 81–85; 102–5; 120–23; 140–43; 153–55.

———. 1881. *Tsuni-//goam: The Supreme Being of the Khoi-khoi.* London: Trübener and Co.

Hall, M. 1988. "At the Frontier: Some Arguments against Hunter-gathering and Farming Modes of Production in Southern Africa." In Ingold, Riches, and Woodburn, pp. 137–47.

Hallowell, A. I. 1967. "Aggression in Saulteaux Society." In *Culture and Experience.* New York: Schocken Books, pp. 177–90.

Hanson, J. 1995. "Hunters and Gatherers." *New Academic* (spring): 12–13.

Haralambos, M. 1980. *Sociology Themes and Perspectives.* Slough: University Tutorial Press.

Harcombe, E. 1928. *Our Missionary Story.* Cape Town: Methodist Book Depot.

Harpending, H. and P. Draper. 1990. "Comment." On Solway and Lee, pp. 127–29.
Havelock, E. 1963. *Preface to Plato.* Cambridge: Harvard University Press.
Heikkinen, T. 1985. *Hai//om and !Xu Stories from North Namibia.* MS.
Heine, B. 1985. "The Mountain People—Some Notes on the Ik of North-East Uganda." *Africa* 55:16–27.
Heinz, H.-J. 1966. "The Social Organization of the !kõ Bushmen." Master's thesis, Pretoria: University of South Africa. (Published as *Social Organization of the !Kõ Bushmen.* Ed. K. Keuthmann. Köln: Rüdiger Köppe Verlag, 1994.)
———. 1971. "The Ethno-Biology of the !kõ-Bushmen: The Anatomical and Physiological Knowledge." *South African Journal of Science* (February): 43–50.
———. 1975a. "Elements of !Kõ Religious Belief." *Anthropos* 70:17–41.
———. 1975b. "!kõ-Buschmänner (Südafrika, Kalhari) Festanz 'guma.'" *Encyclopedia Cinematographica,* E, 1830: 1–15.
———. 1975c. "!kõ Girls Puberty Ceremony." *Encyclopedia Cinematographica,* E, 1849: 6–11.
———. 1976/77. "The Ethno-biology of the !kõ-Bushmen: Knowledge on the Behaviour of Cloven-hoofed Animals (Antelopes and Warthogs)." *Ethnomedizin* 4:241–66.
———. 1978a. "The Bushmen in a Changing World." In Tobias, pp. 173–78.
———. 1978b. "The Bushmen's Store of Scientific Knowledge." In Tobias, pp. 148–61.
———. 1978/79. "The Ethno-Biology of the !kõ-Bushmen: Knowledge Concerning Medium and Smaller Animals." *Ethnomedizin* 5:319–40.
———. 1981/82. "The Ethno-biology of the !kõ-Bushmen: Entomological Knowledge." *Ethnomedizin,* 7:97–116.
Heinz, H.-J. and M. Lee. 1978. *Namkwa.* London: Jonathan Cape.
Heinz, H.-J. and O. Martini. 1980. "The Ethno-biology of the !kõ-Bushmen: The Ornithological Knowledge." *Ethnomedizin* 6:31–59.
Helm, J. 1968. "The Nature of Dogrib Socioterritorial Graoups." In Lee and DeVore, *Man the Hunter*, pp. 118–25.
Henderson, J. L. 1964. "Ancient Myths and Modern Man." In C. G. Jung, ed. *Man and His Symbols.* New York: Laurel, pp. 95–158.
Hepburn, J. D. 1895. *Twenty Years in Khama's Country.* London: Hodder and Stoughton.
Hewitt, R. 1986. *Structure, Meaning and Ritual in the Narratives of the Southern San.* (QKF 2). Hamburg: Helmut Buske Verlag.
Hillman, E. 1990. *Inculturation Applied: Toward an African Christianity.* New York: Paulist Press.
Hirschberg, W. 1933. "Gibt es eine Buschmannkultur?" *Zeitschrift für Ethnologie* 65:19–36.
Hitchcock, R. K. 1996. *Bushmen and the Politics of the Environment in Southern Africa.* IWGIA Document no. 79. Copenhagen: International Work Group for Indigenous Affairs.
Hobsbawm, E. 1965. *Marx's Precapitalist Socio-Economic Formations.* New York: International Publishers.
Hoebel, E. A. 1954. *The Law of Primitive Man.* Cambridge: Harvard University Press.
Holm, E. 1965. *Tier und Gott: Mythik, Mantik und Magie der südafrikanischen Urjäger.* Basel/Stuttgart: Schwabe and Co.
Holub, E. 1881. *Seven Years in South Africa.* 2 vols. London: Sampson Low, Marston, Searle and Rivington.

How, M. W. 1962. *The Mountain Bushmen of Basutoland.* Pretoria: H. J.van Schaik Ltd.

Hunnisett, S. 1993. "Suicide, Alcohol, and Rapid Social Change in a Sub-Arctic Indian Society: An Ethnography of Change, 1920–1990." Ph.D. diss., University of Iowa.

Huruwitz, H. 1956. "Social and Cultural Anthropological Observations on the Bushmen and Other Indigenous Peoples of the Okavango Swamp." *The Leech* 26:19–25.

Hynes, W. J. 1993. "Inconclusive Conclusions: Tricksters—Metaplayers and Revealers." In Hynes and Doty, pp. 202–18.

Hynes, W. J. and T. J. Steele. 1980. "St. Peter: Apostle Transfigured into Trickster." Paper presented at the American Academy of Religion Annual Conference, Dallas, Texas, November. (Published in Hynes and Doty, pp. 159–73.)

Hynes, W. J. and W. G. Doty, eds. 1993. *Mythical Trickster Figures.* Tuscaloosa: The University of Alabama Press.

Ikeya, K. 1993. "Goat Raising among the San in the Central Kalahari." *African Studies Monographs* 14:39–52.

———. 1994. "Hunting with Dogs among the San in the Central Kalahari." *African Studies Monographs* 15:119–34.

———. 1996a. "Road Construction and Handicraft Production in the Xade Area, Botswana." *African Studies Monographs* 22, Supplement:67–84.

———. 1996b. "Dry Farming among the San in the Central Kalahari." *African Studies Monographs* 22, Supplement:85–100.

Ingold, T. 1986. "Comment." On Béteille, pp. 129–30.

———. 1988. "Notes on the Foraging Mode of Production." Ingold, Riches, and Woodburn, pp. 269–85.

———. 1990. "Comment." On Solway and Lee, p. 130.

Ingold, T., D. Riches, and J. Woodburn, eds. 1988. *Hunters and Gatherers,* vol. 1: *History, Evolution and Social Change.* Oxford: Berg.

Iwasaki-Goodman, M. and M. M. R. Freeman. 1994. "Social and Cultural Significance of Whaling in Contemporary Japan: A Case Study of Small-Type Coastal Whaling." In Burch and Ellanna, pp. 377–400.

Jeffreys, M. D. W. 1978. "An Epitaph to the Bushmen." In Tobias, pp. 88–93.

Jolly, P. 1996. "Symbiotic Interaction between Black Farmers and South-Eastern San." *Current Anthropology* 37:277–305.

Jung, C. G. 1972. "On the Psychology of the Trickster Figure." In Radin, *The Trickster*, pp. 195–211. [1956]

Kapferer, B., ed. 1976. *Transaction and Meaning: Directions in the Anthropology of Exchange and Symbolic Behaviour.* Philadelphia: Institute for the Study of Human Issues.

Katz, R. 1976. "Education for Transcendence: !Kia-Healing and the Kalahari !Kung." In Lee and DeVore, *Kalahari Hunter-Gatherers*, pp. 281–301.

———. 1982. *Boiling Energy.* Cambridge: Harvard University Press.

Katz, R., M. Biesele, and V. St. Denis. 1997. *Healing Makes our Hearts Happy: Spirituality and Transformation among the Kalahari Ju/'hoansi*. Rochester, Vermont: Inner Traditions.

Kaufmann, H. 1910. "Die ≠Auin. Ein Beitrag zur Buschmannforschung." *Mitteilungen aus den deutschen Schutzgebieten* 23:135–60.

Kehoe, A. 1989. *The Ghost Dance: Ethnohistory and Revitalization.* New York: Holt, Rinehart and Winston.

Kelly, R. 1995. *The Foraging Spectrum.* Washington: Smithsonian Institution Press.
Kent, S. 1989a. "And Justice for All: The Development of Political Centralization among Newly Sedentary Foragers." *American Anthropologist* 91:703–12.
———. 1989b. "Cross-Cultural Perceptions of Farmers as Hunters and the Value of Meat." In S. Kent, ed. *Farmers as Hunters—The Implications of Sedentism.* Cambridge: Cambridge University Press, pp. 1–17.
———. 1992. "The Current Forager Controversy: Real Versus Ideal Views of Hunter-Gatherers." *Man*, n.s., 27:45–70.
———. 1993a. "Sharing in an Egalitarian Kalahari Community" *Man*, n.s., 28:479–514.
———. 1993b. "Does Sedentism Impact Traditional Gender Roles? A Case Study from the Kalahari." Paper presented at the 7th CHAGS, Moscow.
———. 1993c. "Comment." On Boehm, p. 243.
Kerenyi, K. 1972. "The Trickster in Relation to Greek Mythology." In Radin, *The Trickster*, pp. 171–91.
Kicherer, J. 1804. "Narrative of the Mission to the Hottentots and Boschesmens." *Transactions of the Mission Society* 2:1–48.
King-Odjig, A. 1993. "If Jesus Met Nanbush." Play, premiered at Humber College, Toronto, 22 November.
Kirby, P., ed. 1940. *The Journal of Dr. Andrew Smith.* Cape Town: Van Riebeck Society.
Knappert, J. 1981. *Namibia Land and Peoples Myths and Fables.* Nisaba, vol. 2. Religious Texts Translation Series. Leiden: E. J. Brill.
Koepping, K.-P. 1985. "Absurdity and Hidden Truth: Cunning Intelligence and Grotesque Body Images as Manifestations of the Trickster." *History of Religions* 25:191–214.
Köhler, O. 1978/79 "Mythus, Glaube und Magie bei den Kxoe-Buschleuten." *Journal of the S.W.A.S. Society* 33:9–49.
Konner, M. 1976. "Maternal Care, Infant Behaviour and Development among the !Kung." In Lee and DeVore, *Kalahari Hunter-Gatherers*, pp. 218–45.
Konner, M. and M. Shostak. 1986. "Ethnographic Romanticism and the Idea of Human Nature: Parallels between Samoa and !Kung San." In Biesele et al., *The Past and Future of !Kung Ethnography,* pp. 69–78.
Kuru Development Trust 1991/92. *Annual Report* May 1991–April 1992. Ghanzi: Kuru Development Trust.
Lau, B. 1987. *Namibia in Jonker Afrikaner's Time.* Windhoek: National Archives.
Leacock, E. 1978. "Women's Status in Egalitarian Society: Implications for Social Evolution." *Current Anthropology* 19:247–75.
Leacock, E. and R. B. Lee, eds. 1982. *Politics and History in Band Societies.* Cambridge/Paris: Cambridge University Press/Editions de la Maison des Sciences de l'Homme.
Lebzelter, V. 1934. *Eingeborenenkulturen von Südwestafrika Die Buschmänner.* Leipzig: Verlag Karl W. Hiersemann.
Lee, D. 1976. *Valuing the Self.* Englewood Cliffs, New Jersey: Prentice-Hall.
Lee, R. B. 1967. "Trance Cure of the !Kung Bushmen." *Natural History* (November): 30–37.
———. 1968. "The Sociology of !Kung Bushman Dance Performances." In R. Prince, ed. *Trance and Possession States.* Montreal: R. M. Bucke Memorial Society, pp. 35–54.
———. 1969. "Eating Christmas in the Kalahari." *Natural History* (December): 14–22.

———. 1976. "!Kung Bushman Spatial Organization: An Ecological and Historical Perspective." In Lee and DeVore, *Kalahari Hunter-Gatherers*, pp. 73–97.

———. 1978. "Ecology of a Contemporary San People." In Tobias, pp. 94–114.

———. 1979. *The !Kung San: Men, Women, and Work in a Foraging Society.* Cambridge: Cambridge University Press.

———. 1981. "Is there a Foraging Mode of Production?" *Canadian Journal of Anthropology* 2:13–19.

———. 1982. "Politics, Sexual and Non-sexual, in an Egalitarian Society." In Leacock and Lee, pp. 37–60.

———. 1988. "Reflections on Primitive Communism." In Ingold, Riches, and Woodburn, pp. 252–68.

———. 1992. "Art, Science, or Politics? The Crisis of Representation in Gatherer-Hunter Studies." *American Anthropologist* 94:31–54.

———. 1993. *The Dobe Ju/'hoansi.* 2nd. ed. Fort Worth: Harcourt Brace College Publishers.

Lee, R. B. and I. DeVore, eds. 1968. *Man the Hunter.* Chicago: Aldine.

———. 1976. *Kalahari Hunter-Gatherers.* Cambridge: Harvard University Press.

Lee, R. B. and M. Guenther. 1993. "Problems in Kalahari Historical Ethnography and the Tolerance of Error." *History in Africa* 20: 185–235.

Lee, R. B., M. Biesele, and R. Hitchcock. 1996. "Three Decades of Ethnographic Research among the Ju/'hoansi of Northwestern Botswana: 1963–1996." *Botswana Notes and Records* 28:107–20.

Lenssen-Erz, T. 1989. "The Catalogue." In Pager, *The Rock Paintings of the Upper Brandberg*, pp. 343–502.

———. 1994. "Facts of Fantasy? The Rock Paintings of the Brandberg, Namibia, and a Concept of Textualization for Purposes of Data Processing." *Semiotica* 100:169–200.

Le Roux, W. 1995a. "The Largest San 'Settlement' in the World?" *Newsletter Kalahari Support Group* (June): 7–8.

———. 1995b. "The Challenges of Change: A Survey of the Effects of Preschool on Basarwa Primary School Children in the Ghanzi District of Botswana." Ghanzi: Kuru Development Trust.

Lévi-Strauss, C. 1963. *Totemism.* Trans. R. Needham. Boston: Beacon Press.

Lewis-Williams, D. 1981. *Believing and Seeing: Symbolic Meanings in Southern San Rock Paintings.* New York: Academic Press.

———. 1982. "The Economic and Social Context of Southern San Rock Art." *Current Anthropology* 23:429–49.

———. 1983. *New Approaches to Southern African Rock Art.* Goodwin Series 4. Cape Town: South African Archaeological Society.

———. 1988. "'People of the Eland': An Archaeo-Linguistic Crux." In Ingold, Riches, and Woodburn, pp. 203–12.

Lewis-Williams, D. and M. Biesele. 1978. "Eland Hunting Rituals among the Northern and Southern San Groups: Striking Similarities." *Africa* 48:117–34.

Lewis-Williams, D. and T. Dowson. 1988. "Sign of all Times: Entoptic Phenomena in Upper Plaeolithic Art." *Current Anthropology* 29:201–45.

———. 1989. *Images of Power: Understanding Bushman Rock Art.* Johannesburg: Southern Book Publishers.

Lichtenstein, H. 1928. *Travels in Southern Africa in the Years 1803, 1804, 1805, and 1806.* 2 vols. Cape Town: Van Riebeck Society [1811]

Lloyd, L. 1889. *A Short Account of Further Bushman Material Collected.* London: David Nutt.

Luig, U. 1990. "Konfliktlösung als Wiederherstellung von Gleichheit: Die !Kung San." In K.-H. Kohl, H. Muszinski, and I. Strecker, eds. *Die Vielfalt der Kultur.* Berlin: Dietrich Reimer Verlag, pp. 202–21.

Maack, R. n.d. "Die 'Weisse Dame' vom Brandberg." *Ethnologica,* Neue Folge, 3:1–84.

Mackenzie, J. 1871. *Ten Years North of the Orange River.* Edinburgh: Edmonston.

Maler-Sieber, G. 1978. *Völkerkunde die uns angeht.* Gütersloh: Bertelsmann.

Malinowski, B. 1948. *Magic, Science and Religion and Other Essays.* Boston: Beacon Press.

Marais, J. S. 1939. *The Cape Coloured People.* London: Longmans, Green and Co.

Marks, S. 1972. "Khoisan Resistance to the Dutch in the Seventeenth and Eighteenth Century." *Journal of African History* 13:65–80.

Marshall, J. 1982. *N!ai: The Story of a !Kung Woman.* Watertown, Mass.: Documentary Educational Resources. Film.

Marshall, L. 1957. "N!ow." *Africa* 27:232–40.

———. 1959. "Marriage among the !Kung Bushmen." *Africa* 29:335–65.

———. 1962. "!Kung Bushman Religious Beliefs." *Africa* 32:221–52.

———. 1965. "The !Kung Bushmen." In A. Gibbs, ed. *Peoples of Africa.* New York: Holt, Rinehart, and Winston, pp. 241–78.

———. 1969. "The Medicine Dance of the !Kung Bushmen." *Africa* 39:347–81.

———. 1976a. *The !Kung of Nyae Nyae.* Cambridge: Harvard University Press.

———. 1976b. "Sharing, Talking and Giving: Relief of Social Tensions among the !Kung." In Lee and DeVore, *Kalahari Hunter-Gatherers,* pp. 349–71.

———. n.d. *For Food and Health: Beliefs of the Nyae Nyae !Kung.* Cambridge: Harvard University Press, forthcoming.

Marshall-Thomas, E. 1990. "The Old Way." *New Yorker,* 15 October, pp. 78–110.

Mattenklodt, 1931. *A Fugitive in South-West Africa 1908 to 1920.* Trans. O. Williams. London: Thornton Butterworth Ltd. [1923]

Mauss, M. 1905. "Essai sur les variations saisonniéres des sociétés eskimos: étude de morphologie sociale." *L'Année Sociologique* 9:39–132.

Maylam, P. 1980. *Rhodes, the Tswana and the British.* Westport: Greenwood Press.

McCabe, J. 1855. "Journal Kept during Tour into the Interior of South Africa to the Lake N'Gami and to the Country Two-Hundred-and-Fifty Miles Beyond by Mr. Joseph McCabe." In W. C. Holden, *History of the Colony of Natal, South Africa.* London: Alexander Heylin, pp. 413–34.

McCall, D. F. 1970. "Wolf Courts Girl: The Equivalence of Hunting and Mating in Bushman Thought." *Ohio University Papers in International Studies, Africa Series* no. 7.

McCreedy, M. 1994. "The Arms of the *Dibouka.*" In Burch and Ellanna, pp. 15–34.

Metzger, F. 1950. *Naro and his Clan.* Windhoek: Meinert.

Metzger, F. and P. Ettighoffer. 1952. *Und seither lacht die Hyäne.* Windhoek: Meinert.

Moffat, R. 1842. *Missionary Labours and Scenes in South Africa.* London: John Snow.

Molema, S. M. 1920. *The Bantu Past and Present.* Edinburgh: W. Green and Sons.

Mönnig, H. O. 1967. *The Pedi.* Pretoria: J. J. van Schaik.

Morgan, L. H. 1877. *Ancient Society.* New York: World.

Morris, B. 1987. *Anthropological Studies of Religion.* Cambridge: Cambridge University Press.

Morupisi, D. 1992. "Dekar Community of Hope" *Kultwano* (August): 14–15.

Müller, Hauptmann. 1912. "Ein Erkundungsritt in das Kau-Kau-Veld. *Deutsches Kolonialblatt* 23:530–41.

Müller, P. K. 1923. *Georg Schmidt: Die Geschichte der ersten Hottentot Mission 1737–44.* Herrenhut: Missionsbuchhandlung.

Murphy, W. P. 1978. "Oral Literature." *Annual Reviews of Anthropology* 7:113–36.

Myers, F. 1988. "Critical Trends in the Study of Hunter-Gatherers." *Annual Review of Anthropology* 17:261–82.

n. a. 1877. "History of the Bosjesmans or Bushpeople." Pamphlet. Cape Town: National Library.

Nettleton, G. G. 1934. "History of the Ngamiland Tribes up to 1926." *Bantu Studies* 8:343–60.

Nonaka, K. 1996. "Ethnoentomology of the Central Kalahari San." *African Studies Monographs* 22, Supplement:29–46.

Olivier, E. 1998. "The Art of Metamorphosis—or the Ju/'hoan Conception of Plurivocality." In Bank, pp.263–68.

Olpp, J. 1922. *Deutsch Missions- und Segenstätten in Südwest beim Übergang der Kolonie in andere Hände.* Barmen: Rheinische Missionsgesellschaft.

Orpen, J. M. 1908. *Reminiscences of Life in South Africa from 1846 to the Present Day.* Durban: P. Davis and Sons. Reprinted in *Africana Collectana* X. Cape Town: C. Struik, 1964.

Osaki, M. 1984. "The Social Influence of Change in Hunting Technique among the Central Kalahari San." *African Studies Monographs* 5:49–62.

———. 1990. "The Influence of Sedentism on Sharing among the Central Kalahari Hunter-Gatherers." *African Studies Monographs* 12, Supplement:59–87.

Pager, H. 1971. *Ndedema.* Graz: Akademische Druck- und Verlagsanstalt.

———. 1975. *Stone Age Myth and Magic.* Graz: Akademische Druck- und Verlagsanstalt.

———. 1989. *The Rock Paintings of the Upper Brandberg. Part I: Amis Gorge.* Ed. R. Kuper. Cologne: Heinrich-Barth Institut.

Paine, R. 1974. "Second Thoughts about Barth's Models." Occasional Papers no. 32. London: Royal Anthropological Institute.

Park, R. E. 1928. "Human Migration and the Marginal Man." *American Journal of Sociology* 33:881–93.

Passarge, S. 1905. "Die Grundlinien im ethnologischen Bilde der Kalahari Region." *Zeitschrift der Gesellschaft für Erdkunde in Berlin* 40:20–36, 68–88.

———. 1906. "Berichtigung zu der Besprechung über 'Die Buschmänner der Kalahari.'" *Zeitschrift für Ethnologie* 38:411–14.

———. 1907. *Die Buschmänner der Kalahari.* Berlin: Dietrich Reimer.

Pelto, R. D. 1993. "West African Tricksters: Web of Purpose, Dance of Delight." In Hynes and Doty, pp. 122–40.

Penn, N. 1991. "The /Xam and the Colony." Paper presented at the Bleek and Lloyd 1870–1991 Conference, University of Cape Town, 9–11 September.

———. 1996. "'Fated to Perish': The Destruction of the Cape San." In Skotnes, pp. 81–92.

Pfitzner, E. and D. Wangemann 1891. *Wilhelm Posselt, der Kaffern Missionar.* Berlin: Buchhandlung der evangelischen Missionsgesellschaft.

Philip, J. 1828. *Researches in South Africa.* 2 vols. London: Duncan.
Potgieter, E. F. 1955. *The Disappearing Bushmen of Lake Chrissie: A Preliminary Survey.* Pretoria: J. L. van Schaik.
Radin, P. 1957. *Primitive Religion.* New York: Dover. [1937]
———. 1972. *The Trickster.* New York: Schocken Books. [1956]
Rahner, H. 1967. *Man at Play.* New York: Herder and Herder.
Rao, A. 1993. "Zur Problematik der Wildbeuterkategorie." In T. Schweitzer, M. Schweitzer, and W. Kokot, eds. *Handbuch der Ethnologie.* Berlin: Dietrich Reimer Verlag, pp. 491–520.
Richter, D. J. 1922. *Geschichte der evangelischen Mission in Afrika.* Gütersloh: Bertelsmann.
Ricketts, M. L. 1993. "The Shaman and the Trickster." In Hynes and Doty, pp. 87–105.
Ridington, R. 1982. "Technology, World View and Adaptive Strategy in a Northern Hunting Society." *Canadian Review of Sociology and Anthropology* 19:469–81.
Roberts, J. 1989. *From Trickster to Badman: The Black Folk Hero in Slavery and Freedom.* Philadelphia: University of Pennsylvania Press.
Rosaldo, R. 1989. *Culture and Truth.* Boston: Beacon Press.
Rosenberg, H. 1990. "Complaint Discourse, Aging, and Caregiving among the !Kung San of Botswana." In Jay Sokolovsky, ed. *The Cultural Context of Aging.* New York: Bergin and Garvey, pp. 19–41.
Rudner, J. and I. Rudner. 1978. "Bushman Art." In Tobias, pp. 57–75.
Russell, J. B. 1984. *Lucifer: The Devil in the Middle Ages.* Ithaca: Cornell University Press.
Russell, M. and M. Russell. 1979. *Afrikaners in the Kalahari.* Cambridge: Cambridge University Press.
Rybak, B. 1977. "Une convergence remarquable entre langages tambourinés, codes nerveux et langages machine." *L'Homme* 17:117–21.
Sadr, K. 1997. "Kalahari Archaeology and the Bushman Debate." *Current Anthropology* 38:104–12.
Saliba, J. 1976/77. "Religion and the Anthropologists, 1960–76." Parts I and II. *Anthropologica* 18:179–214; 19:177–208.
Schapera, I. 1930. *The Khoisan Peoples of South Africa.* London: Routledge and Kegan Paul.
———. 1953. *The Tswana.* London: International African Institute.
Schatz, I. 1993. *Unter Buschleuten.* Tsumeb: Ilse Schatz.
Schebesta, P. 1923. "Die religösen Anschauungen Südafrikas." *Anthropos* 18/19:114–24.
Schinz, H. 1891. *Deutsch-Südwest-Afrika.* Oldenburg und Leipzig: Schulzesche Hof-Buchhandlung und Hof-Buchdruckerei.
Schmidt, S. 1970. "Europäische Volkerzählungen bei den Nama und Bergdama." *Fabula* 11:32–53.
———. 1973. "Die Mantis religiosa in den Glaubensvorstellungen der Khoisan-Völker." *Zeitschrift für Ethnologie* 98:102–27.
———. 1974/75. "Einige Bemerkungen zum Lochspiel (Mankala) in Südwestafrika." *Journal of the SWA Scientific Society* 29:67–77.
———. 1977. "Europäische Märchen am kap der Guten Hoffnung des 18. Jahrhunderts. Ein Rekonstruktionsversuch der AaTh-Typen 300–1199 anhand der Ü berlieferungen in Südwestafrika." *Fabula* 18:40–74.

———. 1977/78. "Der Trickster der Khoisan-Volkserzählungen als Regenkämpfer." *Journal of the South West African Scientific Society* 31:69–93.

———. 1980. *Märchen aus Namibia.* Cologne: Eugen Diederichs Verlag.

———. 1985. "Europäische Sagen bei den Nama und Damara in Südwestafrika/ Namibia." *Fabula* 26:298–316.

———. 1986a. "Heiseb-Trickster und Gott der Nama und Dama in Südwestafrika (Namibia)." In R. Vossen and K. Keuthmann, eds. *Contemporary Studies on Khoisan,* vol. 2 (QKF 5), pp. 205–56.

———. 1986b. "Tales and Beliefs about Eyes-on-his-Feet: The Interrelatedness of Khoisan Folklore." In Biesele et al., *The Past and Future of !Kung Ethnography,* pp. 169–94.

———. 1989. *Catalogue of the Khoisan Folktales of Southern Africa.* 2 vols. (QKF 6.1 and 6.2). Hamburg: Helmut Buske Verlag.

———. 1991. *Aschenputtel und Eulenspiegel in Afrika Entlehntes Erzählungen der Nama und Damara in Namibia.* Cologne: Rüdiger Köppe Verlag.

———. 1993. "KhoeKhoe Gowag (Nama/Damara) Oral Traditions." *Fasette/Facets/ Facetten* 12:1–14.

———. 1994. *Zaubermärchen in Afrika Erzählungen der Damara und Nama.* Cologne: Rüdiger Köppe Verlag.

———. 1995. *Als die Tiere noch Menschen waren Urzeit- und Trickstergeschichten der Damara und Nama.* Cologne: Rüdiger Köppe Verlag.

Schmidt, W. 1933. *Der Ursprung der Gottesidee,* vol. 4: "Die Religionen der Urvölker Afrikas." Münster: Aschaffendorfer Verlagsbuchhnadlung.

Schott, R. 1955. "Die Buschmänner in Südafrika Eine Studie über Schwierigkeiten der Akkulturation." *Sociologus* 5:1320–49.

Seiler-Dietrich, A. 1980. *Märchen der Bantu.* Cologne: Eugen Diederichs Verlag.

Seiner, F. 1911. "Aus den deutschsüdwestafrikanischen Schutzgebieten. Die Omaheke." *Mitteilungen aus den deutschen Schutzgebieten* 24:336–41.

———. 1913. "Ergebnisse einer Bereisung der Omaheke in den Jahren 1910–12." *Mitteilungen aus den deutschen Schutzgebieten* 26:225–316.

Serpell, J. 1986. *In the Company of Animals.* Oxford: Basil Blackwell.

Service, E. 1979. *The Hunters.* 2nd. ed. Englewood Cliffs: Prentice-Hall.

Sharp, H. 1994. "The Power of Weakness." In Burch and Ellanna, pp. 35–58.

Sharp, L. 1968. "Comment." In Lee and DeVore, *Man the Hunter,* p. 160.

Shaw, B. 1841. *Memorials of Southern Africa.* London: Mason.

Shepard, P. 1973. *Thinking Animals. Animals and the Development of Human Intelligence.* New York: The Viking Press.

Shostak, M. 1976. "A !Kung Woman's Memory of Childhood." In Lee and DeVore, *Kalahari Hunter-Gatherers,* pp. 246–78.

———. 1981. *Nisa: The Life and Words of a !Kung Woman.* New York: Vintage Books.

Shott, Michael J. "On Recent Trends in the Anthropology of Foragers: Kalahari Revisionism and Its Archaeological Implications." *Man,* n.s., 27: 843–71.

Silberbauer, G. 1963. "Marriage and the Girl's Puberty Ceremony of the G/wi Bushmen." *Africa* 33:12–24.

———. 1965. *Bushman Survey Report.* Gaberones: Government Printer.

———. 1972. "The G/wi Bushmen." In M. G. Bicchieri, ed. *Hunter-Gatherers Today.* New York: Holt, Rinehart and Winston, pp. 271–326.

———. 1981. *Hunter and Habitat in the Central Kalahari Desert.* Cambridge: Cambridge University Press.

———. 1982. "Political Process in G/wi Bands." In Leacock and Lee, pp. 23–35.

———. 1996. "Neither Are your Ways my Ways." In S. Kent, ed. *Cultural Diversity among Twentieth-Century Foragers.* Cambridge: Cambridge University Press, pp. 21–64.

Silberbauer, G. and A. Kuper 1966. "Kgalagari Masters and Bushman Serfs: Some Observations." *African Studies* 25:171–79.

Sillery, A. 1952. *The Bechuanaland Protectorate.* Oxford: Oxford University Press.

Simmel, G. S. 1971. *On Individualism and Social Forms.* Ed. D. N. Levine. Chicago: University of Chicago Press.

Skotnes, P., ed. 1996. *Miscast: Negotiating the Presence of the Bushmen.* Cape Town: University of Cape Town Press.

Smith, A. 1975. *Andrew Smith's Journal of his Expedition into the Interior of South Africa 1834–1836.* Ed. William F. Lye. Cape Town: Balkema.

Smith, P. 1987. "Transhumant Europeans Overseas: The Newfoundland Case." *Current Anthropology* 28:241–50.

Solomon, A. 1992. "Gender, Representation, and Power in San Ethnography and Rock Art." *Journal of Anthropological Archaeology* 11:291–29.

———. 1994. "Mythic Women: A Study in Variability in San Rock Art and Narrative." In Dowson and Lewis-Williams, pp. 331–71.

Solway, J. and R. B. Lee. 1990. "Foragers, Genuine or Spurious? Situating the Kalahari San in History." *Current Anthropology* 31: 109–46.

Speth, J. D. 1990. "Seasonality, Resource Stress, and Food-Sharing in So-Called 'Egalitarian' Foraging Societies." *Journal of Anthropological Research* 9:148–88.

Spoelstra, C. 1902. *Are the Boers Hostile to Mission Work?* London: Adelphi.

Stals, E .L .P., ed. 1991. *The Commissions of W. C. Palgrave.* Cape Town: Van Riebeck Society.

Stow, G. 1905. *The Native Races of South Africa.* London: Swan and Sonnenschein.

Strassberger, E. 1969. *The Rhenish Mission Society in South Africa 1830–1950.* Cape Town: C. Struik.

Sugawara, K. 1991. "The Economic and Social Life among the Kalaharai San (//Ganakhwe and G/wikhwe) in the Sedentary Community at !Koi!kom." In N. Peterson and T. Matysa, eds. *Cash, Commoditisation and Changing Foragers.* Osaka: National Museum of Ethnology, pp. 91–116.

Sundkler, B. 1961. *Bantu Prophets in South Africa.* 2nd. ed. Oxford: Oxford University Press.

———. 1962. *The Christian Ministry in Africa.* London: SCM Press Ltd.

Sylvain, R. 1998. "Survival Strategies of San Women on Commercial Farms in the Omaheke Region, Namibia." In Bank, pp. 336–43.

Szalay, M. 1983. *Ethnologie und Geschichte.* Berlin: Dietrich Reimer. (English Translation: *The San and the Colonization of the Cape: 1770–1879.* Cologne: Rüdiger Köppe Verlag, 1995.)

———. 1986. *Die Kunst Schwarzafrikas.* Part 1. Zürich: Völkerkundemuseum der Universität Zürich.

Tanaka, J. 1976. "Subsistence Ecology of Central Kalahari San." In Lee and DeVore, *Kalahari Hunter-Gatherers,* pp. 98–119.

———. 1980. The San Hunter-Gatherers of the Kalahari. Tokyo: The University of Tokyo Press.

———. 1996. "The World of Animals Viewed by the San Hunter-Gatharers in Kalahari [*sic*]." *African Studies Monographs* 22, Supplement:11–28.

Taylor, C. 1992. *The Malaise of Modernity.* Concord: Anansi.

Theal, G. M. n.d. *Record of the Cape Colony, 1806–1815,* vol. 5. Cape Town: Government Printer.

Thomas, E. W. 1950. *Bushman Folktales.* Cape Town: Oxford University Press.

Tindall, B. A. 1856. *Two Lectures on Great Namaqualand and its Inhabitants.* Cape Town: Pike.

Tlou, T. 1975. "Documents of Botswana: How Rhodes Tried to Seize Ngamiland." *Botswana Notes and Records* 7:61–65.

Tobias, P., ed. 1978. *The Bushmen.* Cape Town: Human and Rousseau.

Toelken, B. 1969. "The 'Pretty language' of Yellowman: Genre, Mode, and Texture in Navaho Coyote Narratives." *Genre* 2:211–35.

———. 1979. *The Dynamics of Folklore.* Boston: Houghton Mifflin Co.

Tonkinson, R. 1978. *The Mardudjara Aborigines: Living the Dream in Australia's Desert.* New York: Holt, Rinehart and Winston.

Townshend, P. 1976/77. "The SWA Game of //hus (das Lochspiel) in the Wider Context of African Mankala." *Journal of the SWA Scientific Society* 31:85–94.

Trenk, P. 1910. "Die Buschleute der Namib, ihre Rechts- und Familienverhältnisse." *Mitteilungen aus den deutscehn Schutzgebieten* 23:166–70.

Trueblood, E. 1964. *The Humor of Christ.* New York: Farrar and Rinehart.

Turkinson, T. 1992. "Nharo Painters." *Marung* (October): 13–15.

Turnbull, C. 1966. *Wayward Servants: The Two Worlds of the African Pygmies.* London: Eyre and Spottiswoode.

———. 1972. *The Mountain People.* New York: Simon and Schuster.

Turner, V. 1969. *The Ritual Process.* Chicago: Aldine.

———. 1970a. "Betwixt and Between: The Liminal Period in *Rites de Passage.*" In *The Forest of Symbols*, pp. 93–111.

———. 1970b. *The Forest of Symbols.* Ithaca: Cornell University Press.

———. 1974. "Passages, Margins and Poverty: Religious Symbols of Communitas." In *Drama, Fields and Metaphors.* Ithaca: Cornell University Press, pp. 231–71.

van der Merwe, W. J. 1936. *The Development of Missionary Attitudes in the Dutch Reformed Church in South Africa.* Cape Town: Nasionale Pers.

van der Post, L. 1958. *The Lost World of the Kalahari.* Harmondsworth: Penguin.

———. 1961. *The Heart of the Hunter.* Harmondsworth: Penguin.

———. 1975. *A Mantis Carol.* London: The Hogarth Press.

———. 1984. *Testament to the Bushmen.* Harmondsworth: Penguin.

van Gennep, A. 1960. *The Rites of Passage.* Chicago: Phoenix Books. [1908]

van Onselen, L. 1961. *Trekboer.* Cape Town: Howard Timmins.

Vedder, H. 1922. *Skizzen aus dem Leben der Mission in Südwest Afrika.* Barmen: Rheinische Missionsgesellschaft.

———. 1934. *Das alte Südwestafrika.* Berlin: Martin Warneck.

Vedder, H. and A. Unterkeller. n.d. "Von den Buschmännern und der Buschmannmission." MS.

Vinnicombe, P. 1976. *People of the Eland.* Pietermaritzburg: University of Natal Press.

Visser, H. n.d. *Naro in a Quarter of an Hour.* Mimeographed.

———. 1994. *Naro Dictionary.* Mimeographed.
Volkman, T. 1982. *The San in Transition,* vol. 1: A Guide to N!ai, the Story of a !Kung Woman. Boston: Cultural Survival.
von Eckenbrecher, M. 1907. *Was Afrika mir gab und nahm.* Berlin: Ernst Siegfried Mittner and Sohn.
Vorster, L. P. 1994. "Towery by die !Xu van Schmidtsdrift: 'n verklaring." *South African Journal of Ethnology* 17:69–81.
———. 1995. "The !Xu of Schmidtsdrift and Sorcery." In A. J. M. Sanders, ed. *Speaking for the Bushmen.* Gaborone: The Botswana Society, pp. 101–15.
Wagner-Robertz, D. 1976. "Schamanentum bei den Hain//om in Südwestafrika." *Anthropos* 71:533–54.
Waitz, T. 1858–1872. *Anthropologie der Naturvölker.* 6 vols. Leipzig: Friedrich Fleischer.
Weiner, A. 1996. "Reciprocity." In D. Levinson and M. Ember, eds. *Encyclopedia of Cultural Anthropology,* vol.3. New York: Henry Holt and Company, pp. 1060–68.
Whiting, 1968. "Comment." In Lee and DeVore, *Man the Hunter,* pp. 336–39.
Wiessner, P. 1982. "Risk, Reciprocity, and Social Influence on !Kung San Economics." In Leacock and Lee, pp. 61–84.
———. 1984. "Reconsidering the Behavioural Basis for Style: A Case Study among the Kalahari San." *Journal of Anthropological Archaeology* 3:190–234.
———. 1986. "!Kung San Networks in a Generational Perspective." In Biesele et al., *The Past and Future of !Kung Ethnography,* pp. 103–36.
Wiessner, P. and F. T. Larsen. 1979. "'Mother! Sing Loudly to Me!': The Annotated Dialogue of a Basarw Healer in Trance." *Botswana Notes and Records* 11:25–31.
Wilhelm, J. H. 1955. "Die !Kung-Buschleute." *Museum für Völkerkunde zu Leipzig* 14:91–189.
Williams, D. 1967. *When Races Meet.* Johannesburg: A. P. B. Publications.
Wilmsen, E. 1989. *Land Filled with Flies: A Political Economy of the Kalahari.* Chicago: University of Chicago Press.
———, ed. 1997. *The Kalahari Ethnographies (1896–1898) of Siegfried Passarge.* Cologne: Rüdiger Köppe Verlag.
Wilmsen, E. and J. R. Denbow. 1990. "Paradigmatic History of San-speaking Peoples and Current Attempts at Revision." *Current Anthropology* 31: 489–524.
Wily, E. 1973. "An Analysis of the Bere Bushman Settlement Scheme." Gaborone Ministry of Local Government and Lands.
———. 1982. "A Strategy of Self-Determination for the Kalahari San (The Botswana Government's Program of Action in the Ghanzi Farms)." *Development and Change* 13:291–398.
Wood, J. G. 1877. *The Uncivilized Races of Men in all Countries around the World.* 2 vols. Hartford: J. B. Burr Pub. Co.
Woodburn, J. 1982. "Egalitarian Societies." *Man,* n.s., 17:431–51.
———. 1988. "African Hunter-gatherer Social Organization: Is it Best Understood as a Product of Encapsulation?" In Ingold, Riches, and Woodburn, pp. 31–72.
Wright, J. B. 1971. *Bushman Raiders of the Drakensberg.* Pietermaritzberg: University of Natal Press.
Wust, Pater. 1938. "Ein sterbendes Volk." *Monatsblätter der Oblaten* 45:254–59, 292–97, 325–29.
Zucker, W. 1967. "The Clown Is the Lord of Disorder." *Theology Today* 24:306–17.

Index

MATHIAS GUENTHER, Professor of Sociology and Anthropology at Wilfrid Laurier University, Ontario, is the author of *The Farm Bushmen of the Ghanzi District, Botswana; The Nharo Bushmen of Botswana: Tradition and Change;* and *Bushman Folktales: Oral Traditions of the Nharo of Botswana and the Xam of the Cape.*